Thank you for picking up *Haikyu!!* volume 7. I have a bad habit of taking a pen (or other drawing implement) with me when I get up to go somewhere—like the foyer—then leaving that pen there and promptly forgetting about it. Then I wander around everywhere looking for it. I think I spend at least 100 hours a year looking for stuff I've lost that way.

HARUICHI FURUDATE began his manga career when he was 25 years old with the one-shot *Ousama Kid* (King Kid), which won an honorable mention for the 14th Jump Treasure Newcomer Manga Prize. His first series, *Kiben Gakuha, Yotsuya Sensei no Kaidan* (Philosophy School, Yotsuya Sensei's Ghost Stories), was serialized in Weekly Shonen Jump in 2010. In 2012, he began serializing *Haikyu!!* in Weekly Shonen Jump, where it became his most popular work to date.

HAIKYU!!

VOLUME 7
SHONEN JUMP Manga Edition

Story and Art by
HARUICHI FURUDATE

Translation ☐ **ADRIENNE BECK**
Touch-Up Art & Lettering ☐ **ERIKA TERRIQUEZ**
Design ☐ **FAWN LAU**
Editor ☐ **MARLENE FIRST**

HAIKYU!! © 2012 by Haruichi Furudate
All rights reserved.
First published in Japan in 2012 by SHUEISHA Inc., Tokyo.
English translation rights arranged by SHUEISHA Inc.

The stories, characters and incidents mentioned
in this publication are entirely fictional.

Printed in Italy

Published by VIZ Media, LLC
P.O. Box 77010
San Francisco, CA 94107

10 9 8 7 6 5 4
First printing, January 2017
Fourth printing, December 2021

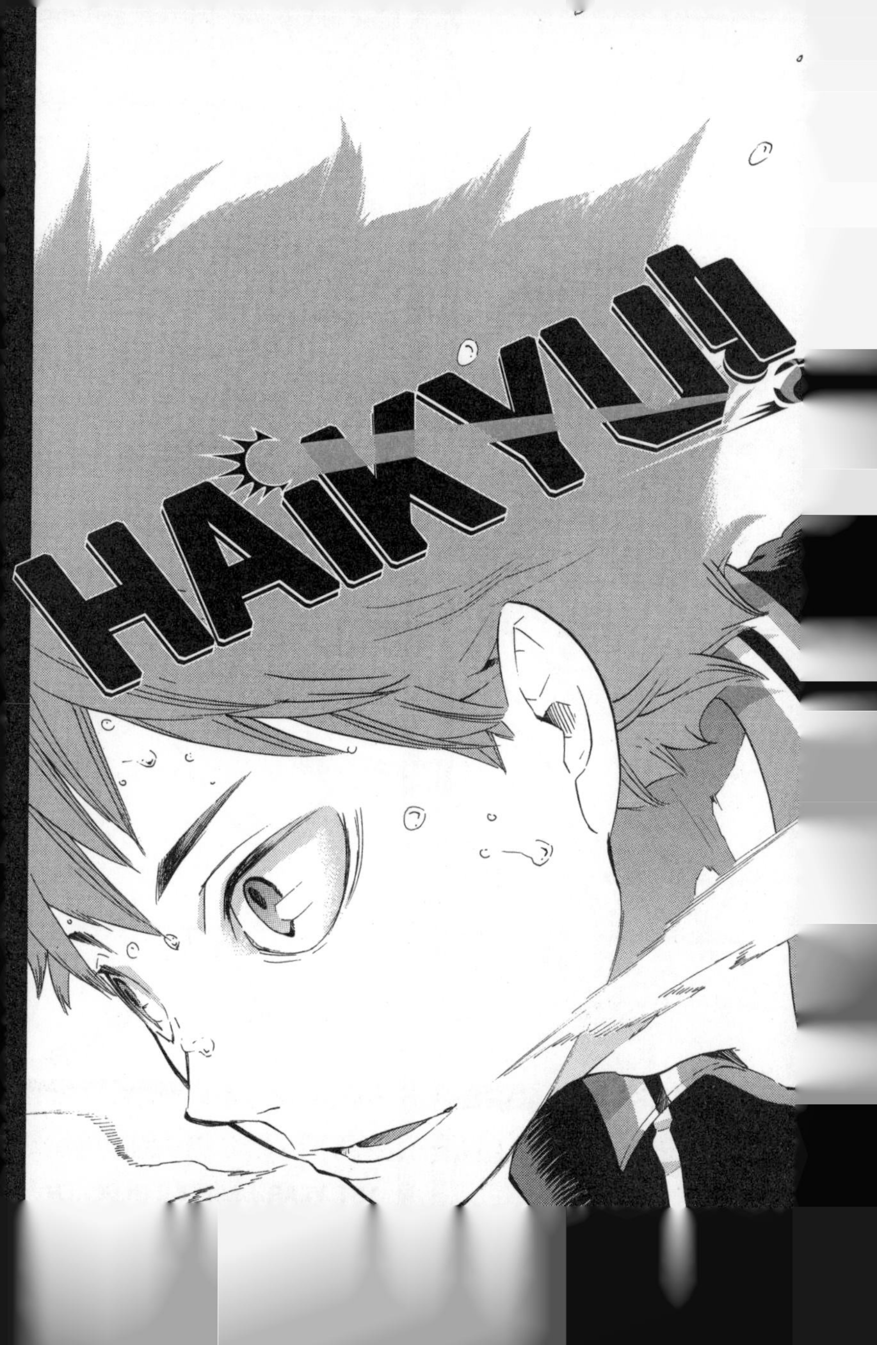
HAIKYU!!

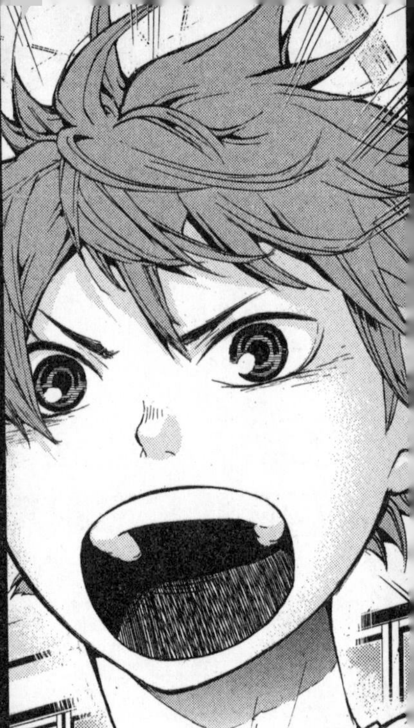

SHOYO HINATA

1ST YEAR / MIDDLE BLOCKER

Even though he doesn't have the best body type for volleyball, he is super athletic. Gets nervous easily.

TOBIO KAGEYAMA

1ST YEAR / SETTER

His instincts and athletic talent are so good that he's like a "king" who rules the court. Demanding and egocentric.

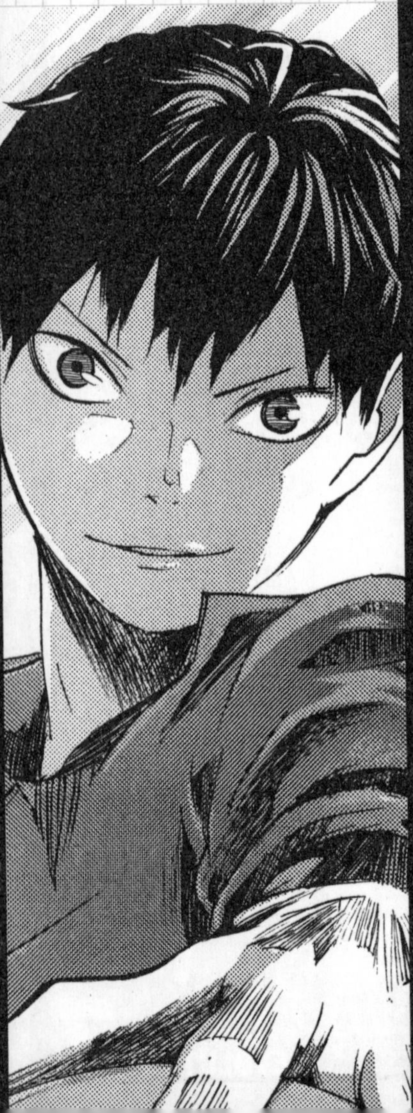

CHARACTERS

Karasuno High School Volleyball Club

YU NISHINOYA

2ND YEAR
LIBERO

KEI TSUKISHIMA

1ST YEAR
MIDDLE BLOCKER

KIYOKO SHIMIZU

3RD YEAR
MANAGER

DAICHI SAWAMURA

3RD YEAR (CAPTAIN)
WING SPIKER

ASAHI AZUMANE

3RD YEAR
WING SPIKER

TADASHI YAMAGUCHI

1ST YEAR
MIDDLE BLOCKER

RYUNOSUKE TANAKA

2ND YEAR
WING SPIKER

KOUSHI SUGAWARA

3RD YEAR (VICE CAPTAIN)
SETTER

KEISHIN UKAI

COACH

ITTETSU TAKEDA

ADVISER

Aoba Johsai High School Volleyball Club

TOHRU OIKAWA

3RD YEAR (CAPTAIN)
SETTER

HAJIME IWAIZUMI

3RD YEAR
WING SPIKER

Ever since he saw the legendary player known as "the Little Giant" compete at the national volleyball finals, Shoyo Hinata has been aiming to be the best volleyball player ever! He decides to join the volleyball club at his middle school and gets to play in an official tournament during his third year. His team is crushed by a team led by volleyball prodigy Tobio Kageyama, also known as "the King of the Court." Swearing revenge on Kageyama, Hinata graduates middle school and enters Karasuno High School, the school where the Little Giant played. However, upon joining the club, he finds out that Kageyama is there too! The two of them bicker constantly, but they bring out the best in each other's talents and become a powerful combo! In Karasuno's practice game against Nekoma, Kageyama and Hinata figure out new ways to improve their skills but ultimately lose to their opponent's consistent teamwork. Promising to get payback on the national stage, Karasuno gets ready for the summer Inter-High Tournament! They win their first two matches, but round 3 is a rematch against Aoba Johsai! Master setter "the Great King" Oikawa figures out the secret behind Kageyama's strategy, throwing Kageyama off guard and ultimately causing him to lose his cool...which gets him benched! And the one replacing him is none other than Sugawara!

HAIKYU!!

7 EVOLUTION

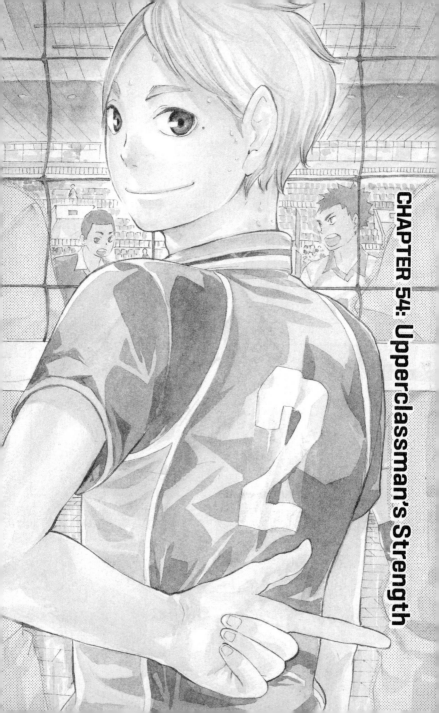

CHAPTER 54: Upperclassman's Strength

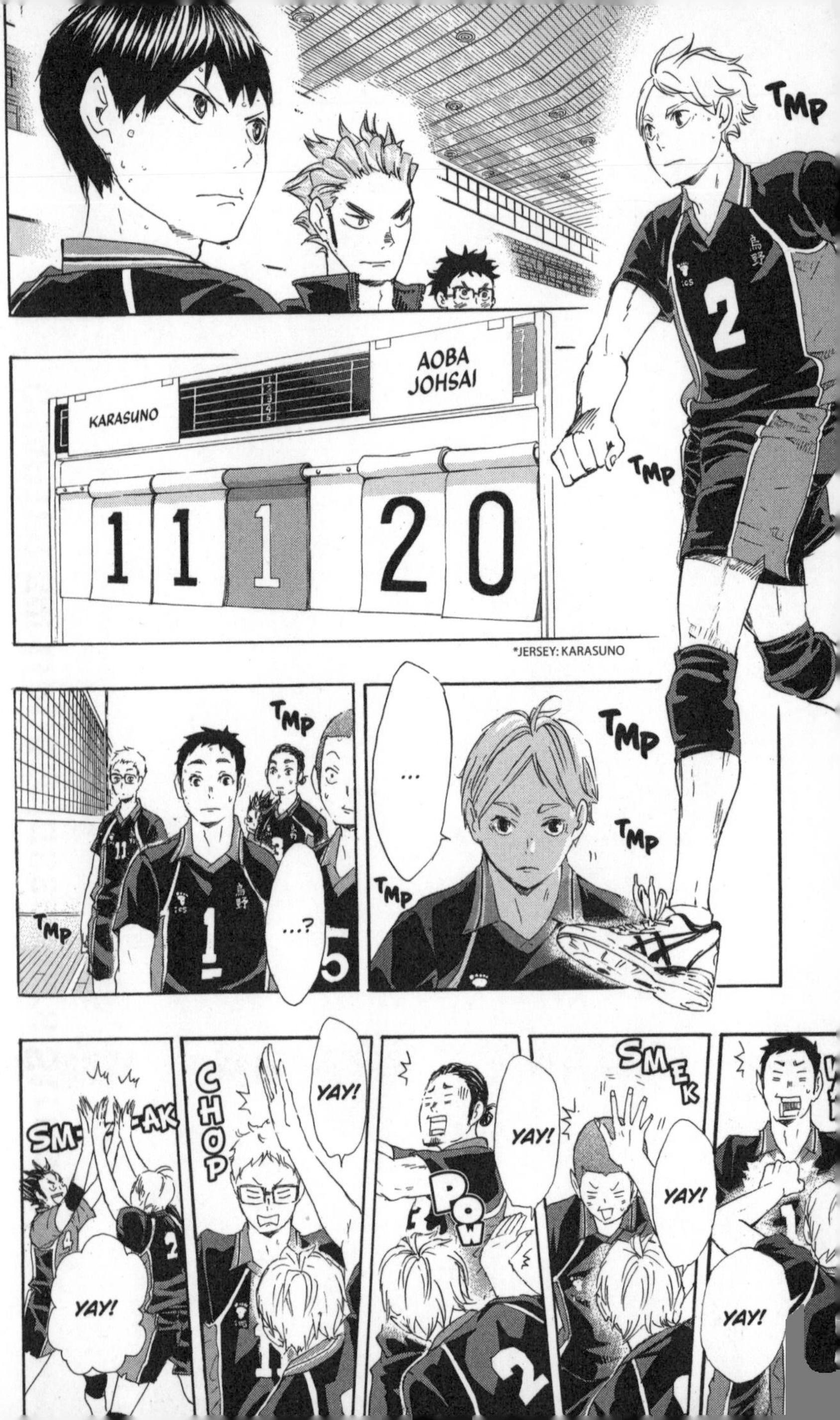
TMP
TMP
TMP
AOBA JOHSAI
KARASUNO
11
1
20
*JERSEY: KARASUNO
TMP
...
TMP
TMP
TMP
...?
TMP
YAY!
SMEK
YAY!
YAY!
POW
YAY!
CHOP
YAY!
SM--AK
YAY!

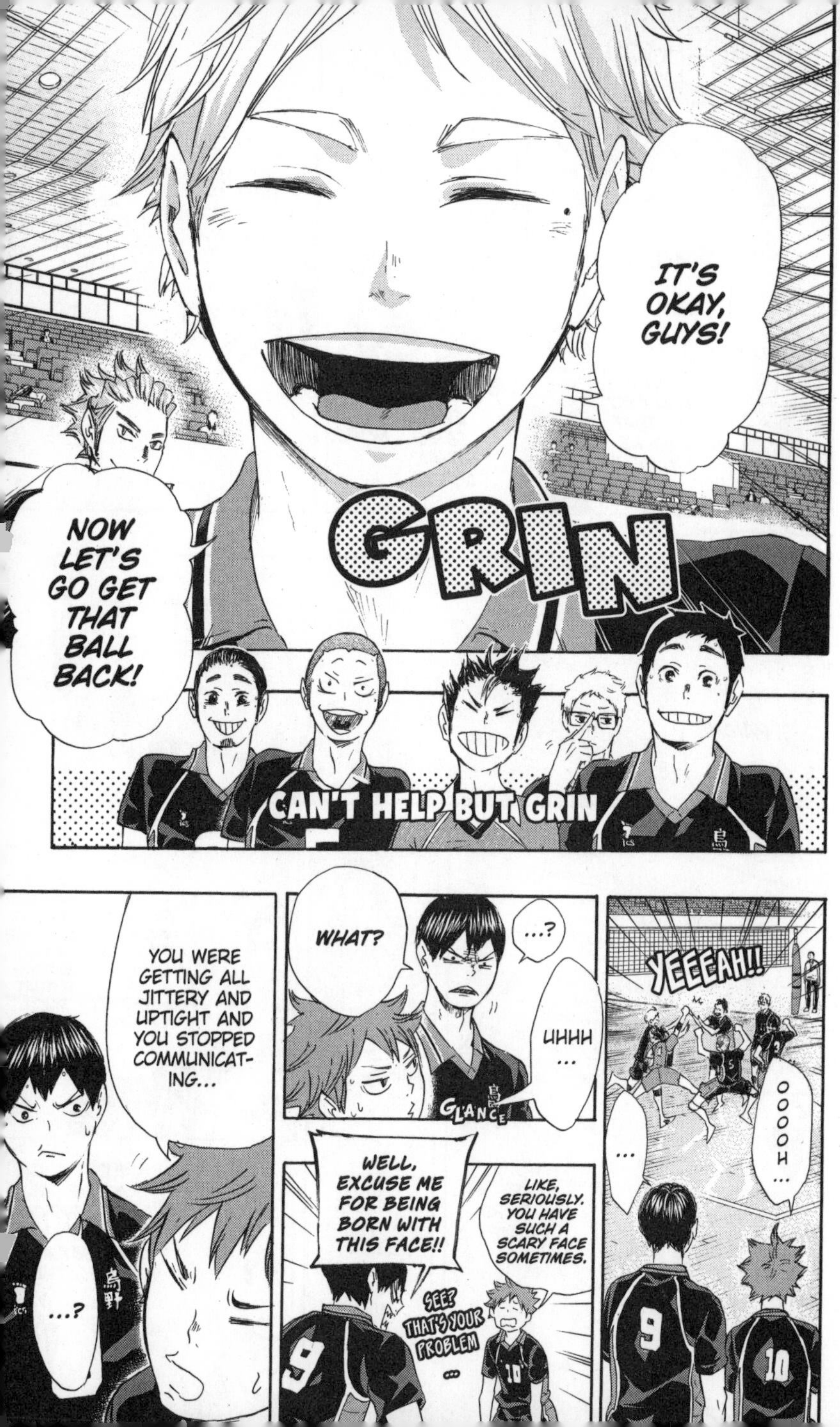
IT'S OKAY, GUYS!
GRIN
NOW LET'S GO GET THAT BALL BACK!
CAN'T HELP BUT GRIN
YEEEAH!!
OOOOH...
...
...?
WHAT?
UHHH...
GLANCE
LIKE, SERIOUSLY. YOU HAVE SUCH A SCARY FACE SOMETIMES.
WELL, EXCUSE ME FOR BEING BORN WITH THIS FACE!!
SEE? THAT'S YOUR PROBLEM
...
YOU WERE GETTING ALL JITTERY AND UPTIGHT AND YOU STOPPED COMMUNICATING...
...?

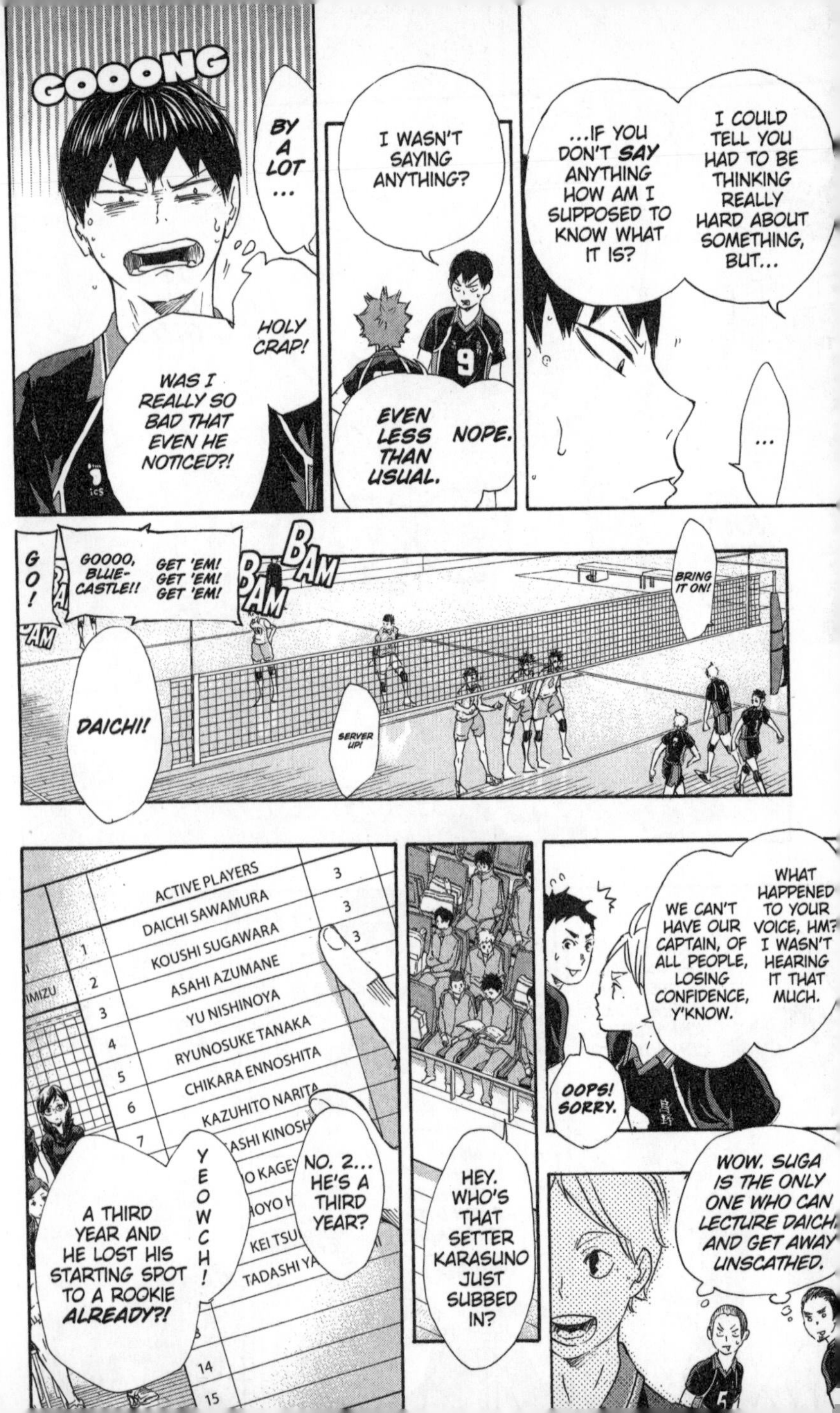
I COULD TELL YOU HAD TO BE THINKING REALLY HARD ABOUT SOMETHING, BUT...
...IF YOU DON'T SAY ANYTHING HOW AM I SUPPOSED TO KNOW WHAT IT IS?
...
I WASN'T SAYING ANYTHING?
NOPE.
EVEN LESS THAN USUAL.
BY A LOT...
GOOONG
HOLY CRAP!
WAS I REALLY SO BAD THAT EVEN HE NOTICED?!
BRING IT ON!
BAM
BAM
BAM
GET 'EM! GET 'EM! GET 'EM!
GOOOO, BLUE-CASTLE!!
GO!
SERVER UP!
DAICHI!
WHAT HAPPENED TO YOUR VOICE, HM? I WASN'T HEARING IT THAT MUCH.
WE CAN'T HAVE OUR CAPTAIN, OF ALL PEOPLE, LOSING CONFIDENCE, Y'KNOW.
OOPS! SORRY.
WOW. SUGA IS THE ONLY ONE WHO CAN LECTURE DAICHI AND GET AWAY UNSCATHED.
HEY. WHO'S THAT SETTER KARASUNO JUST SUBBED IN?
ACTIVE PLAYERS
DAICHI SAWAMURA
KOUSHI SUGAWARA
ASAHI AZUMANE
YU NISHINOYA
RYUNOSUKE TANAKA
CHIKARA ENNOSHITA
NO. 2... HE'S A THIRD YEAR?
YEOWCH!
A THIRD YEAR AND HE LOST HIS STARTING SPOT TO A ROOKIE ALREADY?!

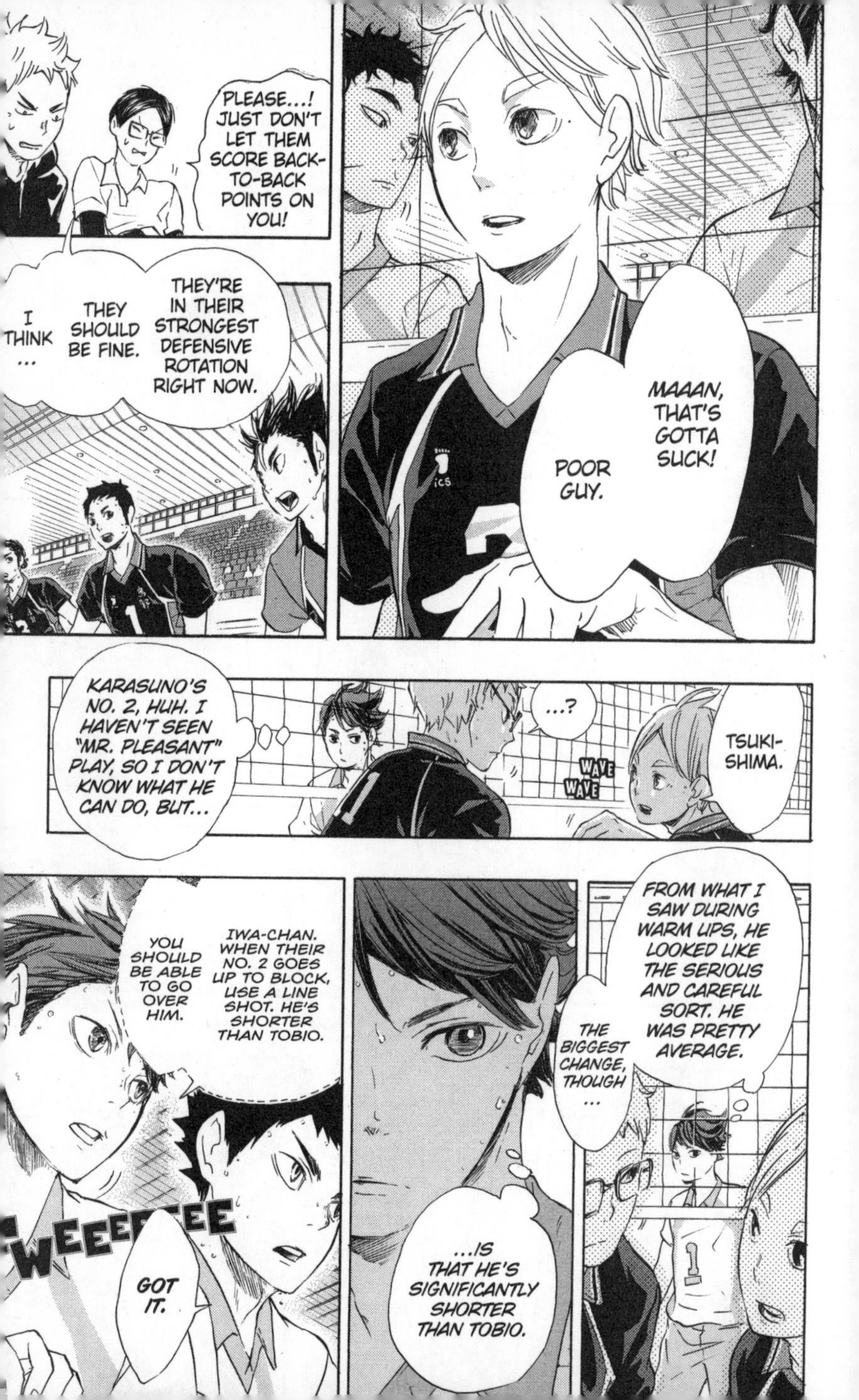
MAAAN, THAT'S GOTTA SUCK!
POOR GUY.
PLEASE...! JUST DON'T LET THEM SCORE BACK-TO-BACK POINTS ON YOU!
THEY'RE IN THEIR STRONGEST DEFENSIVE ROTATION RIGHT NOW.
THEY SHOULD BE FINE.
I THINK...
TSUKI-SHIMA.
...?
WAVE WAVE
KARASUNO'S NO. 2, HUH. I HAVEN'T SEEN "MR. PLEASANT" PLAY, SO I DON'T KNOW WHAT HE CAN DO, BUT...
FROM WHAT I SAW DURING WARM UPS, HE LOOKED LIKE THE SERIOUS AND CAREFUL SORT. HE WAS PRETTY AVERAGE.
THE BIGGEST CHANGE, THOUGH...
...IS THAT HE'S SIGNIFICANTLY SHORTER THAN TOBIO.
IWA-CHAN. WHEN THEIR NO. 2 GOES UP TO BLOCK, USE A LINE SHOT. HE'S SHORTER THAN TOBIO.
YOU SHOULD BE ABLE TO GO OVER HIM.
GOT IT.

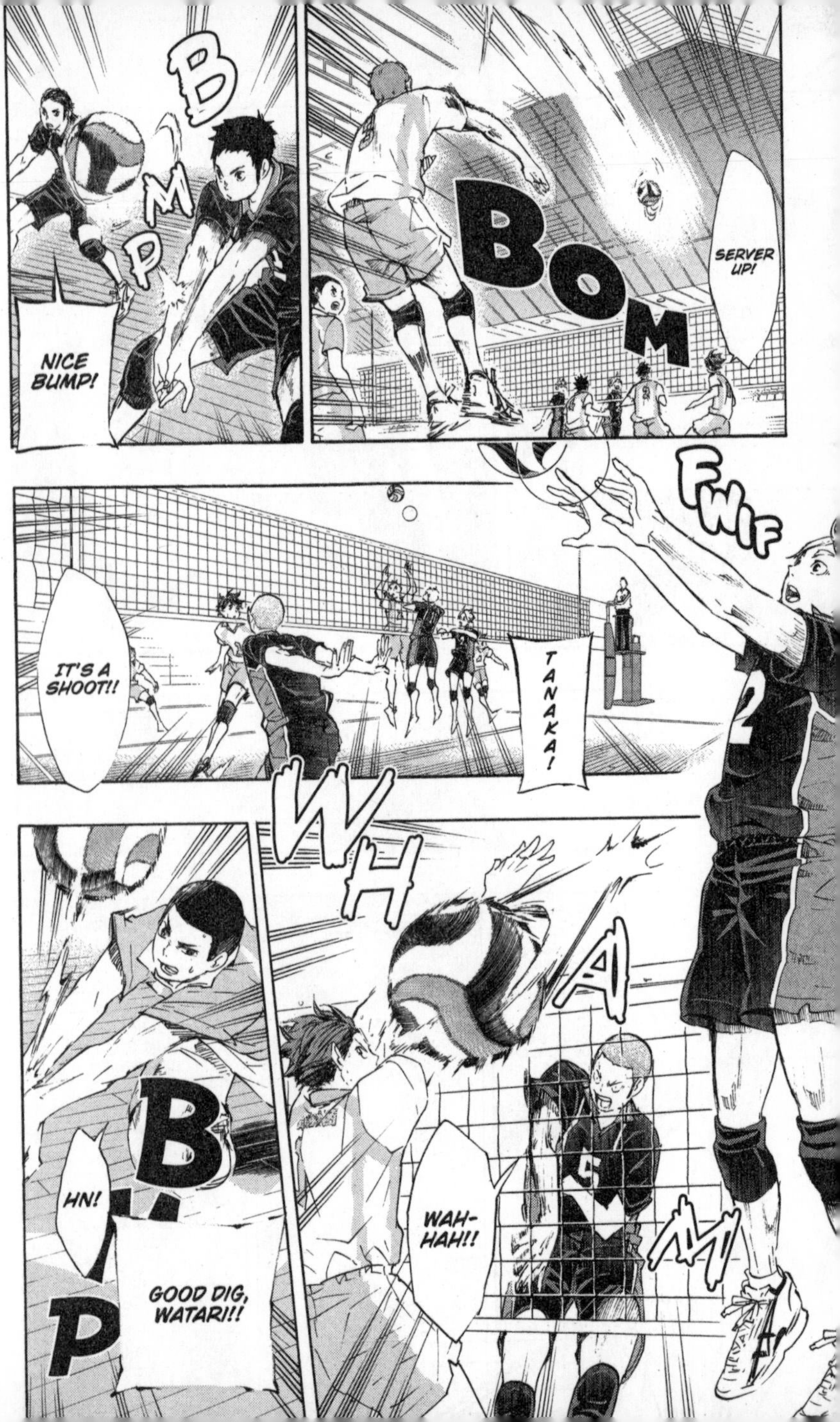
SERVER UP!
BOM
BMP
NICE BUMP!
FWIF
TANAKA!
IT'S A SHOOT!!
WHAM
WAH-HAH!!
HN!
B
P
GOOD DIG, WATARI!!

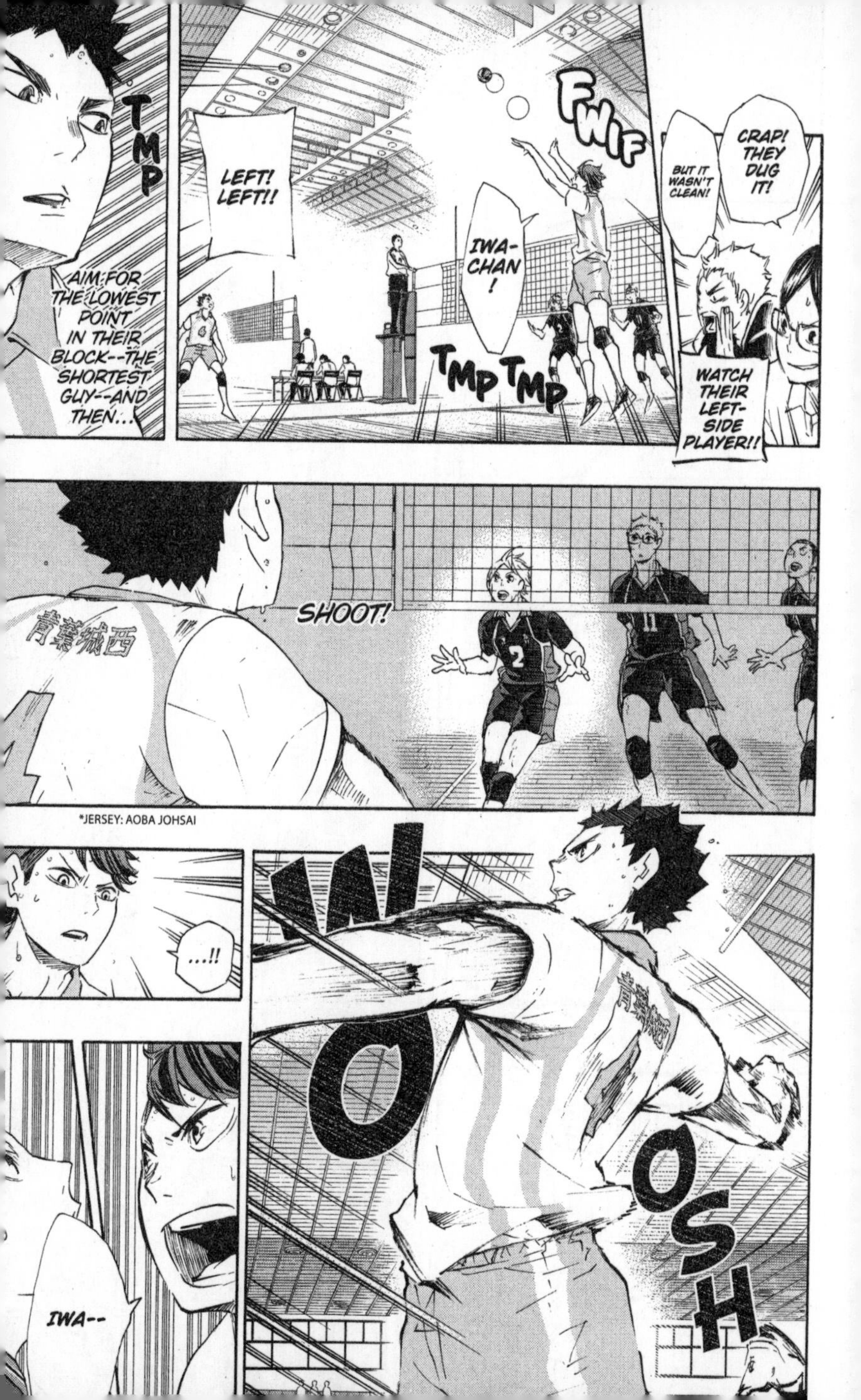
CRAP! THEY DUG IT!
BUT IT WASN'T CLEAN!
WATCH THEIR LEFT-SIDE PLAYER!!
FWIF
IWA-CHAN!
LEFT! LEFT!!
TMP TMP
TMP
TMP
AIM FOR THE LOWEST POINT IN THEIR BLOCK--THE SHORTEST GUY--AND THEN...
SHOOT!
*JERSEY: AOBA JOHSAI
WHOOSH
...!!
IWA--

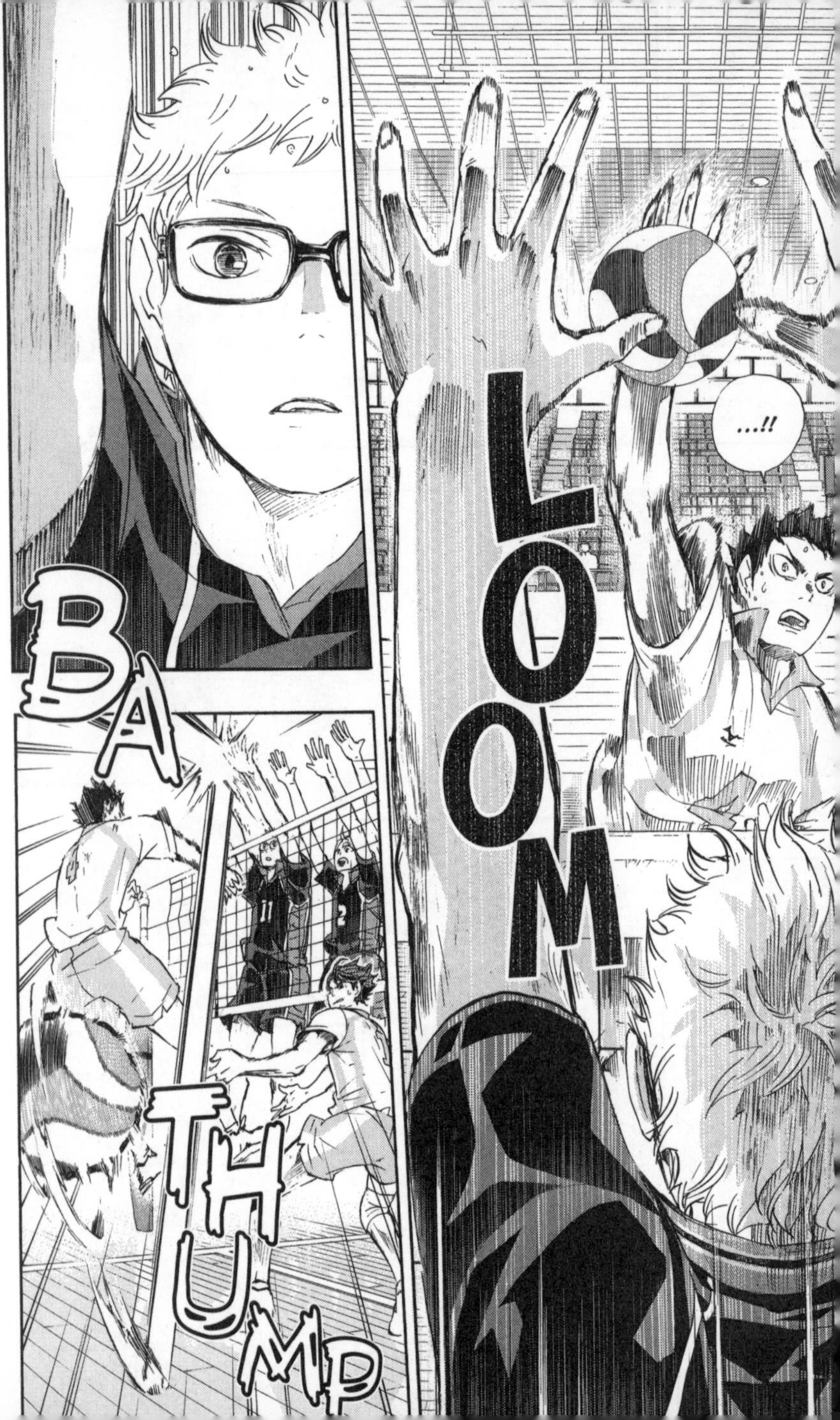
LOOM
...!!
BA
THUMP

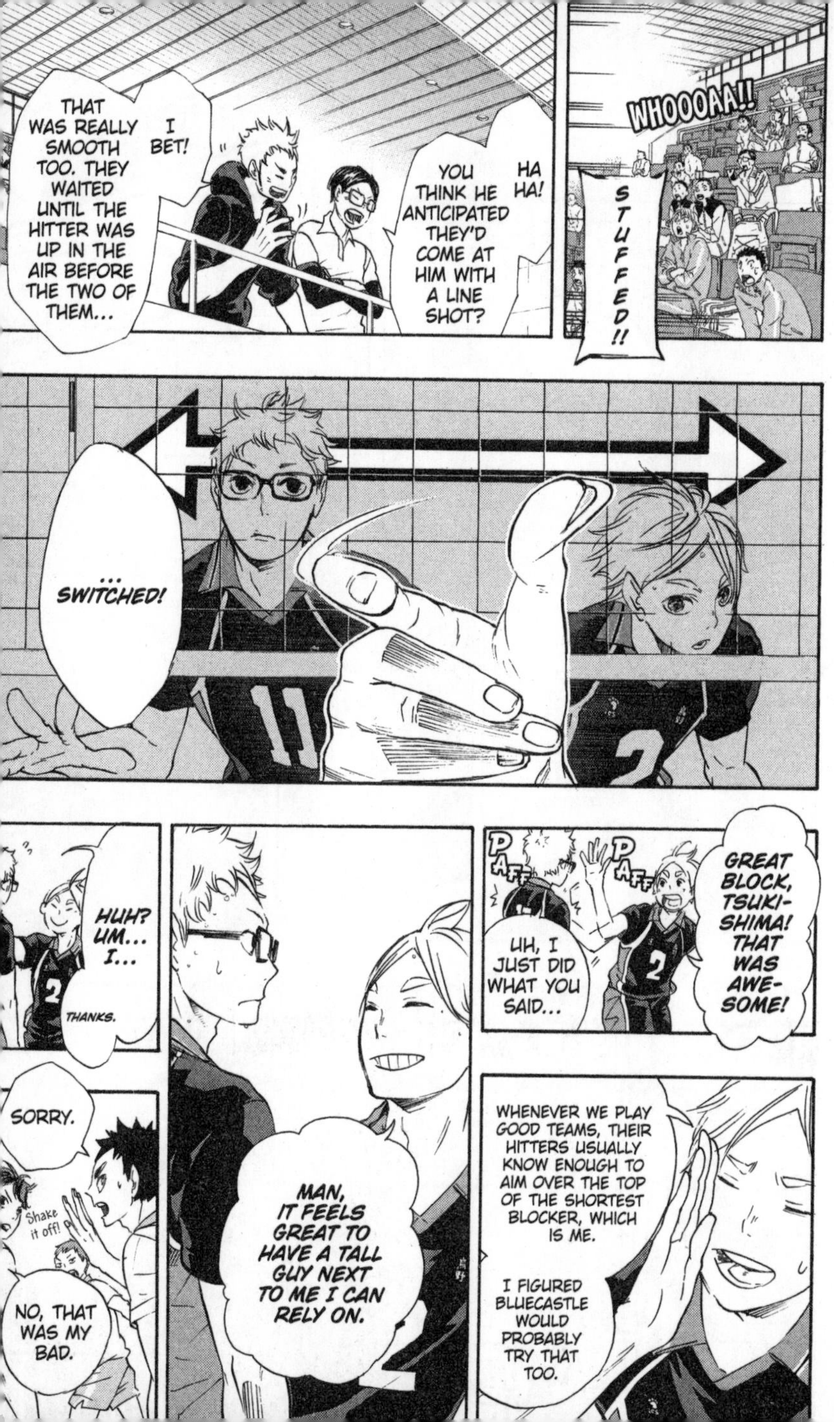
WHOOOAA!!
STUFFED!!
HA HA!
YOU THINK HE ANTICIPATED THEY'D COME AT HIM WITH A LINE SHOT?
I BET!
THAT WAS REALLY SMOOTH TOO. THEY WAITED UNTIL THE HITTER WAS UP IN THE AIR BEFORE THE TWO OF THEM...
...SWITCHED!
GREAT BLOCK, TSUKISHIMA! THAT WAS AWESOME!
PAFF
PAFF
UH, I JUST DID WHAT YOU SAID...
WHENEVER WE PLAY GOOD TEAMS, THEIR HITTERS USUALLY KNOW ENOUGH TO AIM OVER THE TOP OF THE SHORTEST BLOCKER, WHICH IS ME.
I FIGURED BLUECASTLE WOULD PROBABLY TRY THAT TOO.
MAN, IT FEELS GREAT TO HAVE A TALL GUY NEXT TO ME I CAN RELY ON.
HUH? UM... I...
THANKS.
SORRY.
Shake it off!
NO, THAT WAS MY BAD.

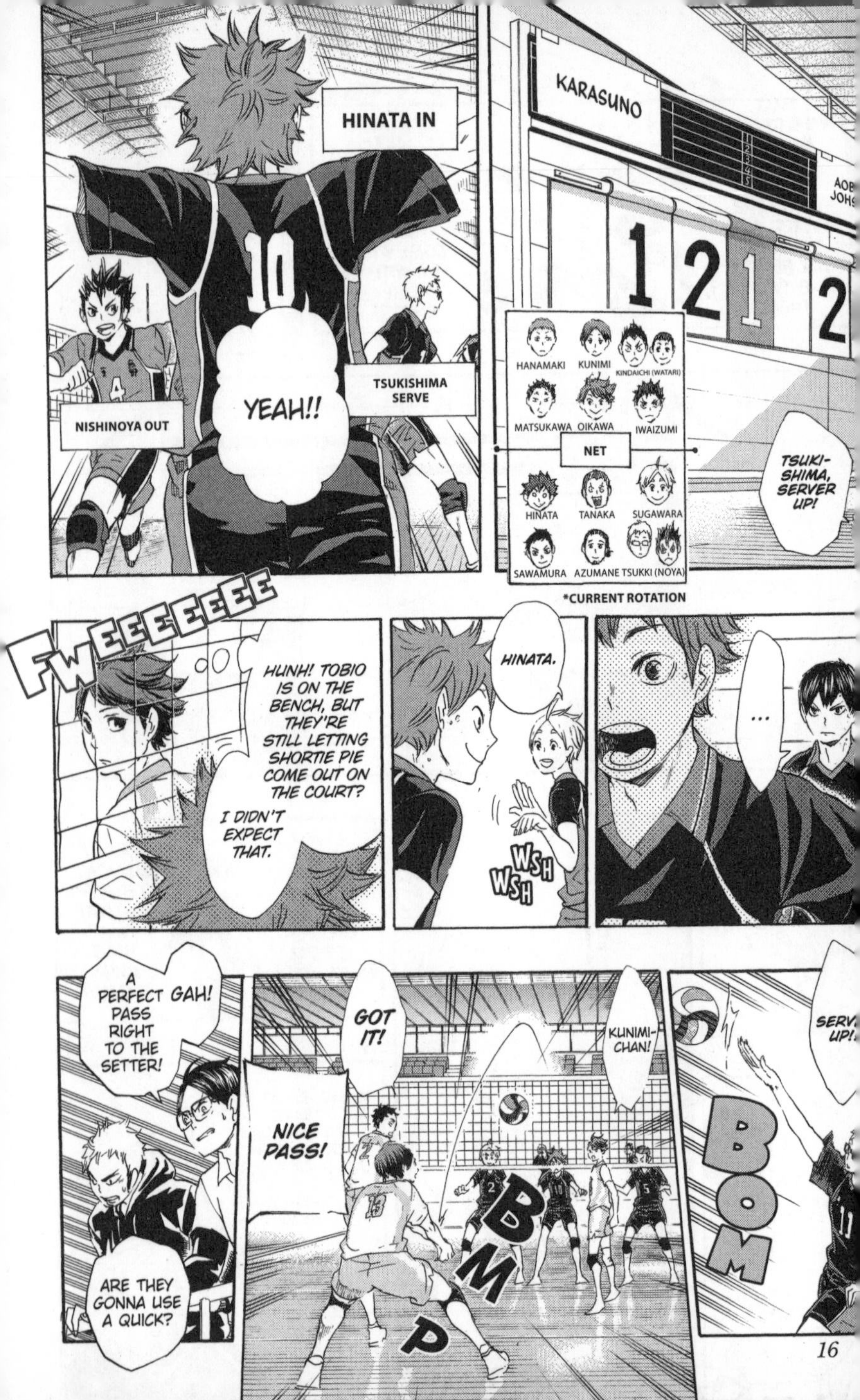
KARASUNO
1 2 3 4 5
1 2 1 2
TSUKI-SHIMA, SERVER UP!
HANAMAKI KUNIMI KINDAICHI (WATARI)
MATSUKAWA OIKAWA IWAIZUMI
NET
HINATA TANAKA SUGAWARA
SAWAMURA AZUMANE TSUKKI (NOYA)
*CURRENT ROTATION
HINATA IN
TSUKISHIMA SERVE
YEAH!!
NISHINOYA OUT
FWEEEEEEE
...
HINATA.
WSH WSH
HUNH! TOBIO IS ON THE BENCH, BUT THEY'RE STILL LETTING SHORTIE PIE COME OUT ON THE COURT?
I DIDN'T EXPECT THAT.
SERV UP!
BOM
KUNIMI-CHAN!
GOT IT!
NICE PASS!
BMP
GAH!
A PERFECT PASS RIGHT TO THE SETTER!
ARE THEY GONNA USE A QUICK?

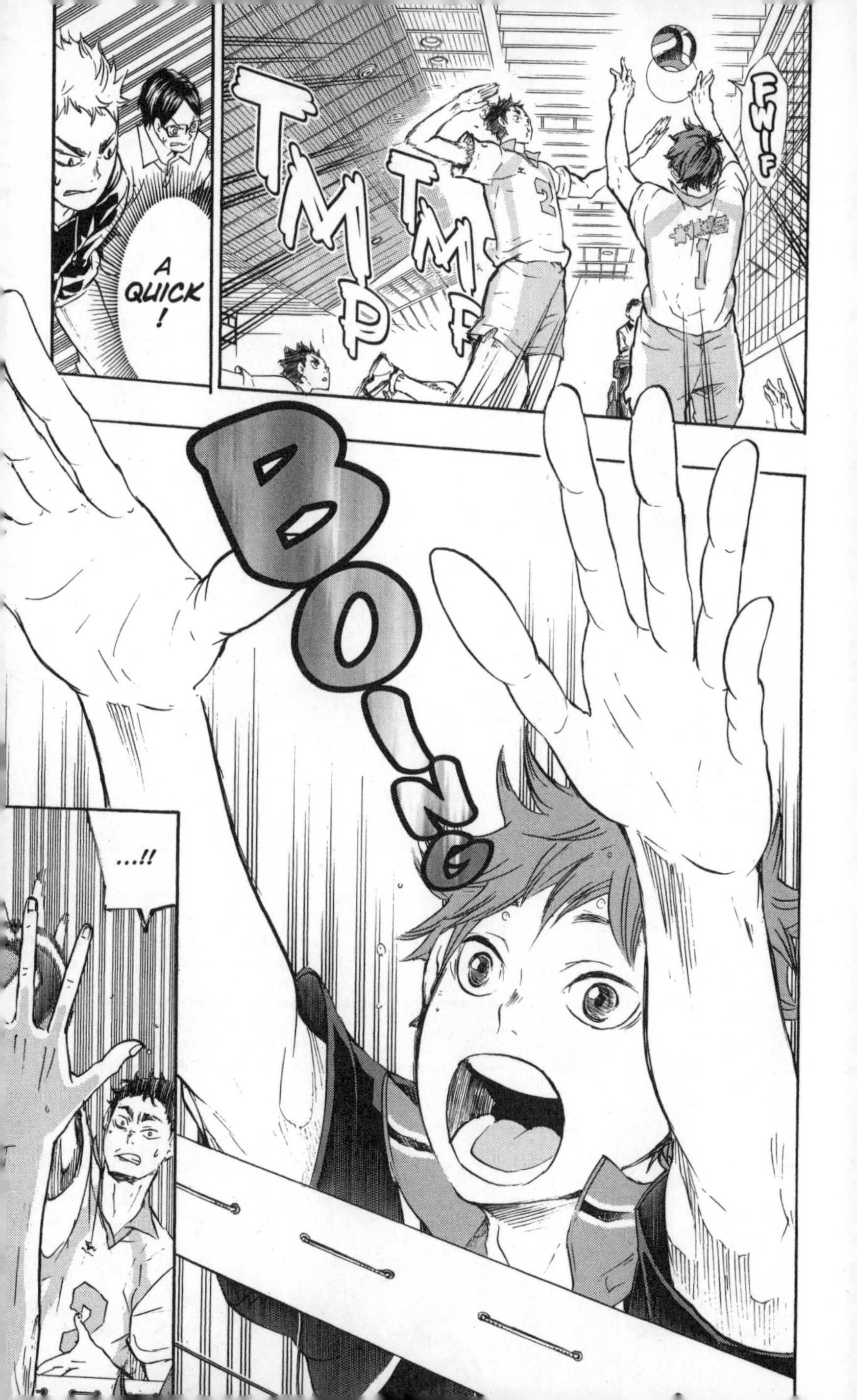
FWIF
TMP
TMP
A QUICK!
BOING
...!!

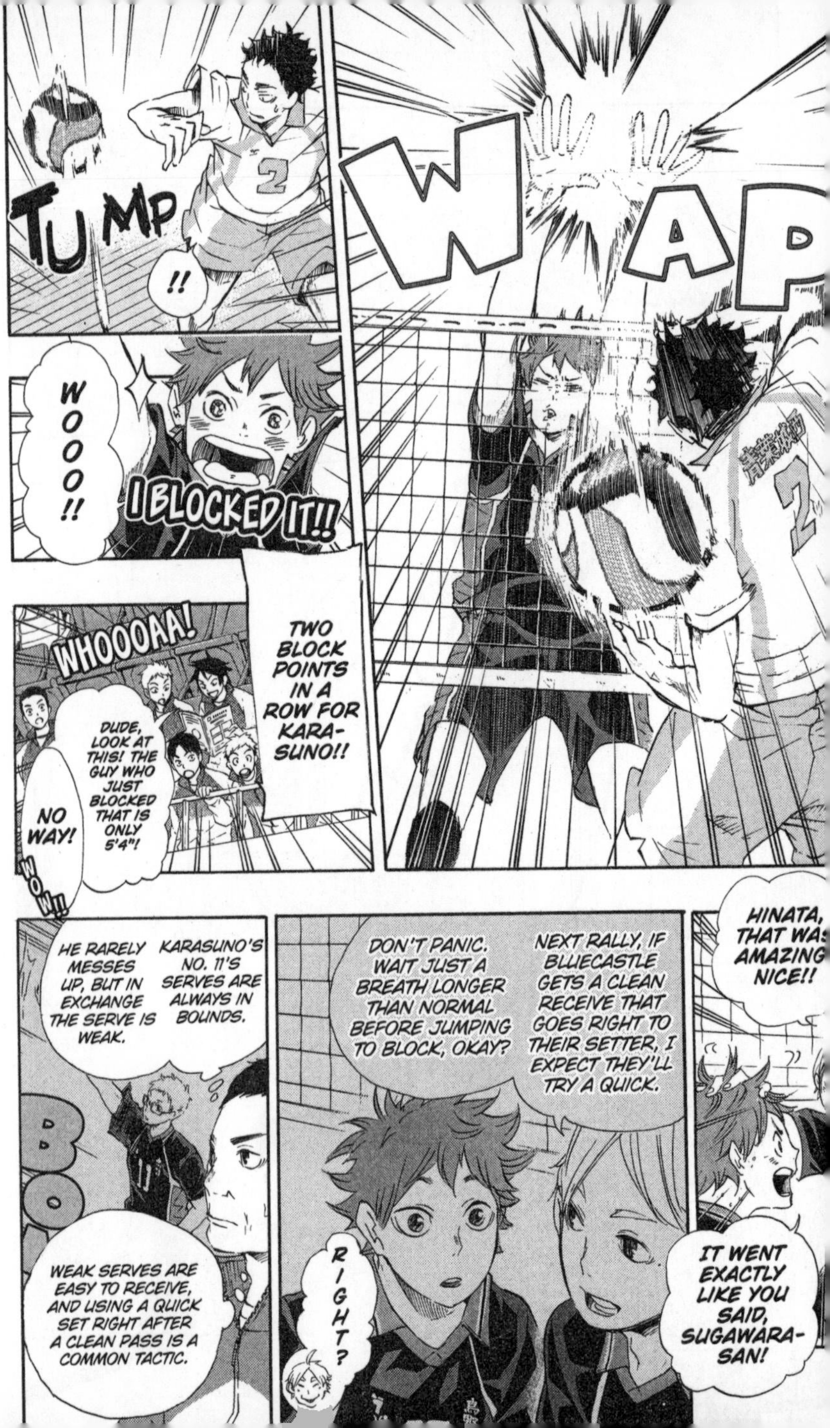
WHAP
TWO BLOCK POINTS IN A ROW FOR KARA-SUNO!!
TUMP
!!
WOOOO!!
I BLOCKED IT!!
WHOOOAA!
DUDE, LOOK AT THIS! THE GUY WHO JUST BLOCKED THAT IS ONLY 5'4"!
NO WAY!
WOW!!
HINATA, THAT WAS AMAZING NICE!!
IT WENT EXACTLY LIKE YOU SAID, SUGAWARA-SAN!
NEXT RALLY, IF BLUECASTLE GETS A CLEAN RECEIVE THAT GOES RIGHT TO THEIR SETTER, I EXPECT THEY'LL TRY A QUICK.
DON'T PANIC. WAIT JUST A BREATH LONGER THAN NORMAL BEFORE JUMPING TO BLOCK, OKAY?
RIGHT?
KARASUNO'S NO. 11'S SERVES ARE ALWAYS IN BOUNDS.
HE RARELY MESSES UP, BUT IN EXCHANGE THE SERVE IS WEAK.
WEAK SERVES ARE EASY TO RECEIVE, AND USING A QUICK SET RIGHT AFTER A CLEAN PASS IS A COMMON TACTIC.

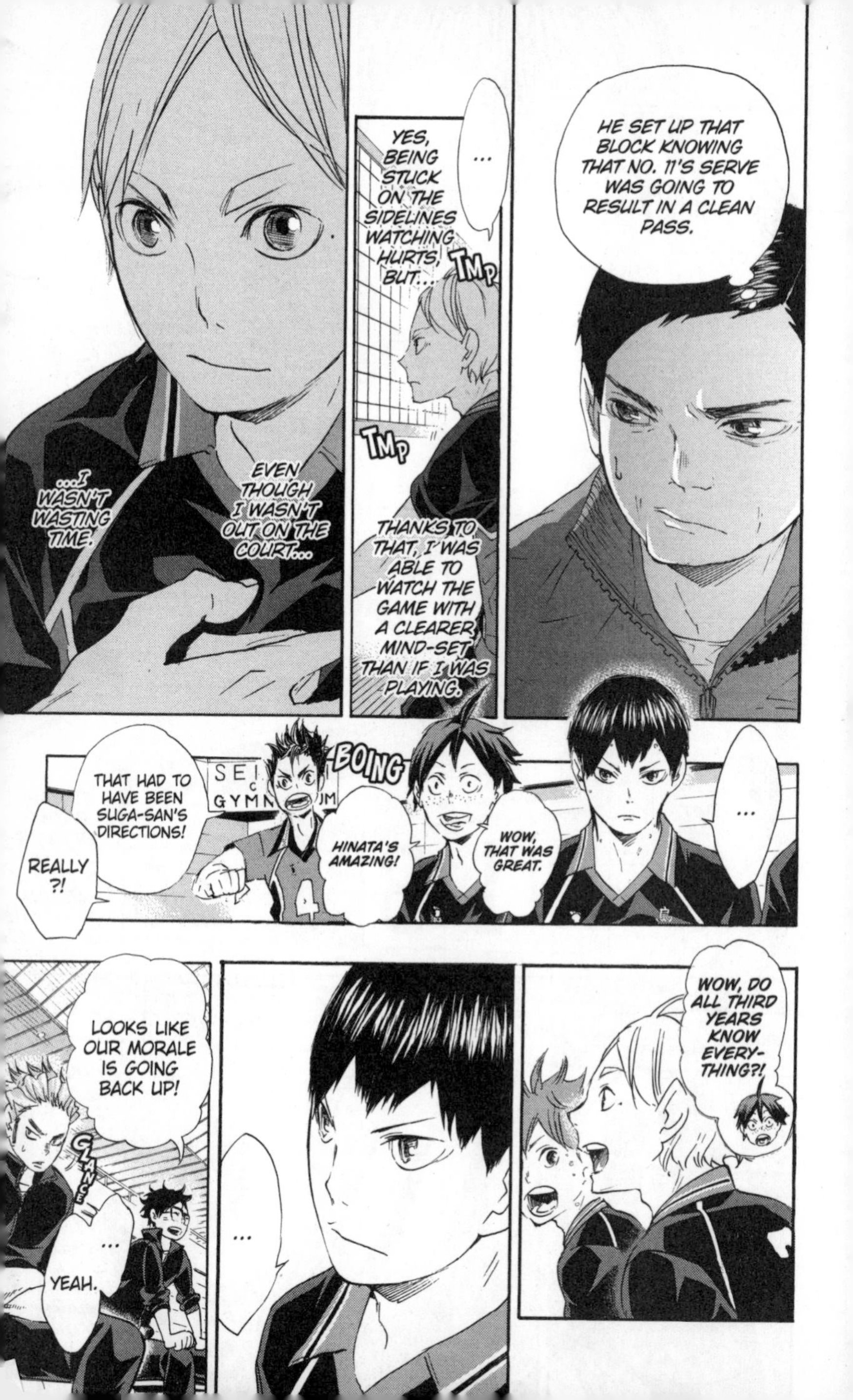
HE SET UP THAT BLOCK KNOWING THAT NO. 11'S SERVE WAS GOING TO RESULT IN A CLEAN PASS.
...
YES, BEING STUCK ON THE SIDELINES WATCHING HURTS, BUT...
TMP
TMP
THANKS TO THAT, I WAS ABLE TO WATCH THE GAME WITH A CLEARER MIND-SET THAN IF I WAS PLAYING.
EVEN THOUGH I WASN'T OUT ON THE COURT...
...I WASN'T WASTING TIME.
...
WOW, THAT WAS GREAT.
HINATA'S AMAZING!
BOING
THAT HAD TO HAVE BEEN SUGA-SAN'S DIRECTIONS!
REALLY?!
WOW, DO ALL THIRD YEARS KNOW EVERY-THING?!
...
LOOKS LIKE OUR MORALE IS GOING BACK UP!
GLANCE
...
YEAH.

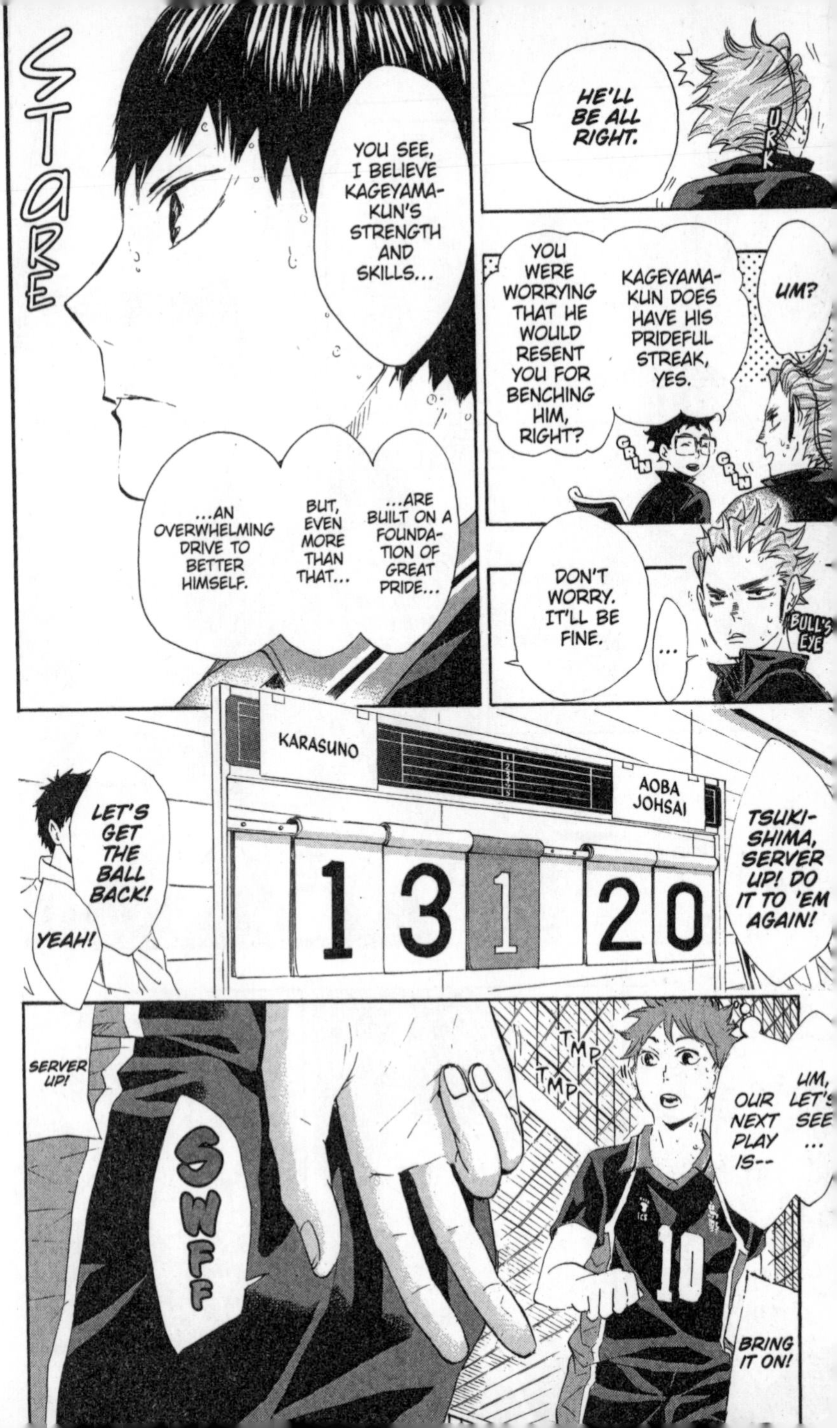
URK
HE'LL BE ALL RIGHT.
UM?
KAGEYAMA-KUN DOES HAVE HIS PRIDEFUL STREAK, YES.
YOU WERE WORRYING THAT HE WOULD RESENT YOU FOR BENCHING HIM, RIGHT?
GRIN
GRIN
...
DON'T WORRY. IT'LL BE FINE.
BULL'S EYE
STARE
YOU SEE, I BELIEVE KAGEYAMA-KUN'S STRENGTH AND SKILLS...
...ARE BUILT ON A FOUNDATION OF GREAT PRIDE...
BUT, EVEN MORE THAN THAT...
...AN OVERWHELMING DRIVE TO BETTER HIMSELF.
TSUKISHIMA, SERVER UP! DO IT TO 'EM AGAIN!
KARASUNO
AOBA JOHSAI
13 1 20
LET'S GET THE BALL BACK!
YEAH!
UM, LET'S SEE...
OUR NEXT PLAY IS--
TMP
TMP
BRING IT ON!
SWFF
SERVER UP!

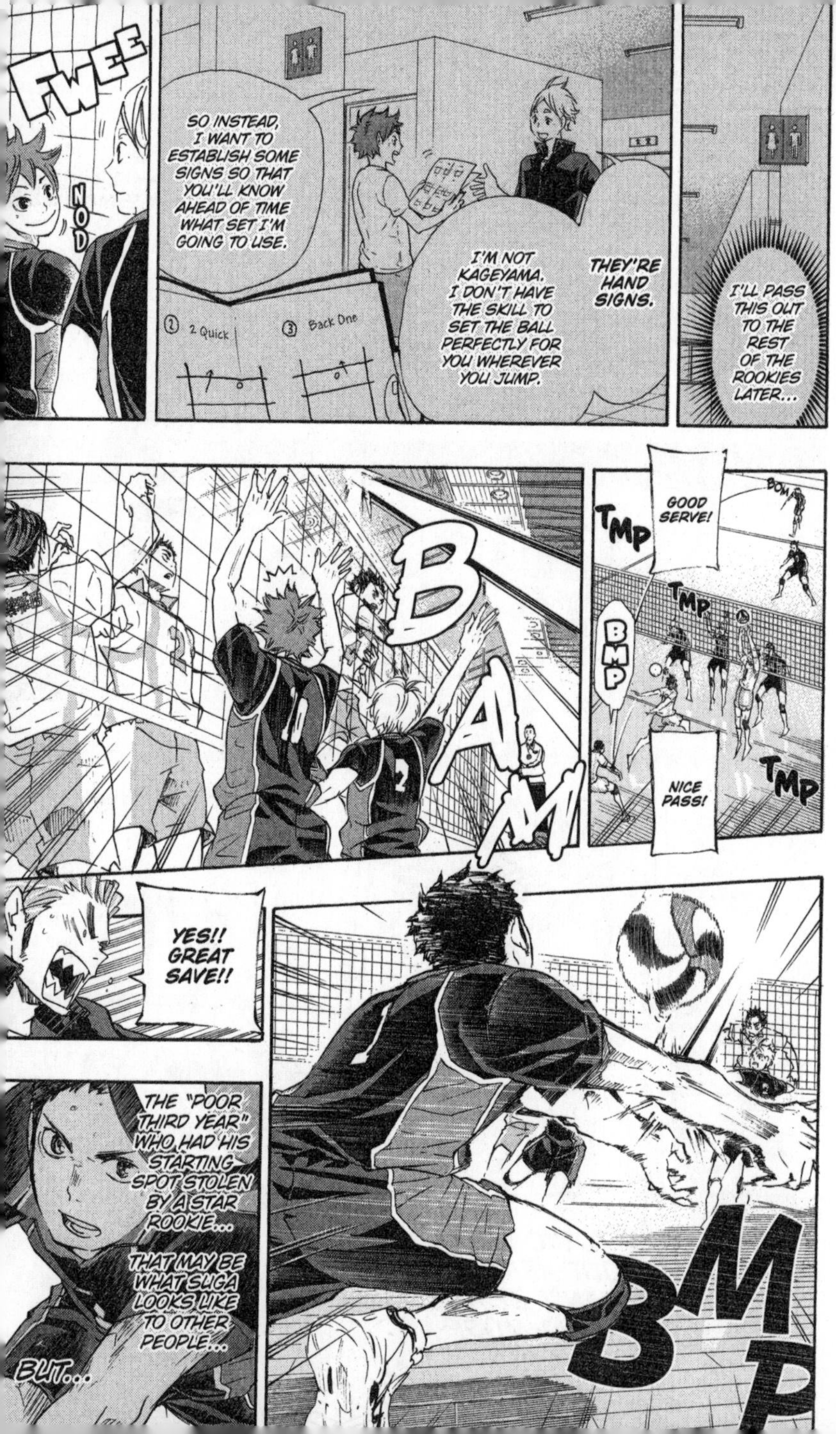
I'LL PASS THIS OUT TO THE REST OF THE ROOKIES LATER...
THEY'RE HAND SIGNS.
I'M NOT KAGEYAMA. I DON'T HAVE THE SKILL TO SET THE BALL PERFECTLY FOR YOU WHEREVER YOU JUMP.
SO INSTEAD, I WANT TO ESTABLISH SOME SIGNS SO THAT YOU'LL KNOW AHEAD OF TIME WHAT SET I'M GOING TO USE.
③ Back One
② 2 Quick
FWEE
NOD
BOM
GOOD SERVE!
TMP
TMP
BMP
NICE PASS!
TMP
BAM
BMP
YES!! GREAT SAVE!!
THE "POOR THIRD YEAR" WHO HAD HIS STARTING SPOT STOLEN BY A STAR ROOKIE...
THAT MAY BE WHAT SUGA LOOKS LIKE TO OTHER PEOPLE...
BUT...

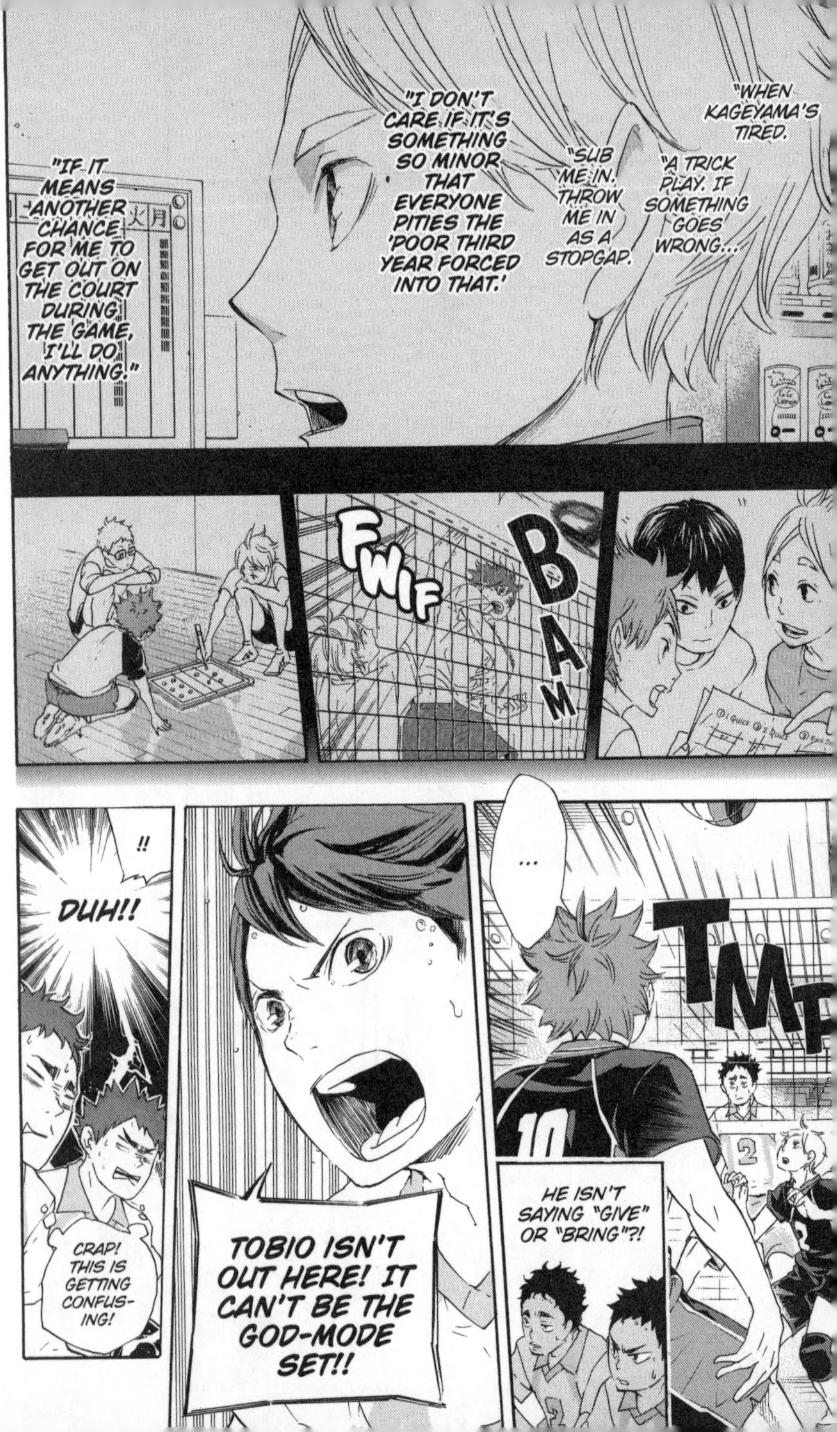
"WHEN KAGEYAMA'S TIRED.
"A TRICK PLAY. IF SOMETHING GOES WRONG...
"SUB ME IN. THROW ME IN AS A STOPGAP.
"I DON'T CARE IF IT'S SOMETHING SO MINOR THAT EVERYONE PITIES THE 'POOR THIRD YEAR FORCED INTO THAT.'
"IF IT MEANS ANOTHER CHANCE FOR ME TO GET OUT ON THE COURT DURING THE GAME, I'LL DO ANYTHING."
①1 Quick ②2 Quick
BAM
FWIF
...
TMP
HE ISN'T SAYING "GIVE" OR "BRING"?!
TOBIO ISN'T OUT HERE! IT CAN'T BE THE GOD-MODE SET!!
!!
DUH!!
CRAP! THIS IS GETTING CONFUS-ING!

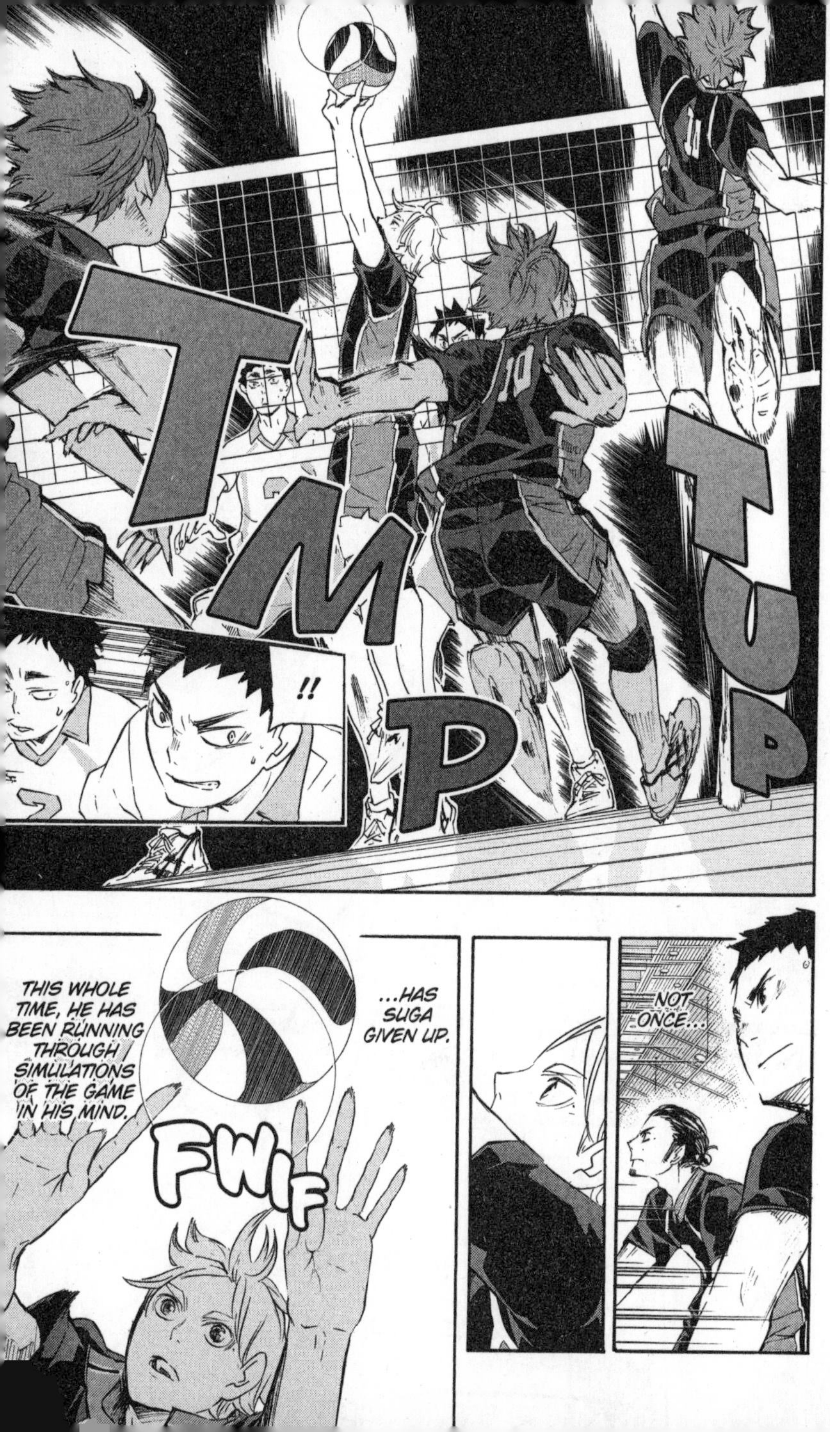
TUP
TMP
!!
NOT ONCE...
...HAS SUGA GIVEN UP.
THIS WHOLE TIME, HE HAS BEEN RUNNING THROUGH SIMULATIONS OF THE GAME IN HIS MIND.
FWIF

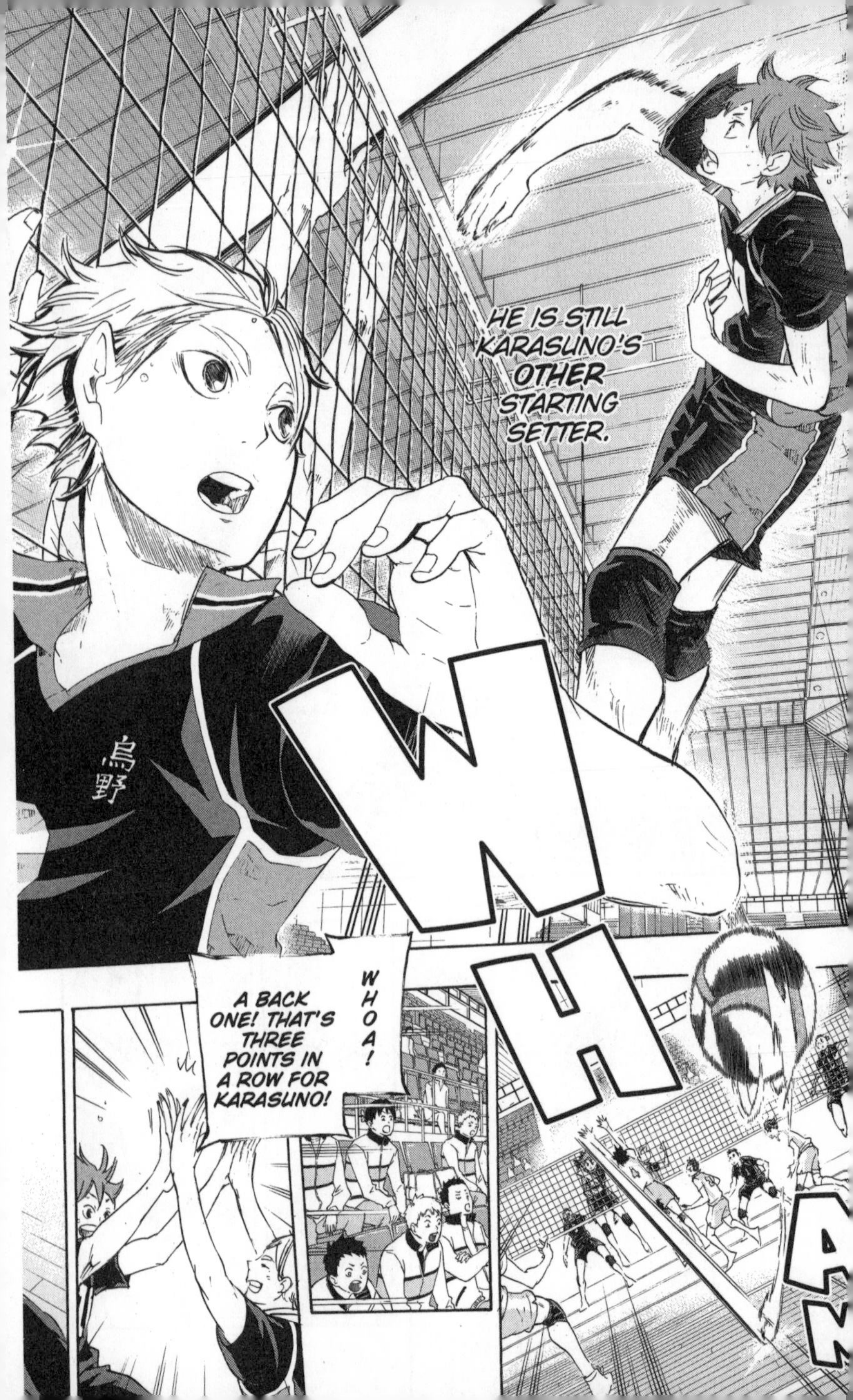
HE IS STILL KARASUNO'S OTHER STARTING SETTER.
WHH
WHOA!
A BACK ONE! THAT'S THREE POINTS IN A ROW FOR KARASUNO!

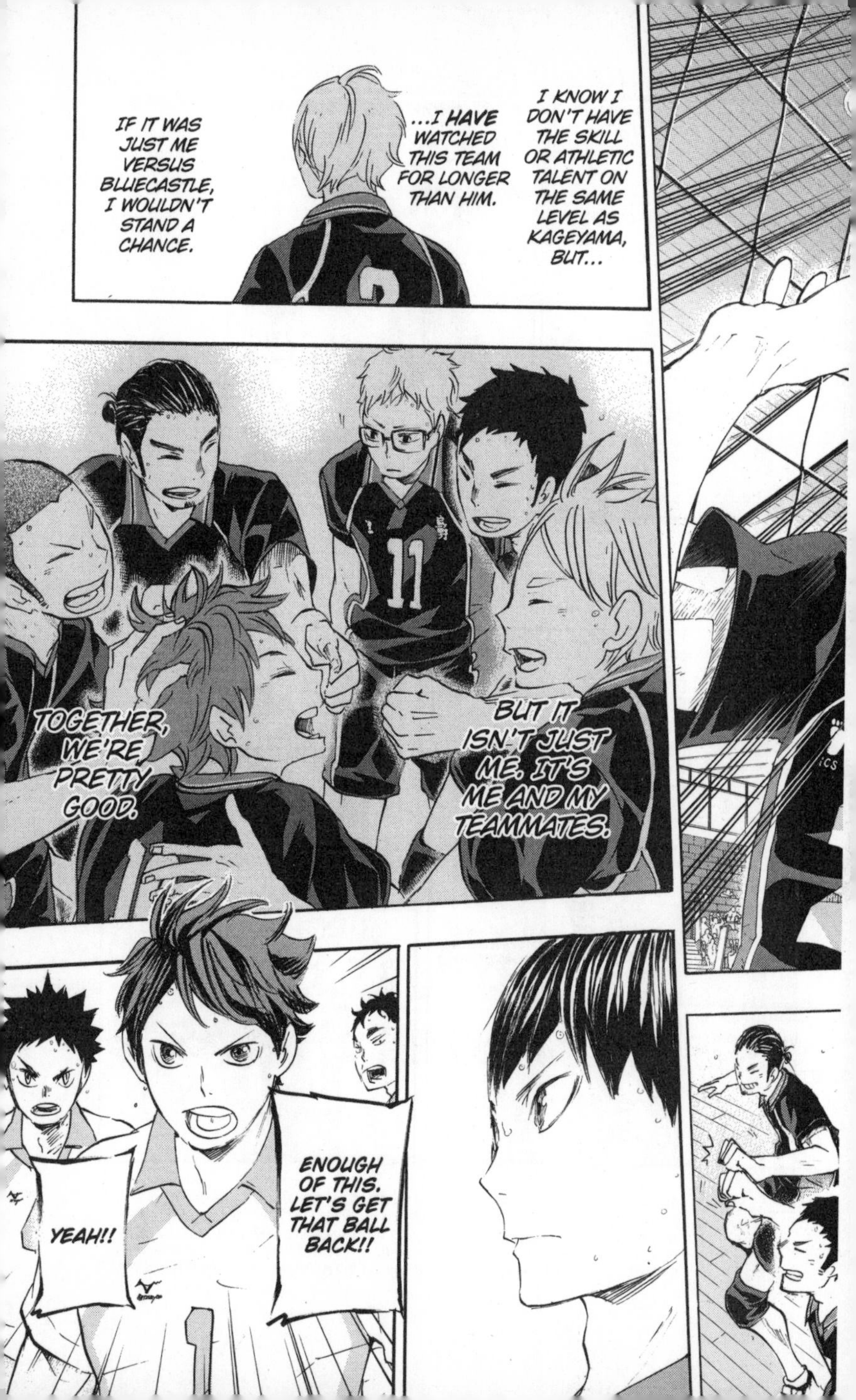
I KNOW I DON'T HAVE THE SKILL OR ATHLETIC TALENT ON THE SAME LEVEL AS KAGEYAMA, BUT...
...I **HAVE** WATCHED THIS TEAM FOR LONGER THAN HIM.
IF IT WAS JUST ME VERSUS BLUECASTLE, I WOULDN'T STAND A CHANCE.
BUT IT ISN'T JUST ME. IT'S ME AND MY TEAMMATES.
TOGETHER, WE'RE PRETTY GOOD.
ENOUGH OF THIS. LET'S GET THAT BALL BACK!!
YEAH!!

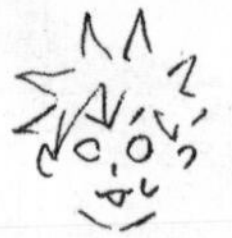

FROM THE DRAWING BOARD!

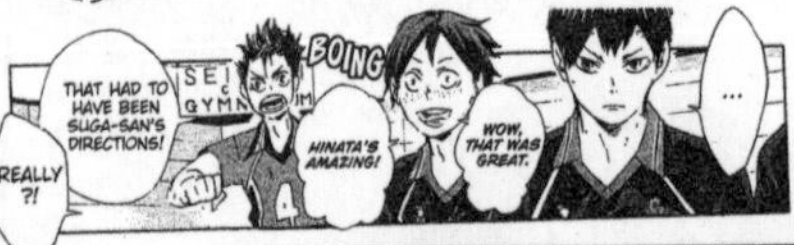
...
WOW, THAT WAS GREAT.
HINATA'S AMAZING!
BOING
THAT HAD TO HAVE BEEN SUGA-SAN'S DIRECTIONS!
REALLY?!

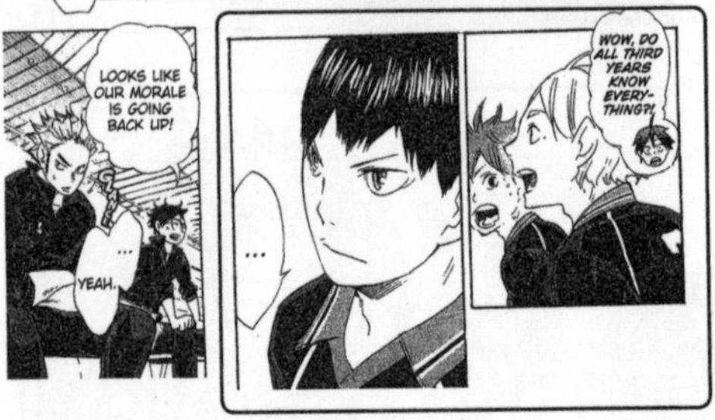
WOW, DO ALL THIRD YEARS KNOW EVERY-THING?!
...
LOOKS LIKE OUR MORALE IS GOING BACK UP!
...
YEAH.

← THESE TWO PANELS HERE…

…USED TO BE THIS.

↓

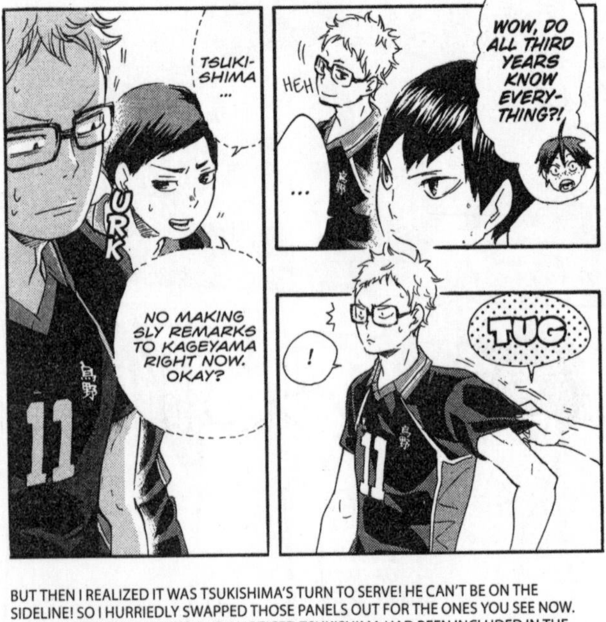
WOW, DO ALL THIRD YEARS KNOW EVERY-THING?!
HEH
...
TUG
!
TSUKISHIMA...
URK
NO MAKING SLY REMARKS TO KAGEYAMA RIGHT NOW. OKAY?

BUT THEN I REALIZED IT WAS TSUKISHIMA'S TURN TO SERVE! HE CAN'T BE ON THE SIDELINE! SO I HURRIEDLY SWAPPED THOSE PANELS OUT FOR THE ONES YOU SEE NOW. AFTER THOSE EDITS WERE DONE, I NOTICED TSUKISHIMA HAD BEEN INCLUDED IN THE PANEL DIRECTLY ABOVE THEM, SO I EDITED HIM OUT FOR NISHINOYA. BUT NISHINOYA IS SHORTER THAN TSUKISHIMA, SO TO HAVE HIM FIT IN THE BLANK SPACE I HAD HIM JUMP.

CHAPTER 55: My Best and Your Best

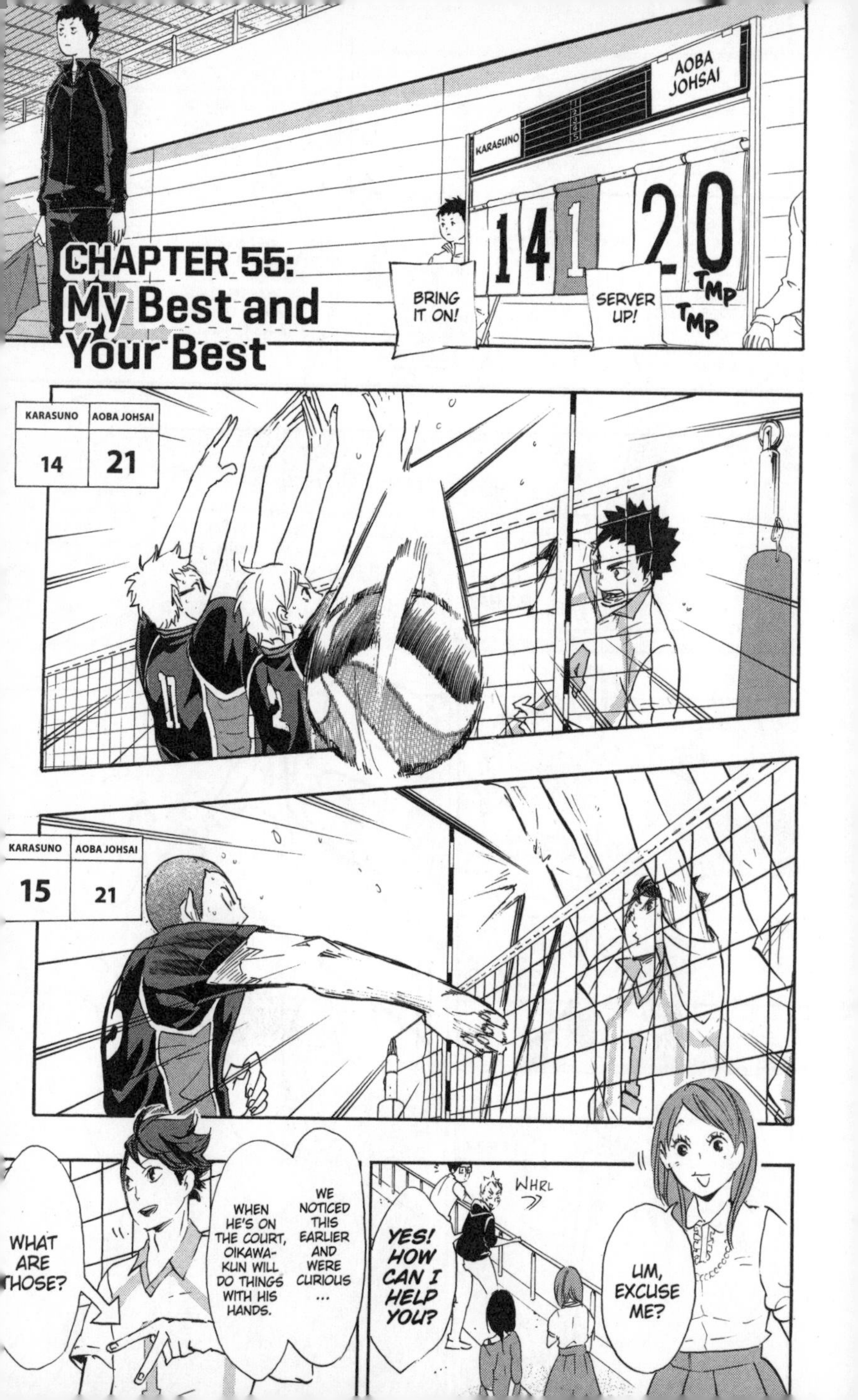
AOBA JOHSAI
KARASUNO
14 1 20
SERVER UP!
TMP TMP
BRING IT ON!
KARASUNO AOBA JOHSAI
14 21
KARASUNO AOBA JOHSAI
15 21
UM, EXCUSE ME?
WHRL
YES! HOW CAN I HELP YOU?
WE NOTICED THIS EARLIER AND WERE CURIOUS...
WHEN HE'S ON THE COURT, OIKAWA-KUN WILL DO THINGS WITH HIS HANDS.
WHAT ARE THOSE?

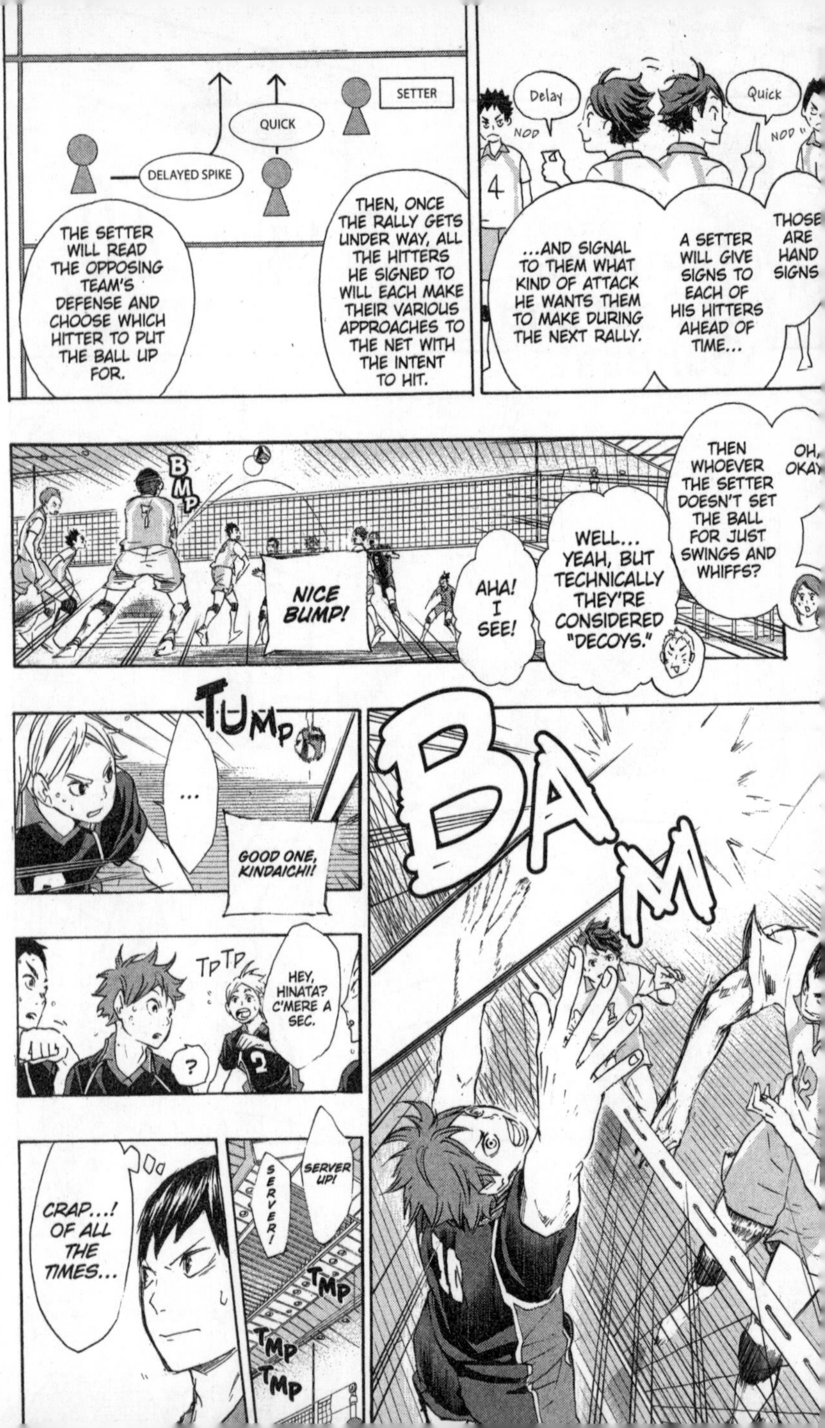
Quick
NOD
Delay
NOD
THOSE ARE HAND SIGNS
A SETTER WILL GIVE SIGNS TO EACH OF HIS HITTERS AHEAD OF TIME...
...AND SIGNAL TO THEM WHAT KIND OF ATTACK HE WANTS THEM TO MAKE DURING THE NEXT RALLY.
SETTER
QUICK
DELAYED SPIKE
THEN, ONCE THE RALLY GETS UNDER WAY, ALL THE HITTERS HE SIGNED TO WILL EACH MAKE THEIR VARIOUS APPROACHES TO THE NET WITH THE INTENT TO HIT.
THE SETTER WILL READ THE OPPOSING TEAM'S DEFENSE AND CHOOSE WHICH HITTER TO PUT THE BALL UP FOR.
OH, OKAY
THEN WHOEVER THE SETTER DOESN'T SET THE BALL FOR JUST SWINGS AND WHIFFS?
WELL... YEAH, BUT TECHNICALLY THEY'RE CONSIDERED "DECOYS."
AHA! I SEE!
NICE BUMP!
BMP
BAM
TUMP
...
GOOD ONE, KINDAICHI!
HEY, HINATA? C'MERE A SEC.
TPTP
?
SERVER UP!
SERVER!
TMP
TMP
TMP
CRAP...! OF ALL THE TIMES...

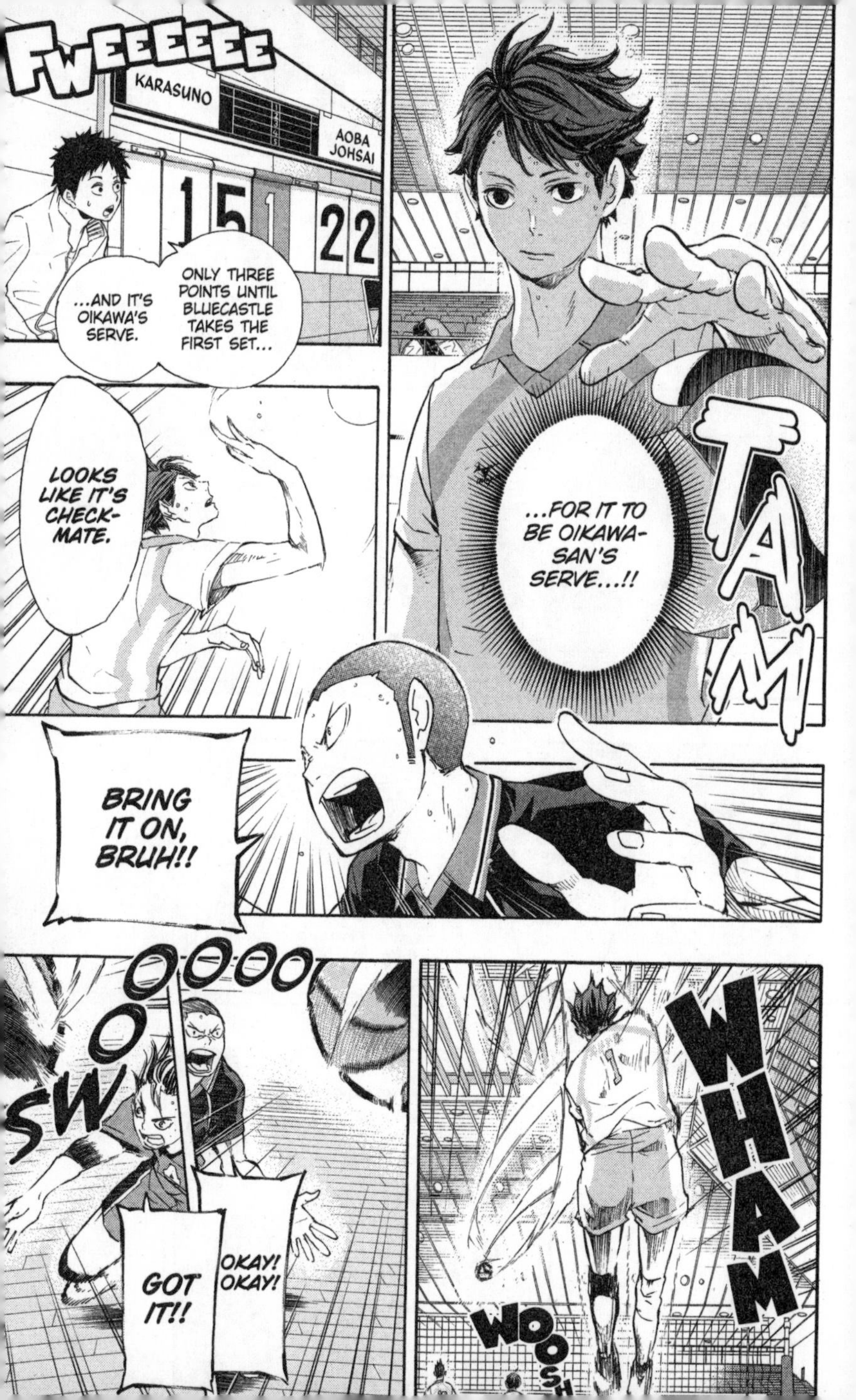
TAM
...FOR IT TO BE OIKAWA-SAN'S SERVE...!!
FWEEEEEE
KARASUNO
AOBA JOHSAI
15
1
22
ONLY THREE POINTS UNTIL BLUECASTLE TAKES THE FIRST SET...
...AND IT'S OIKAWA'S SERVE.
LOOKS LIKE IT'S CHECK-MATE.
BRING IT ON, BRUH!!
WHAM
WOOSH
SWOOOOOOO
OKAY! OKAY!
GOT IT!!

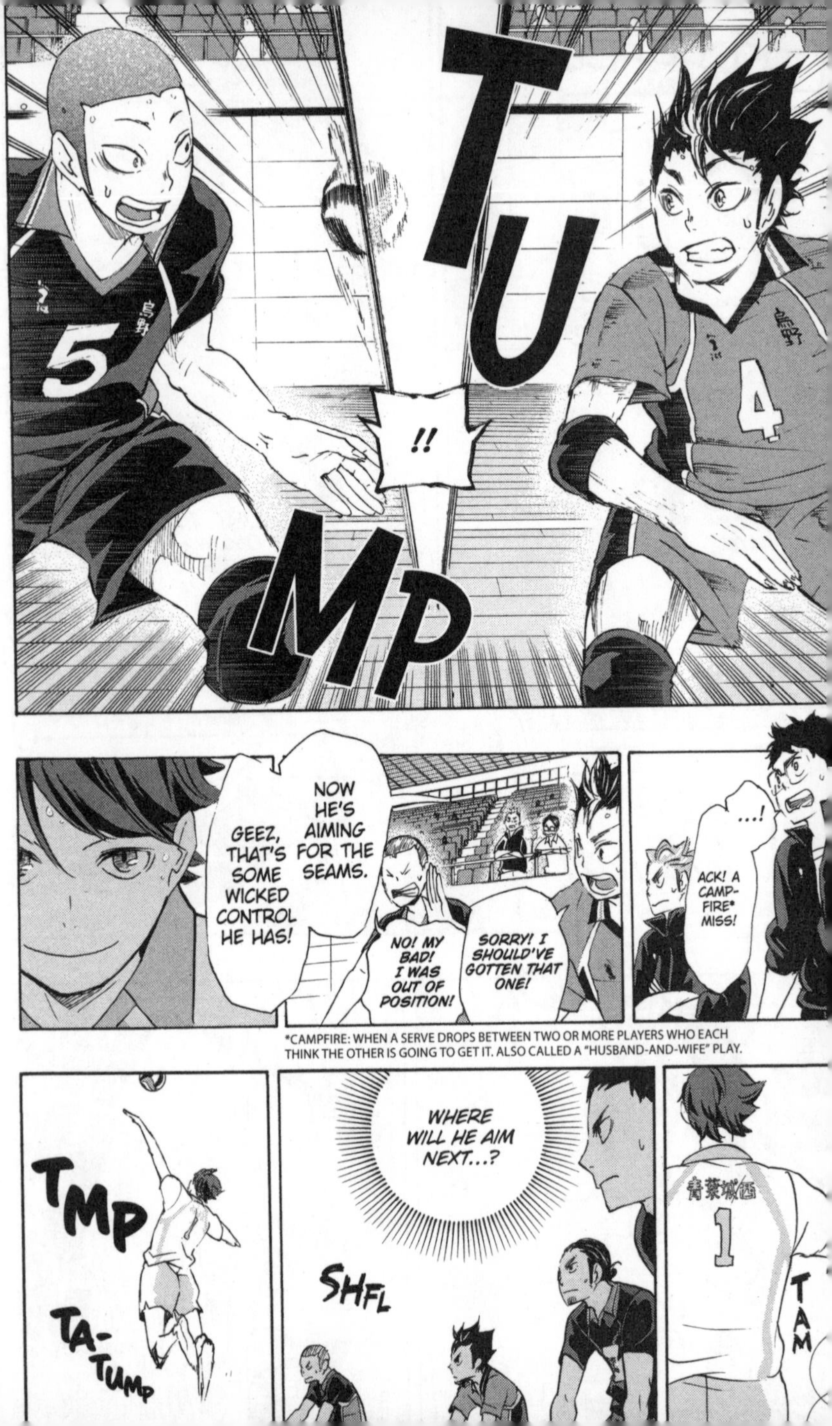
TUMP
!!
...!
ACK! A CAMPFIRE* MISS!
NOW HE'S AIMING FOR THE SEAMS.
GEEZ, THAT'S SOME WICKED CONTROL HE HAS!
SORRY! I SHOULD'VE GOTTEN THAT ONE!
NO! MY BAD! I WAS OUT OF POSITION!
TAM
WHERE WILL HE AIM NEXT...?
SHFL
TMP
TA-TUMP

*CAMPFIRE: WHEN A SERVE DROPS BETWEEN TWO OR MORE PLAYERS WHO EACH THINK THE OTHER IS GOING TO GET IT. ALSO CALLED A "HUSBAND-AND-WIFE" PLAY.

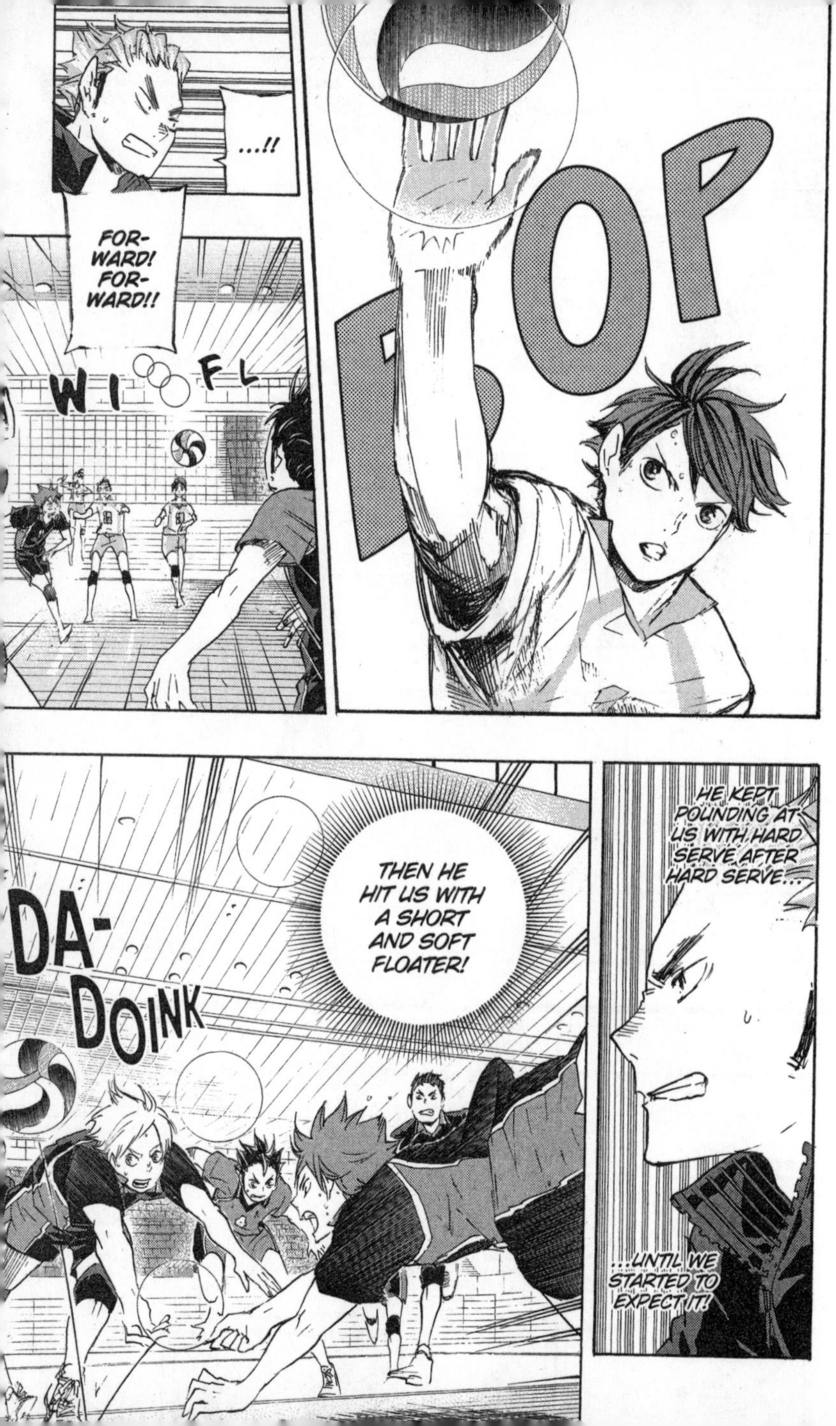
POP
...!!
FOR-WARD! FOR-WARD!!
WIFFL
HE KEPT POUNDING AT US WITH HARD SERVE AFTER HARD SERVE...
...UNTIL WE STARTED TO EXPECT IT!
THEN HE HIT US WITH A SHORT AND SOFT FLOATER!
DA-DOINK

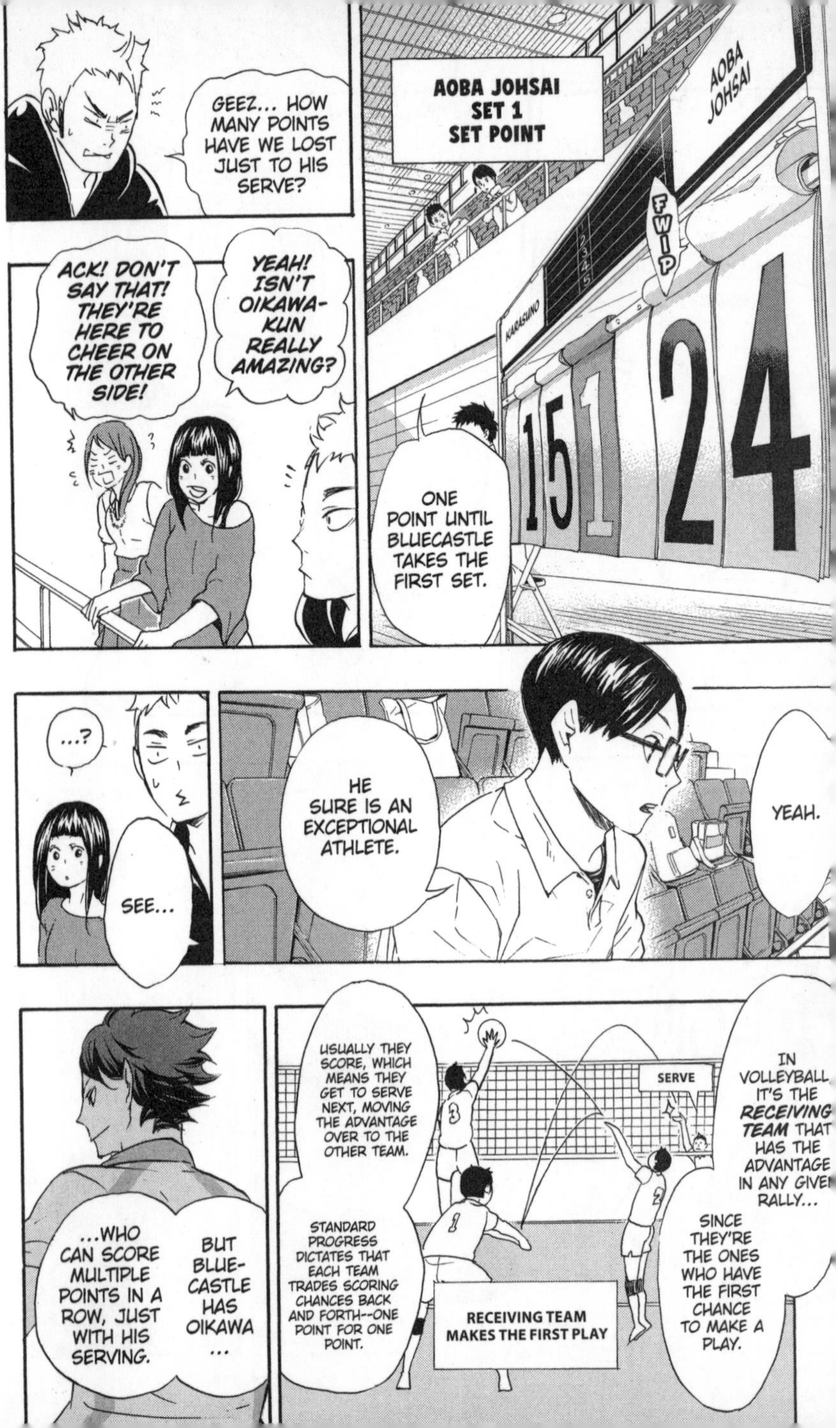
AOBA JOHSAI SET 1 SET POINT
AOBA JOHSAI
FWIP
KARASUNO
15 1 24
ONE POINT UNTIL BLUECASTLE TAKES THE FIRST SET.
GEEZ... HOW MANY POINTS HAVE WE LOST JUST TO HIS SERVE?
YEAH! ISN'T OIKAWA-KUN REALLY AMAZING?
ACK! DON'T SAY THAT! THEY'RE HERE TO CHEER ON THE OTHER SIDE!
YEAH.
HE SURE IS AN EXCEPTIONAL ATHLETE.
...?
SEE...
IN VOLLEYBALL IT'S THE ***RECEIVING TEAM*** THAT HAS THE ADVANTAGE IN ANY GIVE RALLY...
SINCE THEY'RE THE ONES WHO HAVE THE FIRST CHANCE TO MAKE A PLAY.
SERVE
USUALLY THEY SCORE, WHICH MEANS THEY GET TO SERVE NEXT, MOVING THE ADVANTAGE OVER TO THE OTHER TEAM.
RECEIVING TEAM MAKES THE FIRST PLAY
STANDARD PROGRESS DICTATES THAT EACH TEAM TRADES SCORING CHANCES BACK AND FORTH--ONE POINT FOR ONE POINT.
BUT BLUE-CASTLE HAS OIKAWA...
...WHO CAN SCORE MULTIPLE POINTS IN A ROW, JUST WITH HIS SERVING.

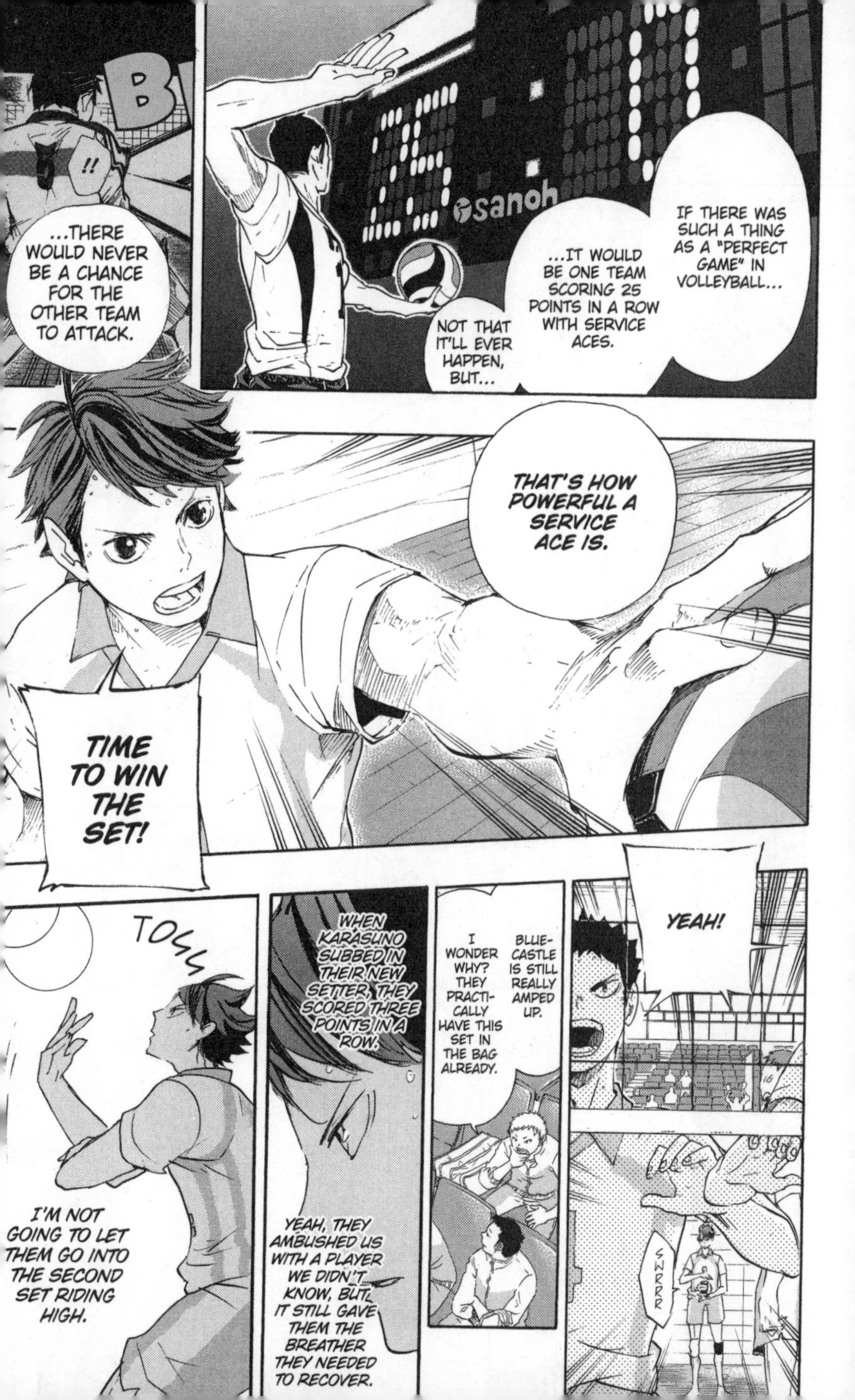
IF THERE WAS SUCH A THING AS A "PERFECT GAME" IN VOLLEYBALL...
...IT WOULD BE ONE TEAM SCORING 25 POINTS IN A ROW WITH SERVICE ACES.
NOT THAT IT'LL EVER HAPPEN, BUT...
sanoh
B
!!
...THERE WOULD NEVER BE A CHANCE FOR THE OTHER TEAM TO ATTACK.
THAT'S HOW POWERFUL A SERVICE ACE IS.
TIME TO WIN THE SET!
YEAH!
SWRRR
BLUE-CASTLE IS STILL REALLY AMPED UP.
I WONDER WHY? THEY PRACTICALLY HAVE THIS SET IN THE BAG ALREADY.
WHEN KARASUNO SUBBED IN THEIR NEW SETTER, THEY SCORED THREE POINTS IN A ROW.
YEAH, THEY AMBUSHED US WITH A PLAYER WE DIDN'T KNOW, BUT IT STILL GAVE THEM THE BREATHER THEY NEEDED TO RECOVER.
TOSS
I'M NOT GOING TO LET THEM GO INTO THE SECOND SET RIDING HIGH.

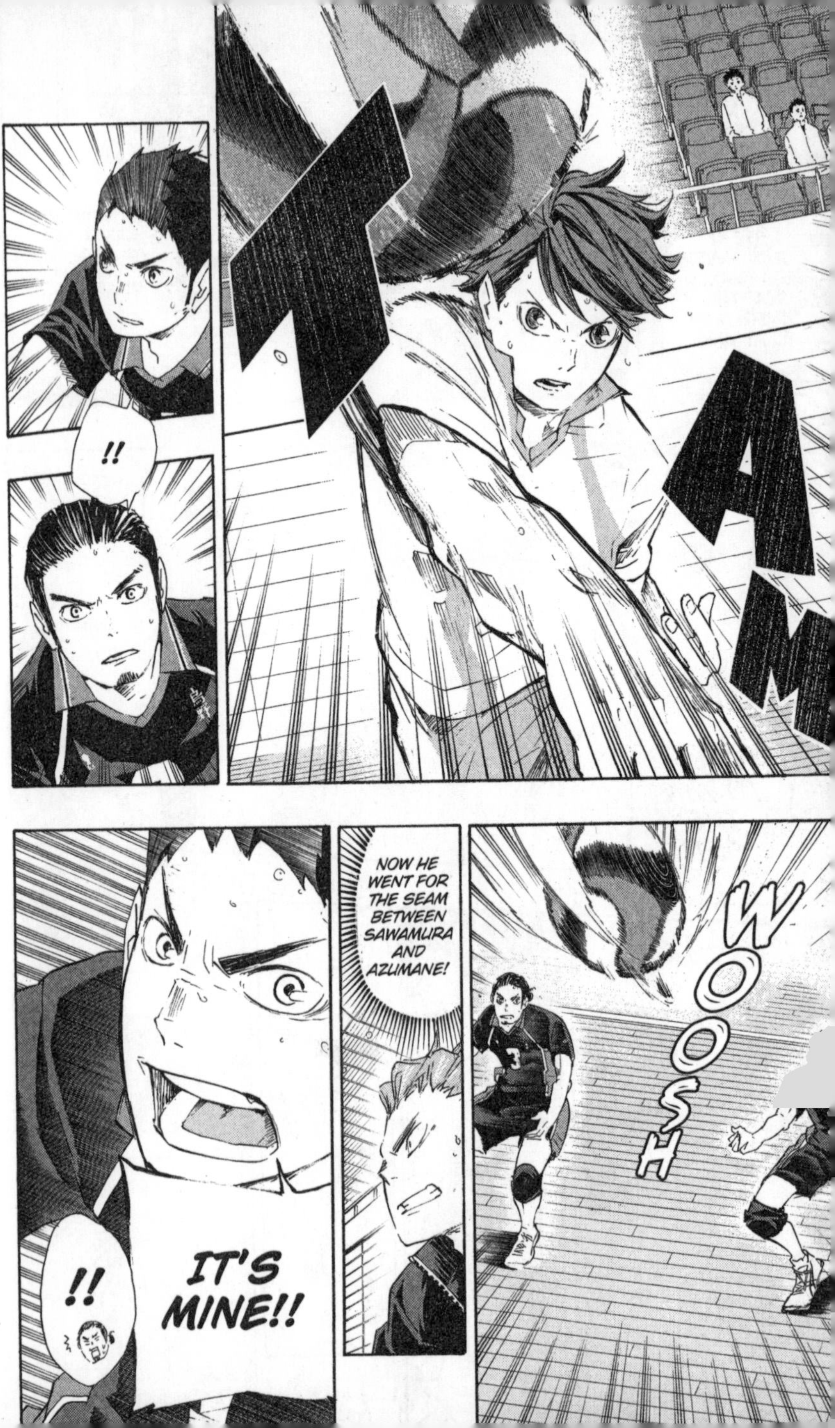
!!
WOOSH
NOW HE WENT FOR THE SEAM BETWEEN SAWAMURA AND AZUMANE!
IT'S MINE!!
!!

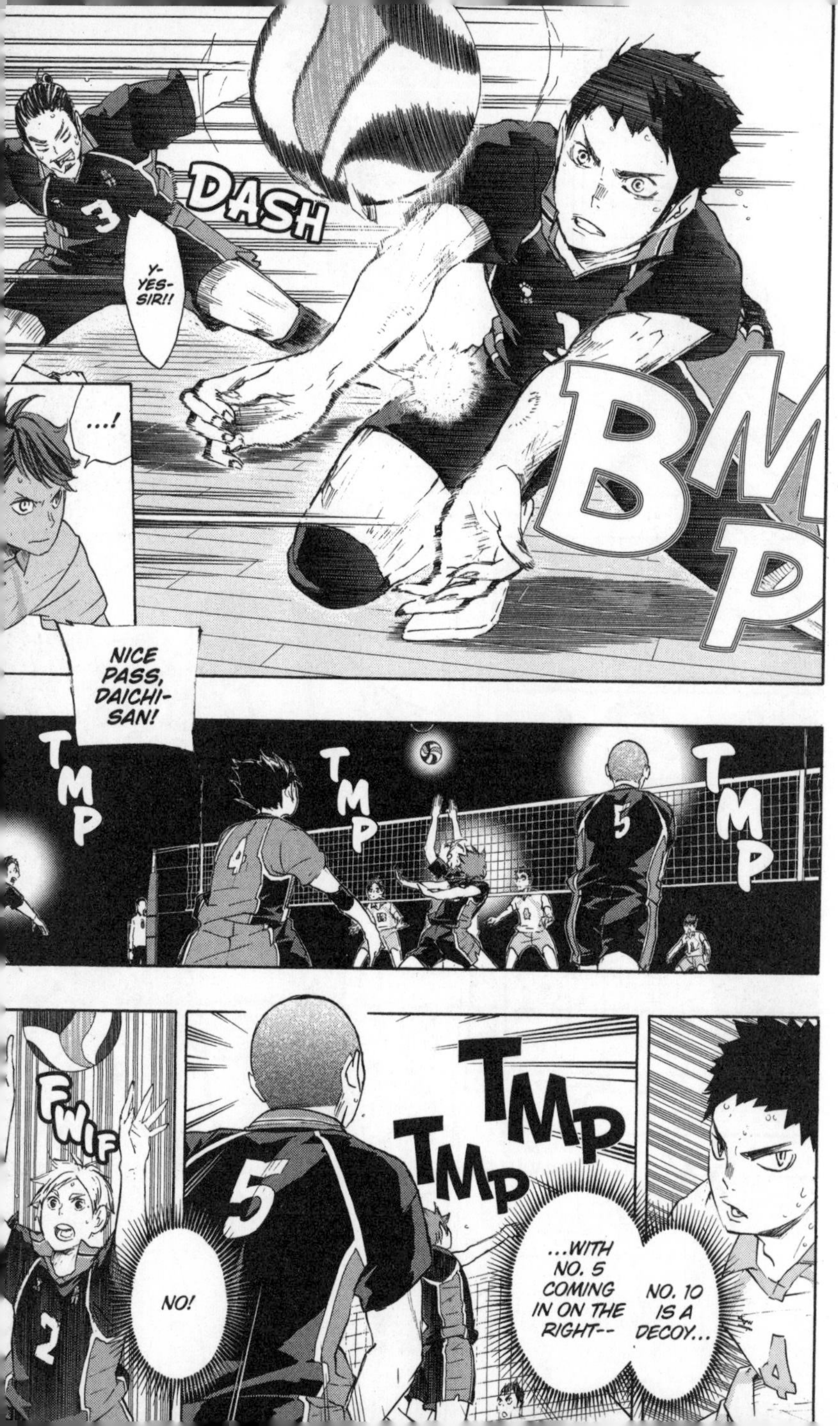
DASH
Y-YES-SIR!!
BMP
...!
NICE PASS, DAICHI-SAN!
TMP
TMP
TMP
NO. 10 IS A DECOY...
...WITH NO. 5 COMING IN ON THE RIGHT--
TMP
TMP
FWIF
NO!

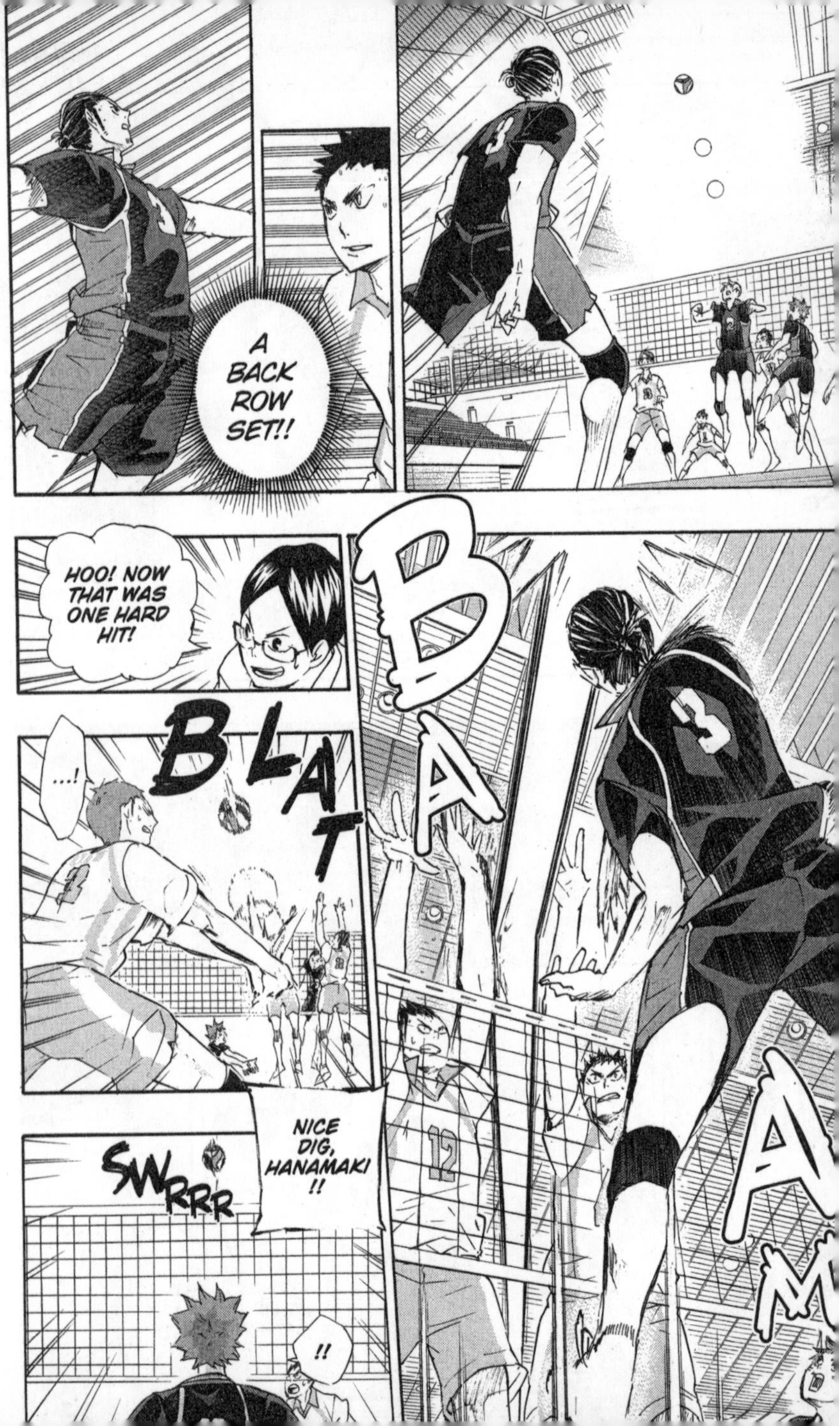
A BACK ROW SET!!
BAAM
HOO! NOW THAT WAS ONE HARD HIT!
...!
BLAT
NICE DIG, HANAMAKI!!
SWRRR
!!

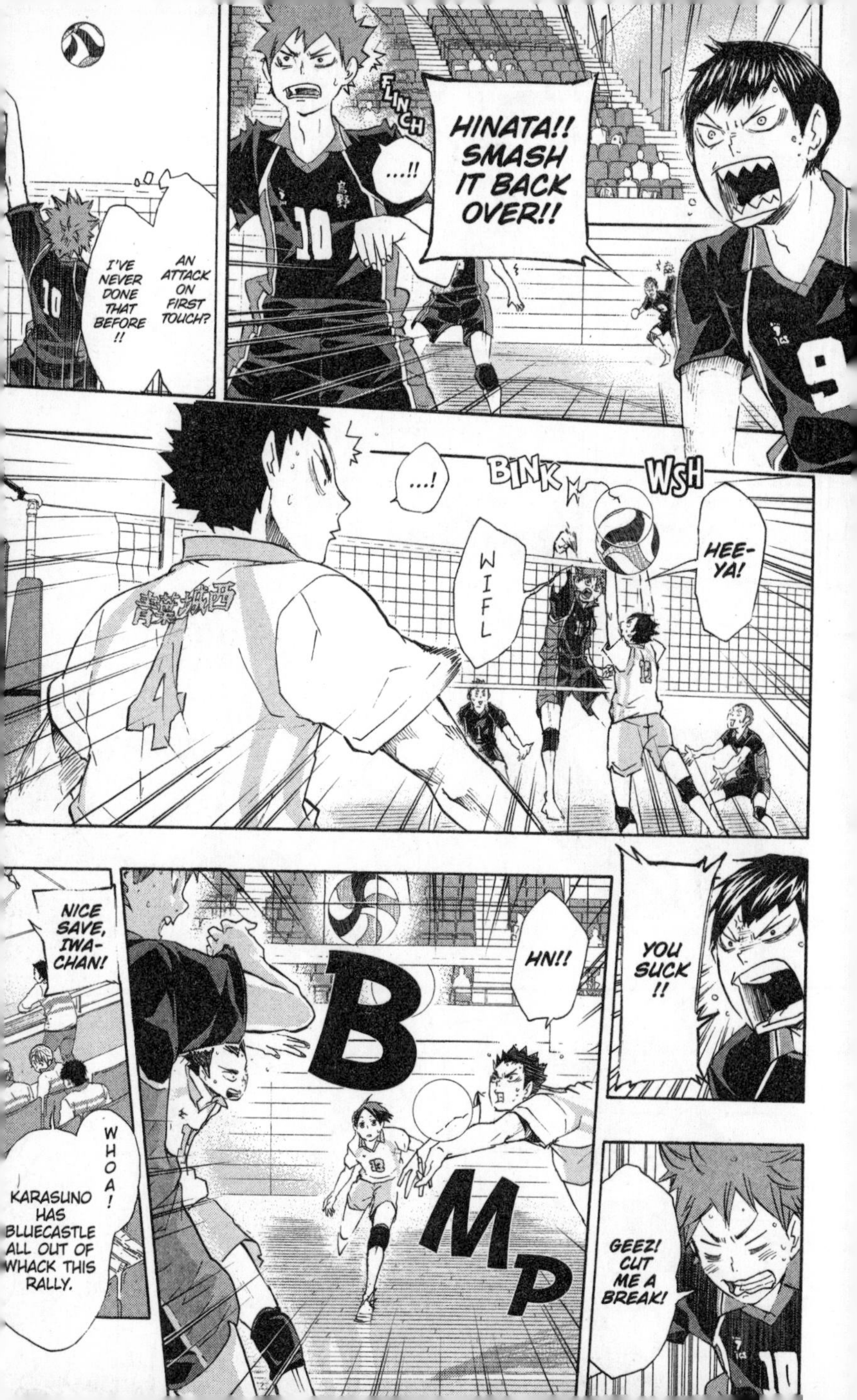
HINATA!! SMASH IT BACK OVER!!
FLINCH
...!!
AN ATTACK ON FIRST TOUCH?
I'VE NEVER DONE THAT BEFORE !!
WSH
BINK
HEE-YA!
...!
WIFL
YOU SUCK !!
GEEZ! CUT ME A BREAK!
HN!!
BUMP
NICE SAVE, IWA-CHAN!
WHOA!
KARASUNO HAS BLUECASTLE ALL OUT OF WHACK THIS RALLY.

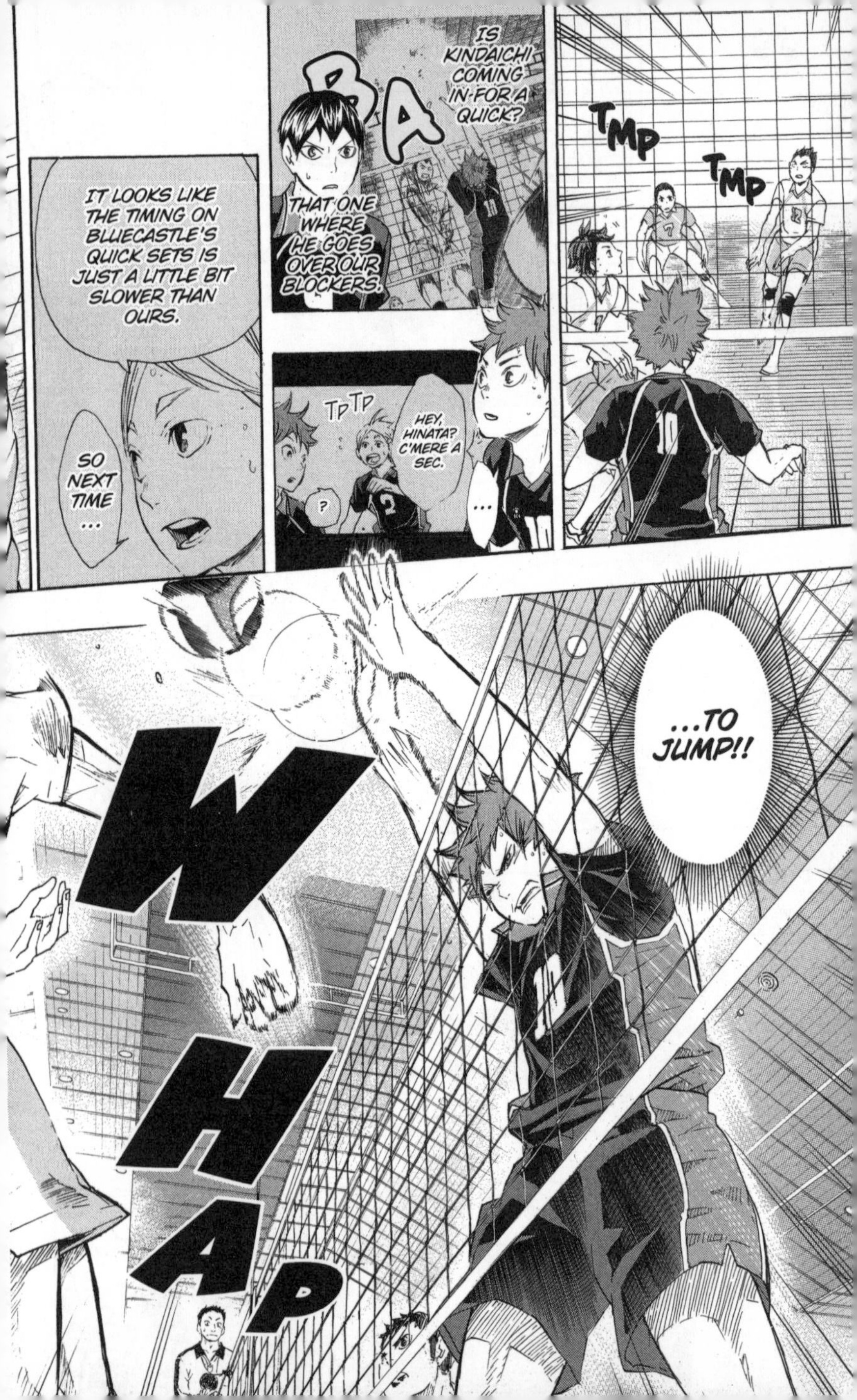
TMP
TMP
IS KINDAICHI COMING IN FOR A QUICK?
BA
THAT ONE WHERE HE GOES OVER OUR BLOCKERS.
HEY, HINATA? C'MERE A SEC.
TP TP
?
...
IT LOOKS LIKE THE TIMING ON BLUECASTLE'S QUICK SETS IS JUST A LITTLE BIT SLOWER THAN OURS.
SO NEXT TIME ...
...TO JUMP!!
WHAP

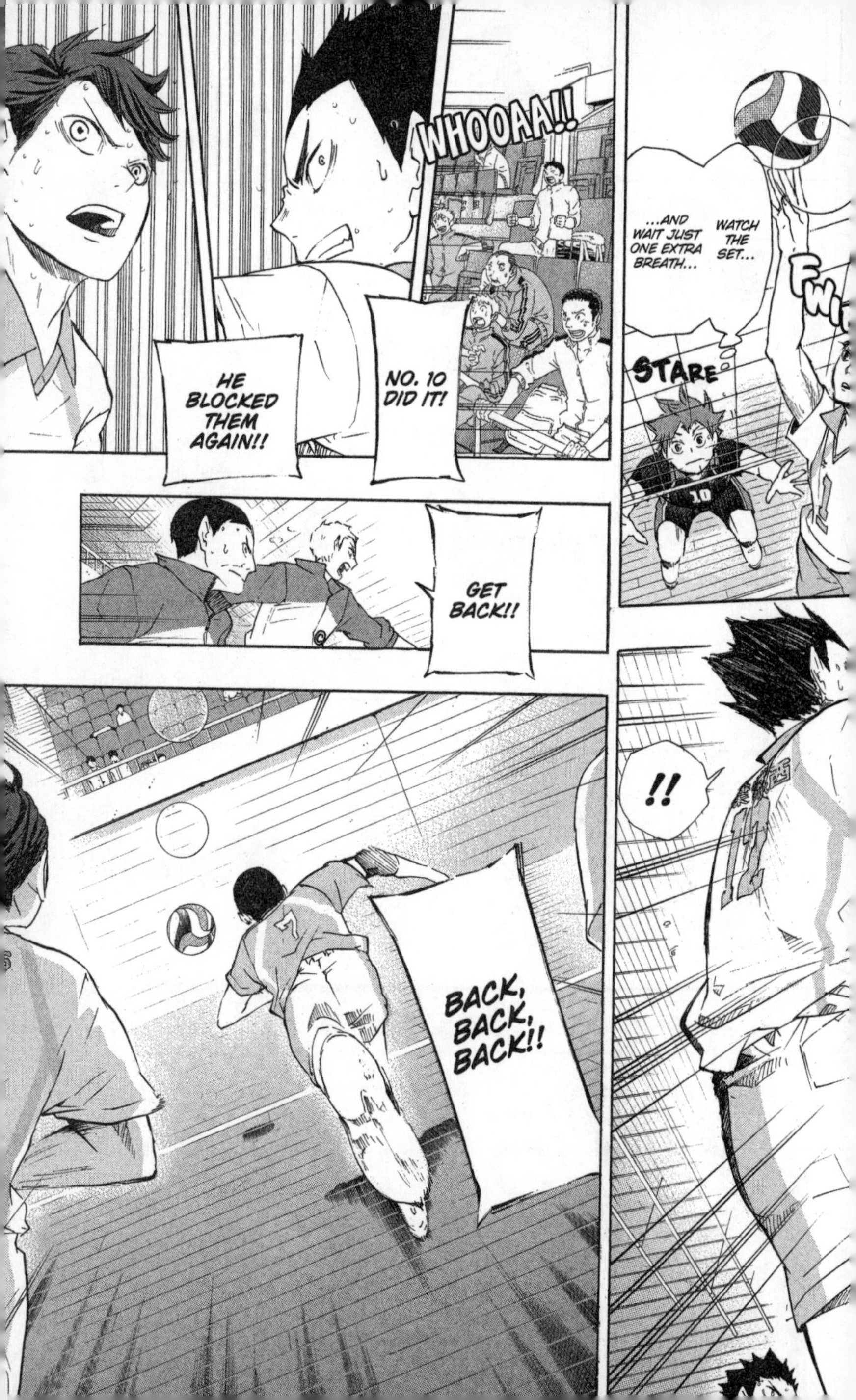
WATCH THE SET...
...AND WAIT JUST ONE EXTRA BREATH...
FWI
STARE
WHOOAA!!
NO. 10 DID IT!
HE BLOCKED THEM AGAIN!!
GET BACK!!
!!
BACK, BACK, BACK!!

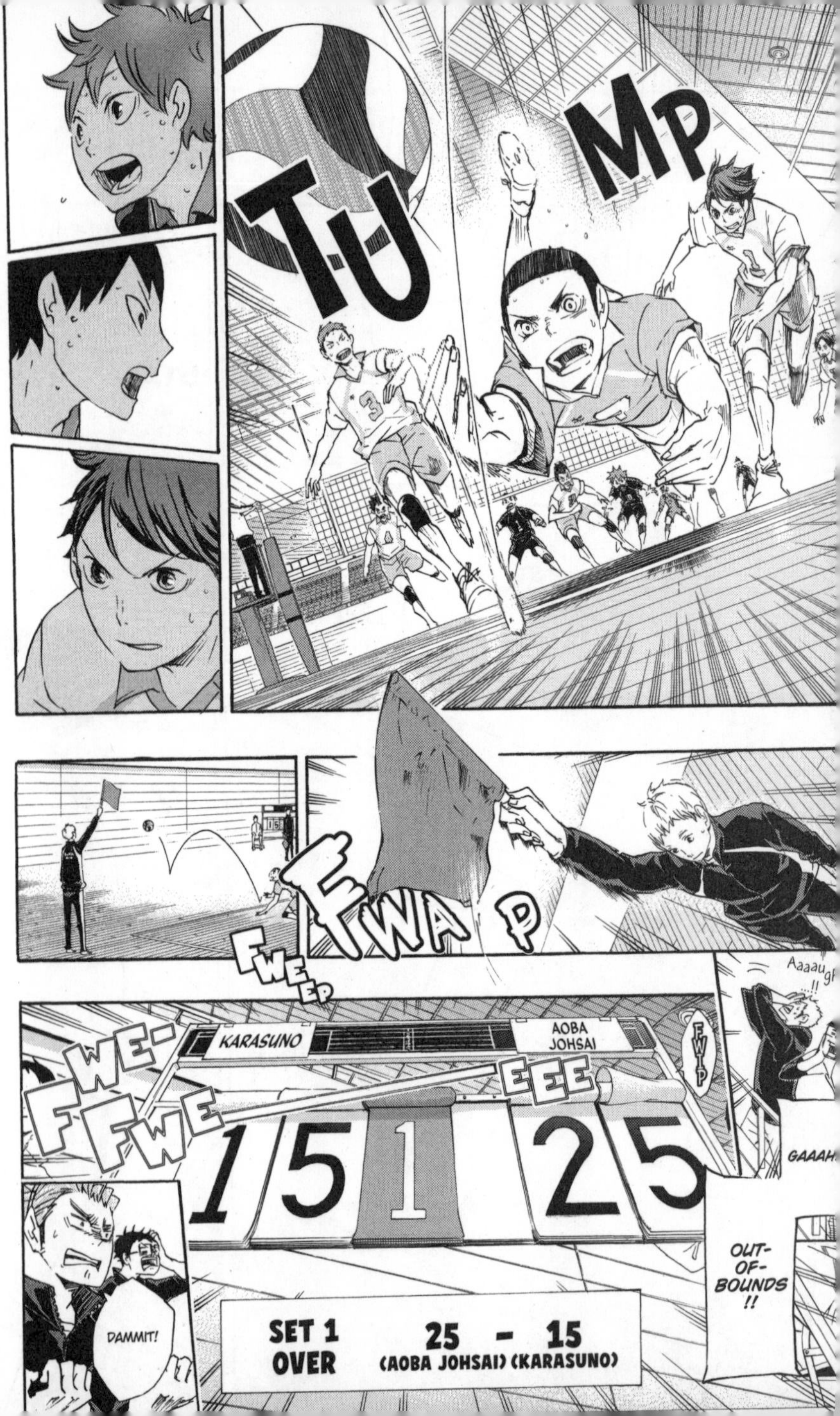
TUMP
FWAP
FWEEP
Aaaaugh!!
FWIP
GAAAH
KARASUNO
AOBA JOHSAI
FWE-FFWE-EEE
15 1 25
OUT-OF-BOUNDS!!
SET 1 OVER 25 - 15 (AOBA JOHSAI) (KARASUNO)
DAMMIT!

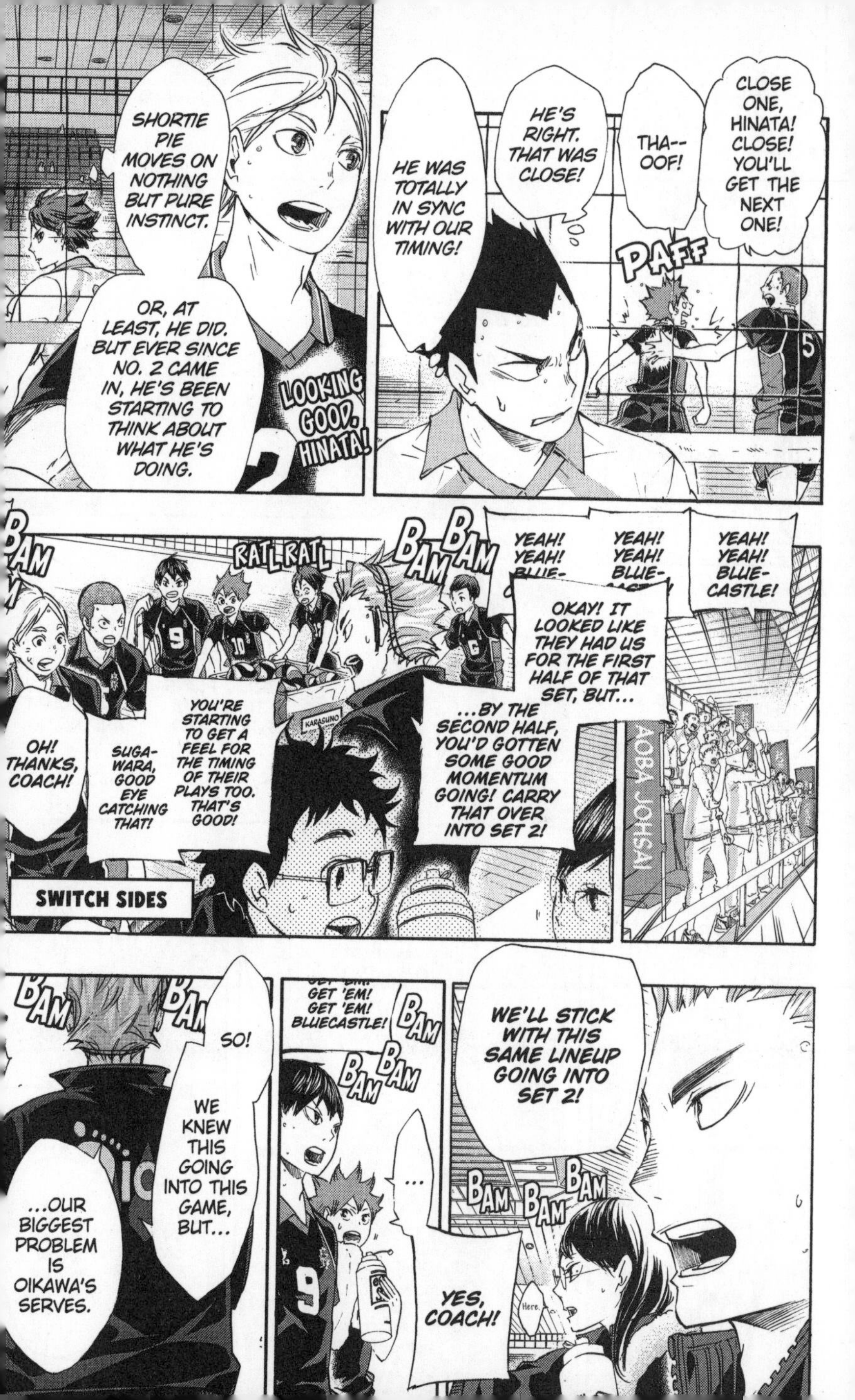
CLOSE ONE, HINATA! CLOSE! YOU'LL GET THE NEXT ONE!
THA-- OOF!
PAFF
HE'S RIGHT. THAT WAS CLOSE!
HE WAS TOTALLY IN SYNC WITH OUR TIMING!
SHORTIE PIE MOVES ON NOTHING BUT PURE INSTINCT.
LOOKING GOOD, HINATA!
OR, AT LEAST, HE DID. BUT EVER SINCE NO. 2 CAME IN, HE'S BEEN STARTING TO THINK ABOUT WHAT HE'S DOING.
YEAH! YEAH! BLUE-CASTLE!
BAM BAM
OKAY! IT LOOKED LIKE THEY HAD US FOR THE FIRST HALF OF THAT SET, BUT...
...BY THE SECOND HALF, YOU'D GOTTEN SOME GOOD MOMENTUM GOING! CARRY THAT OVER INTO SET 2!
AOBA JOHSAI
RATL RATL
KARASUNO
YOU'RE STARTING TO GET A FEEL FOR THE TIMING OF THEIR PLAYS TOO. THAT'S GOOD!
SUGA-WARA, GOOD EYE CATCHING THAT!
OH! THANKS, COACH!
BAM
SWITCH SIDES
WE'LL STICK WITH THIS SAME LINEUP GOING INTO SET 2!
BAM BAM BAM
Here.
YES, COACH!
GET 'EM! GET 'EM! BLUECASTLE!
BAM BAM BAM
...
BAM BAM
SO!
WE KNEW THIS GOING INTO THIS GAME, BUT...
...OUR BIGGEST PROBLEM IS OIKAWA'S SERVES.

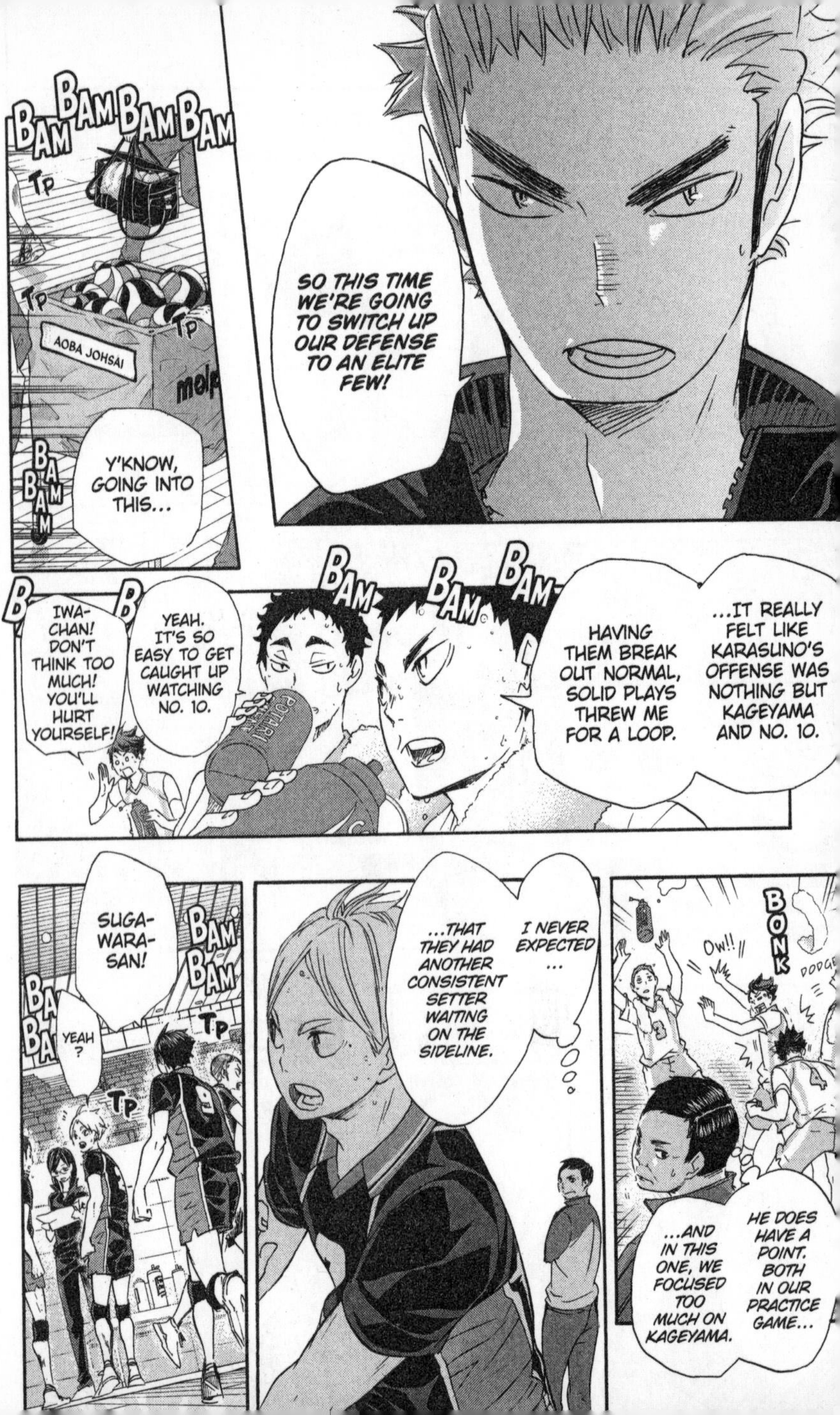
SO THIS TIME WE'RE GOING TO SWITCH UP OUR DEFENSE TO AN ELITE FEW!
BAM BAM BAM BAM
Tp
Tp
Tp
AOBA JOHSAI
molten
Y'KNOW, GOING INTO THIS...
BAM BAM
...IT REALLY FELT LIKE KARASUNO'S OFFENSE WAS NOTHING BUT KAGEYAMA AND NO. 10.
HAVING THEM BREAK OUT NORMAL, SOLID PLAYS THREW ME FOR A LOOP.
BAM BAM BAM
YEAH. IT'S SO EASY TO GET CAUGHT UP WATCHING NO. 10.
B
IWA-CHAN! DON'T THINK TOO MUCH! YOU'LL HURT YOURSELF!
B
BONK
OW!!
DODGE
HE DOES HAVE A POINT. BOTH IN OUR PRACTICE GAME...
...AND IN THIS ONE, WE FOCUSED TOO MUCH ON KAGEYAMA.
I NEVER EXPECTED...
...THAT THEY HAD ANOTHER CONSISTENT SETTER WAITING ON THE SIDELINE.
SUGA-WARA-SAN!
BAM BAM
YEAH?
BAM BAM
Tp
Tp

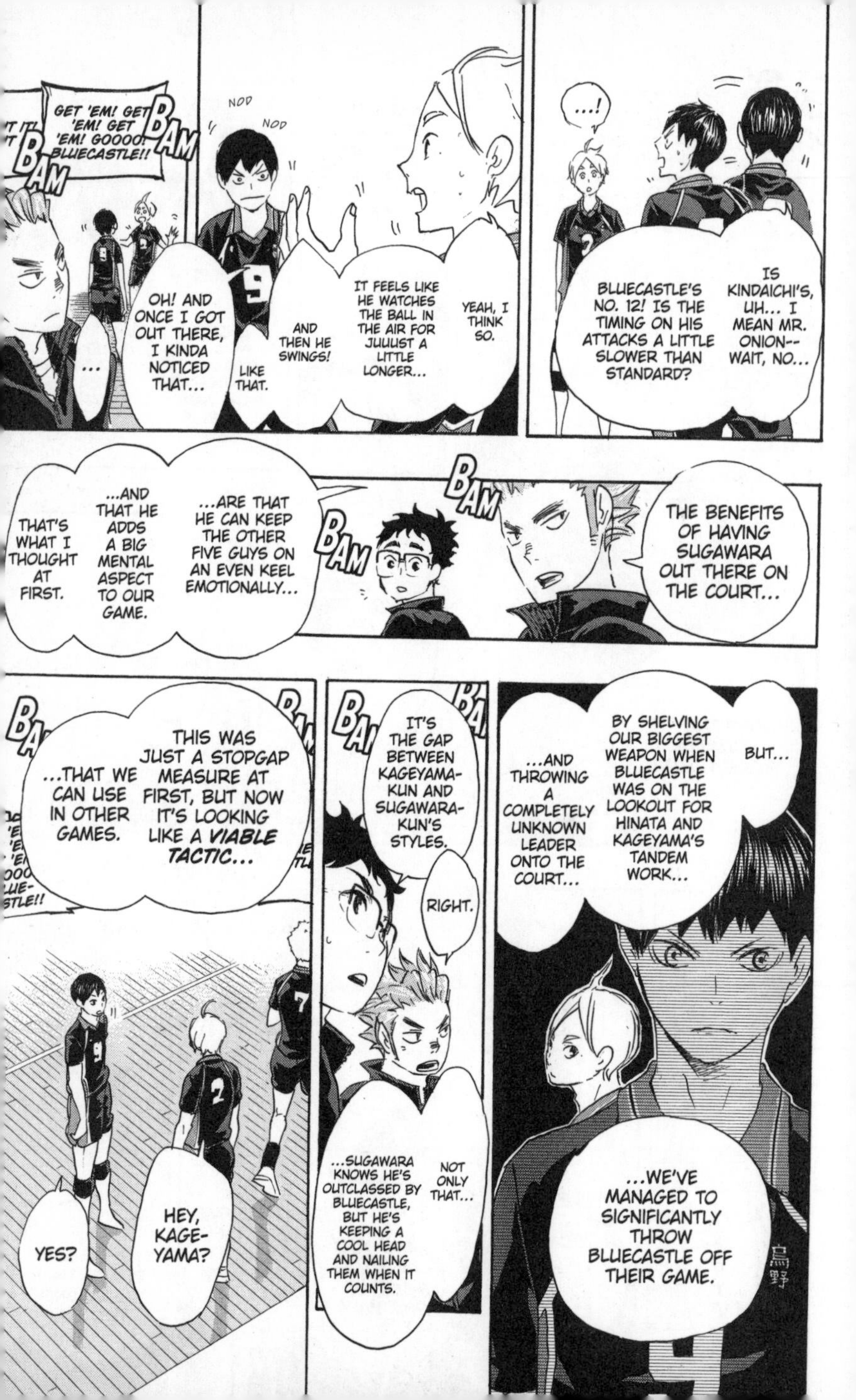
...!
IS KINDAICHI'S, UH... I MEAN MR. ONION-- WAIT, NO...
BLUECASTLE'S NO. 12! IS THE TIMING ON HIS ATTACKS A LITTLE SLOWER THAN STANDARD?
NOD
NOD
YEAH, I THINK SO.
IT FEELS LIKE HE WATCHES THE BALL IN THE AIR FOR JUUUST A LITTLE LONGER...
AND THEN HE SWINGS!
LIKE THAT.
OH! AND ONCE I GOT OUT THERE, I KINDA NOTICED THAT...
GET 'EM! GET 'EM! GET 'EM! GOOOO! BLUECASTLE!!
BAM
BAM
...
THE BENEFITS OF HAVING SUGAWARA OUT THERE ON THE COURT...
BAM
BAM
...ARE THAT HE CAN KEEP THE OTHER FIVE GUYS ON AN EVEN KEEL EMOTIONALLY...
...AND THAT HE ADDS A BIG MENTAL ASPECT TO OUR GAME.
THAT'S WHAT I THOUGHT AT FIRST.
BUT...
BY SHELVING OUR BIGGEST WEAPON WHEN BLUECASTLE WAS ON THE LOOKOUT FOR HINATA AND KAGEYAMA'S TANDEM WORK...
...AND THROWING A COMPLETELY UNKNOWN LEADER ONTO THE COURT...
...WE'VE MANAGED TO SIGNIFICANTLY THROW BLUECASTLE OFF THEIR GAME.
烏野
IT'S THE GAP BETWEEN KAGEYAMA-KUN AND SUGAWARA-KUN'S STYLES.
RIGHT.
NOT ONLY THAT...
...SUGAWARA KNOWS HE'S OUTCLASSED BY BLUECASTLE, BUT HE'S KEEPING A COOL HEAD AND NAILING THEM WHEN IT COUNTS.
THIS WAS JUST A STOPGAP MEASURE AT FIRST, BUT NOW IT'S LOOKING LIKE A *VIABLE TACTIC*...
...THAT WE CAN USE IN OTHER GAMES.
HEY, KAGE-YAMA?
YES?

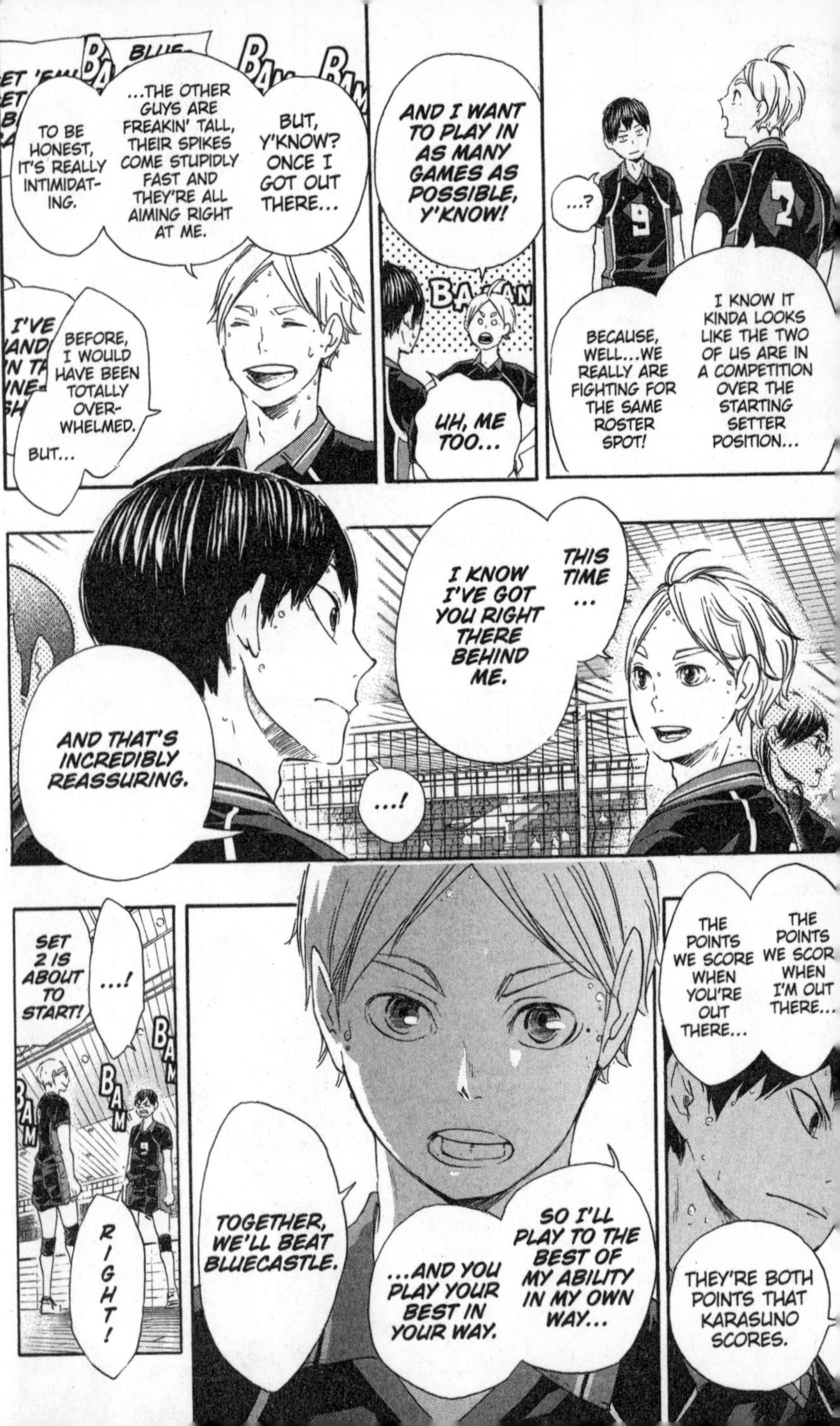
...?
I KNOW IT KINDA LOOKS LIKE THE TWO OF US ARE IN A COMPETITION OVER THE STARTING SETTER POSITION...
BECAUSE, WELL...WE REALLY ARE FIGHTING FOR THE SAME ROSTER SPOT!
AND I WANT TO PLAY IN AS MANY GAMES AS POSSIBLE, Y'KNOW!
UH, ME TOO...
BAM
BAM
BUT, Y'KNOW? ONCE I GOT OUT THERE...
...THE OTHER GUYS ARE FREAKIN' TALL, THEIR SPIKES COME STUPIDLY FAST AND THEY'RE ALL AIMING RIGHT AT ME.
TO BE HONEST, IT'S REALLY INTIMIDAT-ING.
BEFORE, I WOULD HAVE BEEN TOTALLY OVER-WHELMED.
BUT...
THIS TIME...
I KNOW I'VE GOT YOU RIGHT THERE BEHIND ME.
...!
AND THAT'S INCREDIBLY REASSURING.
THE POINTS WE SCOR WHEN I'M OUT THERE...
THE POINTS WE SCORE WHEN YOU'RE OUT THERE...
THEY'RE BOTH POINTS THAT KARASUNO SCORES.
SO I'LL PLAY TO THE BEST OF MY ABILITY IN MY OWN WAY...
...AND YOU PLAY YOUR BEST IN YOUR WAY.
TOGETHER, WE'LL BEAT BLUECASTLE.
...!
SET 2 IS ABOUT TO START!
BAM
BAM
BAM
RIGHT!

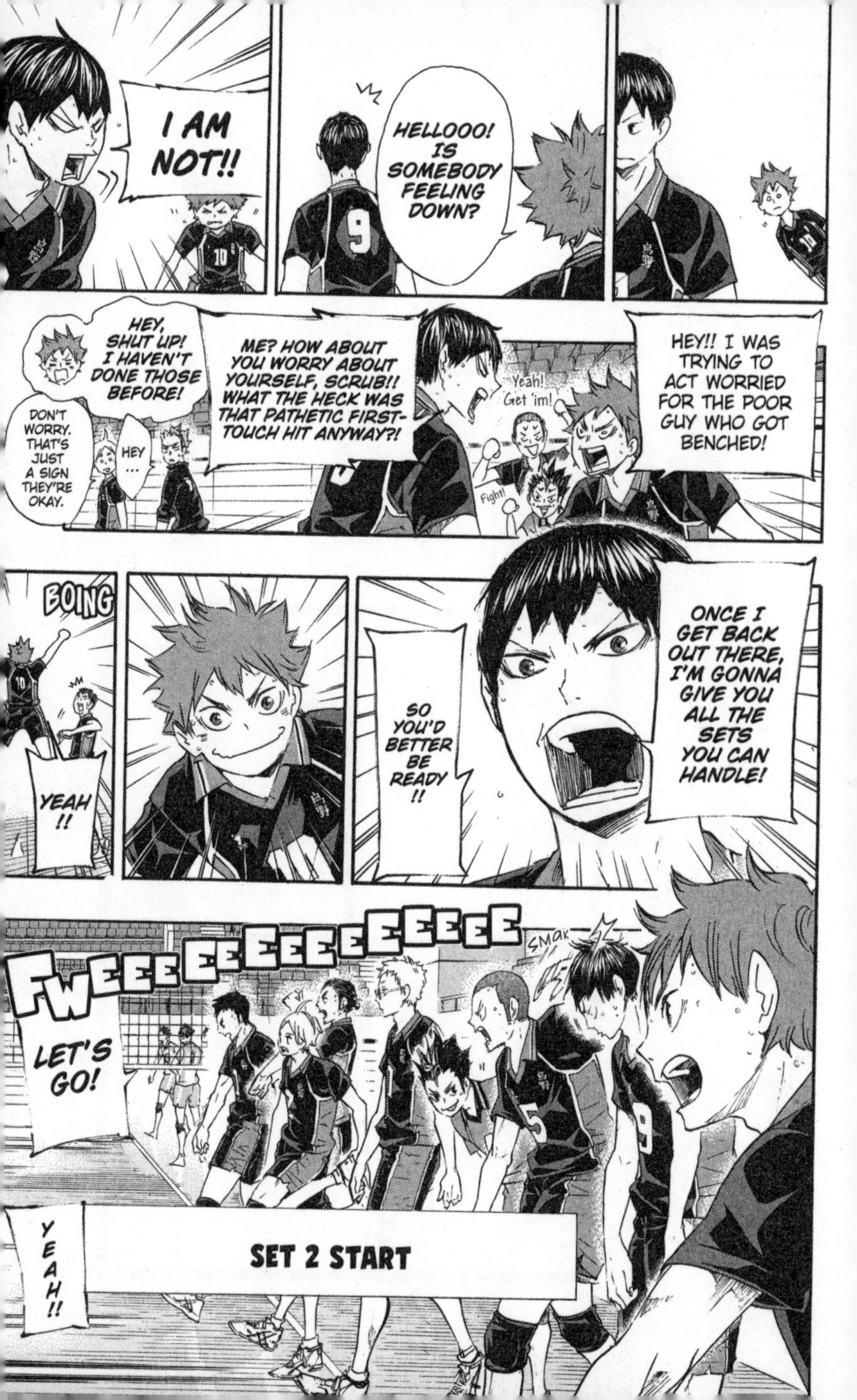
HELLOOO! IS SOMEBODY FEELING DOWN?
I AM NOT!!
HEY!! I WAS TRYING TO ACT WORRIED FOR THE POOR GUY WHO GOT BENCHED!
Yeah! Get 'im!
Fight!
ME? HOW ABOUT YOU WORRY ABOUT YOURSELF, SCRUB!! WHAT THE HECK WAS THAT PATHETIC FIRST-TOUCH HIT ANYWAY?!
HEY, SHUT UP! I HAVEN'T DONE THOSE BEFORE!
HEY ...
DON'T WORRY. THAT'S JUST A SIGN THEY'RE OKAY.
ONCE I GET BACK OUT THERE, I'M GONNA GIVE YOU ALL THE SETS YOU CAN HANDLE!
SO YOU'D BETTER BE READY!!
BOING
YEAH!!
SMAK
FWEEEEEEEEEEEEEE
LET'S GO!
SET 2 START
YEAH!!

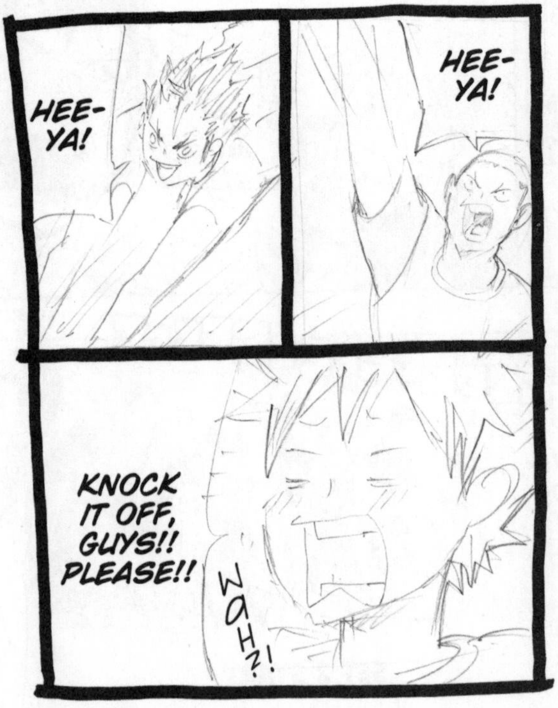
HEE-YA!
HEE-YA!
KNOCK IT OFF, GUYS!! PLEASE!!
WAH?!

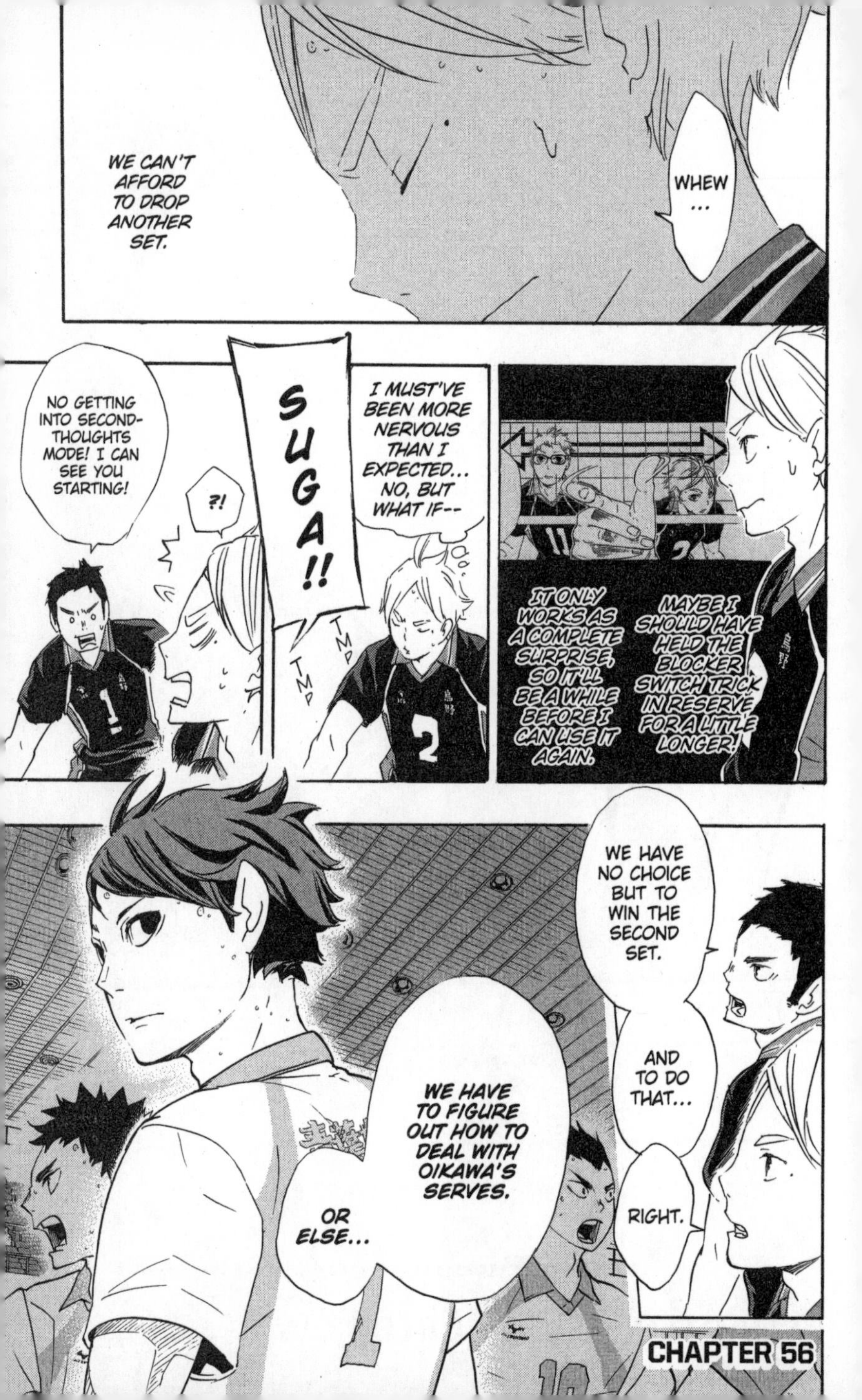
WHEW...
WE CAN'T AFFORD TO DROP ANOTHER SET.
MAYBE I SHOULD HAVE HELD THE BLOCKER SWITCH TRICK IN RESERVE FOR A LITTLE LONGER.
IT ONLY WORKS AS A COMPLETE SURPRISE, SO IT'LL BE A WHILE BEFORE I CAN USE IT AGAIN.
I MUST'VE BEEN MORE NERVOUS THAN I EXPECTED... NO, BUT WHAT IF--
TMP TMP
SUGA!!
?!
NO GETTING INTO SECOND-THOUGHTS MODE! I CAN SEE YOU STARTING!
WE HAVE NO CHOICE BUT TO WIN THE SECOND SET.
AND TO DO THAT...
RIGHT.
WE HAVE TO FIGURE OUT HOW TO DEAL WITH OIKAWA'S SERVES.
OR ELSE...
CHAPTER 56

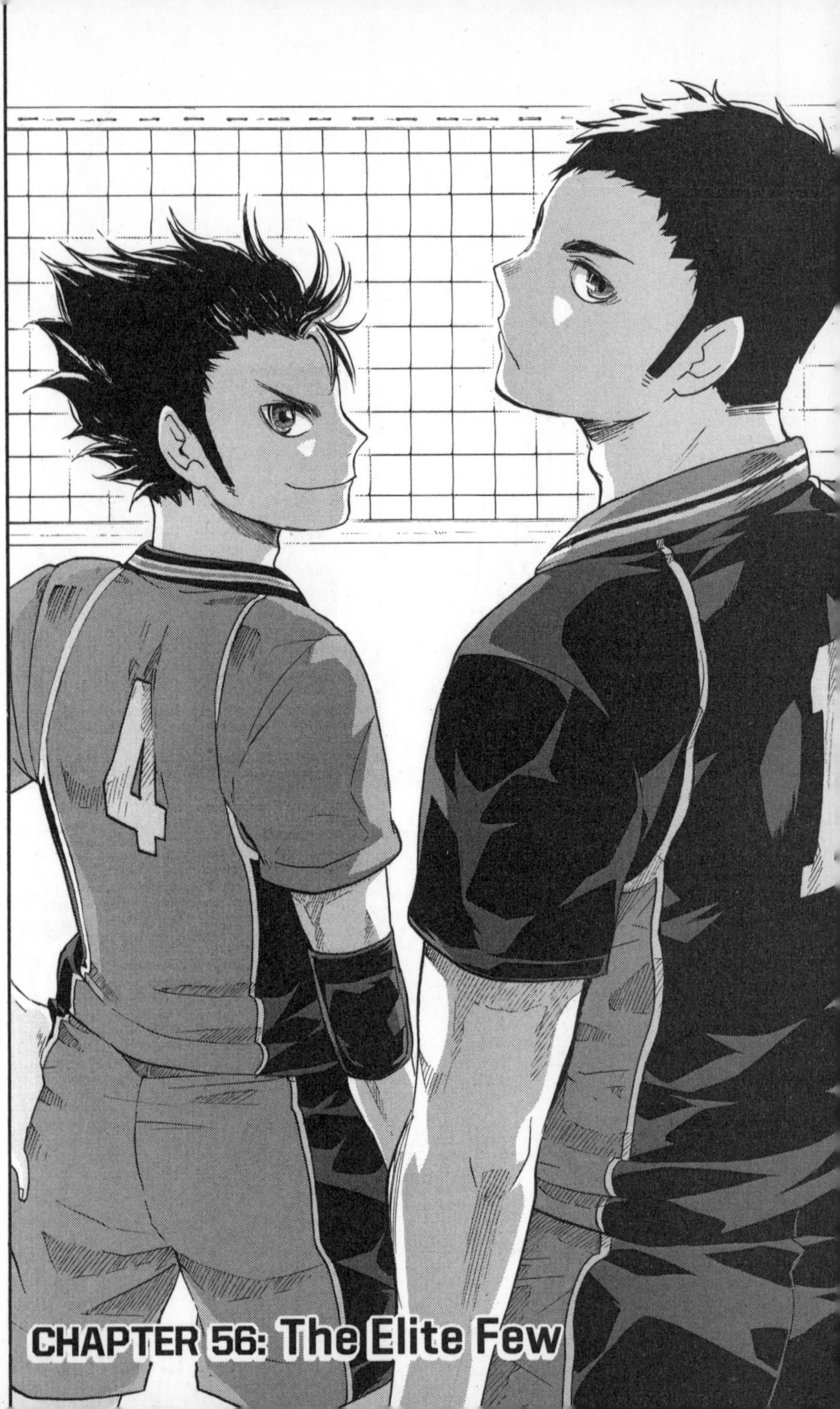
CHAPTER 56: The Elite Few

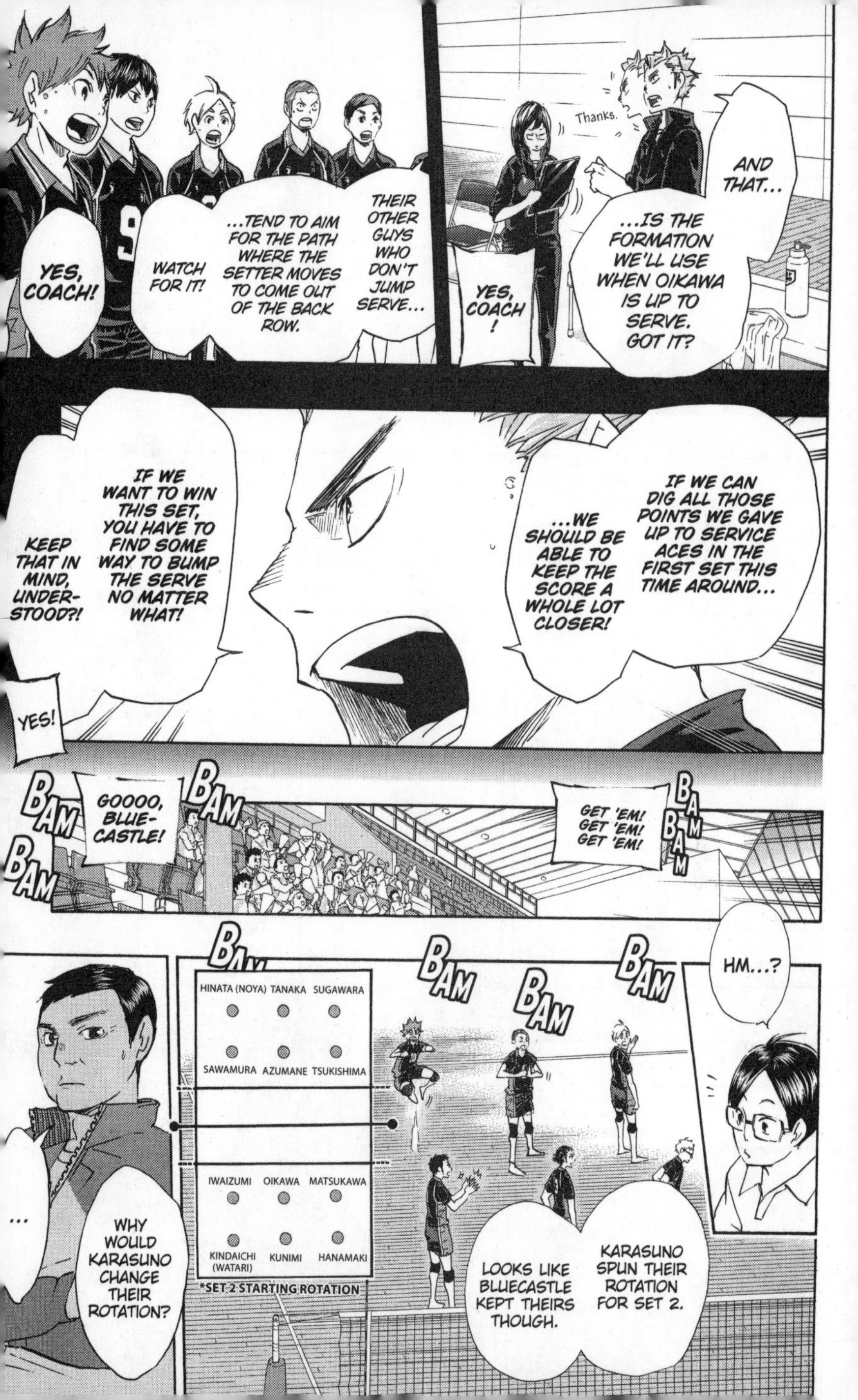
AND THAT...
...IS THE FORMATION WE'LL USE WHEN OIKAWA IS UP TO SERVE. GOT IT?
Thanks.
YES, COACH!
THEIR OTHER GUYS WHO DON'T JUMP SERVE...
...TEND TO AIM FOR THE PATH WHERE THE SETTER MOVES TO COME OUT OF THE BACK ROW.
WATCH FOR IT!
YES, COACH!
IF WE CAN DIG ALL THOSE POINTS WE GAVE UP TO SERVICE ACES IN THE FIRST SET THIS TIME AROUND...
...WE SHOULD BE ABLE TO KEEP THE SCORE A WHOLE LOT CLOSER!
IF WE WANT TO WIN THIS SET, YOU HAVE TO FIND SOME WAY TO BUMP THE SERVE NO MATTER WHAT!
KEEP THAT IN MIND, UNDER-STOOD?!
YES!
BAM BAM
GET 'EM! GET 'EM! GET 'EM!
BAM
GOOOO, BLUE-CASTLE!
BAM
BAM
HM...?
BAM
BAM
BAM
BAM
KARASUNO SPUN THEIR ROTATION FOR SET 2.
LOOKS LIKE BLUECASTLE KEPT THEIRS THOUGH.
HINATA (NOYA) TANAKA SUGAWARA
SAWAMURA AZUMANE TSUKISHIMA
IWAIZUMI OIKAWA MATSUKAWA
KINDAICHI (WATARI) KUNIMI HANAMAKI
*SET 2 STARTING ROTATION
WHY WOULD KARASUNO CHANGE THEIR ROTATION?
...

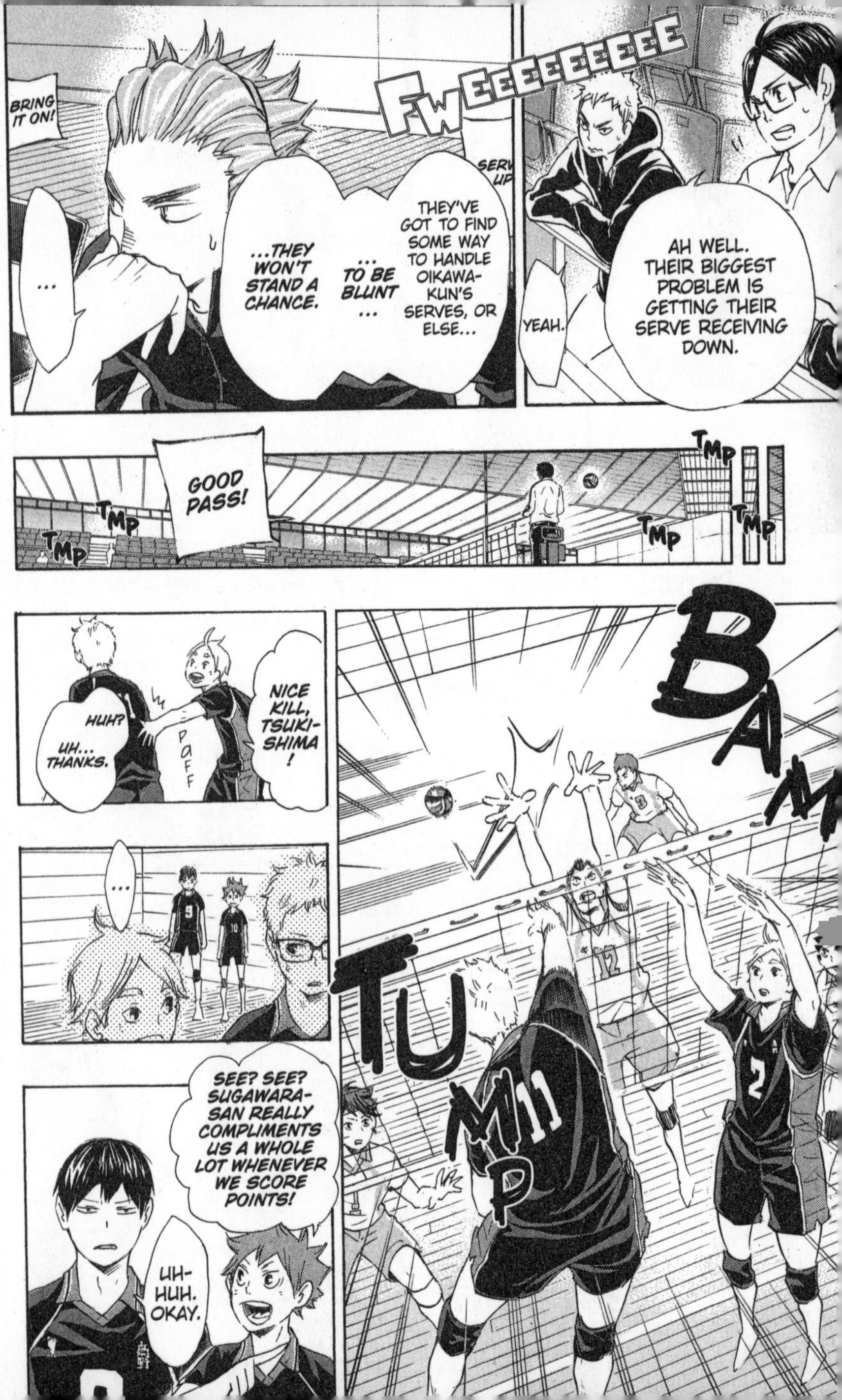
FWEEEEEEEEE
AH WELL. THEIR BIGGEST PROBLEM IS GETTING THEIR SERVE RECEIVING DOWN.
YEAH.
THEY'VE GOT TO FIND SOME WAY TO HANDLE OIKAWA-KUN'S SERVES, OR ELSE...
...TO BE BLUNT...
...THEY WON'T STAND A CHANCE.
...
BRING IT ON!
TMP TMP TMP TMP TMP TMP
GOOD PASS!
BAM
TUMP
NICE KILL, TSUKISHIMA!
PAFF
HUH? UH... THANKS.
...
SEE? SEE? SUGAWARA-SAN REALLY COMPLIMENTS US A WHOLE LOT WHENEVER WE SCORE POINTS!
UH-HUH. OKAY.

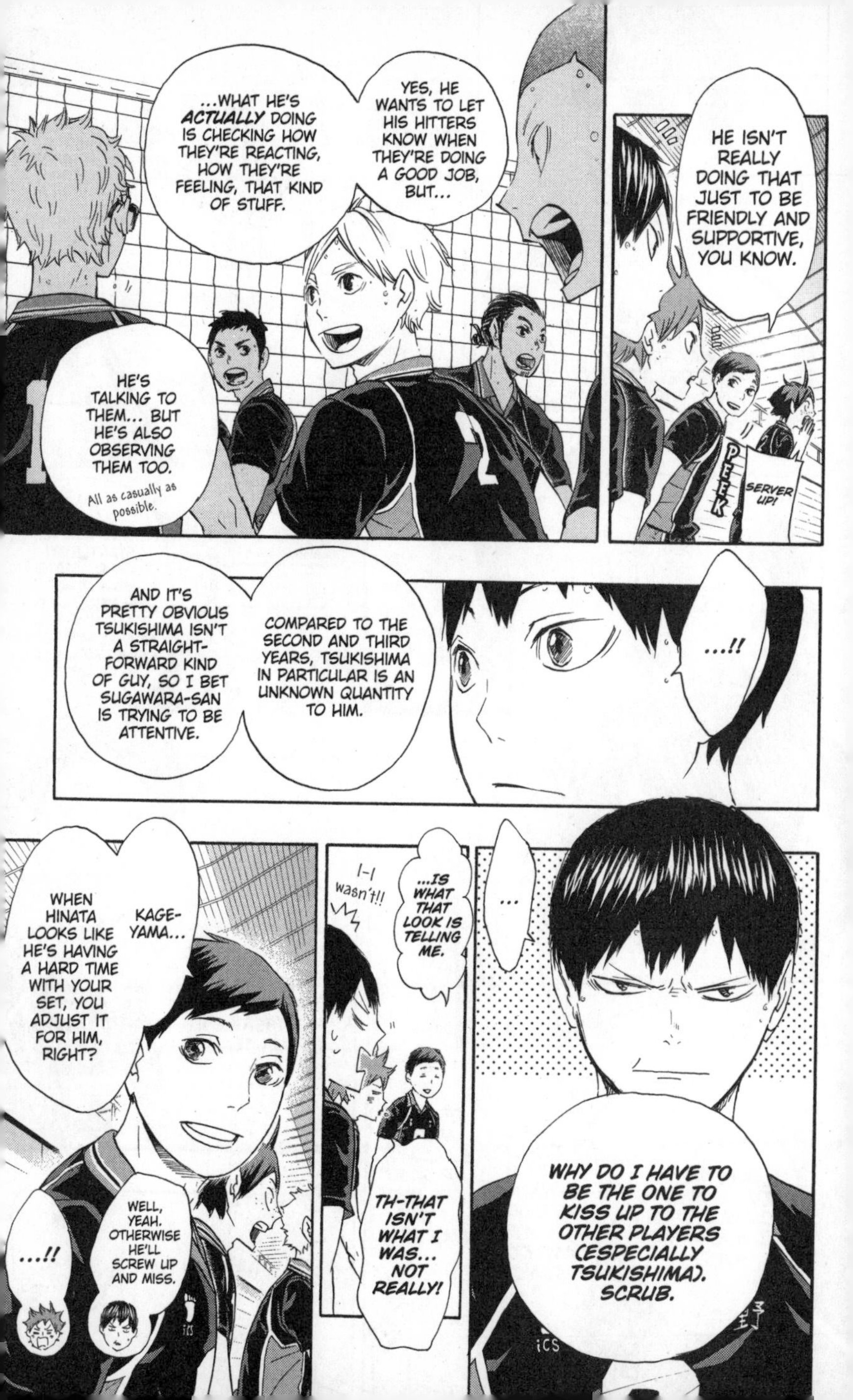
HE ISN'T REALLY DOING THAT JUST TO BE FRIENDLY AND SUPPORTIVE, YOU KNOW.
PEEK
SERVER UP!
YES, HE WANTS TO LET HIS HITTERS KNOW WHEN THEY'RE DOING A GOOD JOB, BUT...
...WHAT HE'S ACTUALLY DOING IS CHECKING HOW THEY'RE REACTING, HOW THEY'RE FEELING, THAT KIND OF STUFF.
HE'S TALKING TO THEM... BUT HE'S ALSO OBSERVING THEM TOO.
All as casually as possible.
...!!
COMPARED TO THE SECOND AND THIRD YEARS, TSUKISHIMA IN PARTICULAR IS AN UNKNOWN QUANTITY TO HIM.
AND IT'S PRETTY OBVIOUS TSUKISHIMA ISN'T A STRAIGHT-FORWARD KIND OF GUY, SO I BET SUGAWARA-SAN IS TRYING TO BE ATTENTIVE.
...
WHY DO I HAVE TO BE THE ONE TO KISS UP TO THE OTHER PLAYERS (ESPECIALLY TSUKISHIMA). SCRUB.
...IS WHAT THAT LOOK IS TELLING ME.
I-I wasn't!!
TH-THAT ISN'T WHAT I WAS... NOT REALLY!
KAGE-YAMA...
WHEN HINATA LOOKS LIKE HE'S HAVING A HARD TIME WITH YOUR SET, YOU ADJUST IT FOR HIM, RIGHT?
WELL, YEAH. OTHERWISE HE'LL SCREW UP AND MISS.
...!!

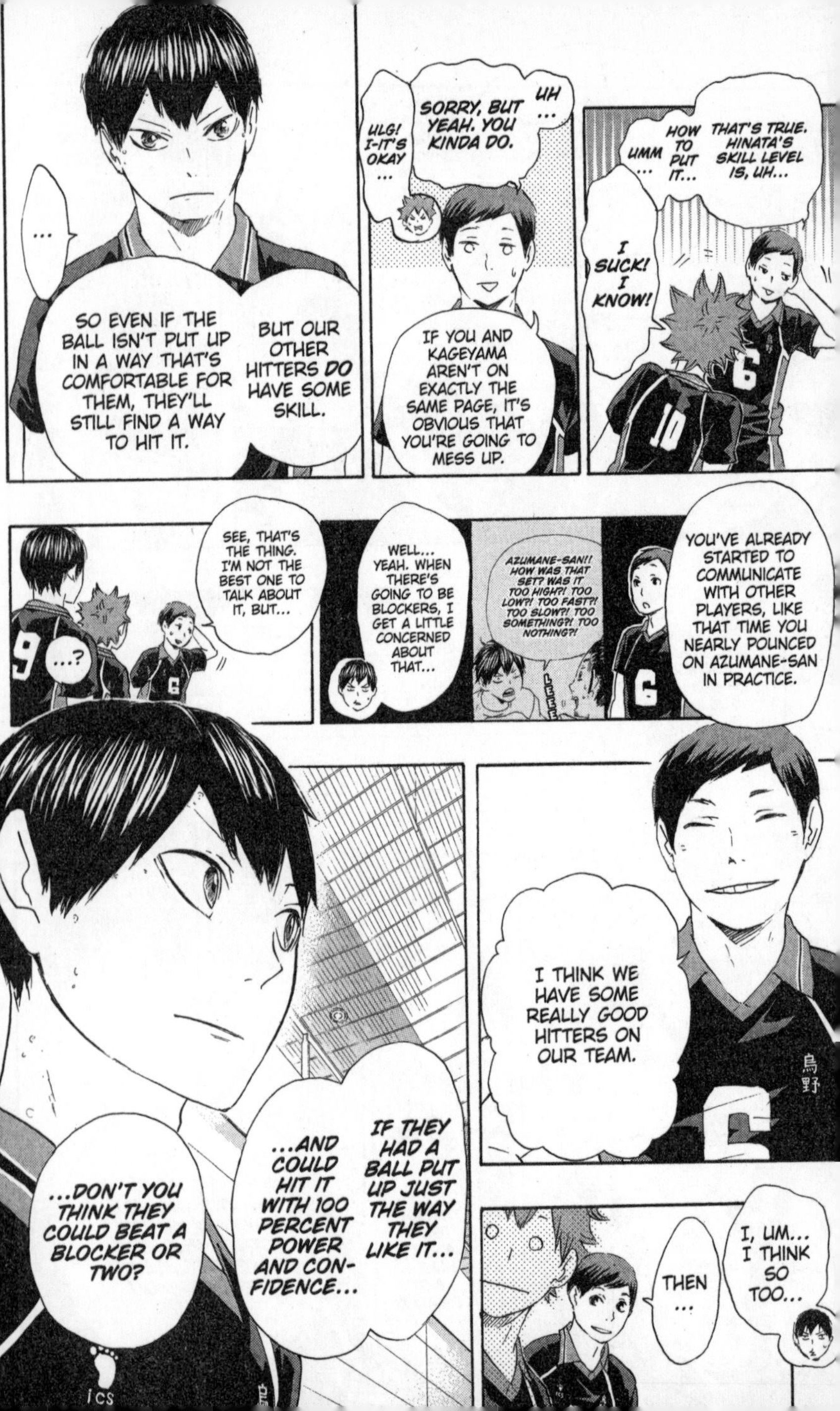

THAT'S TRUE. HINATA'S SKILL LEVEL IS, UH...
HOW TO PUT IT...
UMM...
I SUCK! I KNOW!
UH...
SORRY, BUT YEAH. YOU KINDA DO.
ULG! I-IT'S OKAY...
IF YOU AND KAGEYAMA AREN'T ON EXACTLY THE SAME PAGE, IT'S OBVIOUS THAT YOU'RE GOING TO MESS UP.
...
BUT OUR OTHER HITTERS DO HAVE SOME SKILL.
SO EVEN IF THE BALL ISN'T PUT UP IN A WAY THAT'S COMFORTABLE FOR THEM, THEY'LL STILL FIND A WAY TO HIT IT.
YOU'VE ALREADY STARTED TO COMMUNICATE WITH OTHER PLAYERS, LIKE THAT TIME YOU NEARLY POUNCED ON AZUMANE-SAN IN PRACTICE.
AZUMANE-SAN!! HOW WAS THAT SET? WAS IT TOO HIGH?! TOO LOW?! TOO FAST?! TOO SLOW?! TOO SOMETHING?! TOO NOTHING?!
LEEE
WELL... YEAH. WHEN THERE'S GOING TO BE BLOCKERS, I GET A LITTLE CONCERNED ABOUT THAT...
SEE, THAT'S THE THING. I'M NOT THE BEST ONE TO TALK ABOUT IT, BUT...
...?
I THINK WE HAVE SOME REALLY GOOD HITTERS ON OUR TEAM.
I, UM... I THINK SO TOO...
THEN...
IF THEY HAD A BALL PUT UP JUST THE WAY THEY LIKE IT...
...AND COULD HIT IT WITH 100 PERCENT POWER AND CONFIDENCE...
...DON'T YOU THINK THEY COULD BEAT A BLOCKER OR TWO?

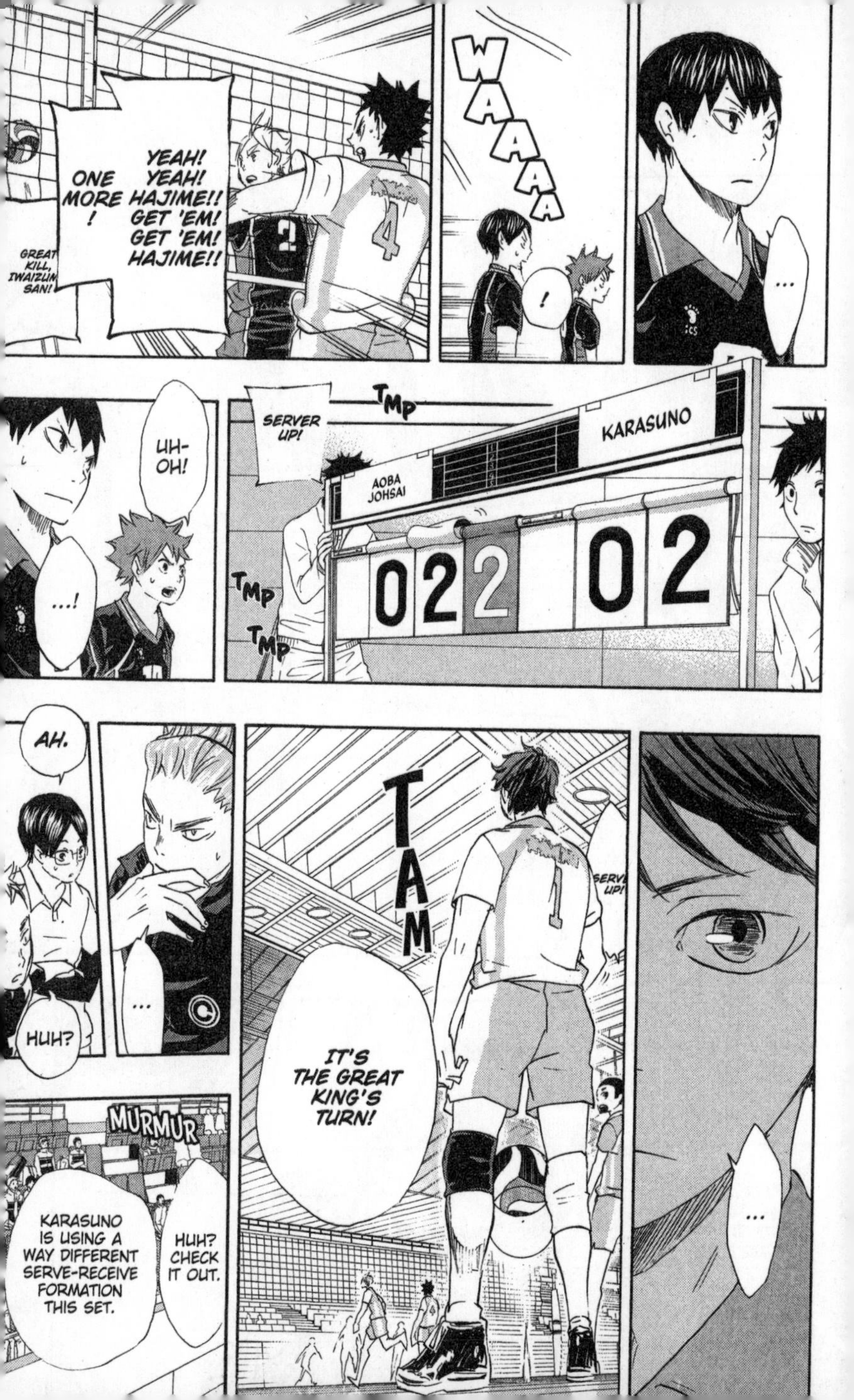
...
WAAAAA
!
YEAH! YEAH! HAJIME!! GET 'EM! GET 'EM! HAJIME!!
ONE MORE!
GREAT KILL, IWAIZUMI-SAN!
KARASUNO
SERVER UP!
TMP
AOBA JOHSAI
02
2
02
TMP
TMP
UH-OH!
...!
...
SERVE UP!
TAM
IT'S THE GREAT KING'S TURN!
...
AH.
HUH?
MURMUR
HUH? CHECK IT OUT.
KARASUNO IS USING A WAY DIFFERENT SERVE-RECEIVE FORMATION THIS SET.

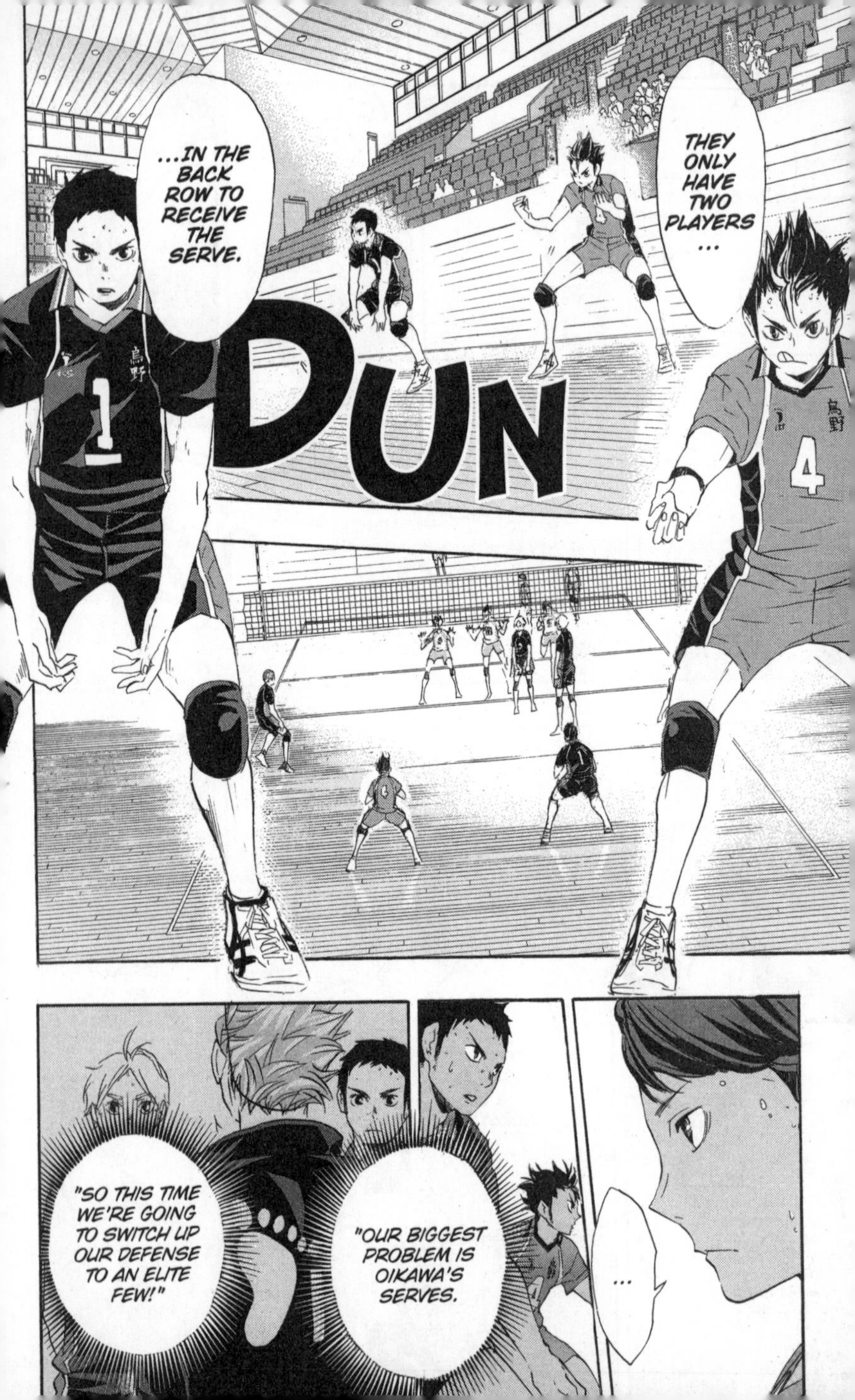
THEY ONLY HAVE TWO PLAYERS...
...IN THE BACK ROW TO RECEIVE THE SERVE.
DUN
...
"OUR BIGGEST PROBLEM IS OIKAWA'S SERVES.
"SO THIS TIME WE'RE GOING TO SWITCH UP OUR DEFENSE TO AN ELITE FEW!"

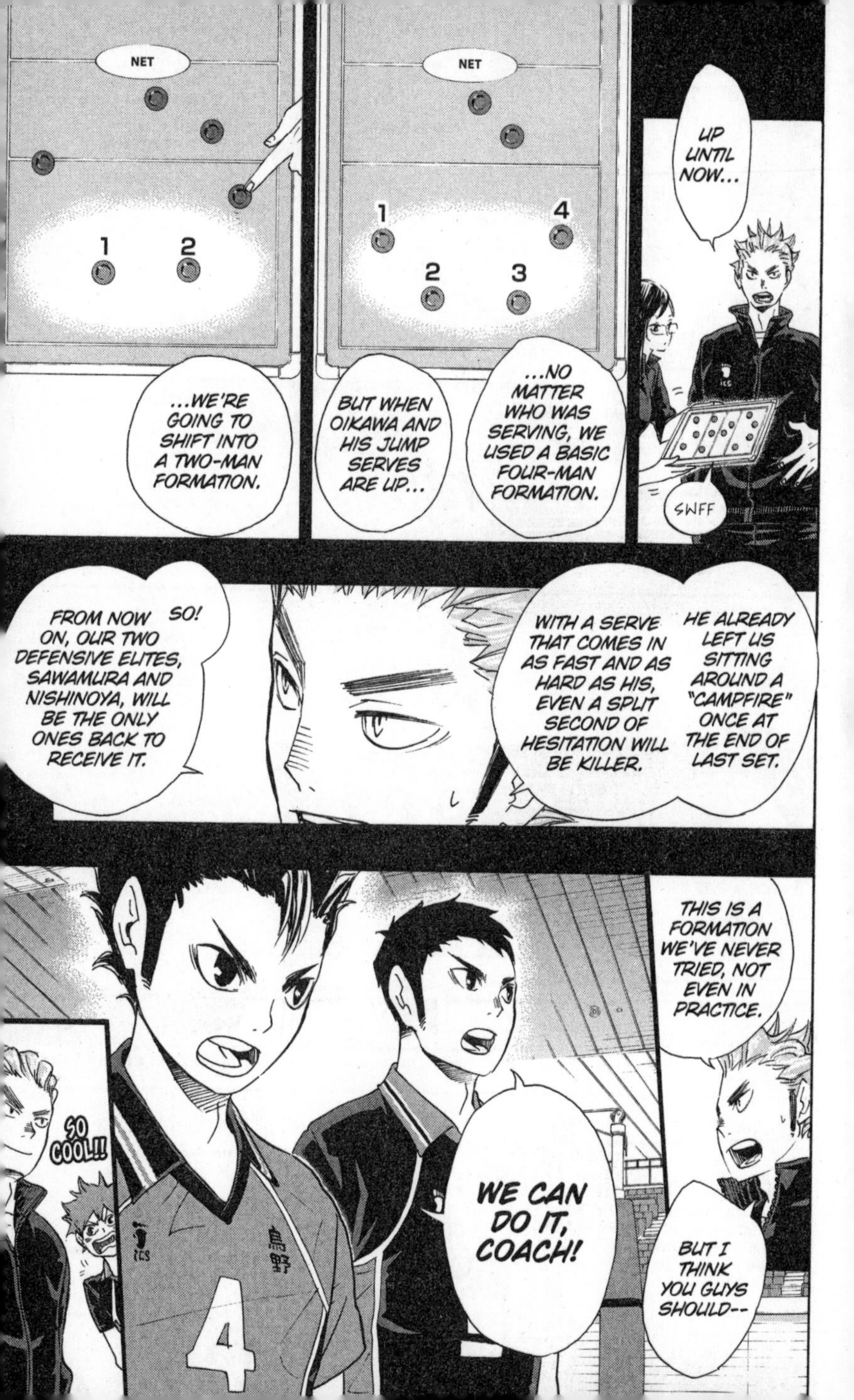
UP UNTIL NOW...
...NO MATTER WHO WAS SERVING, WE USED A BASIC FOUR-MAN FORMATION.
SWFF
NET
1
4
2
3
BUT WHEN OIKAWA AND HIS JUMP SERVES ARE UP...
NET
1
2
...WE'RE GOING TO SHIFT INTO A TWO-MAN FORMATION.
HE ALREADY LEFT US SITTING AROUND A "CAMPFIRE" ONCE AT THE END OF LAST SET.
WITH A SERVE THAT COMES IN AS FAST AND AS HARD AS HIS, EVEN A SPLIT SECOND OF HESITATION WILL BE KILLER.
SO!
FROM NOW ON, OUR TWO DEFENSIVE ELITES, SAWAMURA AND NISHINOYA, WILL BE THE ONLY ONES BACK TO RECEIVE IT.
THIS IS A FORMATION WE'VE NEVER TRIED, NOT EVEN IN PRACTICE.
BUT I THINK YOU GUYS SHOULD--
WE CAN DO IT, COACH!
SO COOL!!

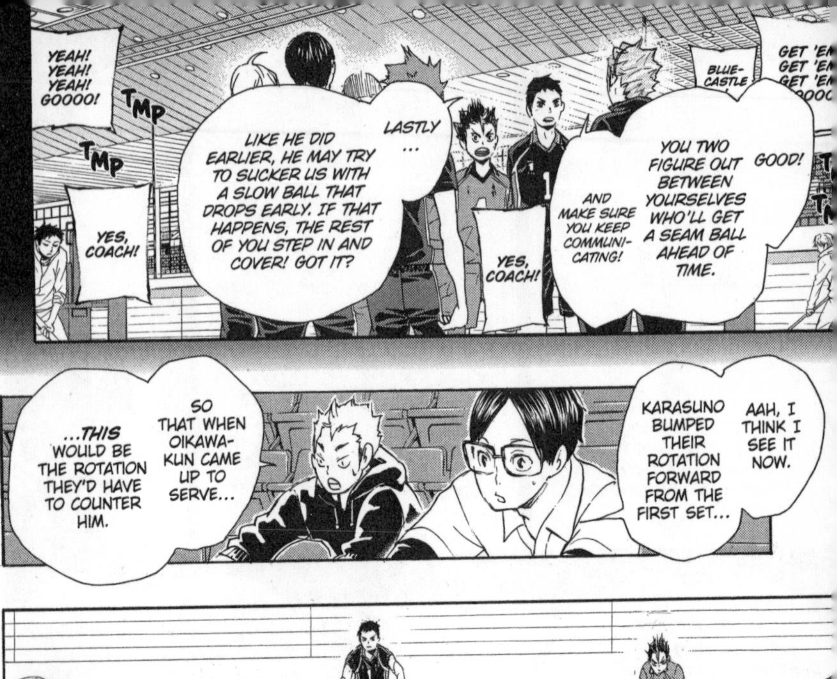
GET 'EM GET 'EM GET 'EM GOOO
BLUE-CASTLE
GOOD!
YOU TWO FIGURE OUT BETWEEN YOURSELVES WHO'LL GET A SEAM BALL AHEAD OF TIME.
AND MAKE SURE YOU KEEP COMMUNICATING!
YES, COACH!
LASTLY...
LIKE HE DID EARLIER, HE MAY TRY TO SUCKER US WITH A SLOW BALL THAT DROPS EARLY. IF THAT HAPPENS, THE REST OF YOU STEP IN AND COVER! GOT IT?
TMP
TMP
YES, COACH!
YEAH! YEAH! YEAH! GOOOO!
AAH, I THINK I SEE IT NOW.
KARASUNO BUMPED THEIR ROTATION FORWARD FROM THE FIRST SET...
SO THAT WHEN OIKAWA-KUN CAME UP TO SERVE...
...THIS WOULD BE THE ROTATION THEY'D HAVE TO COUNTER HIM.
THEIR TWO TOP DEFENDERS, THEIR CAPTAIN AND THEIR LIBERO, ARE IN THE BACK ROW...
AND NOT ONLY THAT...
THEIR TWO POWER HITTERS ARE IN THE PERFECT SPOTS, TOO... BUZZ CUT ON THE FRONT LEFT...
...AND MAN-BUN IN THE BACK RIGHT, READY FOR A PIPE OR SOME OTHER BACK ROW SET.*
*CURRENT ROTATION
AZUMANE
SAWAMURA
HINATA (NOYA)
TSUKISHIMA
SUGAWARA
TANAKA
NET
KUNIMI
KINDAICHI
IWAIZUMI
HANAMAKI
MATSUKAWA (WATARI)
OIKAWA

*THE FRONT LEFT IS USUALLY THE EASIEST SPOT FOR RIGHT-HANDED HITTERS TO ATTACK FROM BECAUSE THE BALL COMES IN FROM THE RIGHT.

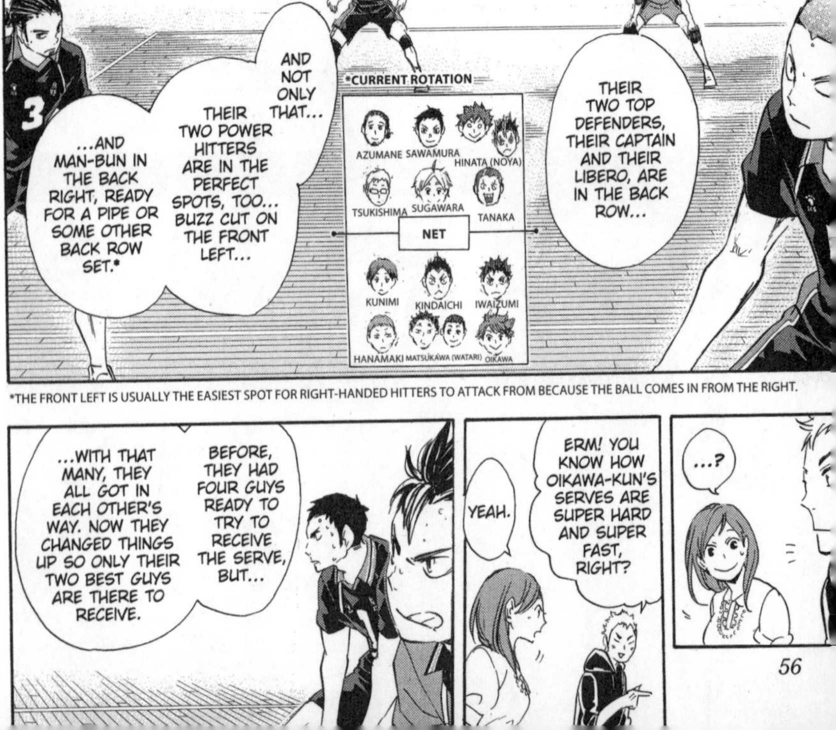
...?
ERM! YOU KNOW HOW OIKAWA-KUN'S SERVES ARE SUPER HARD AND SUPER FAST, RIGHT?
YEAH.
BEFORE, THEY HAD FOUR GUYS READY TO TRY TO RECEIVE THE SERVE, BUT...
...WITH THAT MANY, THEY ALL GOT IN EACH OTHER'S WAY. NOW THEY CHANGED THINGS UP SO ONLY THEIR TWO BEST GUYS ARE THERE TO RECEIVE.

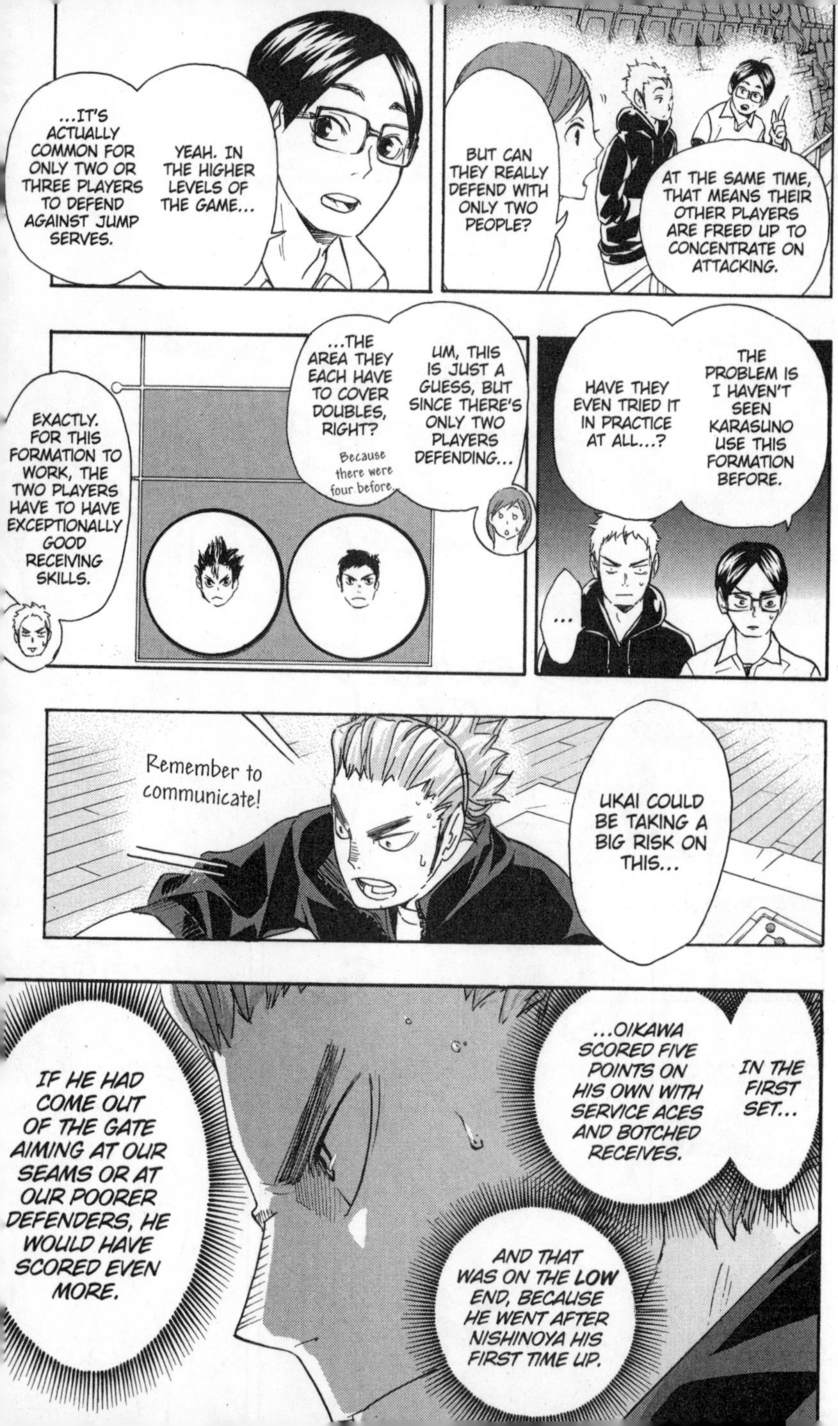
BUT CAN THEY REALLY DEFEND WITH ONLY TWO PEOPLE?
AT THE SAME TIME, THAT MEANS THEIR OTHER PLAYERS ARE FREED UP TO CONCENTRATE ON ATTACKING.
YEAH. IN THE HIGHER LEVELS OF THE GAME...
...IT'S ACTUALLY COMMON FOR ONLY TWO OR THREE PLAYERS TO DEFEND AGAINST JUMP SERVES.
THE PROBLEM IS I HAVEN'T SEEN KARASUNO USE THIS FORMATION BEFORE.
HAVE THEY EVEN TRIED IT IN PRACTICE AT ALL...?
...
UM, THIS IS JUST A GUESS, BUT SINCE THERE'S ONLY TWO PLAYERS DEFENDING...
...THE AREA THEY EACH HAVE TO COVER DOUBLES, RIGHT?
Because there were four before...
EXACTLY. FOR THIS FORMATION TO WORK, THE TWO PLAYERS HAVE TO HAVE EXCEPTIONALLY GOOD RECEIVING SKILLS.
UKAI COULD BE TAKING A BIG RISK ON THIS...
Remember to communicate!
IN THE FIRST SET...
...OIKAWA SCORED FIVE POINTS ON HIS OWN WITH SERVICE ACES AND BOTCHED RECEIVES.
AND THAT WAS ON THE LOW END, BECAUSE HE WENT AFTER NISHINOYA HIS FIRST TIME UP.
IF HE HAD COME OUT OF THE GATE AIMING AT OUR SEAMS OR AT OUR POORER DEFENDERS, HE WOULD HAVE SCORED EVEN MORE.

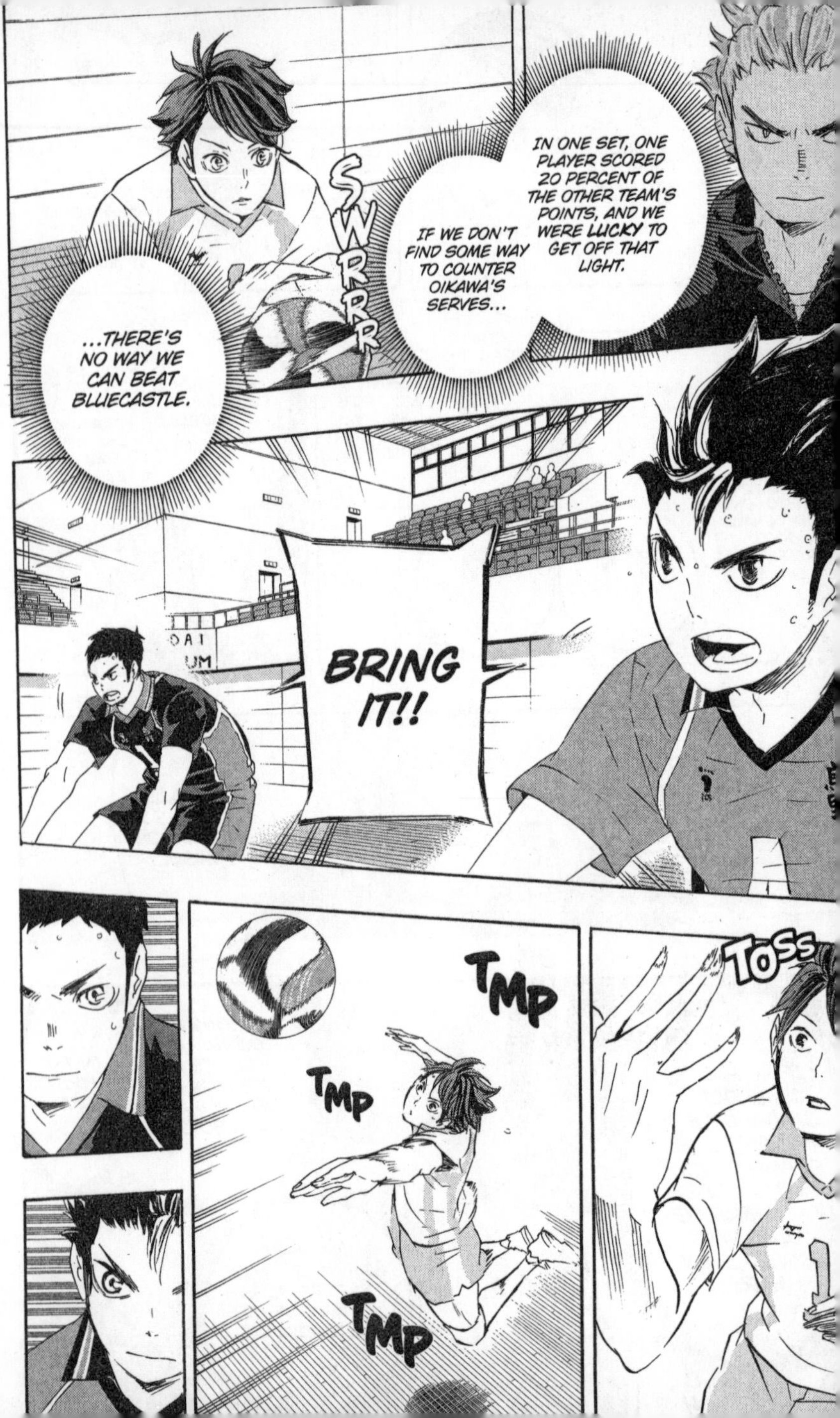
IN ONE SET, ONE PLAYER SCORED 20 PERCENT OF THE OTHER TEAM'S POINTS, AND WE WERE LUCKY TO GET OFF THAT LIGHT.
IF WE DON'T FIND SOME WAY TO COUNTER OIKAWA'S SERVES...
SWRRR
...THERE'S NO WAY WE CAN BEAT BLUECASTLE.
BRING IT!!
TOSS
TMP
TMP
TMP

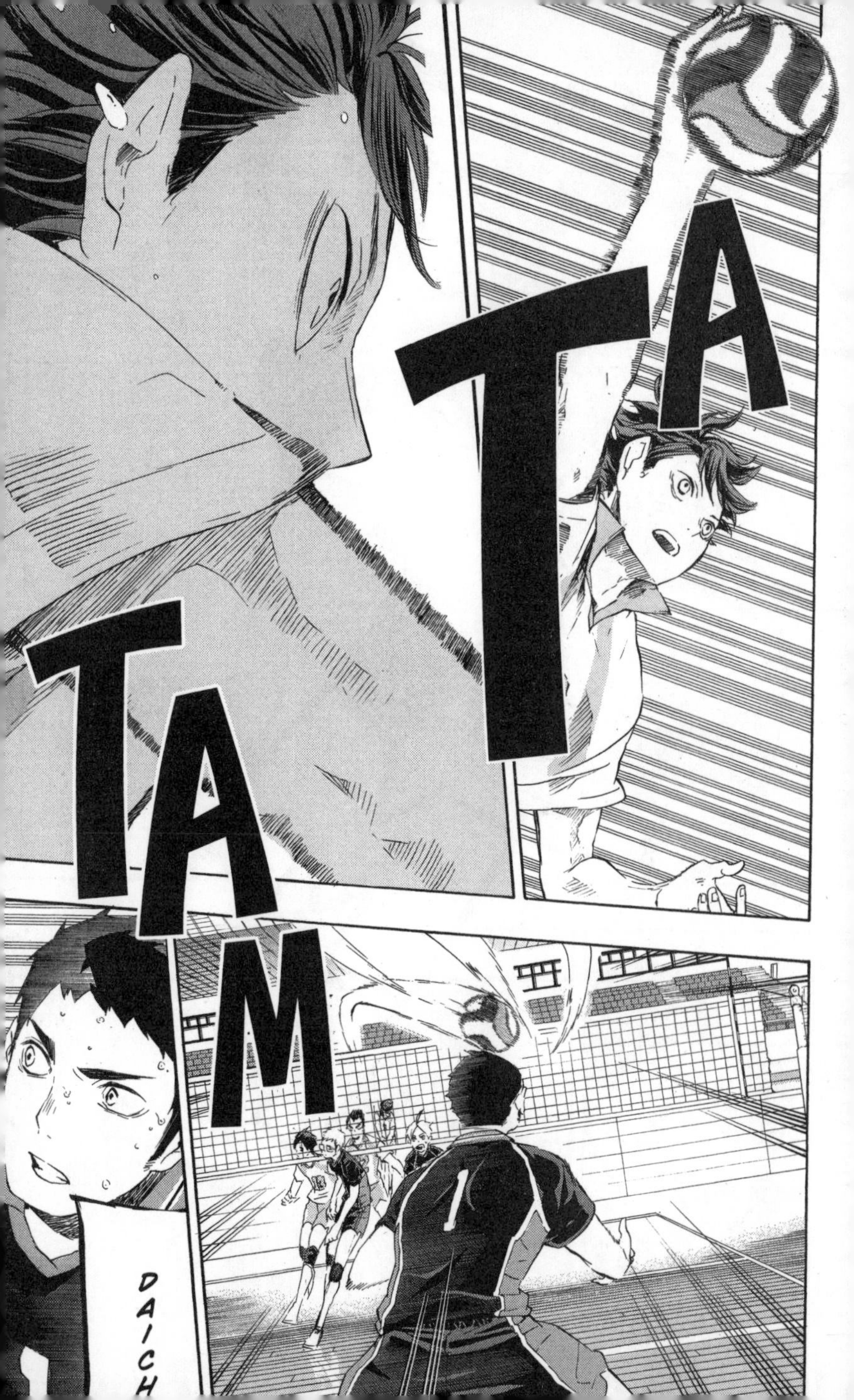
TA
TAM
DAICH

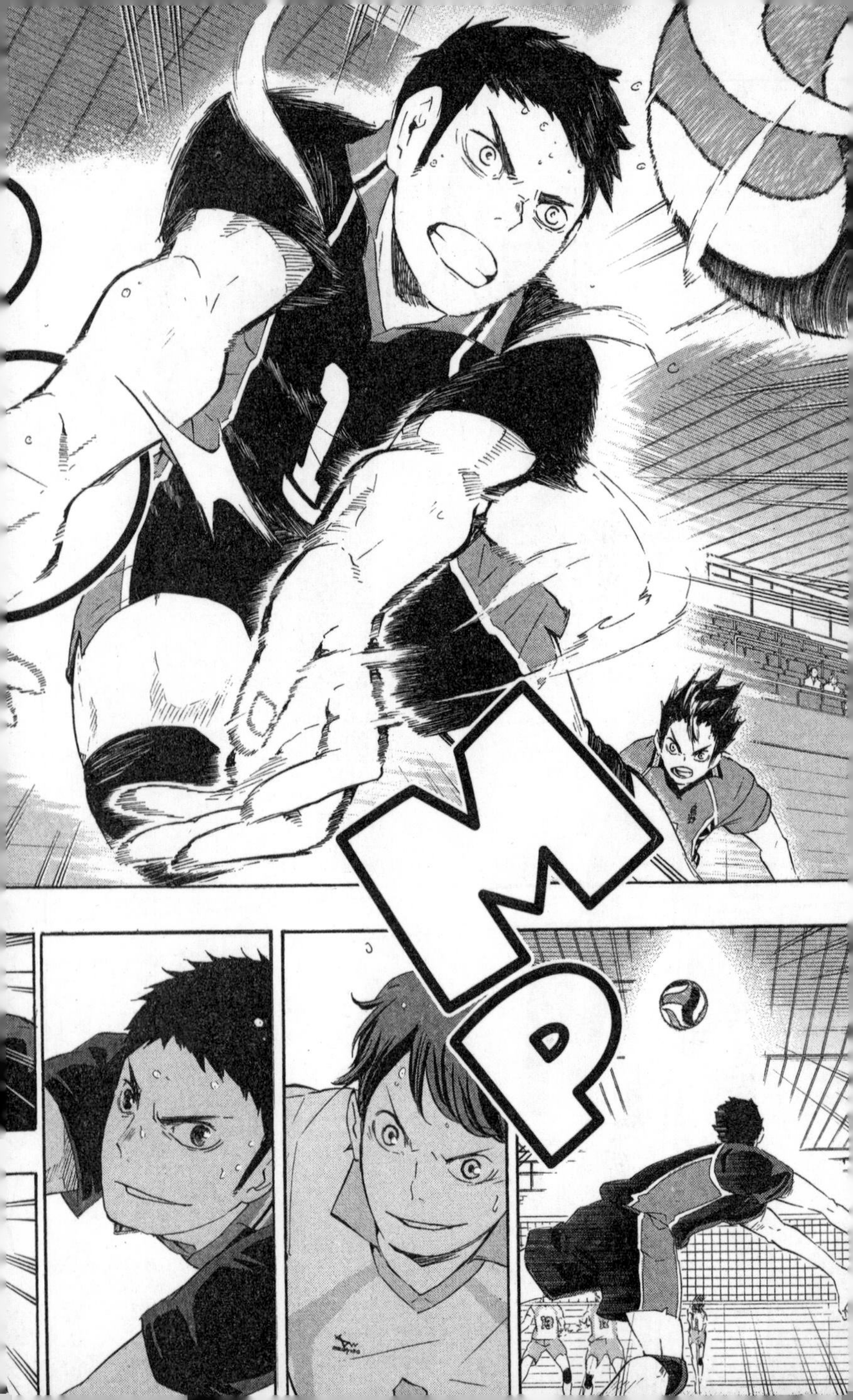
MP

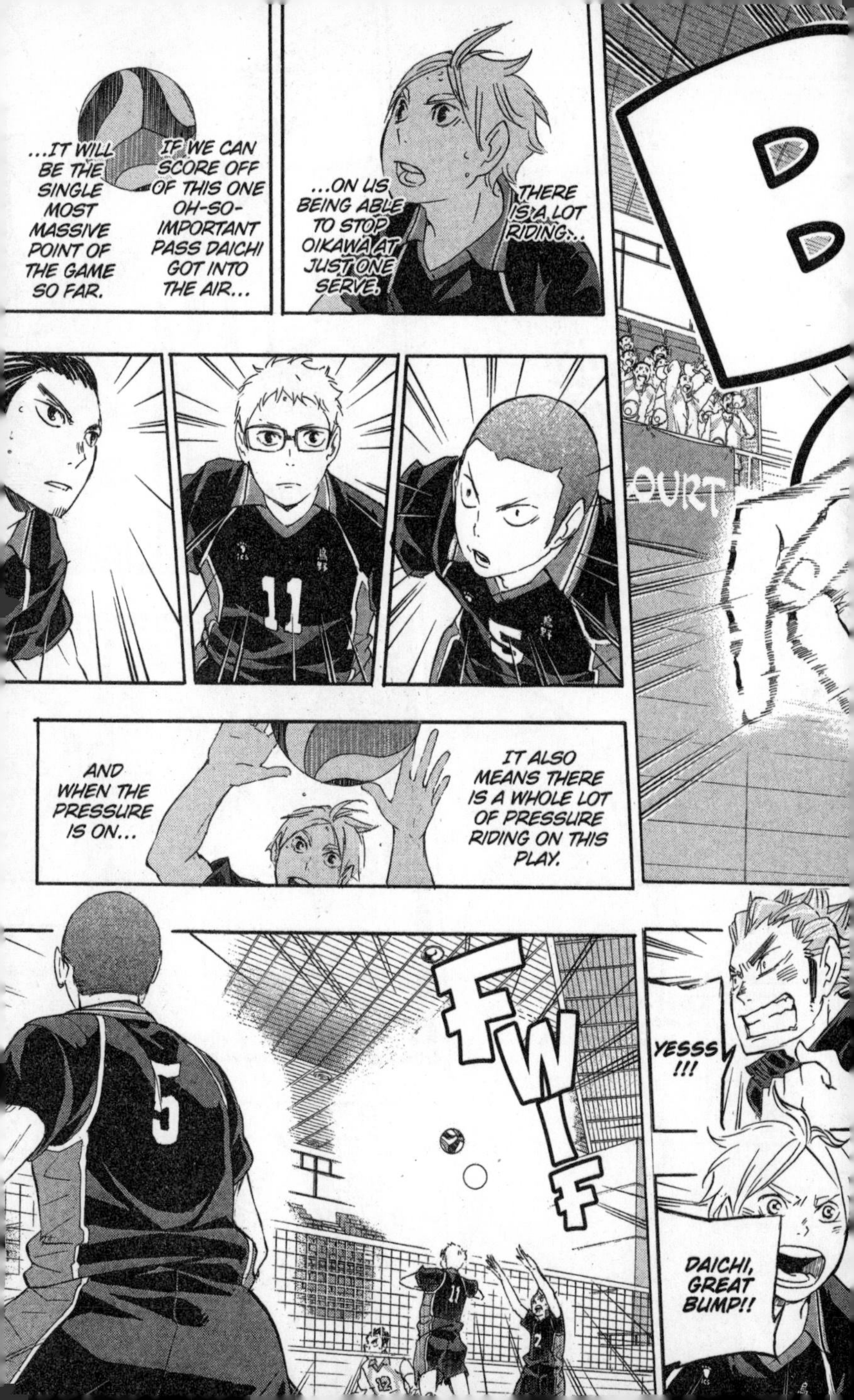
DD
THERE IS A LOT RIDING...
...ON US BEING ABLE TO STOP OIKAWA AT JUST ONE SERVE.
IF WE CAN SCORE OFF OF THIS ONE OH-SO-IMPORTANT PASS DAICHI GOT INTO THE AIR...
...IT WILL BE THE SINGLE MOST MASSIVE POINT OF THE GAME SO FAR.
IT ALSO MEANS THERE IS A WHOLE LOT OF PRESSURE RIDING ON THIS PLAY.
AND WHEN THE PRESSURE IS ON...
YESSS!!!
DAICHI, GREAT BUMP!!
FWIF

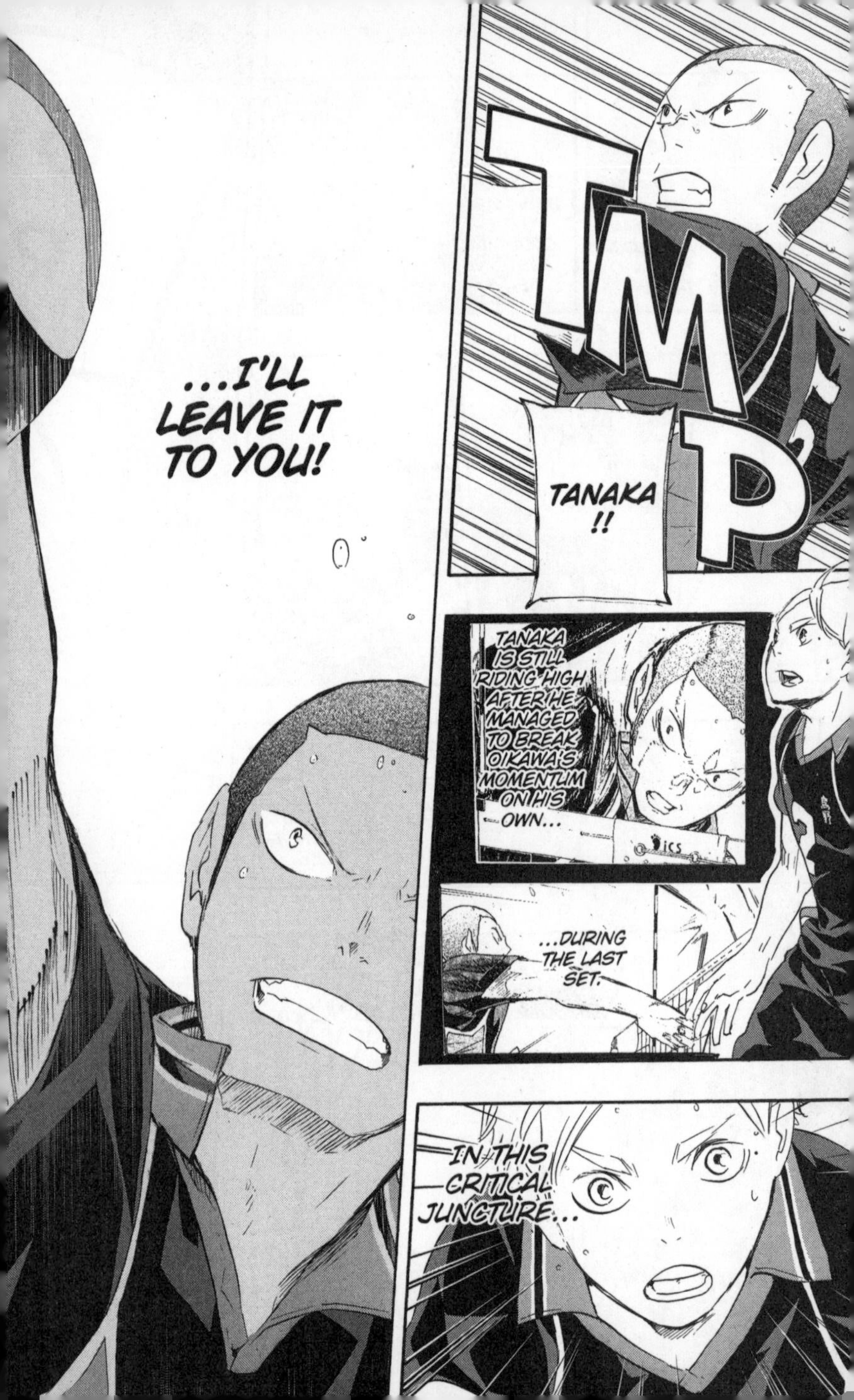
TMP
TANAKA !!
TANAKA IS STILL RIDING HIGH AFTER HE MANAGED TO BREAK OIKAWA'S MOMENTUM ON HIS OWN...
...DURING THE LAST SET.
IN THIS CRITICAL JUNCTURE...
...I'LL LEAVE IT TO YOU!

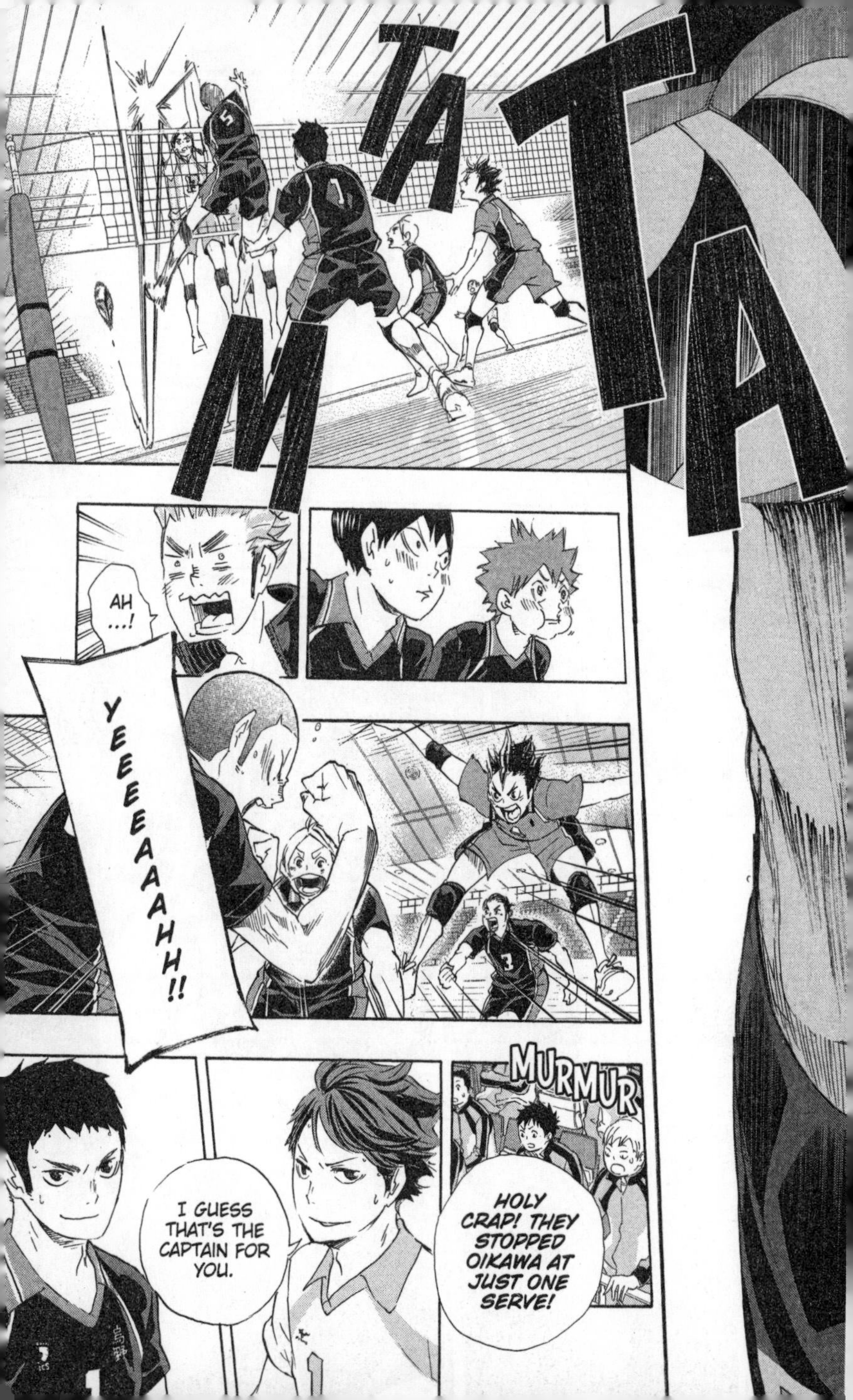
TATAMI
AH ...!
YEEEEAAAAHH!!
MURMUR
HOLY CRAP! THEY STOPPED OIKAWA AT JUST ONE SERVE!
I GUESS THAT'S THE CAPTAIN FOR YOU.

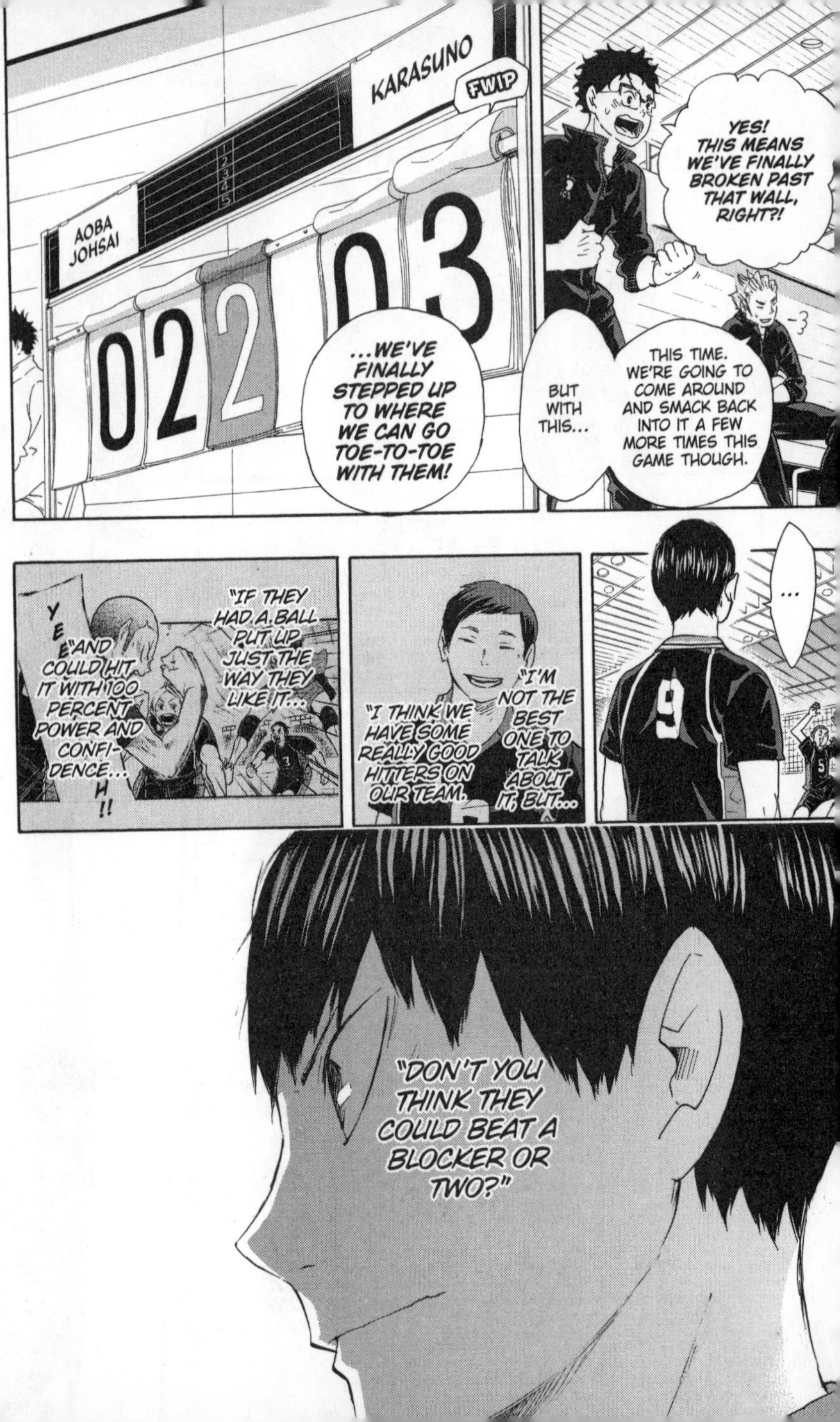
YES! THIS MEANS WE'VE FINALLY BROKEN PAST THAT WALL, RIGHT?!
THIS TIME. WE'RE GOING TO COME AROUND AND SMACK BACK INTO IT A FEW MORE TIMES THIS GAME THOUGH.
BUT WITH THIS...
KARASUNO
FWIP
AOBA JOHSAI
...WE'VE FINALLY STEPPED UP TO WHERE WE CAN GO TOE-TO-TOE WITH THEM!
...
"I'M NOT THE BEST ONE TO TALK ABOUT IT, BUT...
"I THINK WE HAVE SOME REALLY GOOD HITTERS ON OUR TEAM.
"IF THEY HAD A BALL PUT UP JUST THE WAY THEY LIKE IT...
"AND COULD HIT IT WITH 100 PERCENT POWER AND CONFI-DENCE...
"DON'T YOU THINK THEY COULD BEAT A BLOCKER OR TWO?"

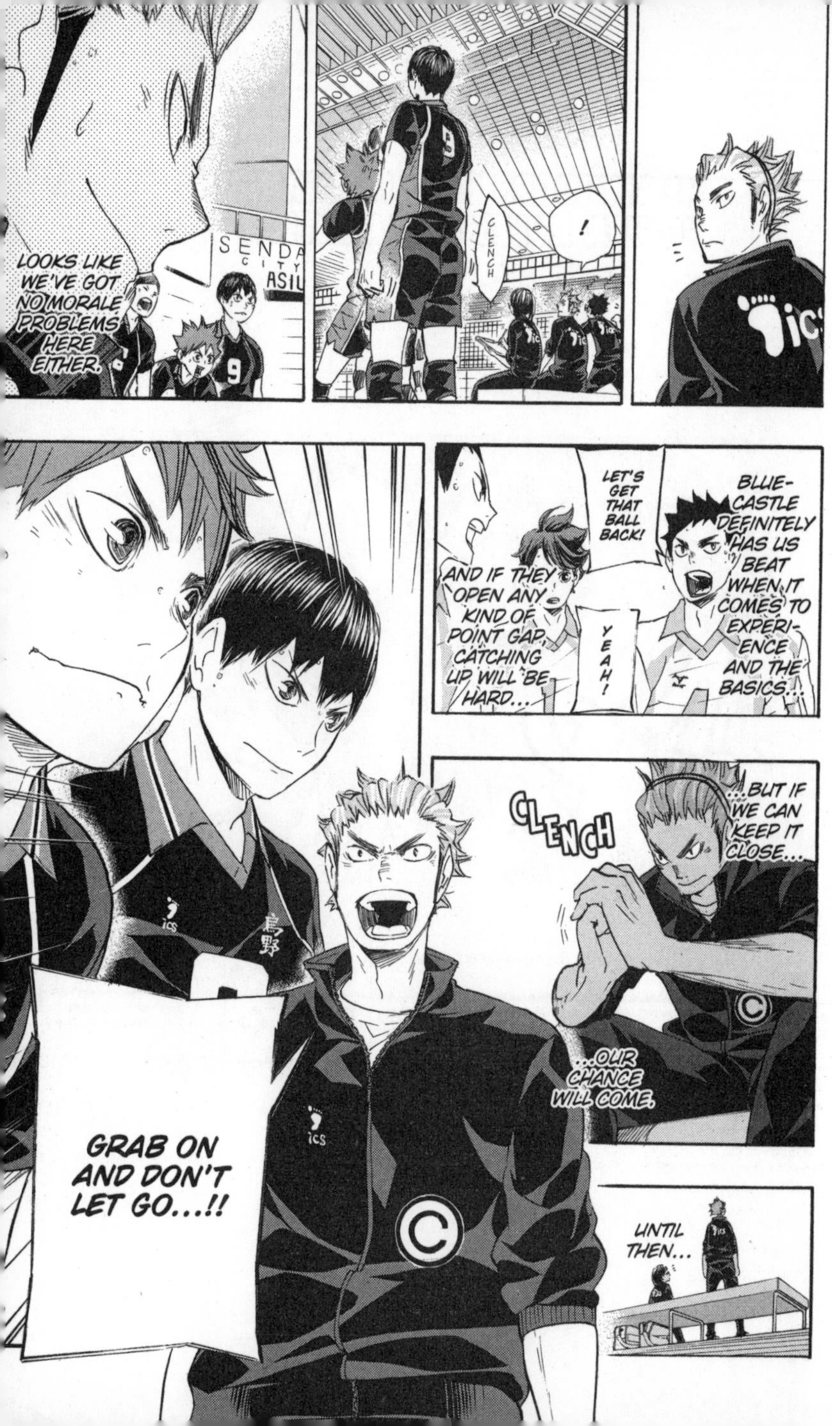
CLENCH
!
LOOKS LIKE WE'VE GOT NO MORALE PROBLEMS HERE EITHER.
BLUE-CASTLE DEFINITELY HAS US BEAT WHEN IT COMES TO EXPERIENCE AND THE BASICS...
LET'S GET THAT BALL BACK!
YEAH!
AND IF THEY OPEN ANY KIND OF POINT GAP, CATCHING UP WILL BE HARD...
...BUT IF WE CAN KEEP IT CLOSE...
CLENCH
...OUR CHANCE WILL COME.
UNTIL THEN...
GRAB ON AND DON'T LET GO...!!

THE "WHOOPS I DID IT AGAIN" & "QUICK RULES EXPLANATION" Corner

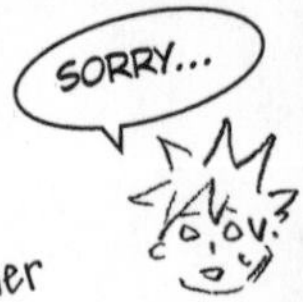
SORRY...

WHEN THIS CHAPTER FIRST RAN IN THE MAGAZINE, THE PANEL WHERE SAWAMURA BUMPS OIKAWA'S SERVE LOOKED LIKE THIS.

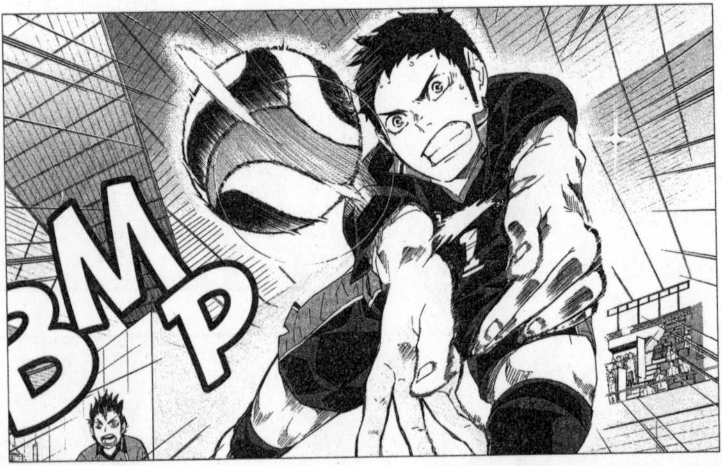
BMP

BUT THIS IS THE CURRENT ROTATION. →

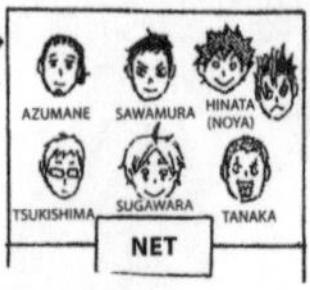
AZUMANE
SAWAMURA
HINATA (NOYA)
TSUKISHIMA
SUGAWARA
TANAKA
NET

(SAWAMURA DRIFTING TO THE LEFT HALF AND NISHINOYA COVERING THE RIGHT)

SO THE ABOVE PANEL ACTUALLY HAS SAWAMURA IN THE OPPOSITE POSITION… A COMPLETE MISTAKE ON MY PART. I APOLOGIZE TO ANY READERS WHO WERE CONFUSED WHEN THIS FIRST RAN. IF THIS REALLY OCCURRED IN A LIVE GAME, IT WOULD BE CONSIDERED A **POSITIONAL FOUL** FOR A PLAYER BEING OUT OF PROPER ALIGNMENT AT THE MOMENT OF SERVICE.

1ST Haikyu!! Character Popularity Poll Results!!

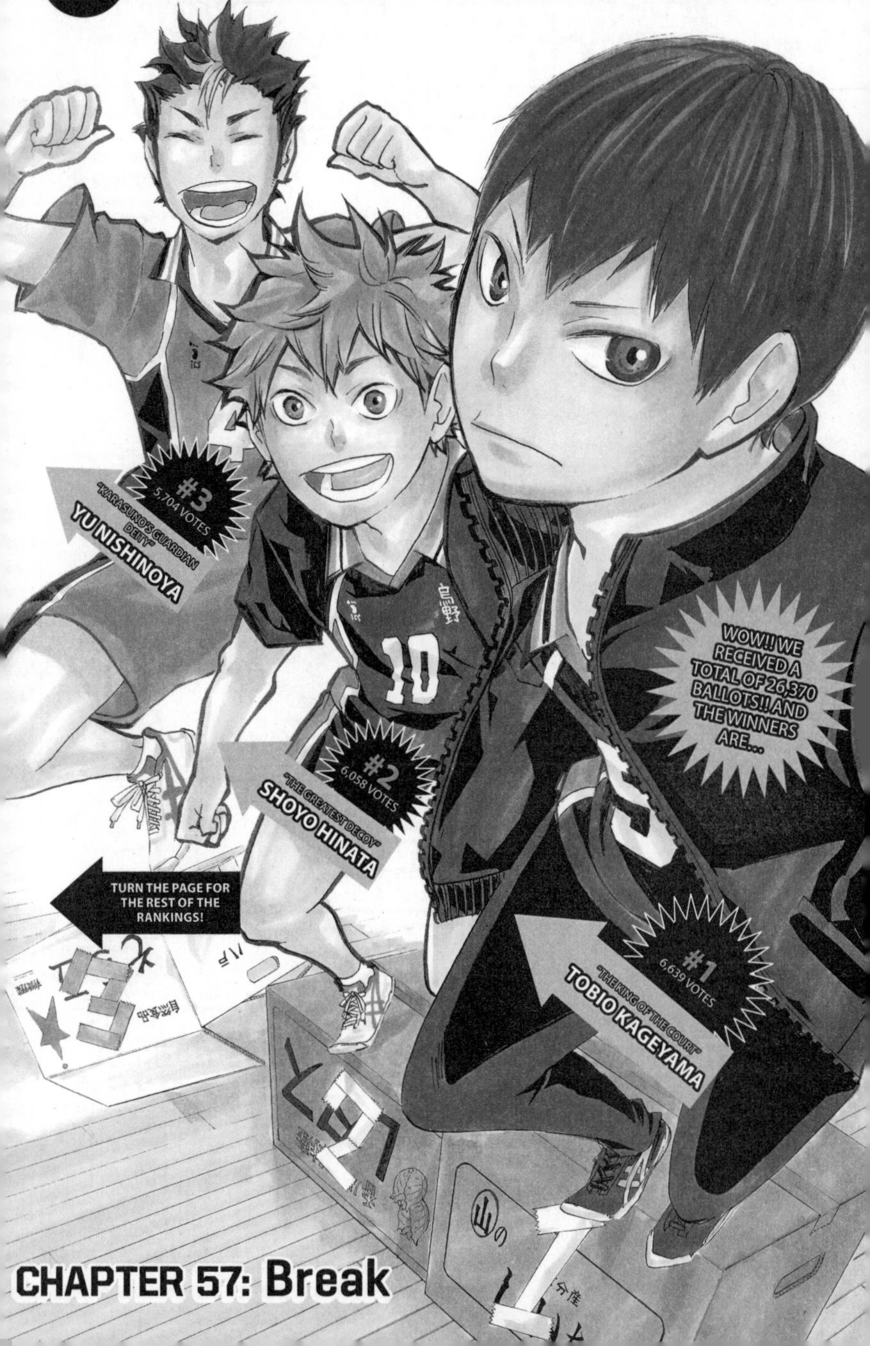

WOW!! WE RECEIVED A TOTAL OF 26,370 BALLOTS!! AND THE WINNERS ARE...
#1 6,639 VOTES
"THE KING OF THE COURT"
TOBIO KAGEYAMA
#2 6,058 VOTES
"THE GREATEST DECOY"
SHOYO HINATA
#3 5,704 VOTES
"KARASUNO'S GUARDIAN DEITY"
YU NISHINOYA
10
TURN THE PAGE FOR THE REST OF THE RANKINGS!

CHAPTER 57: Break

A FREE-FOR-ALL BRAWL!!

ALL OF YOUR FAVORITE CHARACTERS ARE HERE!!

RANKS #4 ~ 10!!

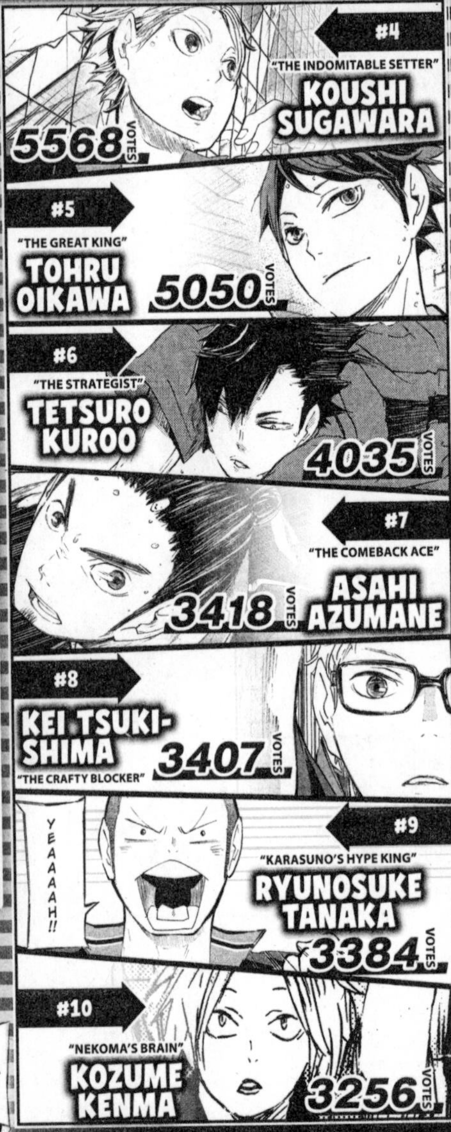
#4
"THE INDOMITABLE SETTER"
KOUSHI SUGAWARA
5568 VOTES
#5
"THE GREAT KING"
TOHRU OIKAWA
5050 VOTES
#6
"THE STRATEGIST"
TETSURO KUROO
4035 VOTES
#7
"THE COMEBACK ACE"
ASAHI AZUMANE
3418 VOTES
#8
KEI TSUKISHIMA
"THE CRAFTY BLOCKER"
3407 VOTES
#9
YEAAAAAH!!
"KARASUNO'S HYPE KING"
RYUNOSUKE TANAKA
3384 VOTES
#10
"NEKOMA'S BRAIN"
KOZUME KENMA
3256 VOTES

JUST ONE STEP SHY OF THE TOP 10! RANKS #11 ~ 20

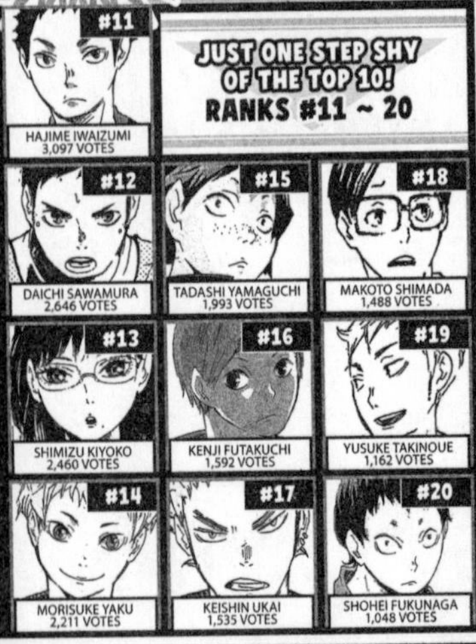
#11
HAJIME IWAIZUMI
3,097 VOTES
#12
DAICHI SAWAMURA
2,646 VOTES
#13
SHIMIZU KIYOKO
2,460 VOTES
#14
MORISUKE YAKU
2,211 VOTES
#15
TADASHI YAMAGUCHI
1,993 VOTES
#16
KENJI FUTAKUCHI
1,592 VOTES
#17
KEISHIN UKAI
1,535 VOTES
#18
MAKOTO SHIMADA
1,488 VOTES
#19
YUSUKE TAKINOUE
1,162 VOTES
#20
SHOHEI FUKUNAGA
1,048 VOTES

DON'T FORGET THESE CHARACTERS, TOO! RANKS #21 ~ 50!!

#21 TAKANOBU AONE	1,003 VOTES	#37 YUKITAKA IZUMI	246 VOTES
#22 CHIKARA ENNOSHITA	954 VOTES	#38 WAKATOSHI USHIJIMA	199 VOTES
#23 YUI MICHIMIYA	928 VOTES	#39 KOJI SEKIMUKAE	195 VOTES
#24 KUNIMI	856 VOTES	#40 YUKI SHIBAYAMA	183 VOTES
#25 HANAMAKI	826 VOTES	#41 THE VICE PRINCIPAL	181 VOTES
#26 HARUICHI FURUDATE	706 VOTES	#42 YASUFUMI NEKOMATA	169 VOTES
#27 ITTETSU TAKEDA	571 VOTES	#43 TAKERU NAKAJIMA	136 VOTES
#28 KANAME MONIWA	558 VOTES	#44 KIYOKO HONDA (FAKE KIYOKO)	128 VOTES
#29T YUTARO KINDAICHI	466 VOTES		
#29T TAKETORA YAMAMOTO	466 VOTES	#45 SHIMADA MART PIG	110 VOTES
#31 HISASHI KINOSHITA	367 VOTES	#46 SADAYUKI MIZOGUCHI	103 VOTES
#32 SOU INUOKA	360 VOTES	#47 THE LITTLE GIANT	100 VOTES
#33 YASUSHI KAMASAKI	338 VOTES	#48 YUKINARI MORI	98 VOTES
#34 NOBUYUKI KAI	324 VOTES	#49 MORI	96 VOTES
#35 HAYATO IKEJIRI	303 VOTES	#50T SUZUKI	95 VOTES
#36 KAZUHITO NARITA	275 VOTES	#50T TAKEHITO SASAYA	95 VOTES

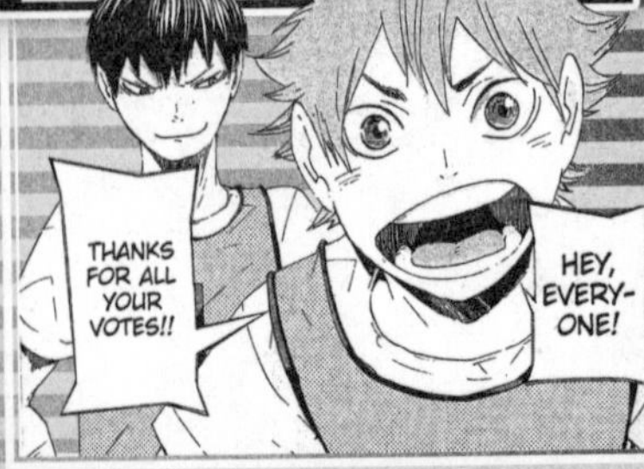
HEY, EVERY-ONE!
THANKS FOR ALL YOUR VOTES!!

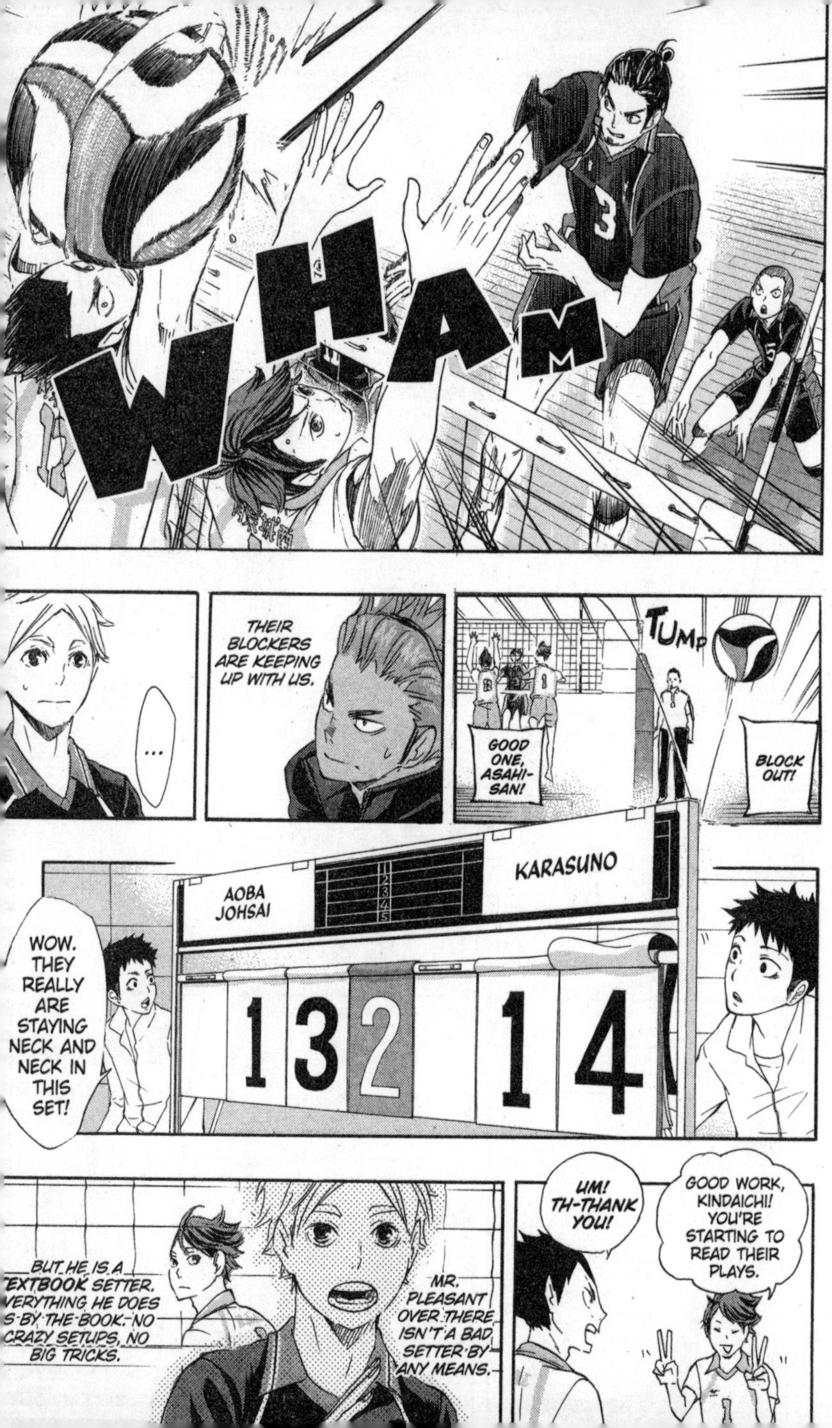
WHAM
TUMP
BLOCK OUT!
GOOD ONE, ASAHI-SAN!
THEIR BLOCKERS ARE KEEPING UP WITH US.
...
KARASUNO
AOBA JOHSAI
1 2 3 4 5
13 2 14
WOW. THEY REALLY ARE STAYING NECK AND NECK IN THIS SET!
GOOD WORK, KINDAICHI! YOU'RE STARTING TO READ THEIR PLAYS.
UM! TH-THANK YOU!
MR. PLEASANT OVER THERE ISN'T A BAD SETTER BY ANY MEANS.
BUT HE IS A TEXTBOOK SETTER. VERYTHING HE DOES S BY THE BOOK. NO CRAZY SETUPS, NO BIG TRICKS.

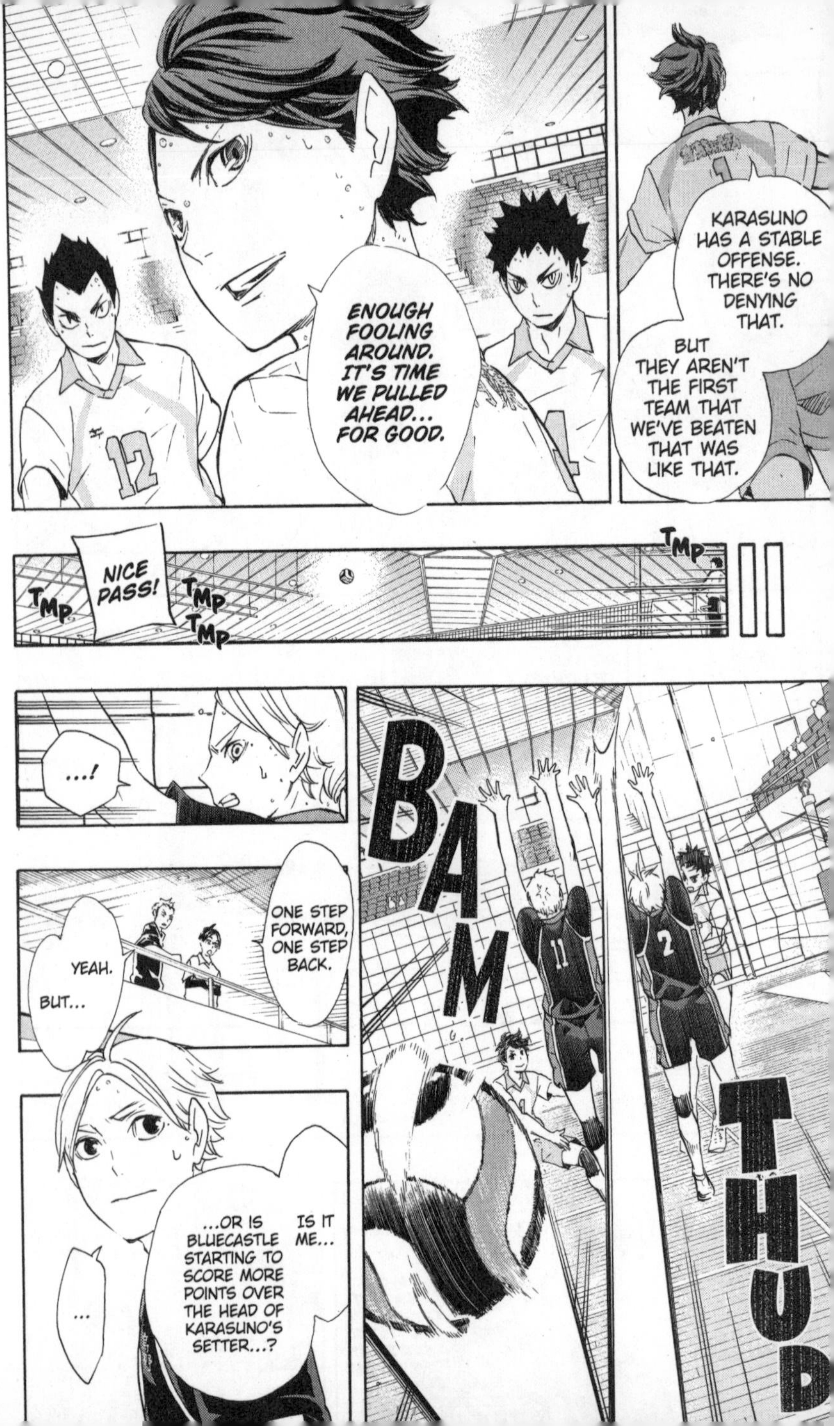
KARASUNO HAS A STABLE OFFENSE. THERE'S NO DENYING THAT.
BUT THEY AREN'T THE FIRST TEAM THAT WE'VE BEATEN THAT WAS LIKE THAT.
ENOUGH FOOLING AROUND. IT'S TIME WE PULLED AHEAD... FOR GOOD.
TMP
NICE PASS!
TMP
TMP
TMP
BAM
THUD
...!
ONE STEP FORWARD, ONE STEP BACK.
YEAH.
BUT...
IS IT ME...
...OR IS BLUECASTLE STARTING TO SCORE MORE POINTS OVER THE HEAD OF KARASUNO'S SETTER...?
...

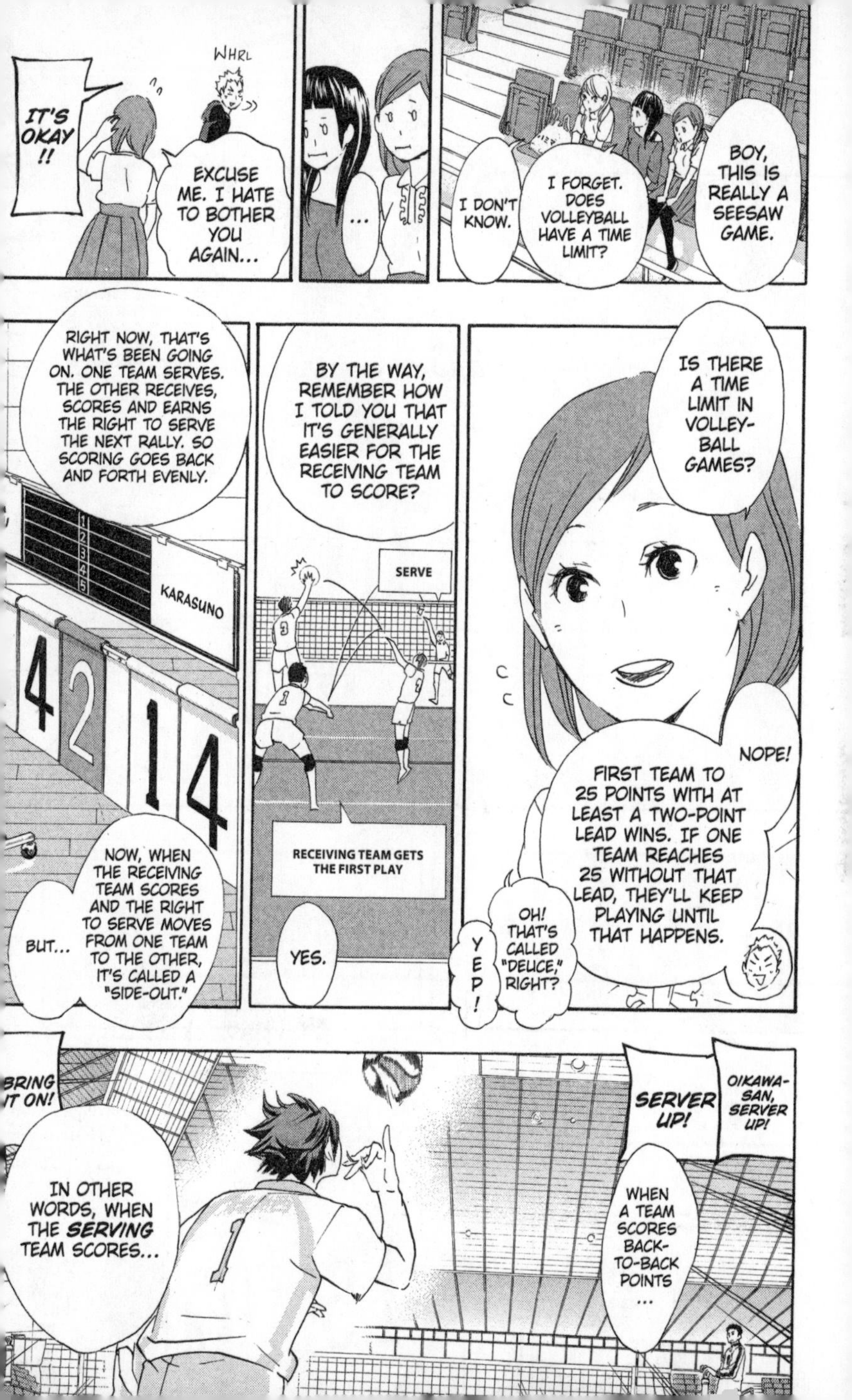
BOY, THIS IS REALLY A SEESAW GAME.
I FORGET. DOES VOLLEYBALL HAVE A TIME LIMIT?
I DON'T KNOW.
...
WHRL
EXCUSE ME. I HATE TO BOTHER YOU AGAIN...
IT'S OKAY!!
IS THERE A TIME LIMIT IN VOLLEY-BALL GAMES?
NOPE!
FIRST TEAM TO 25 POINTS WITH AT LEAST A TWO-POINT LEAD WINS. IF ONE TEAM REACHES 25 WITHOUT THAT LEAD, THEY'LL KEEP PLAYING UNTIL THAT HAPPENS.
OH! THAT'S CALLED "DEUCE," RIGHT?
YEP!
BY THE WAY, REMEMBER HOW I TOLD YOU THAT IT'S GENERALLY EASIER FOR THE RECEIVING TEAM TO SCORE?
SERVE
RECEIVING TEAM GETS THE FIRST PLAY
YES.
RIGHT NOW, THAT'S WHAT'S BEEN GOING ON. ONE TEAM SERVES. THE OTHER RECEIVES, SCORES AND EARNS THE RIGHT TO SERVE THE NEXT RALLY. SO SCORING GOES BACK AND FORTH EVENLY.
KARASUNO
4 2 14
NOW, WHEN THE RECEIVING TEAM SCORES AND THE RIGHT TO SERVE MOVES FROM ONE TEAM TO THE OTHER, IT'S CALLED A "SIDE-OUT."
BUT...
OIKAWA-SAN, SERVER UP!
SERVER UP!
WHEN A TEAM SCORES BACK-TO-BACK POINTS...
BRING IT ON!
IN OTHER WORDS, WHEN THE SERVING TEAM SCORES...

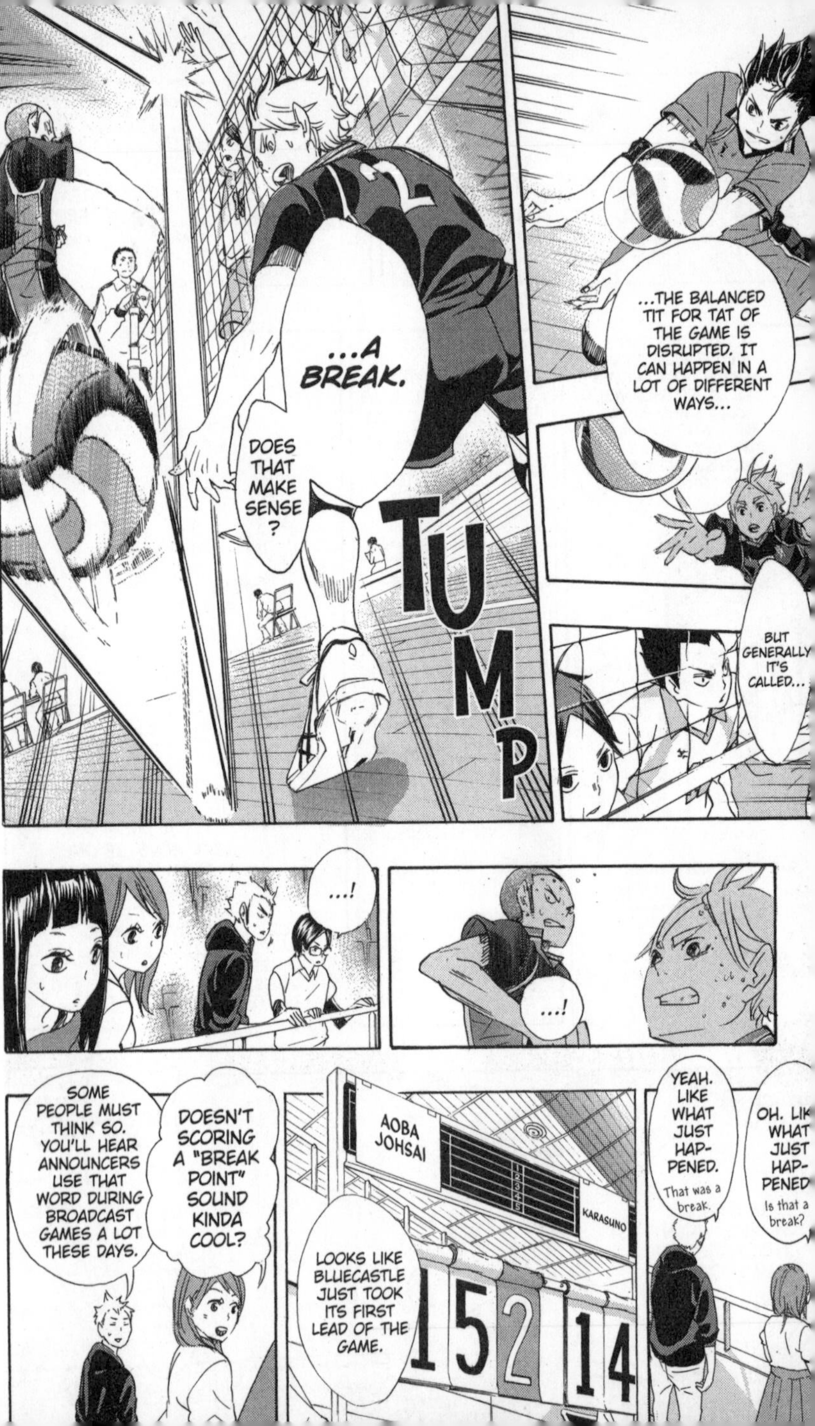
...THE BALANCED TIT FOR TAT OF THE GAME IS DISRUPTED. IT CAN HAPPEN IN A LOT OF DIFFERENT WAYS...
BUT GENERALLY IT'S CALLED...
...A BREAK.
DOES THAT MAKE SENSE?
TUMP
...!
...!
OH. LIK WHAT JUST HAP-PENED
Is that a break?
YEAH. LIKE WHAT JUST HAP-PENED.
That was a break.
AOBA JOHSAI
1 2 3 4 5
KARASUNO
15 2 14
LOOKS LIKE BLUECASTLE JUST TOOK ITS FIRST LEAD OF THE GAME.
DOESN'T SCORING A "BREAK POINT" SOUND KINDA COOL?
SOME PEOPLE MUST THINK SO. YOU'LL HEAR ANNOUNCERS USE THAT WORD DURING BROADCAST GAMES A LOT THESE DAYS.

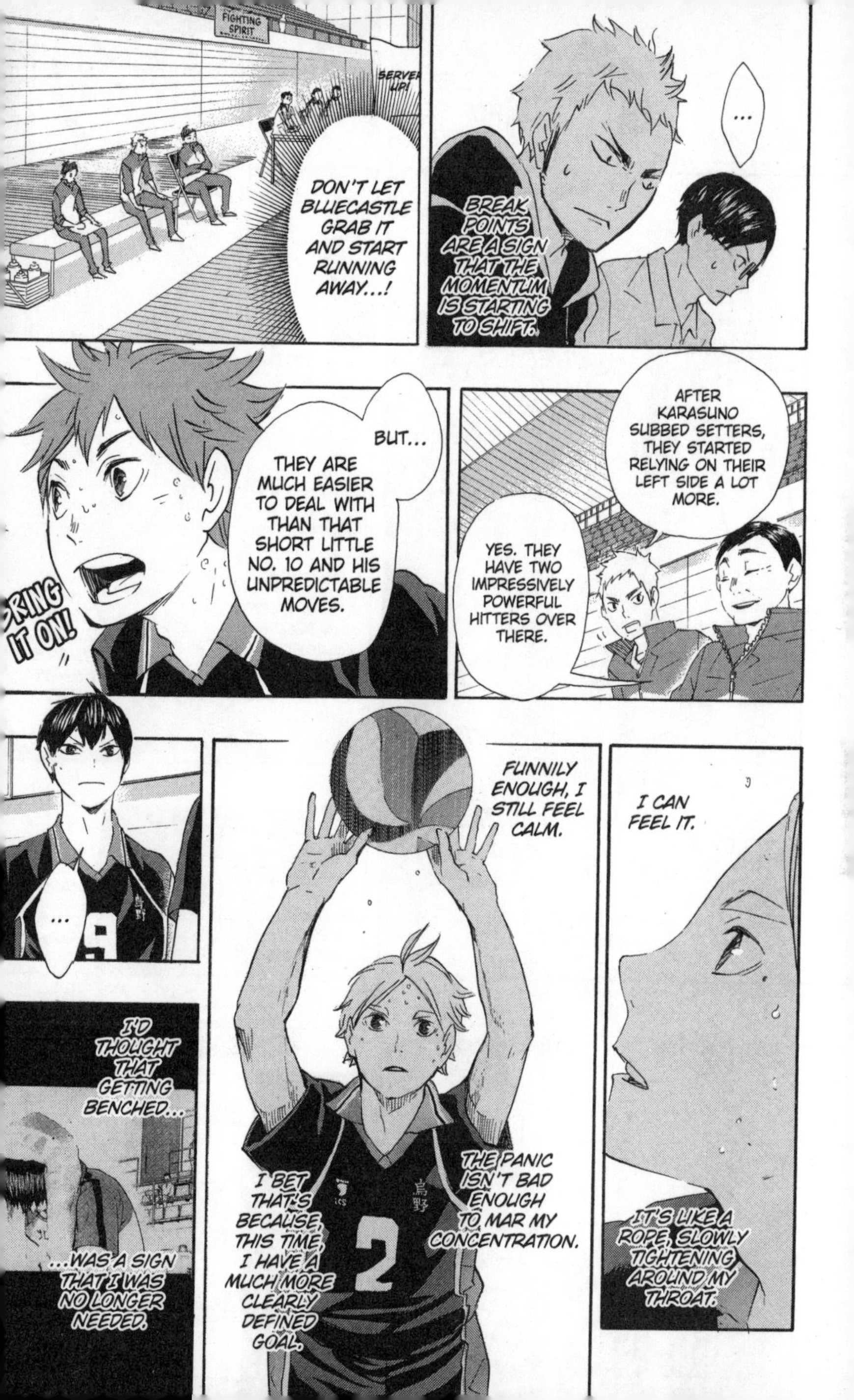
...
BREAK POINTS ARE A SIGN THAT THE MOMENTUM IS STARTING TO SHIFT.
FIGHTING SPIRIT
SERVER UP!
DON'T LET BLUECASTLE GRAB IT AND START RUNNING AWAY...!
AFTER KARASUNO SUBBED SETTERS, THEY STARTED RELYING ON THEIR LEFT SIDE A LOT MORE.
YES. THEY HAVE TWO IMPRESSIVELY POWERFUL HITTERS OVER THERE.
BUT...
THEY ARE MUCH EASIER TO DEAL WITH THAN THAT SHORT LITTLE NO. 10 AND HIS UNPREDICTABLE MOVES.
RING IT ON!
I CAN FEEL IT.
IT'S LIKE A ROPE, SLOWLY TIGHTENING AROUND MY THROAT.
FUNNILY ENOUGH, I STILL FEEL CALM.
THE PANIC ISN'T BAD ENOUGH TO MAR MY CONCENTRATION.
I BET THAT'S BECAUSE, THIS TIME, I HAVE A MUCH MORE CLEARLY DEFINED GOAL.
...
I'D THOUGHT THAT GETTING BENCHED...
...WAS A SIGN THAT I WAS NO LONGER NEEDED.

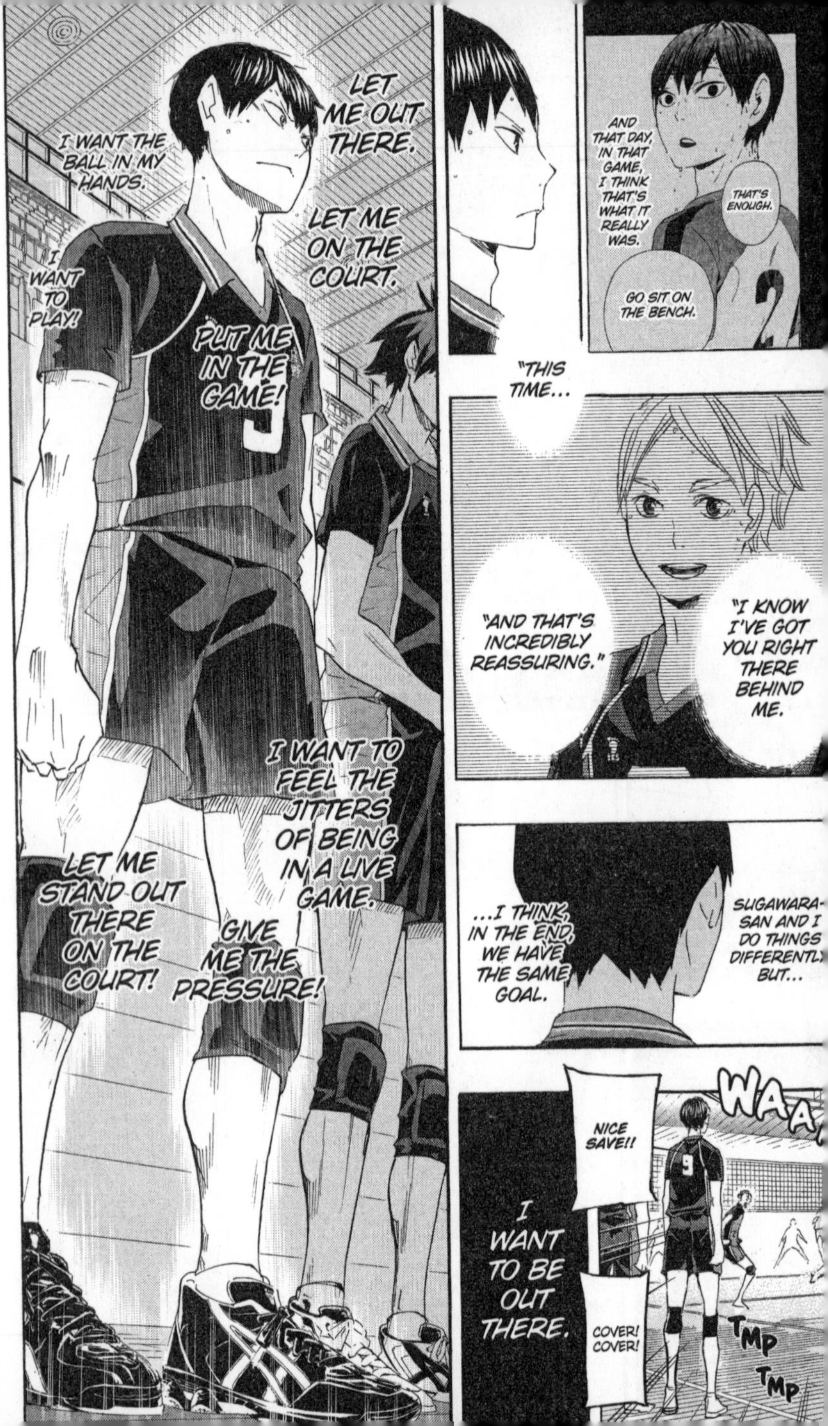
AND THAT DAY, IN THAT GAME, I THINK THAT'S WHAT IT REALLY WAS.
THAT'S ENOUGH.
GO SIT ON THE BENCH.
"THIS TIME...
"I KNOW I'VE GOT YOU RIGHT THERE BEHIND ME.
"AND THAT'S INCREDIBLY REASSURING."
SUGAWARA-SAN AND I DO THINGS DIFFERENTL BUT...
...I THINK, IN THE END, WE HAVE THE SAME GOAL.
WAA
NICE SAVE!!
I WANT TO BE OUT THERE.
COVER! COVER!
TMP
TMP
LET ME OUT THERE.
I WANT THE BALL IN MY HANDS.
LET ME ON THE COURT.
I WANT TO PLAY!
PUT ME IN THE GAME!
I WANT TO FEEL THE JITTERS OF BEING IN A LIVE GAME.
LET ME STAND OUT THERE ON THE COURT!
GIVE ME THE PRESSURE!

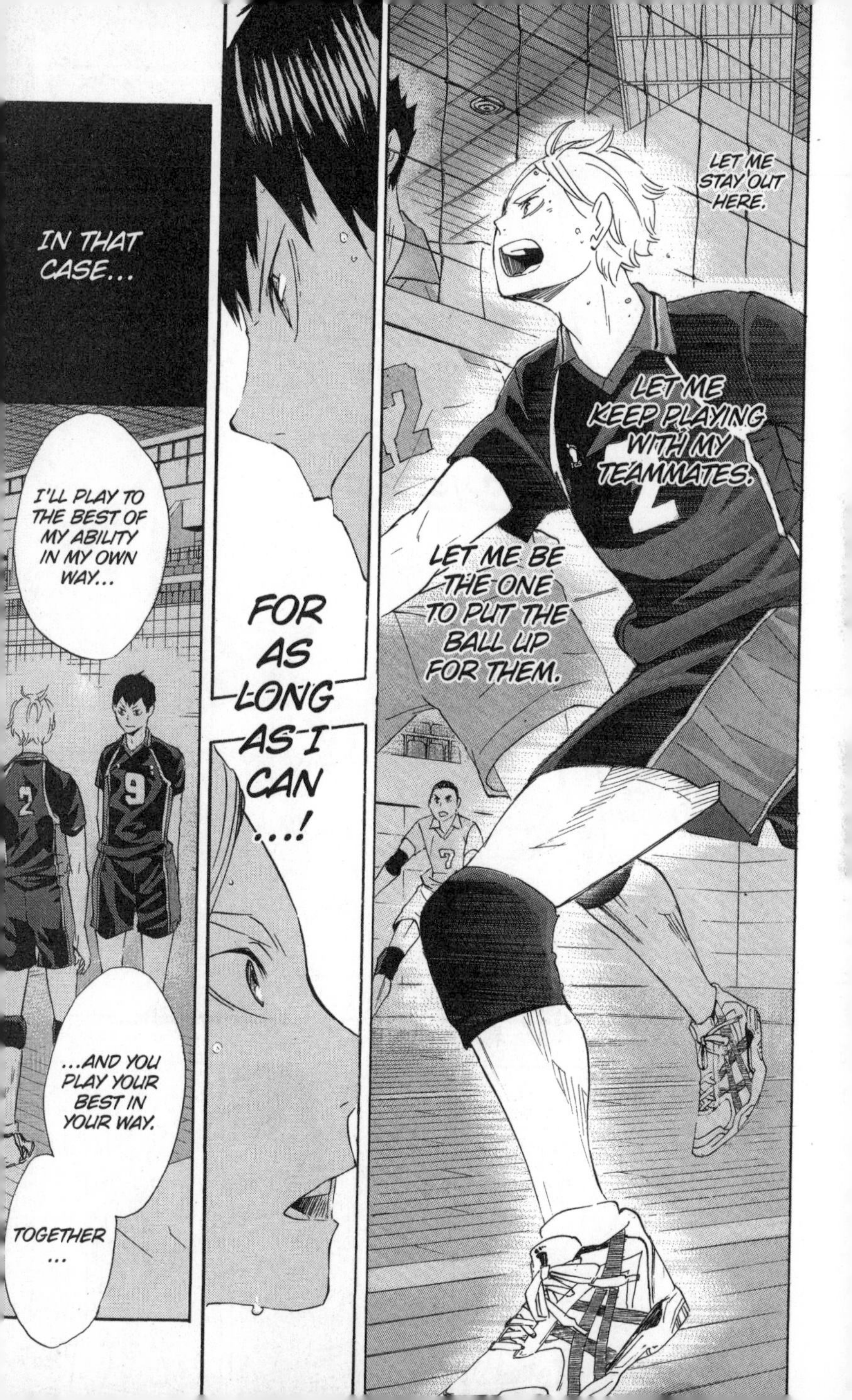
LET ME STAY OUT HERE.
LET ME KEEP PLAYING WITH MY TEAMMATES.
LET ME BE THE ONE TO PUT THE BALL UP FOR THEM.
FOR AS LONG AS I CAN ...!
IN THAT CASE...
I'LL PLAY TO THE BEST OF MY ABILITY IN MY OWN WAY...
...AND YOU PLAY YOUR BEST IN YOUR WAY.
TOGETHER ...

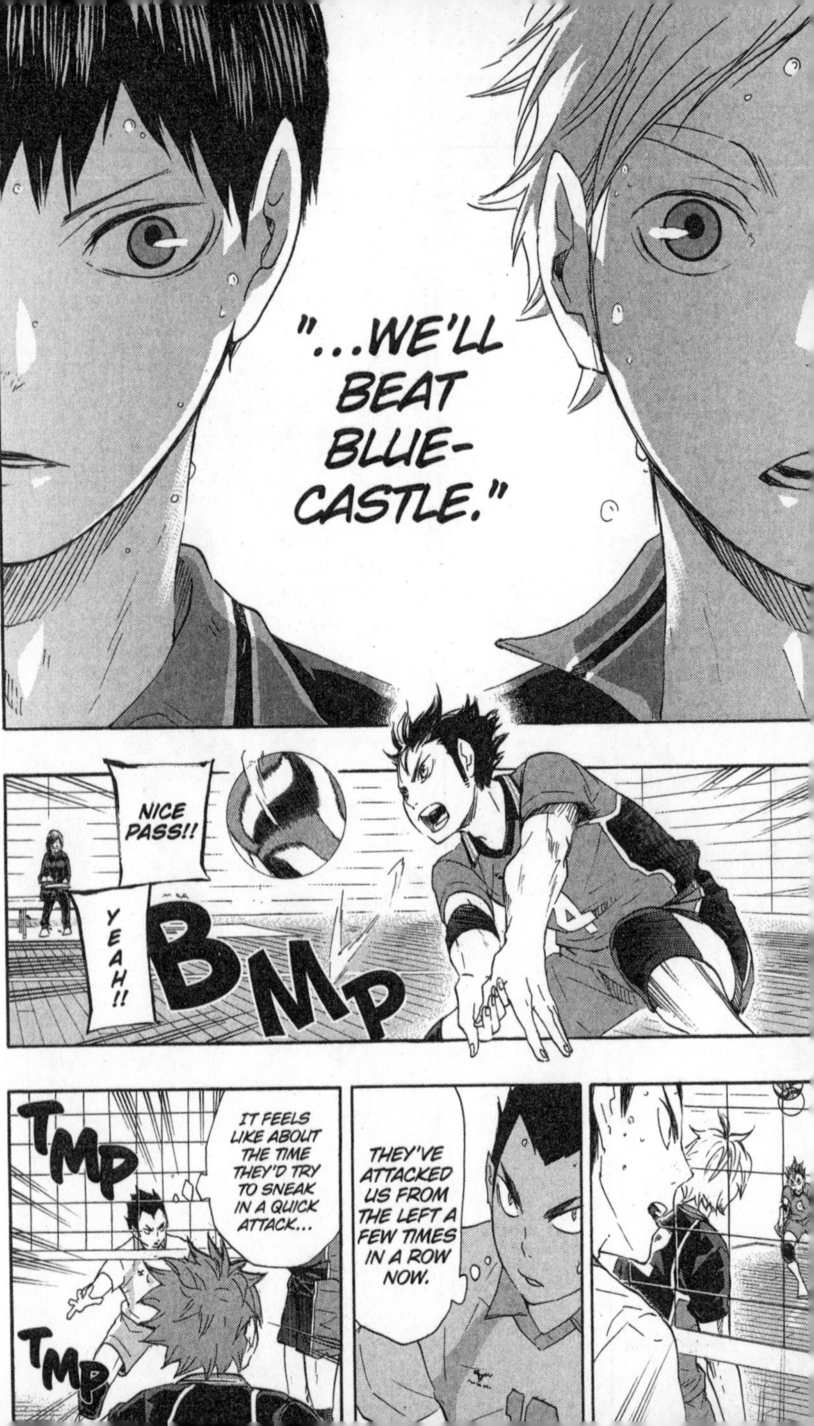
"...WE'LL BEAT BLUE-CASTLE."
BMP
NICE PASS!!
YEAH!!
THEY'VE ATTACKED US FROM THE LEFT A FEW TIMES IN A ROW NOW.
IT FEELS LIKE ABOUT THE TIME THEY'D TRY TO SNEAK IN A QUICK ATTACK...
TMP
TMP

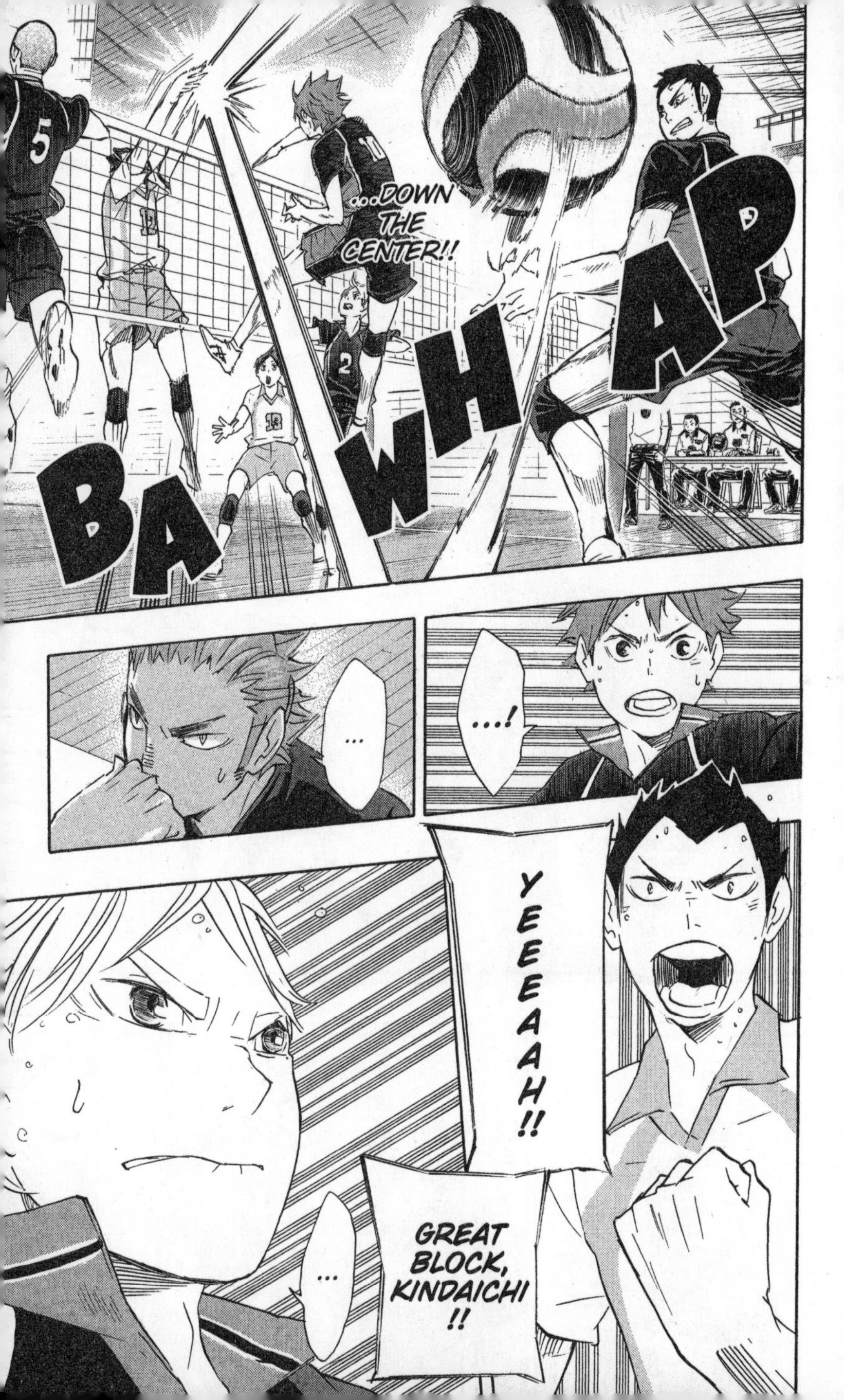
...DOWN THE CENTER!!
BAWHAP
...!
...
YEEEEAAAH!!
GREAT BLOCK, KINDAICHI!!
...

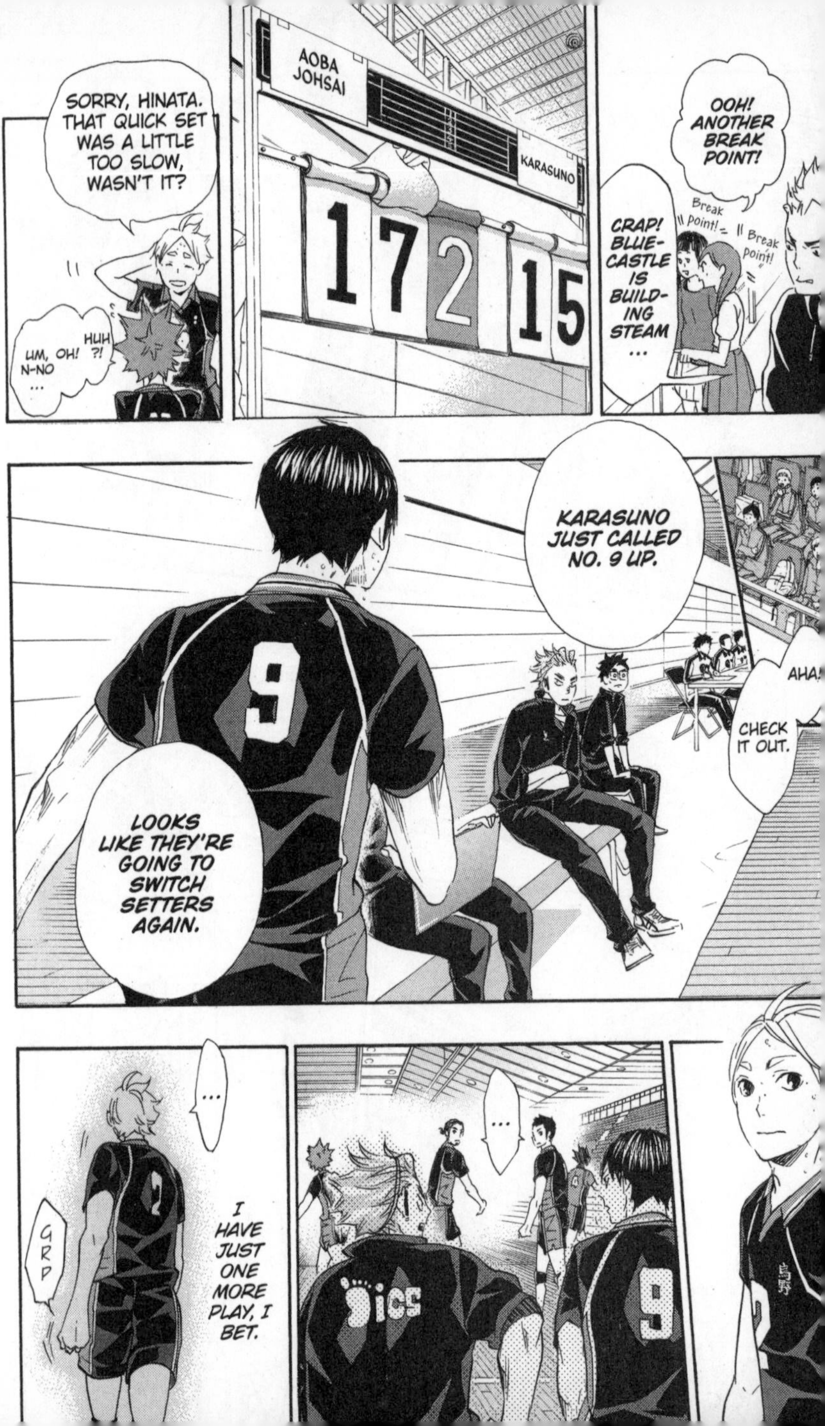
OOH! ANOTHER BREAK POINT!
Break point!
Break point!
CRAP! BLUE-CASTLE IS BUILDING STEAM ...
AOBA JOHSAI
KARASUNO
17
2
15
SORRY, HINATA. THAT QUICK SET WAS A LITTLE TOO SLOW, WASN'T IT?
HUH ?!
UM, OH! N-NO ...
AHA!
CHECK IT OUT.
KARASUNO JUST CALLED NO. 9 UP.
LOOKS LIKE THEY'RE GOING TO SWITCH SETTERS AGAIN.
...
...
I HAVE JUST ONE MORE PLAY, I BET.
GRP

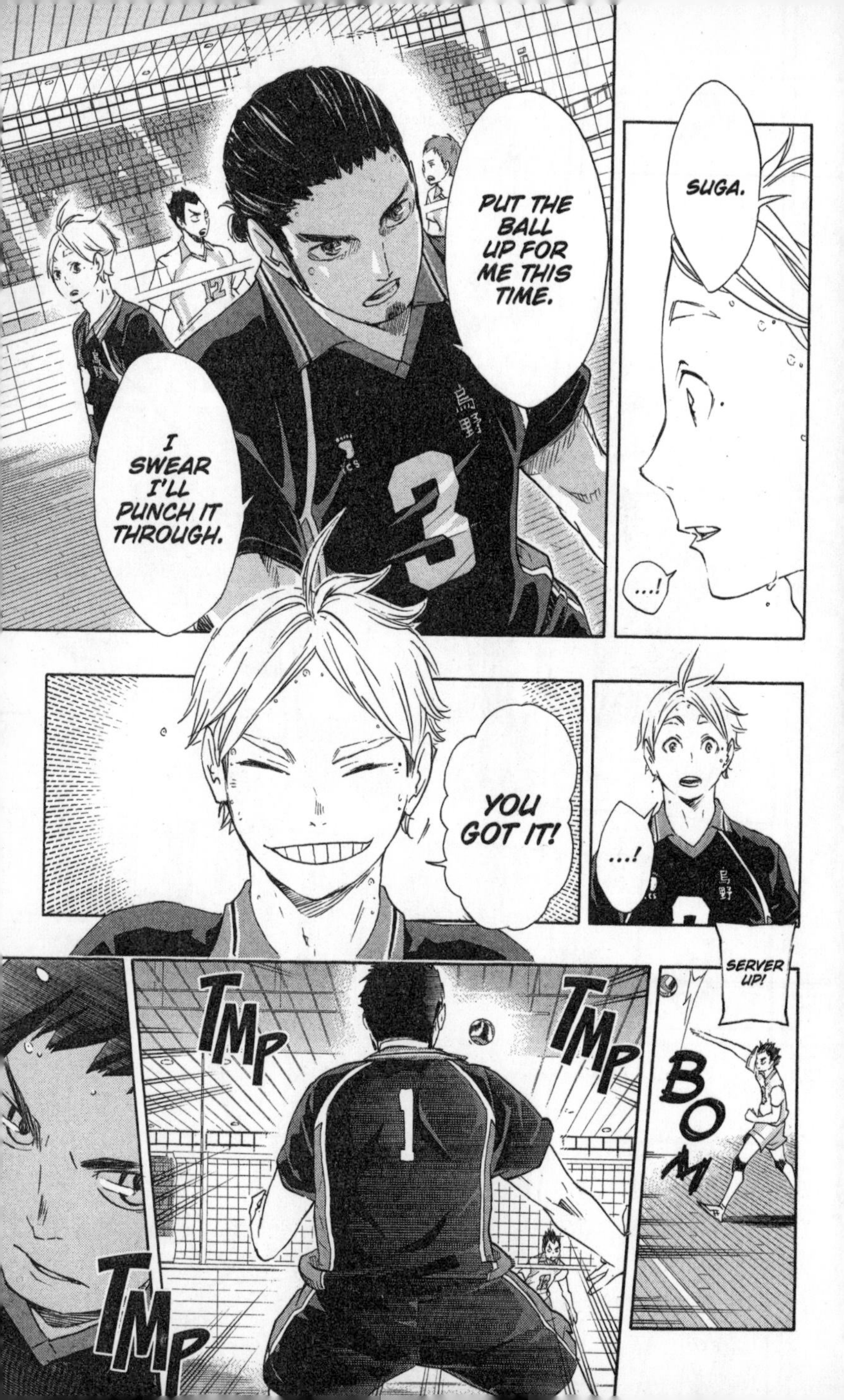
SUGA.
...!
PUT THE BALL UP FOR ME THIS TIME.
I SWEAR I'LL PUNCH IT THROUGH.
...!
YOU GOT IT!
SERVER UP!
BOOM
TMP
TMP
TMP

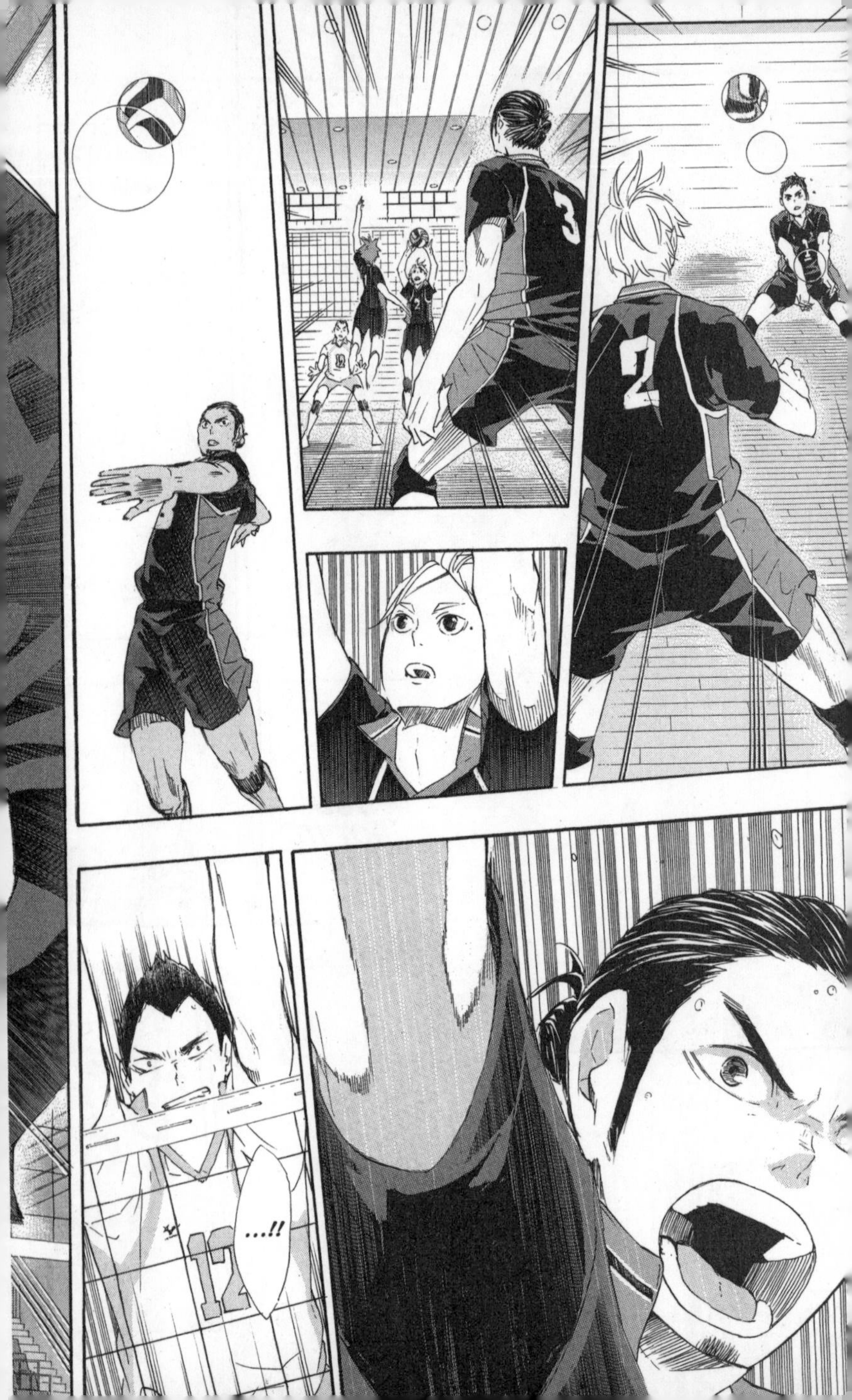
...!!

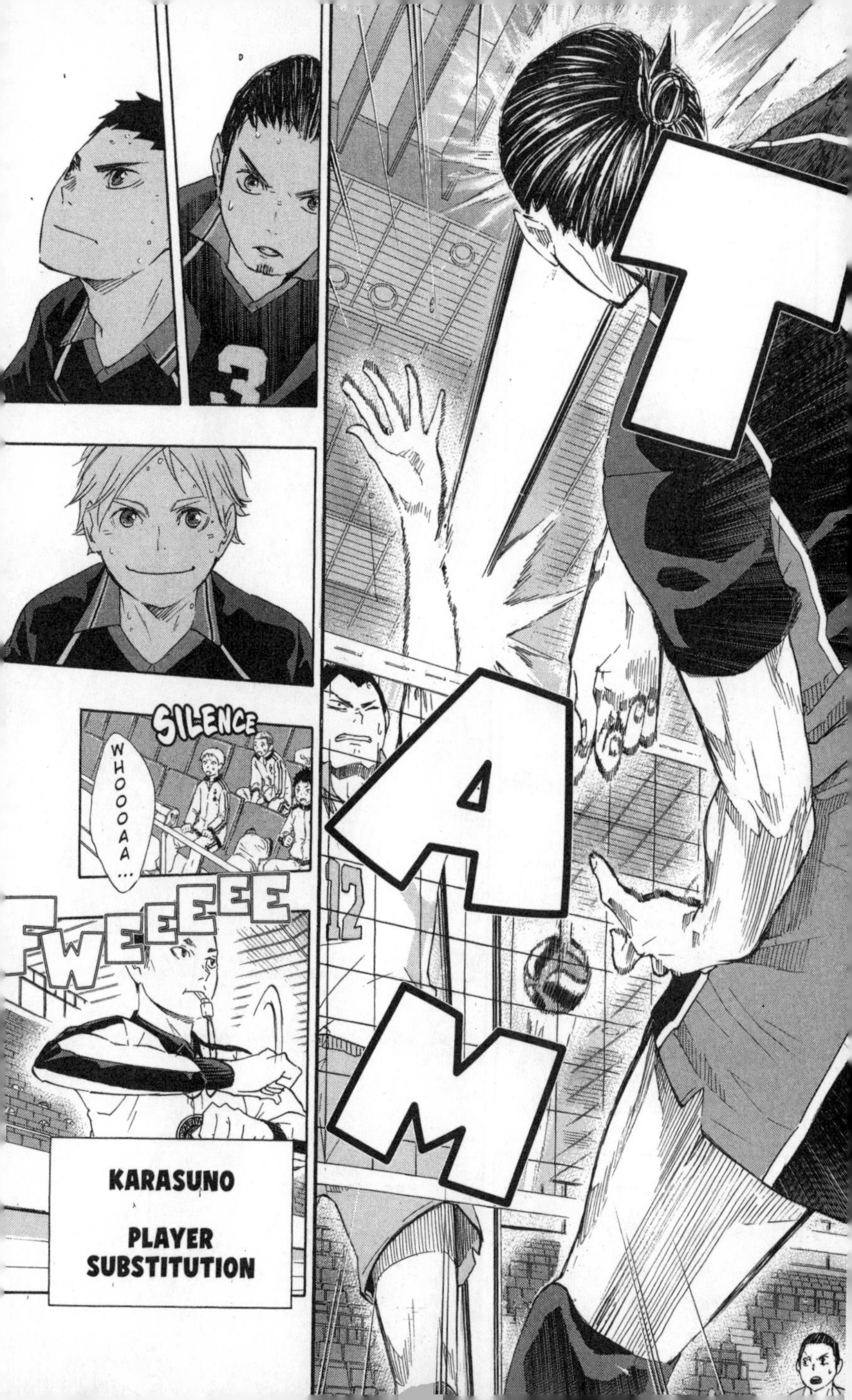
TAM
SILENCE
WHOOOAA...
FWEEEEE
KARASUNO
PLAYER SUBSTITUTION

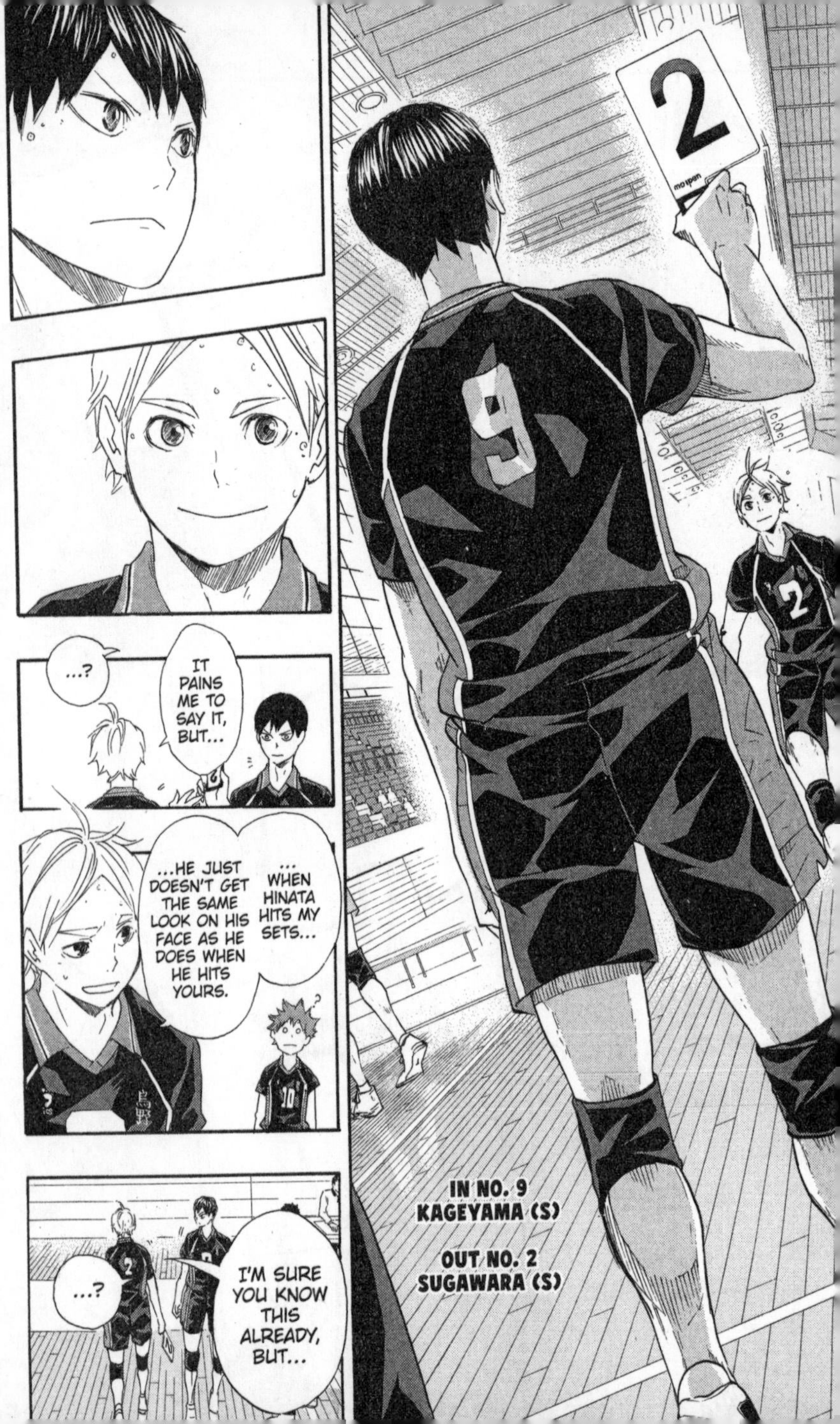
IN NO. 9
KAGEYAMA (S)
OUT NO. 2
SUGAWARA (S)
IT PAINS ME TO SAY IT, BUT...
...?
...WHEN HINATA HITS MY SETS...
...HE JUST DOESN'T GET THE SAME LOOK ON HIS FACE AS HE DOES WHEN HE HITS YOURS.
I'M SURE YOU KNOW THIS ALREADY, BUT...
...?

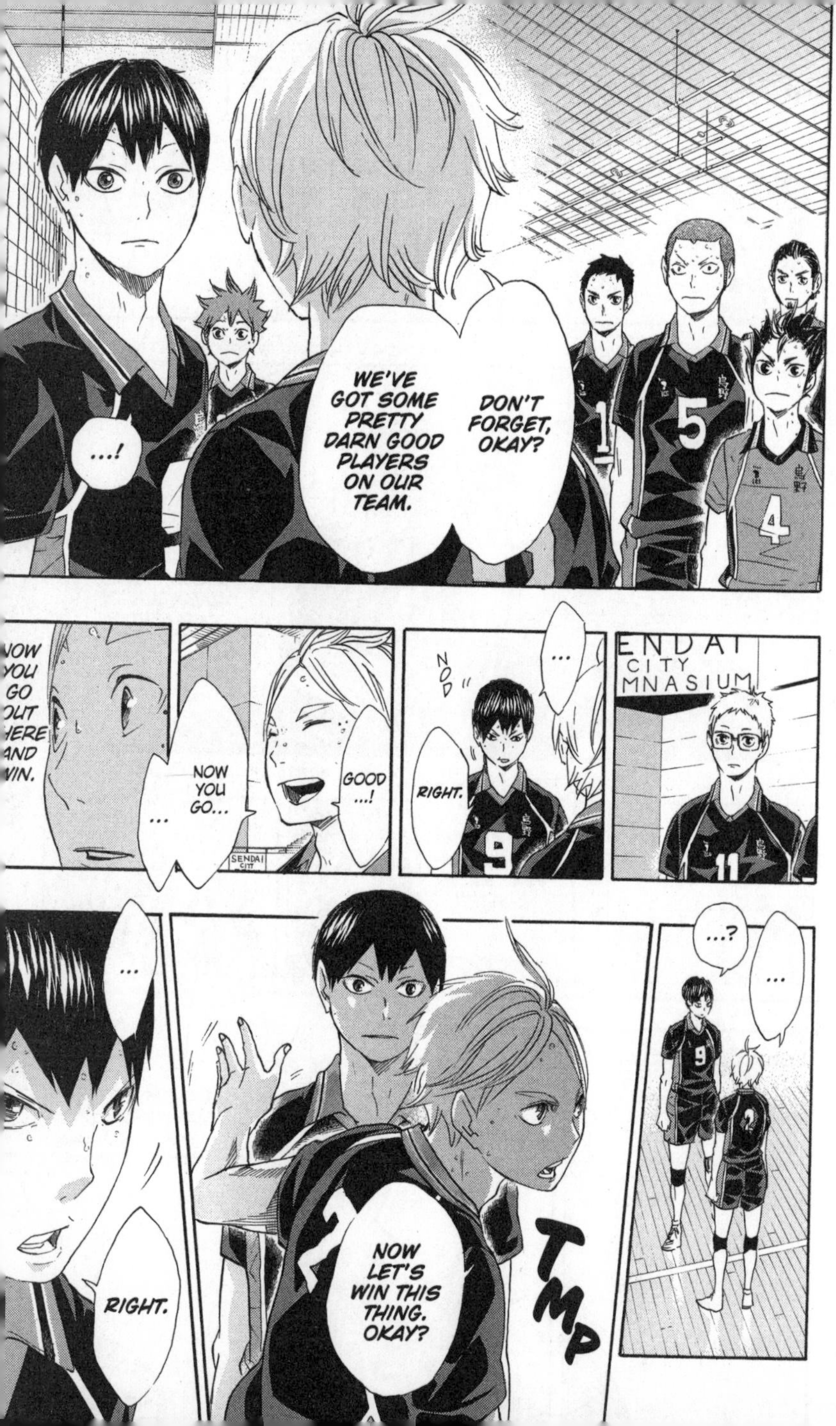

WE'VE GOT SOME PRETTY DARN GOOD PLAYERS ON OUR TEAM.
DON'T FORGET, OKAY?
...!
ENDAI CITY MNASIUM
...
NOD
RIGHT.
GOOD ...!
NOW YOU GO...
...
SENDAI CITY
NOW YOU GO OUT HERE AND WIN.
...?
...
NOW LET'S WIN THIS THING. OKAY?
TMP
...
RIGHT.

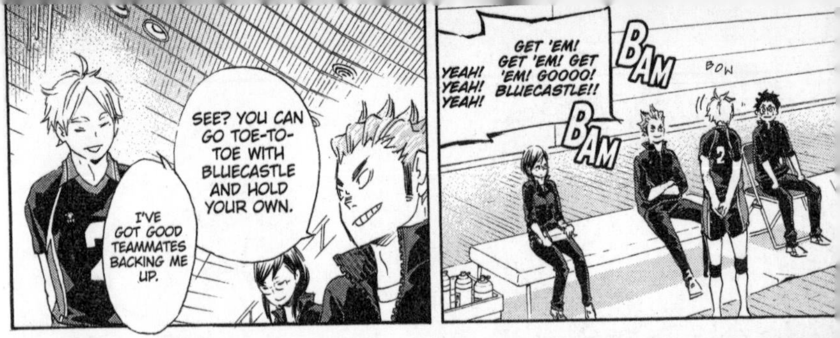
GET 'EM! GET 'EM! GET 'EM! GOOOO! BLUECASTLE!!
YEAH! YEAH! YEAH!
BAM
BOW
BAM
SEE? YOU CAN GO TOE-TO-TOE WITH BLUECASTLE AND HOLD YOUR OWN.
I'VE GOT GOOD TEAMMATES BACKING ME UP.

*CENTER: PLAYERS WHOSE POSITIONS ARE IN THE MIDDLE OF THE COURT. FOR KARASUNO, THAT'S TSUKISHIMA AND HINATA.

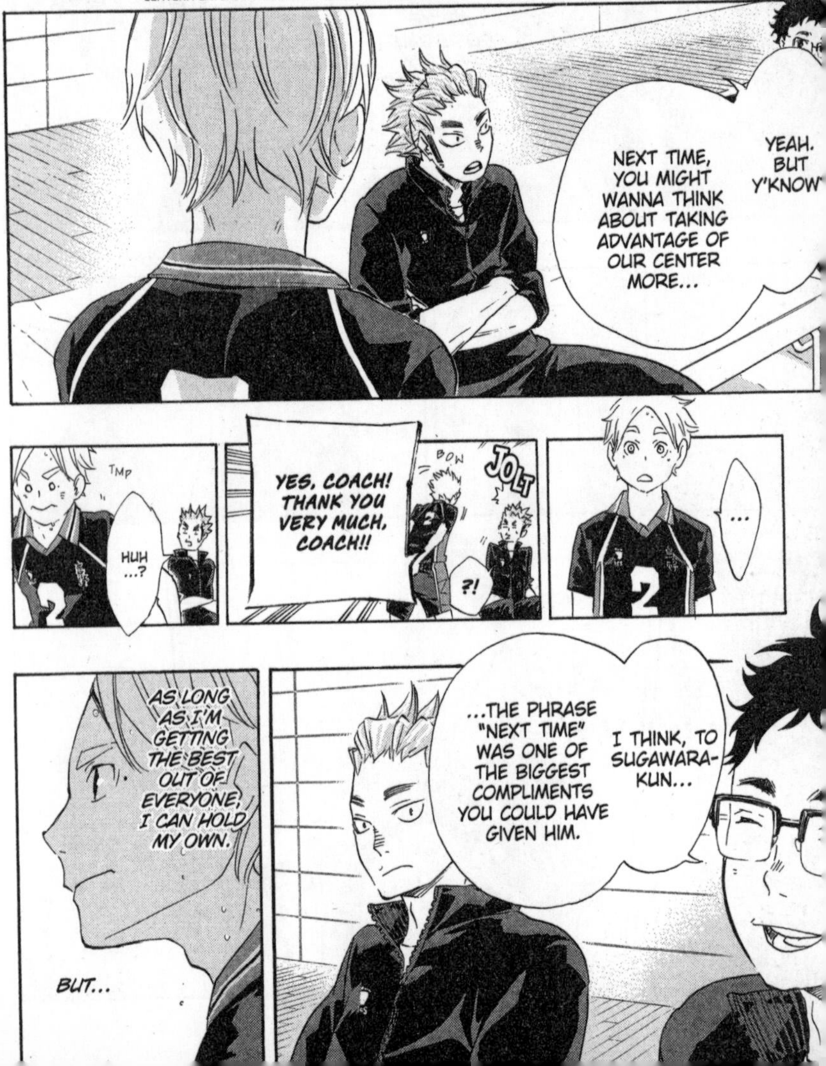
YEAH. BUT Y'KNOW
NEXT TIME, YOU MIGHT WANNA THINK ABOUT TAKING ADVANTAGE OF OUR CENTER MORE...
...
YES, COACH! THANK YOU VERY MUCH, COACH!!
BOW
JOLT
?!
TMP
HUH ...?
I THINK, TO SUGAWARA-KUN...
...THE PHRASE "NEXT TIME" WAS ONE OF THE BIGGEST COMPLIMENTS YOU COULD HAVE GIVEN HIM.
AS LONG AS I'M GETTING THE BEST OUT OF EVERYONE, I CAN HOLD MY OWN.
BUT...

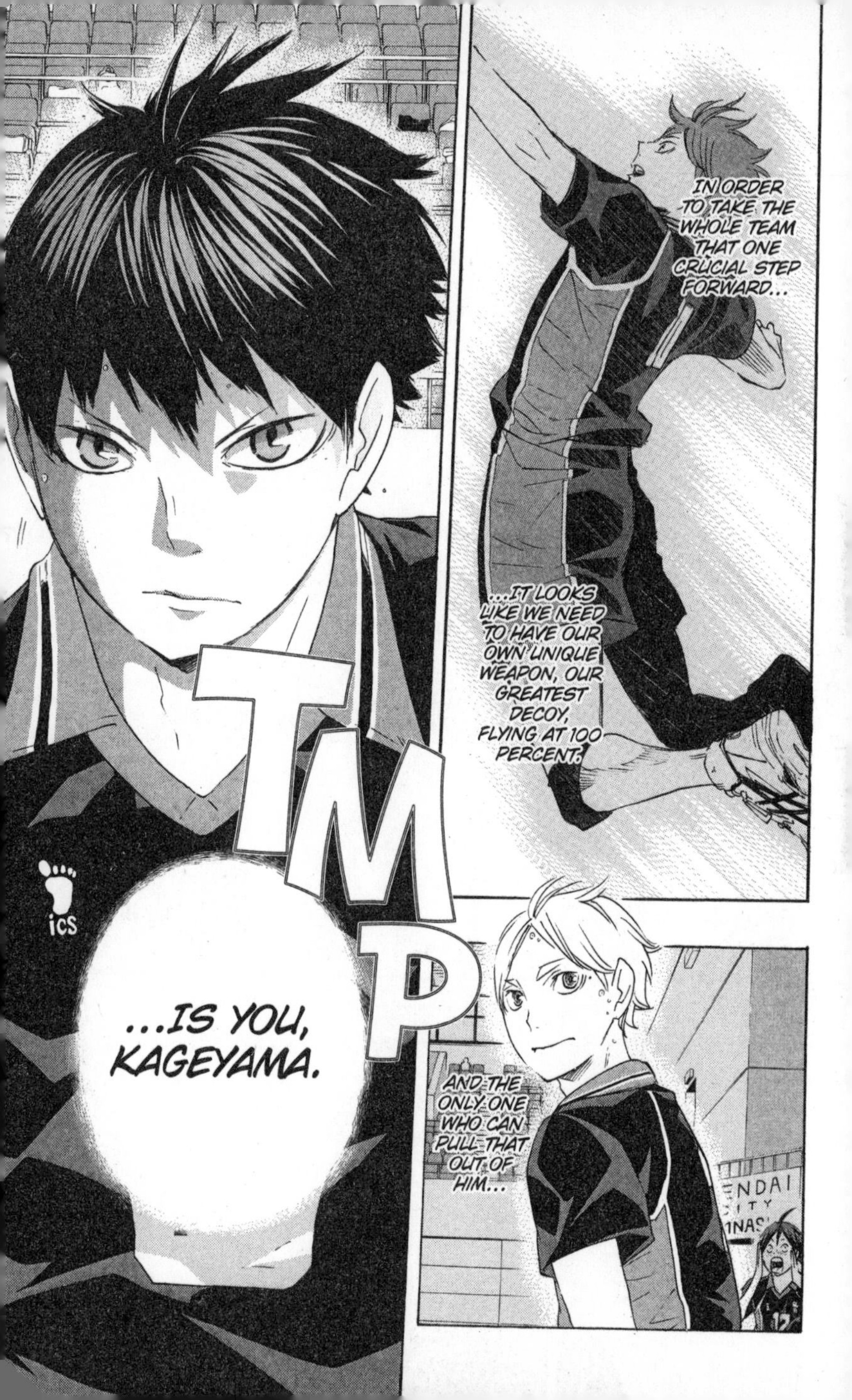
IN ORDER TO TAKE THE WHOLE TEAM THAT ONE CRUCIAL STEP FORWARD...
...IT LOOKS LIKE WE NEED TO HAVE OUR OWN UNIQUE WEAPON, OUR GREATEST DECOY, FLYING AT 100 PERCENT.
AND THE ONLY ONE WHO CAN PULL THAT OUT OF HIM...
TMP
...IS YOU, KAGEYAMA.

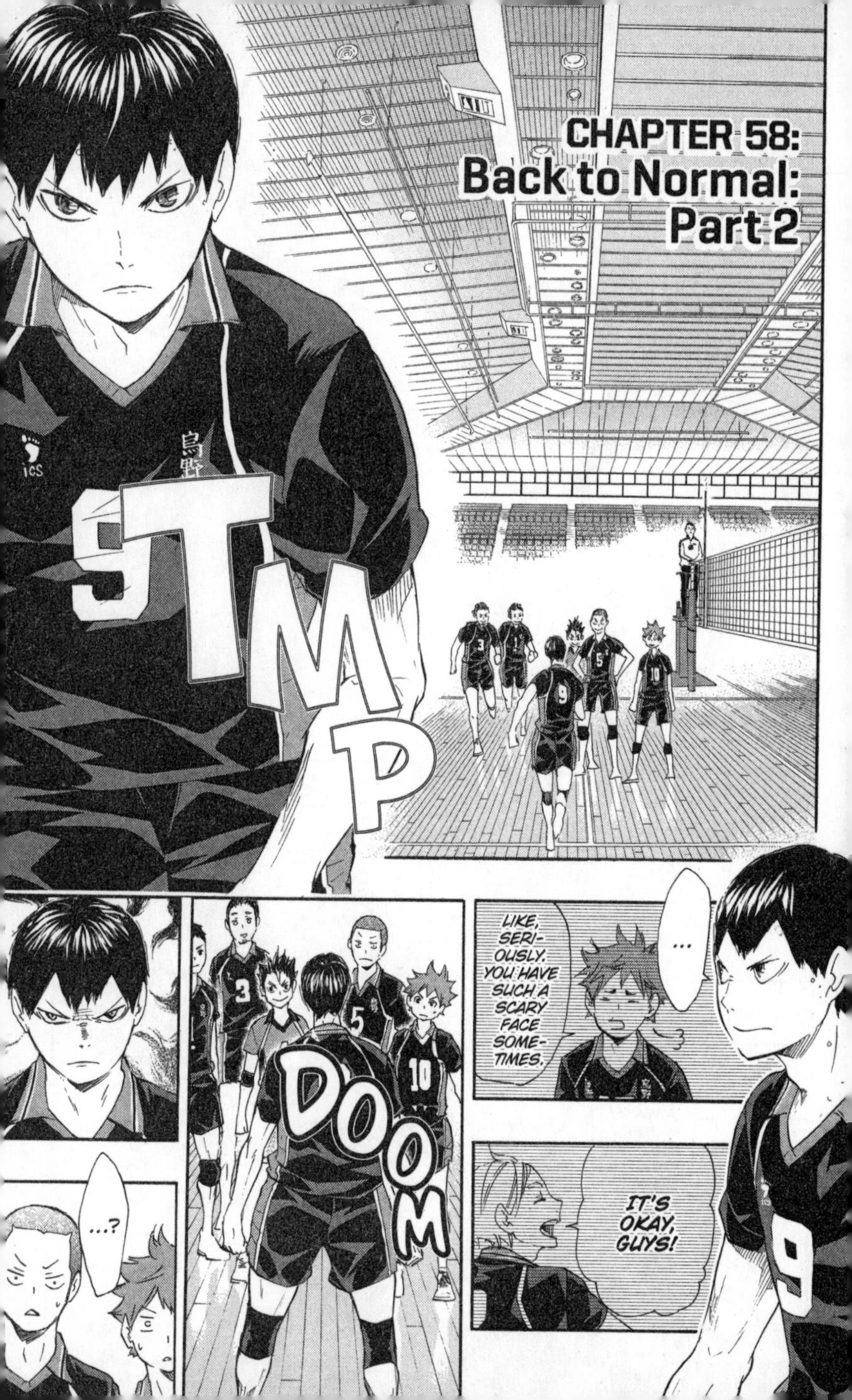
CHAPTER 58:
Back to Normal:
Part 2
STMP
...
LIKE, SERIOUSLY. YOU HAVE SUCH A SCARY FACE SOMETIMES.
IT'S OKAY, GUYS!
DOOOM
...?

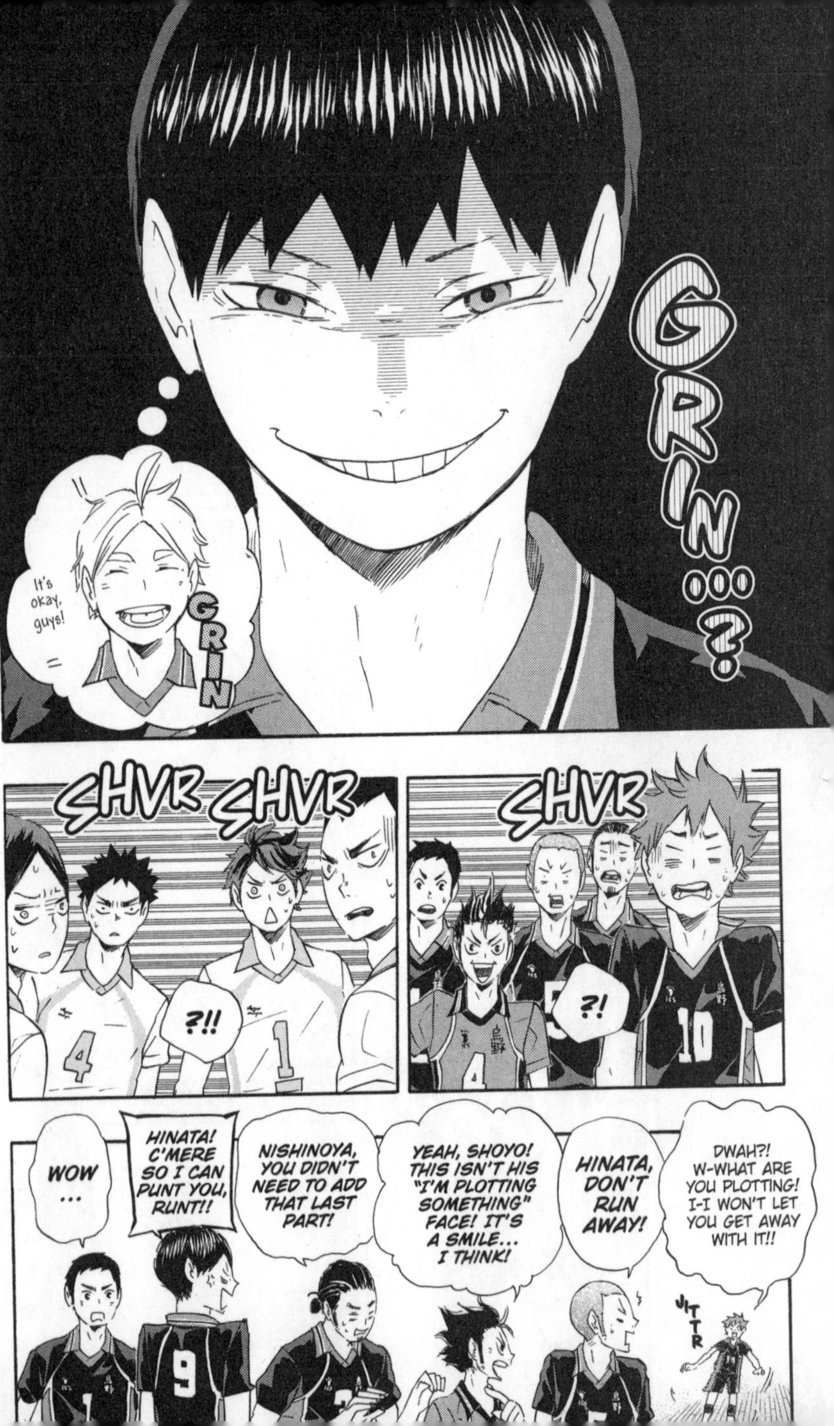
GRIN...?
It's okay, guys!
GRIN
SHVR
?!
SHVR SHVR
?!!
DWAH?! W-WHAT ARE YOU PLOTTING! I-I WON'T LET YOU GET AWAY WITH IT!!
JITTR
HINATA, DON'T RUN AWAY!
YEAH, SHOYO! THIS ISN'T HIS "I'M PLOTTING SOMETHING" FACE! IT'S A SMILE... I THINK!
NISHINOYA, YOU DIDN'T NEED TO ADD THAT LAST PART!
HINATA! C'MERE SO I CAN PUNT YOU, RUNT!!
WOW ...

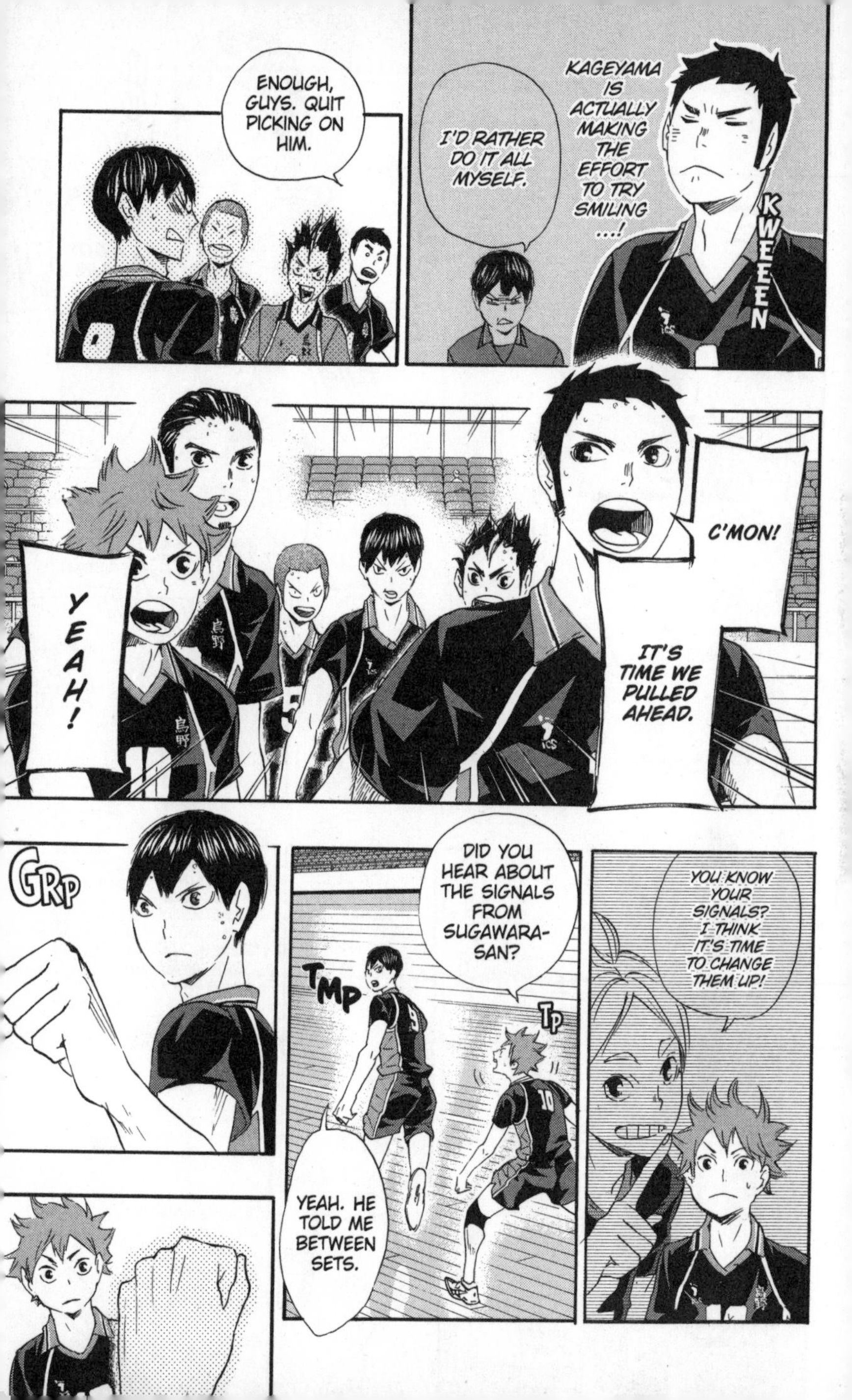
KAGEYAMA IS ACTUALLY MAKING THE EFFORT TO TRY SMILING...!
KWEEEN
I'D RATHER DO IT ALL MYSELF.
ENOUGH, GUYS. QUIT PICKING ON HIM.
C'MON!
IT'S TIME WE PULLED AHEAD.
YEAH!
YOU KNOW YOUR SIGNALS? I THINK IT'S TIME TO CHANGE THEM UP!
DID YOU HEAR ABOUT THE SIGNALS FROM SUGAWARA-SAN?
TMP
TP
YEAH. HE TOLD ME BETWEEN SETS.
GRP

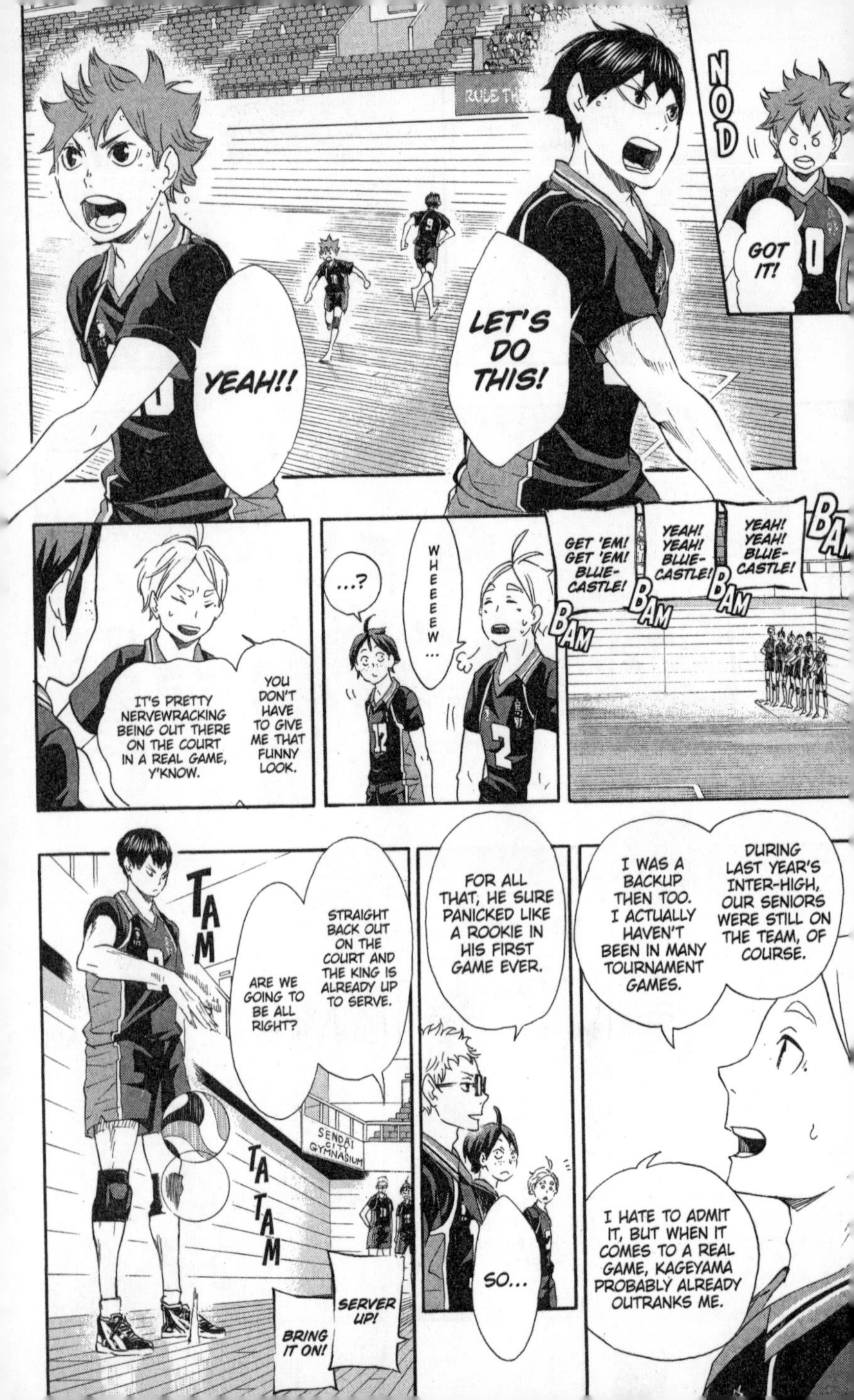
NOD
GOT IT!
LET'S DO THIS!
RULE TH
YEAH!!
BAM
YEAH! YEAH! BLUE-CASTLE!
BAM
YEAH! YEAH! BLUE-CASTLE!
BAM
GET 'EM! GET 'EM! BLUE-CASTLE!
BAM
WHEEEEW...
...?
YOU DON'T HAVE TO GIVE ME THAT FUNNY LOOK.
IT'S PRETTY NERVEWRACKING BEING OUT THERE ON THE COURT IN A REAL GAME, Y'KNOW.
DURING LAST YEAR'S INTER-HIGH, OUR SENIORS WERE STILL ON THE TEAM, OF COURSE.
I WAS A BACKUP THEN TOO. I ACTUALLY HAVEN'T BEEN IN MANY TOURNAMENT GAMES.
I HATE TO ADMIT IT, BUT WHEN IT COMES TO A REAL GAME, KAGEYAMA PROBABLY ALREADY OUTRANKS ME.
FOR ALL THAT, HE SURE PANICKED LIKE A ROOKIE IN HIS FIRST GAME EVER.
SO...
STRAIGHT BACK OUT ON THE COURT AND THE KING IS ALREADY UP TO SERVE.
ARE WE GOING TO BE ALL RIGHT?
TAM
SENDAI CITY GYMNASIUM
TA TAM
SERVER UP!
BRING IT ON!

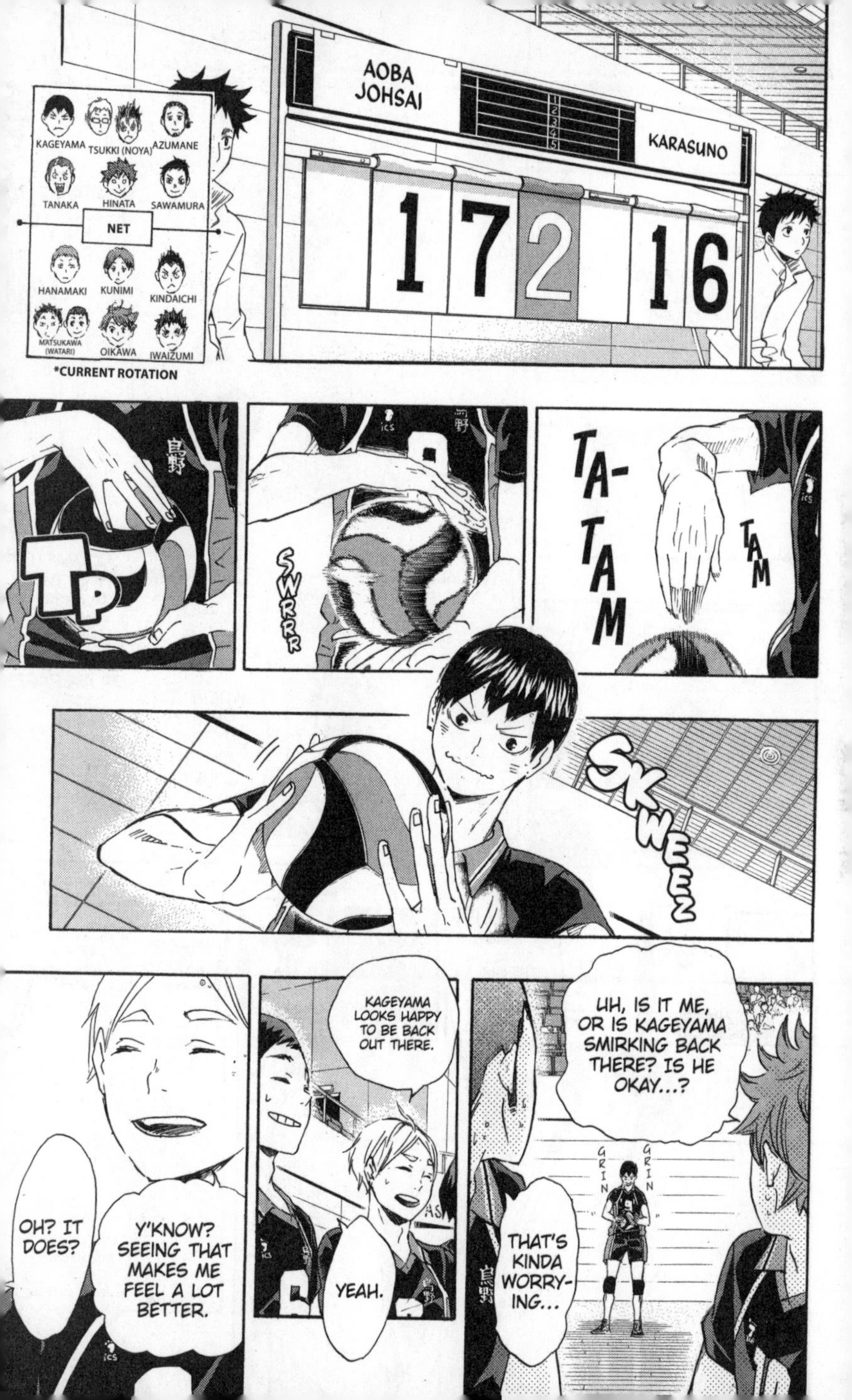
AOBA JOHSAI
1
2
3
4
5
KARASUNO
17
2
16
KAGEYAMA
TSUKKI (NOYA)
AZUMANE
TANAKA
HINATA
SAWAMURA
NET
HANAMAKI
KUNIMI
KINDAICHI
MATSUKAWA (WATARI)
OIKAWA
IWAIZUMI
*CURRENT ROTATION
TA-TAM
TAM
SWRRR
TP
SKWEEZ
UH, IS IT ME, OR IS KAGEYAMA SMIRKING BACK THERE? IS HE OKAY...?
GRIN
GRIN
THAT'S KINDA WORRY-ING...
KAGEYAMA LOOKS HAPPY TO BE BACK OUT THERE.
YEAH.
Y'KNOW? SEEING THAT MAKES ME FEEL A LOT BETTER.
OH? IT DOES?

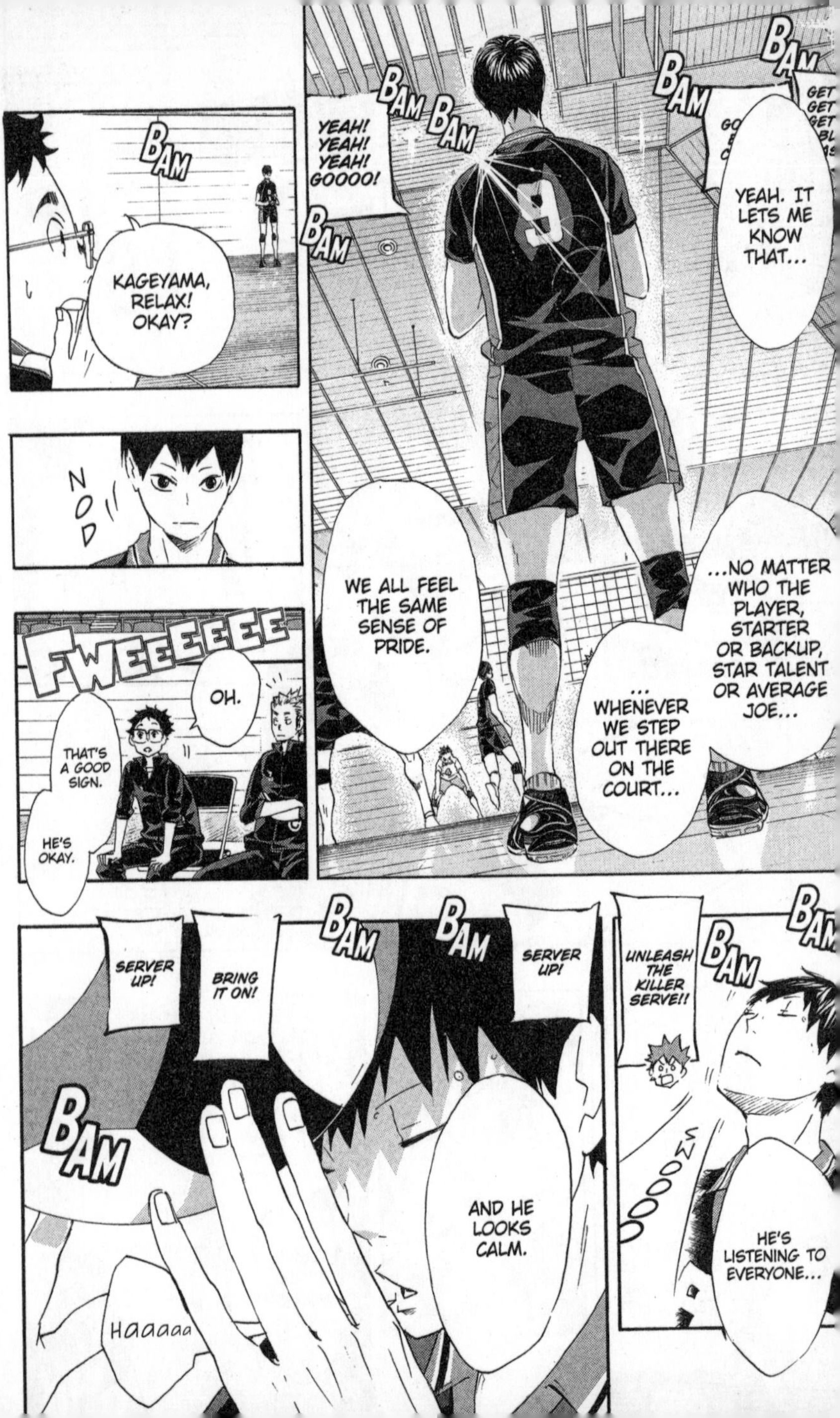
BAM
BAM
GET
GET
GET
YEAH. IT LETS ME KNOW THAT...
BAM BAM
YEAH! YEAH! YEAH! GOOOO!
BAM
...NO MATTER WHO THE PLAYER, STARTER OR BACKUP, STAR TALENT OR AVERAGE JOE...
... WHENEVER WE STEP OUT THERE ON THE COURT...
WE ALL FEEL THE SAME SENSE OF PRIDE.
BAM
KAGEYAMA, RELAX! OKAY?
NOD
FWEEEEEE
OH.
THAT'S A GOOD SIGN.
HE'S OKAY.
BAM
BAM
UNLEASH THE KILLER SERVE!!
SWOOOOO
HE'S LISTENING TO EVERYONE...
SERVER UP!
BAM
BAM
BRING IT ON!
SERVER UP!
BAM
AND HE LOOKS CALM.
Haaaaa

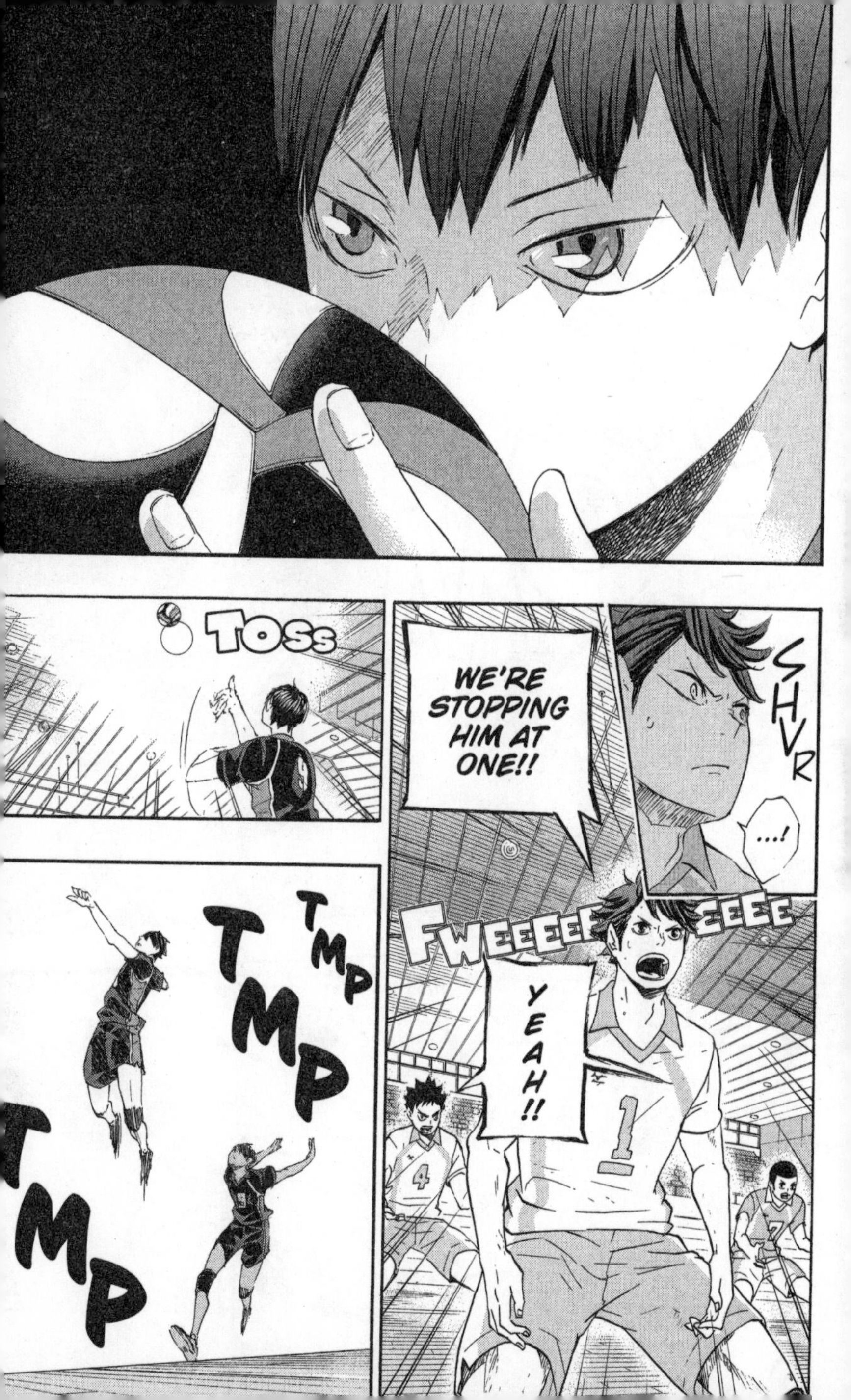

SHVR
WE'RE STOPPING HIM AT ONE!!
...!
FWEEEEEEEEE
YEAH!!
TOSS
TMP
TMP
TMP

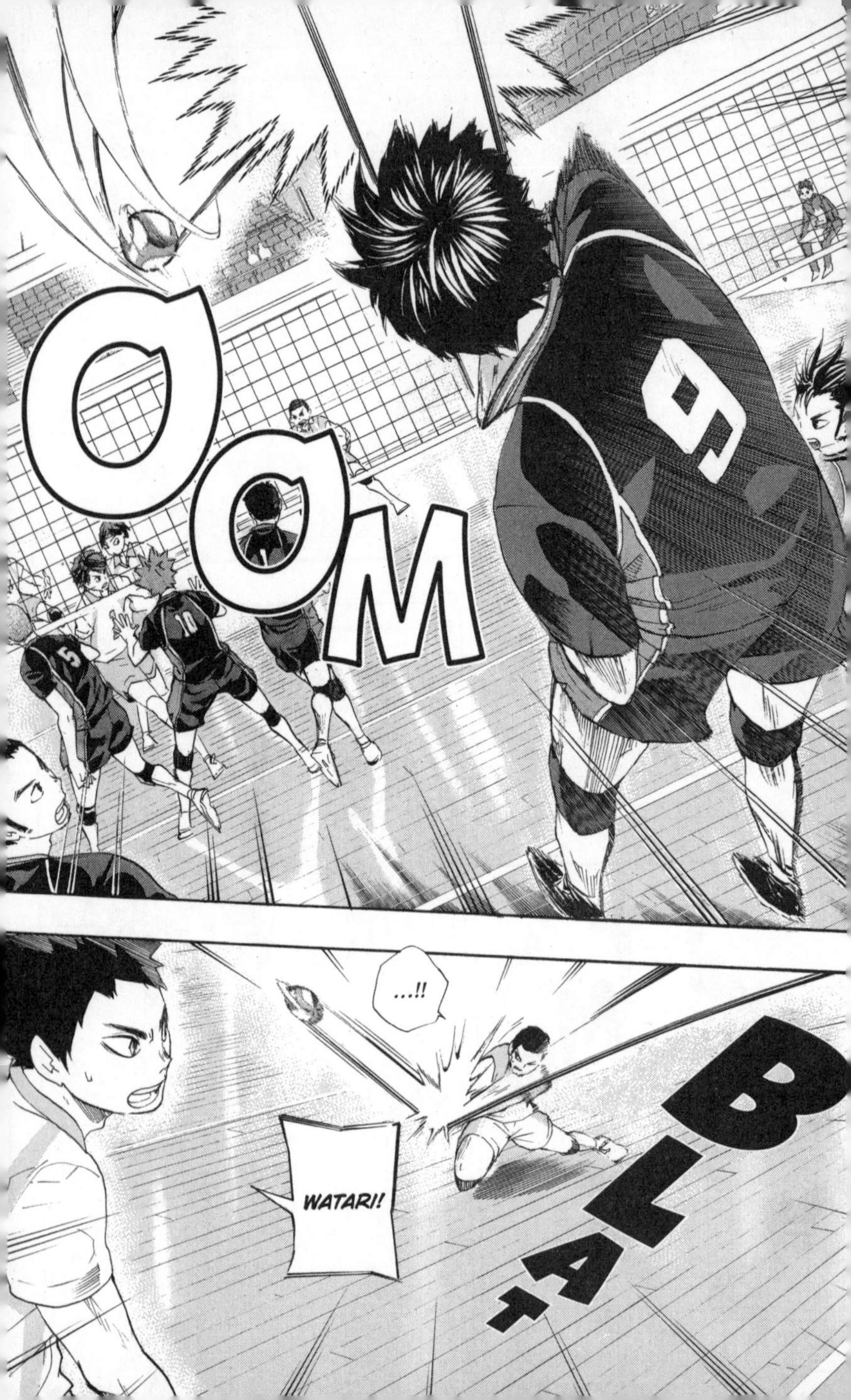
DOOM
BLAT
...!!
WATARI!

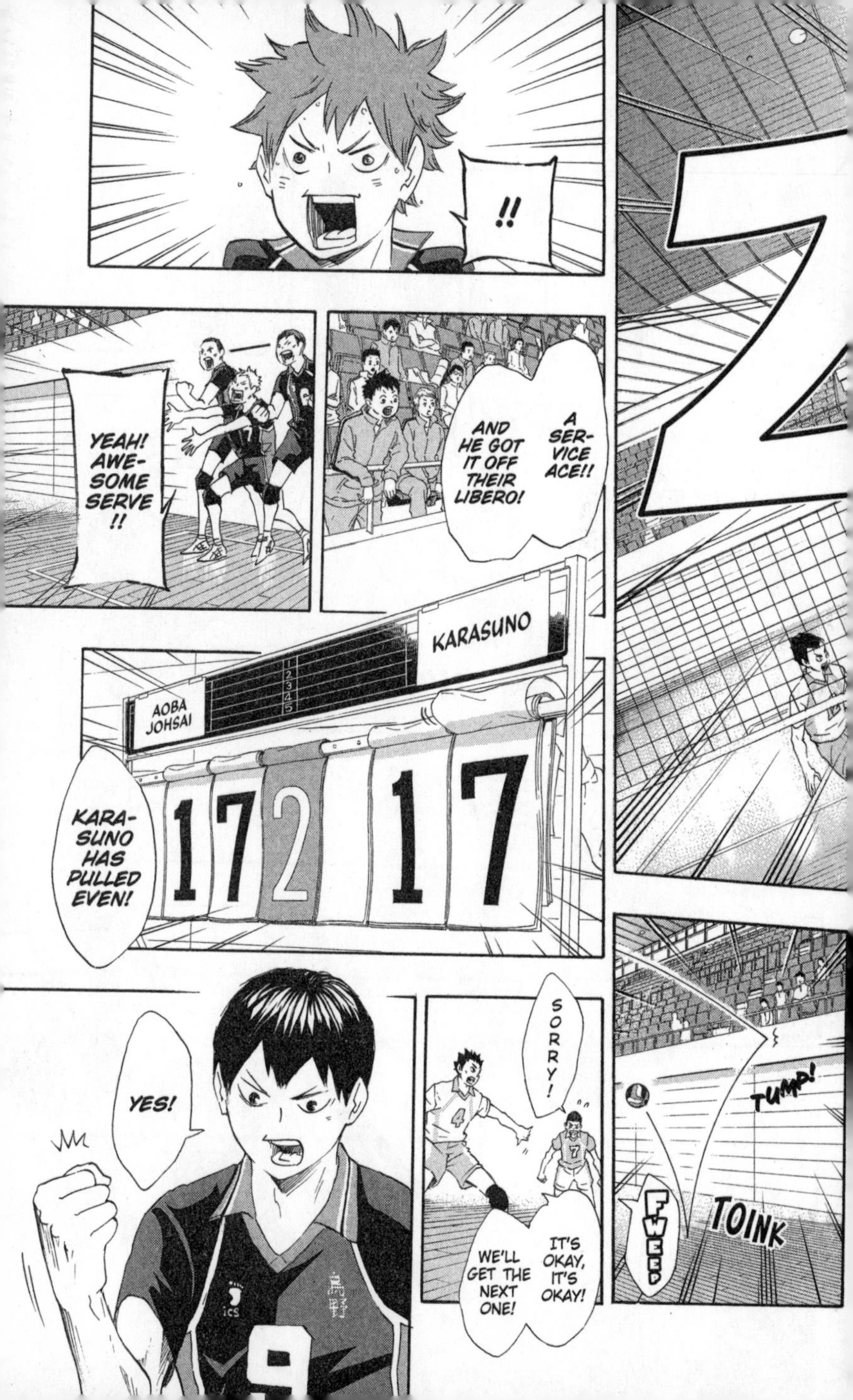
!!
A SERVICE ACE!!
AND HE GOT IT OFF THEIR LIBERO!
YEAH! AWESOME SERVE!!
KARASUNO
AOBA JOHSAI
1 2 3 4 5
17 2 17
KARASUNO HAS PULLED EVEN!
TUMP!
TOINK
FWEEP
SORRY!
IT'S OKAY, IT'S OKAY!
WE'LL GET THE NEXT ONE!
YES!

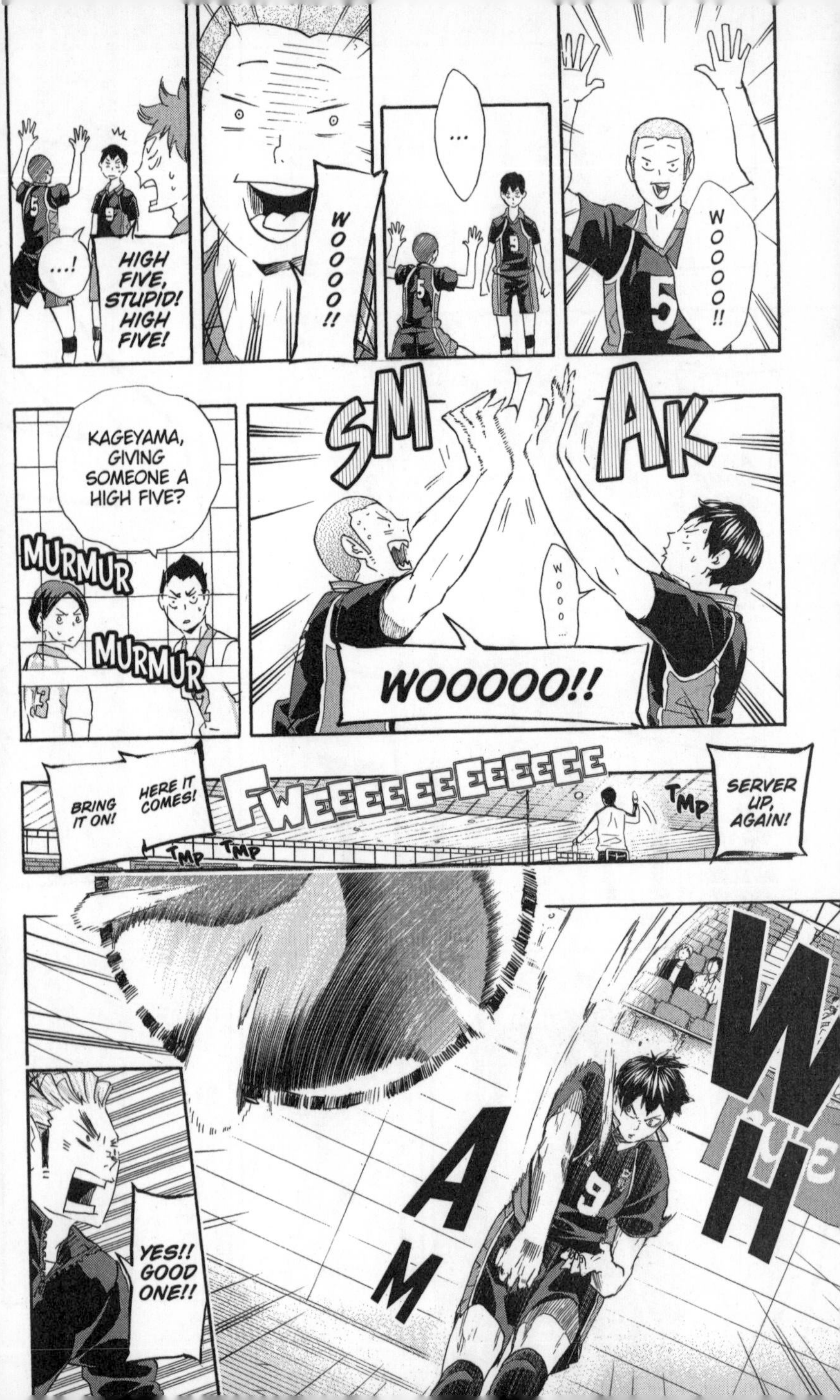

WOOOOO!!
...
WOOOOO!!
HIGH FIVE, STUPID! HIGH FIVE!
...!
SMAK
WOOO...
WOOOOO!!
KAGEYAMA, GIVING SOMEONE A HIGH FIVE?
MURMUR
MURMUR
SERVER UP, AGAIN!
TMP
FWEEEEEEEEEEE
TMP TMP
HERE IT COMES!
BRING IT ON!
WHAM
YES!! GOOD ONE!!

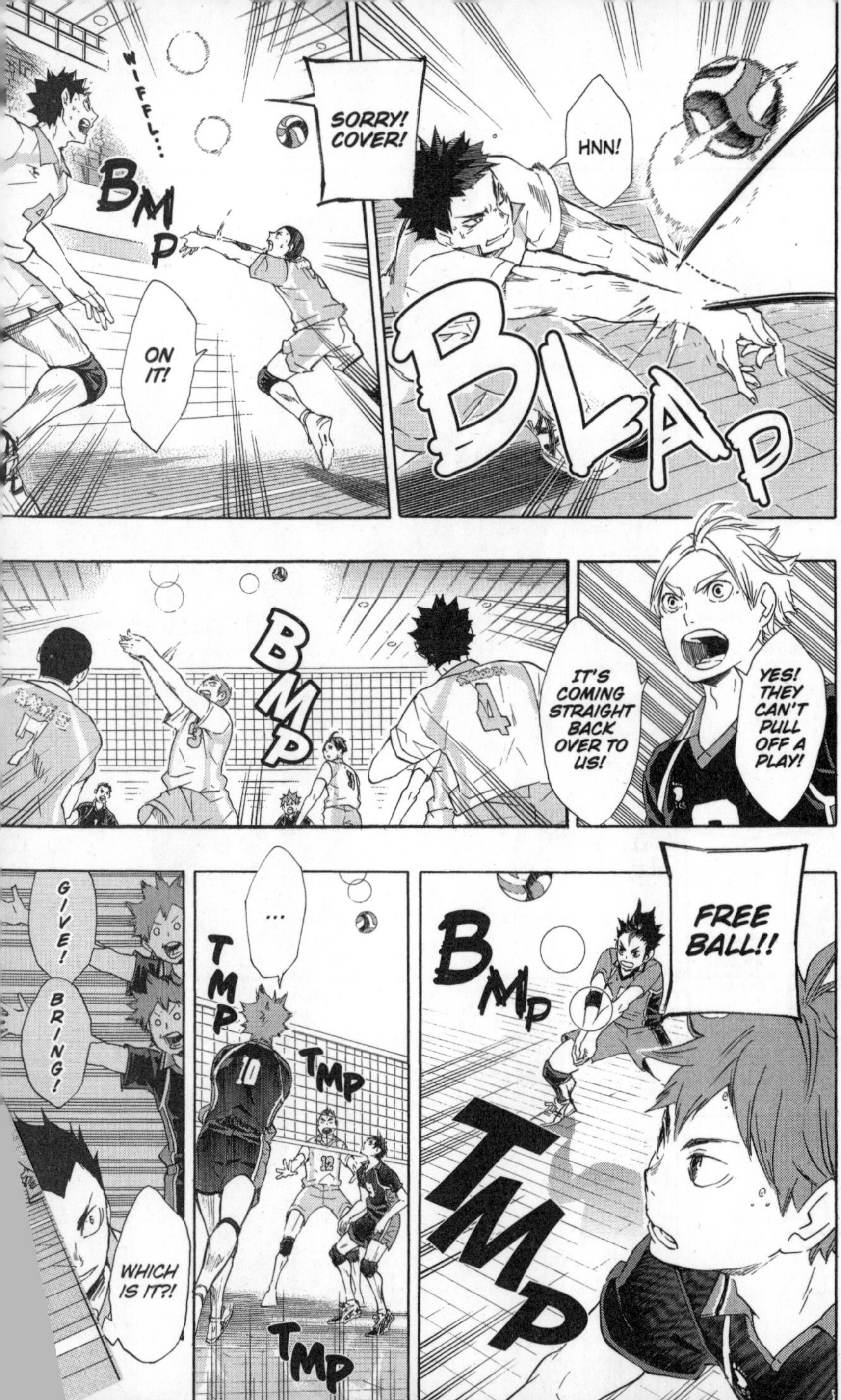
HNN!
BLAP
SORRY! COVER!
WIFFL...
BMP
ON IT!
YES! THEY CAN'T PULL OFF A PLAY!
IT'S COMING STRAIGHT BACK OVER TO US!
BMP
FREE BALL!!
BMP
TMP
...
TMP
TMP
TMP
GIVE!
BRING!
WHICH IS IT?!

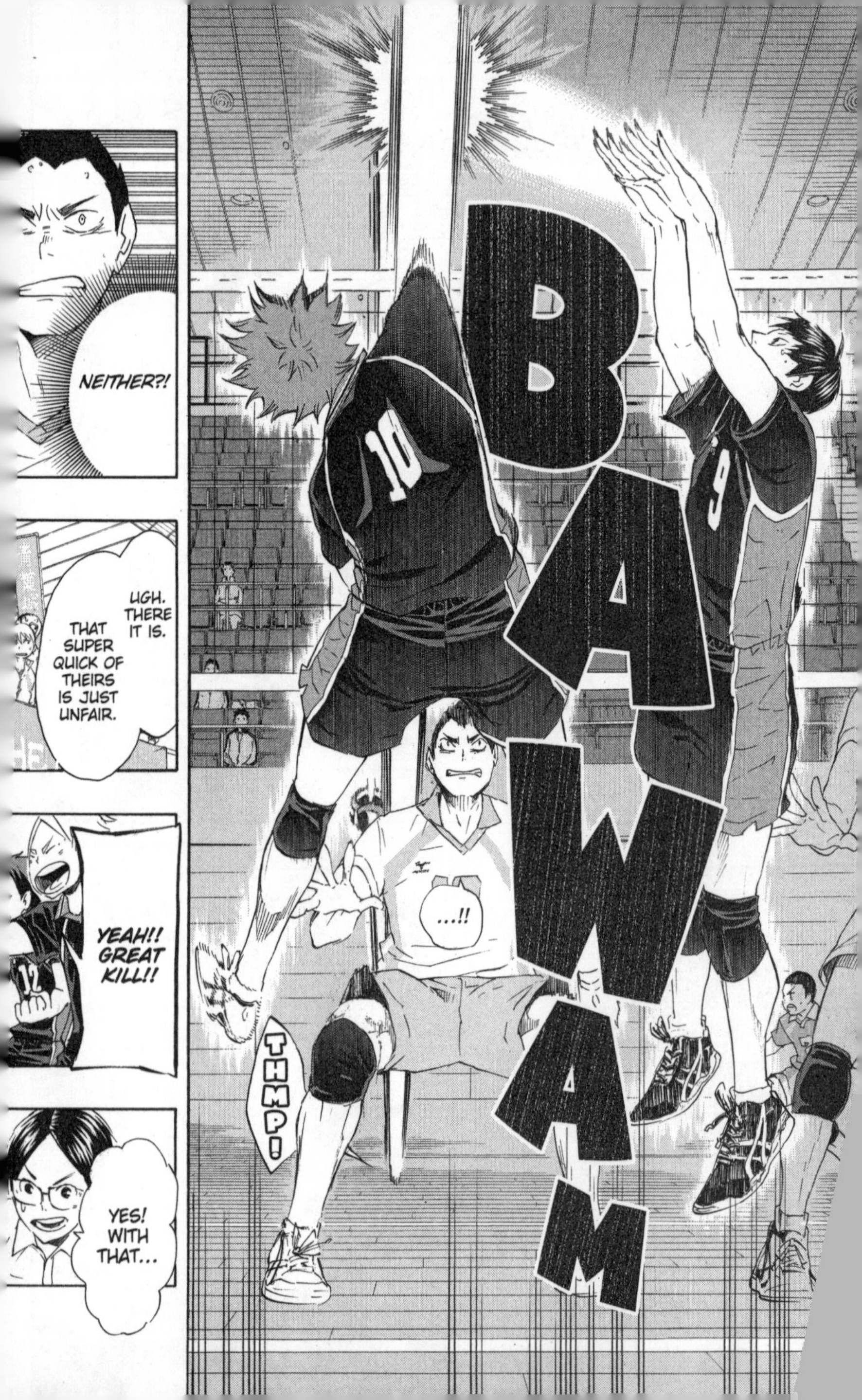
BAWAM
...!!
THMP!
NEITHER?!
UGH. THERE IT IS.
THAT SUPER QUICK OF THEIRS IS JUST UNFAIR.
YEAH!! GREAT KILL!!
YES! WITH THAT...

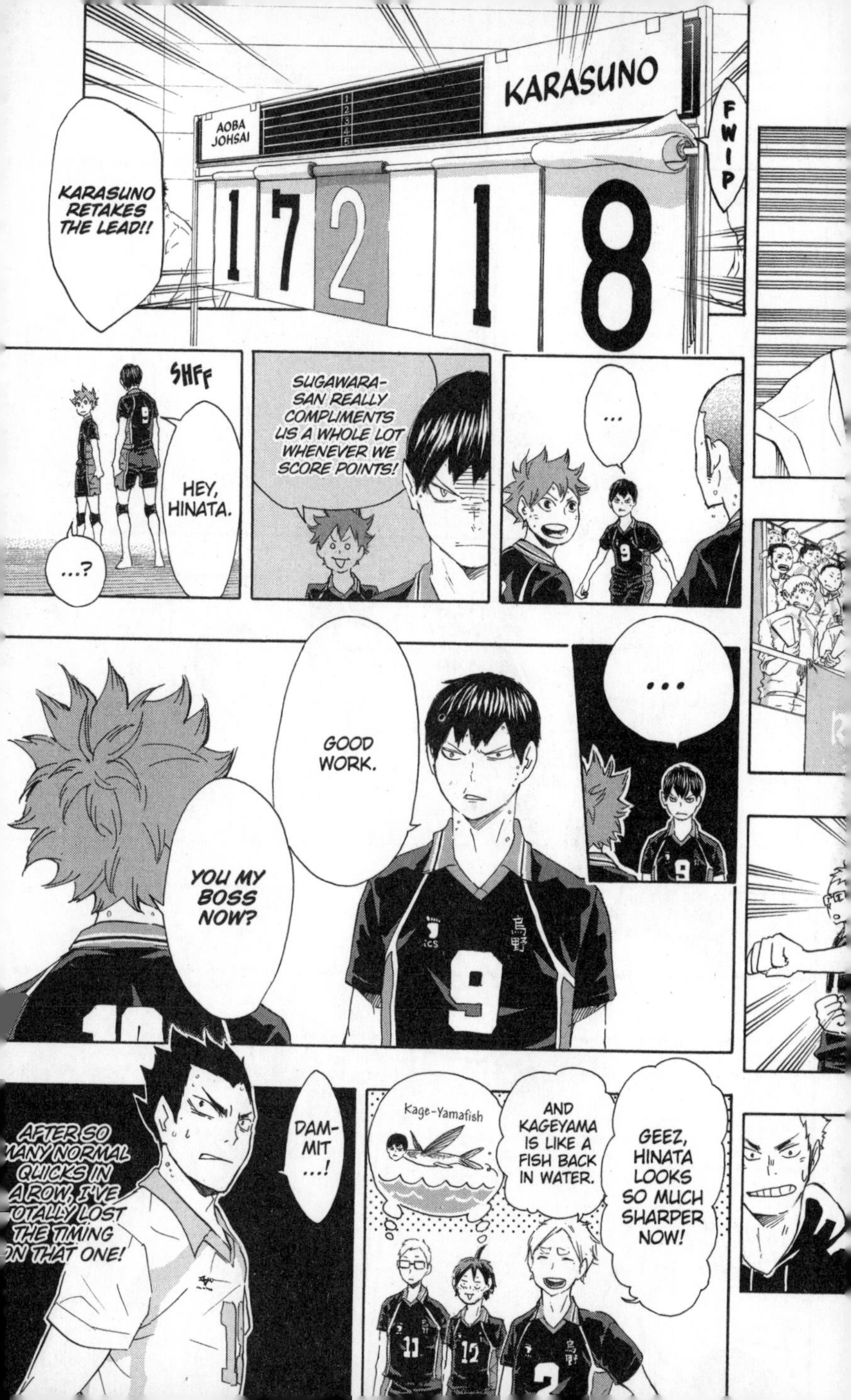
FWIP
KARASUNO
AOBA JOHSAI
1 2 3 4 5
17 2 1 8
KARASUNO RETAKES THE LEAD!!
...
SUGAWARA-SAN REALLY COMPLIMENTS US A WHOLE LOT WHENEVER WE SCORE POINTS!
SHFF
HEY, HINATA.
...?
...
GOOD WORK.
YOU MY BOSS NOW?
GEEZ, HINATA LOOKS SO MUCH SHARPER NOW!
AND KAGEYAMA IS LIKE A FISH BACK IN WATER.
Kage-Yamafish
DAM-MIT ...!
AFTER SO ANY NORMAL QUICKS IN A ROW, I'VE OTALLY LOST THE TIMING N THAT ONE!

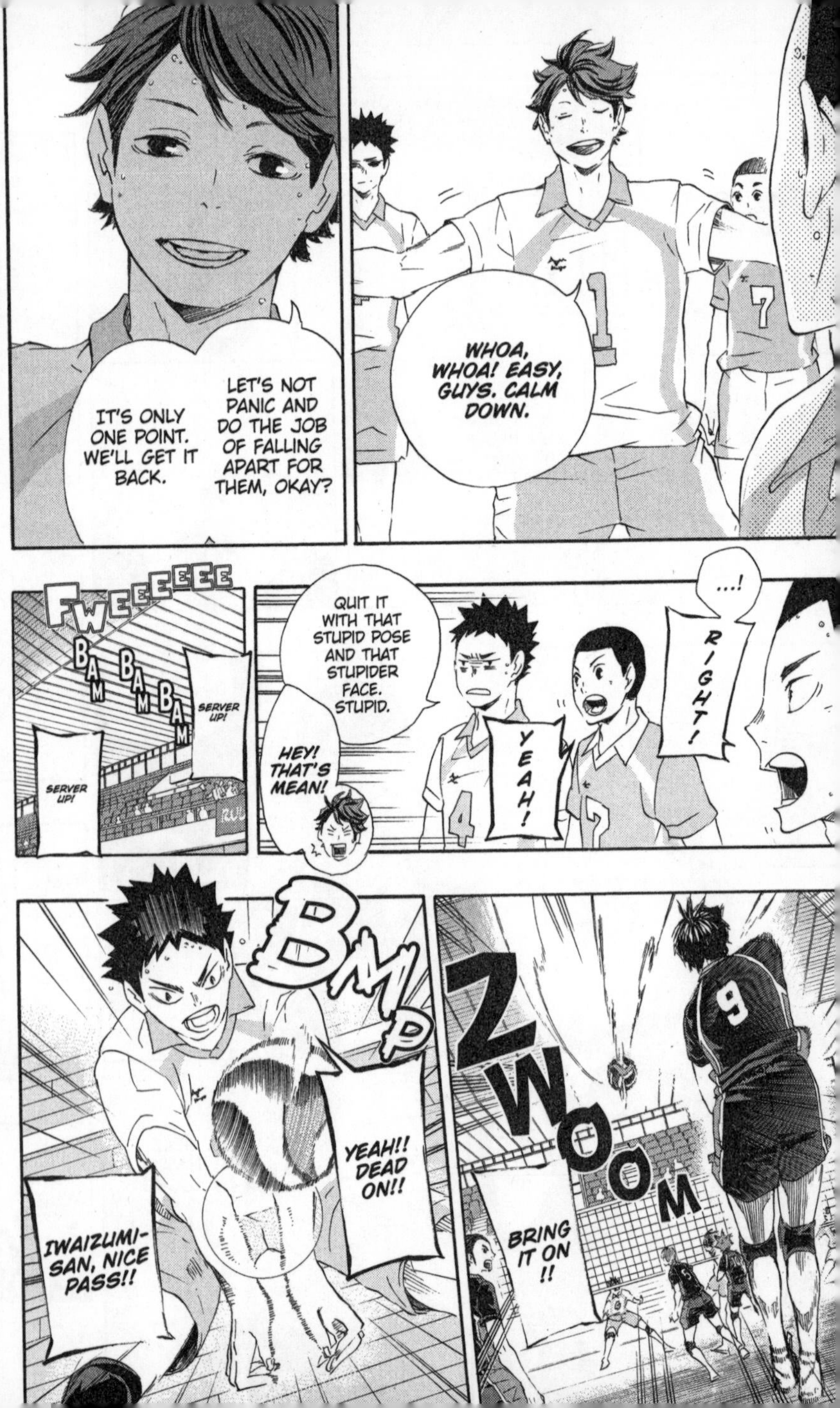
WHOA, WHOA! EASY, GUYS. CALM DOWN.
LET'S NOT PANIC AND DO THE JOB OF FALLING APART FOR THEM, OKAY?
IT'S ONLY ONE POINT. WE'LL GET IT BACK.
...!
RIGHT!
QUIT IT WITH THAT STUPID POSE AND THAT STUPIDER FACE. STUPID.
YEAH!
HEY! THAT'S MEAN!
FWEEEEEE
BAM BAM BAM
SERVER UP!
SERVER UP!
ZWOOOM
BRING IT ON!!
BMP
YEAH!! DEAD ON!!
IWAIZUMI-SAN, NICE PASS!!

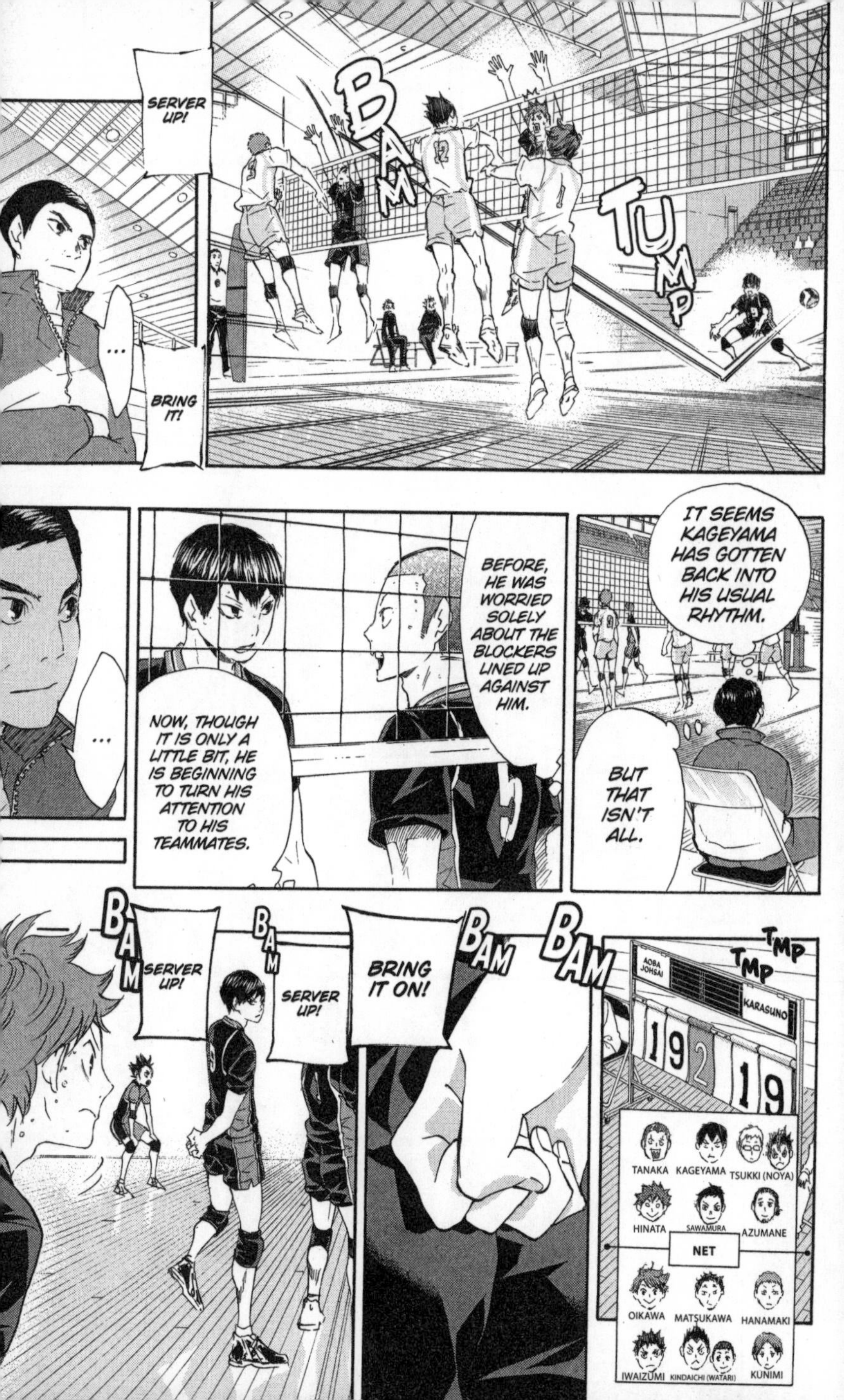
BAM
TUMP
SERVER UP!
...
BRING IT!
IT SEEMS KAGEYAMA HAS GOTTEN BACK INTO HIS USUAL RHYTHM.
BUT THAT ISN'T ALL.
BEFORE, HE WAS WORRIED SOLELY ABOUT THE BLOCKERS LINED UP AGAINST HIM.
NOW, THOUGH IT IS ONLY A LITTLE BIT, HE IS BEGINNING TO TURN HIS ATTENTION TO HIS TEAMMATES.
...
TMP
TMP
AOBA JOHSAI
KARASUNO
19 2 19
TANAKA
KAGEYAMA
TSUKKI (NOYA)
HINATA
SAWAMURA
AZUMANE
NET
OIKAWA
MATSUKAWA
HANAMAKI
IWAIZUMI
KINDAICHI (WATARI)
KUNIMI
BAM
BAM
BRING IT ON!
BAM
SERVER UP!
BAM
SERVER UP!

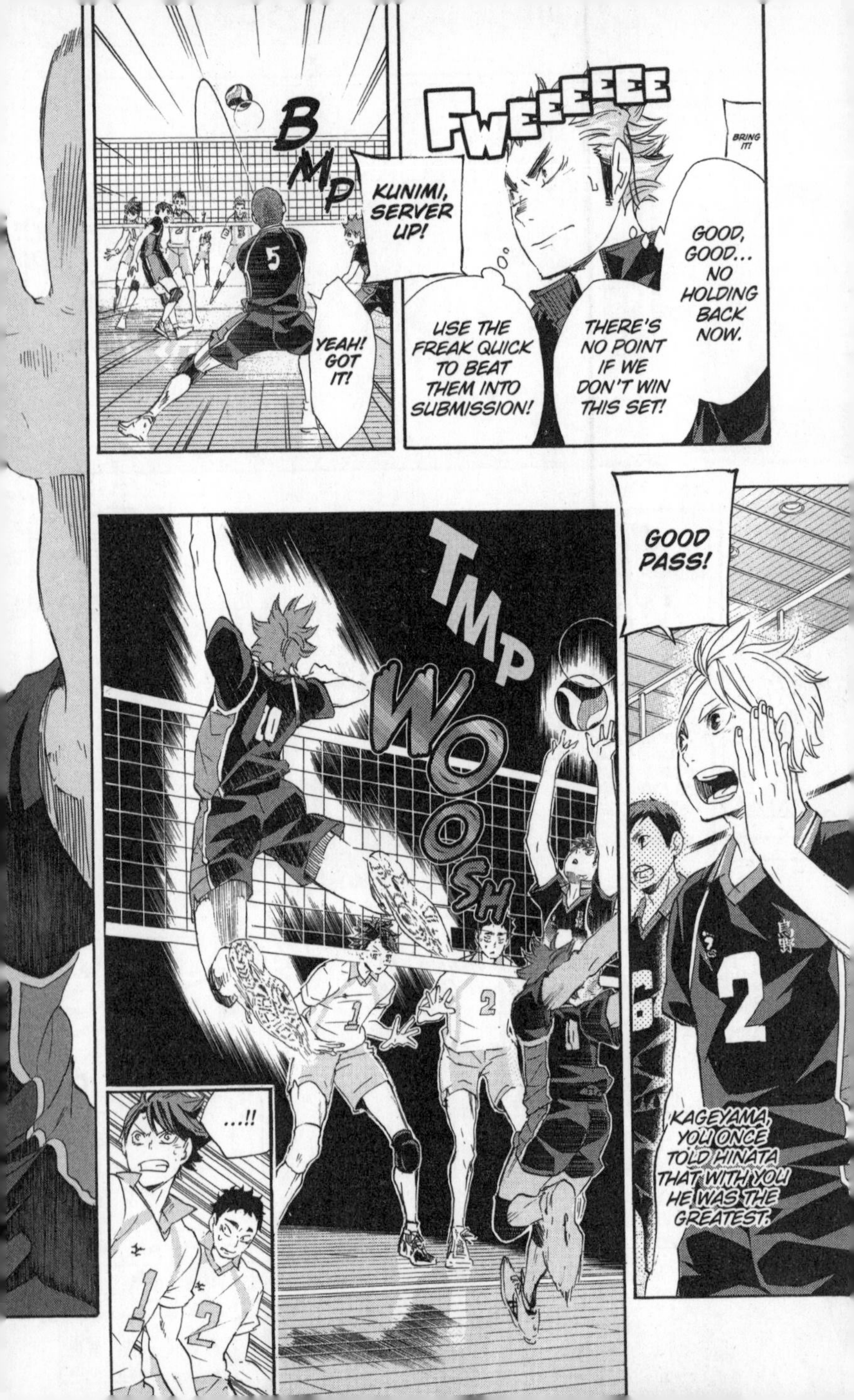
FWEEEEEE
BRING IT!
GOOD, GOOD... NO HOLDING BACK NOW.
THERE'S NO POINT IF WE DON'T WIN THIS SET!
USE THE FREAK QUICK TO BEAT THEM INTO SUBMISSION!
KUNIMI, SERVER UP!
BMP
YEAH! GOT IT!
GOOD PASS!
KAGEYAMA, YOU ONCE TOLD HINATA THAT WITH YOU HE WAS THE GREATEST.
TMP
WOOSH
...!!

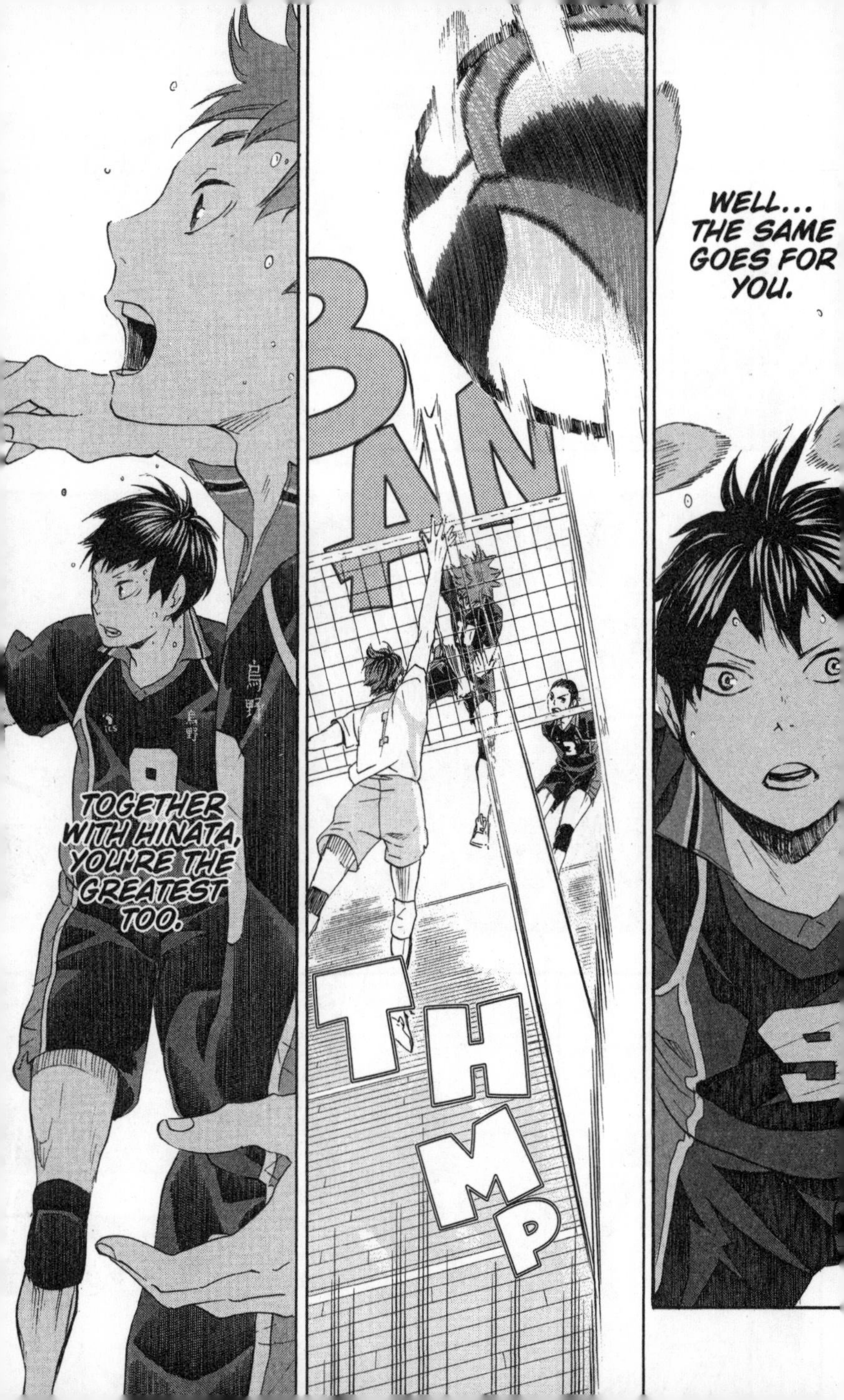
WELL... THE SAME GOES FOR YOU.
THMP
TOGETHER WITH HINATA, YOU'RE THE GREATEST TOO.

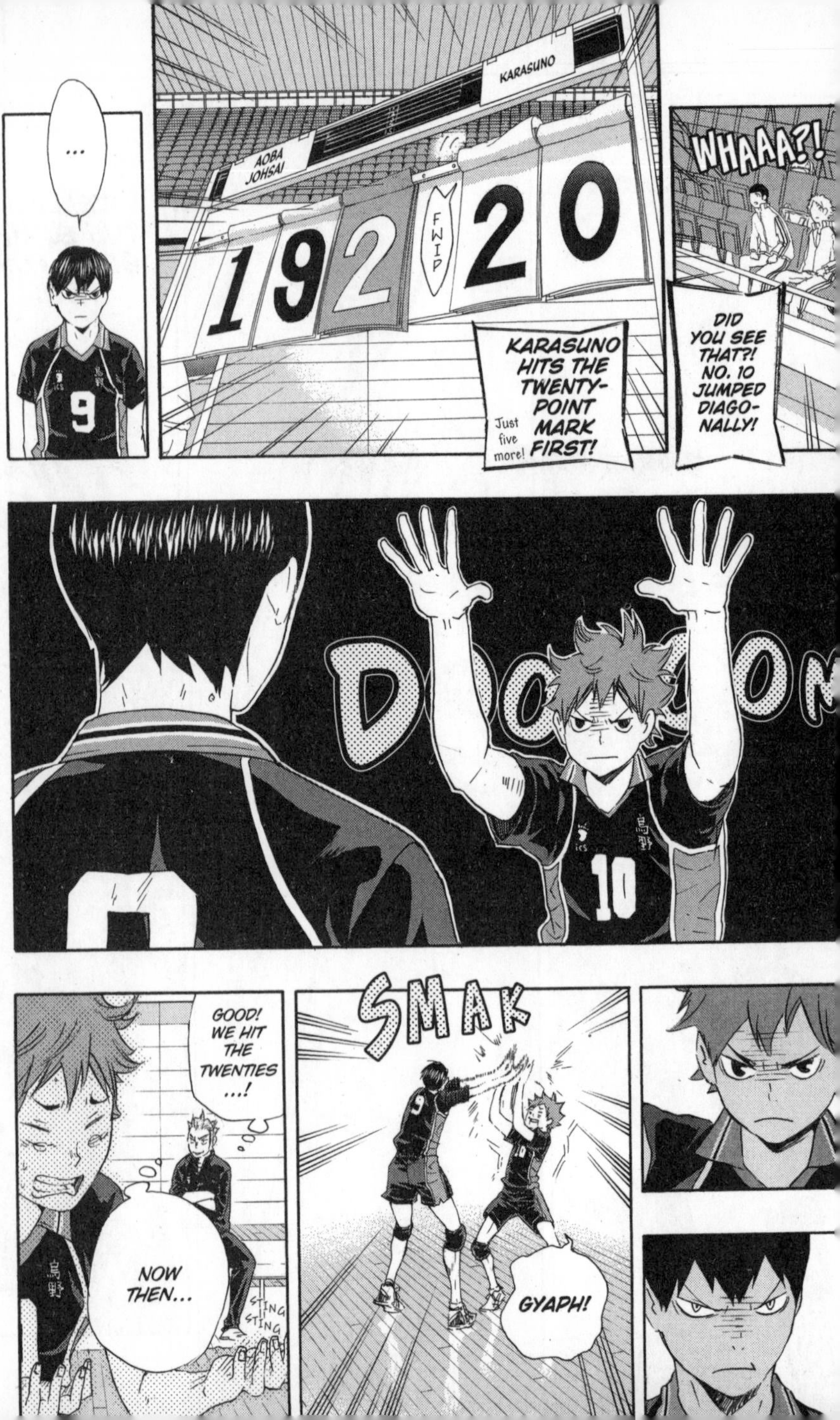
WHAAA?!
DID YOU SEE THAT?! NO. 10 JUMPED DIAGONALLY!
KARASUNO
AOBA JOHSAI
19
20
FWIP
KARASUNO HITS THE TWENTY-POINT MARK FIRST!
Just five more!
...
SMAK
GYAPH!
GOOD! WE HIT THE TWENTIES...!
NOW THEN...
STING STING

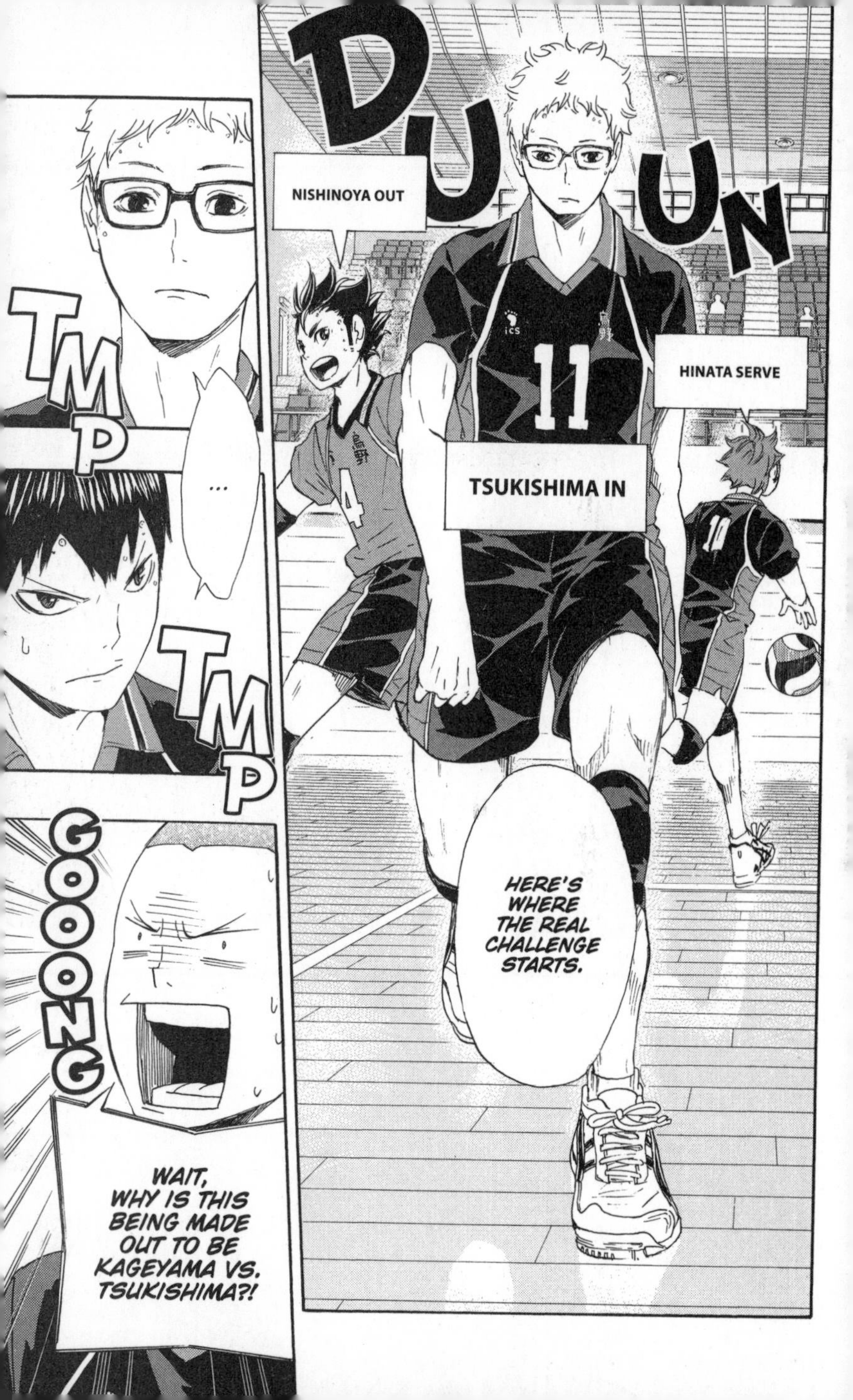
DUUN
NISHINOYA OUT
HINATA SERVE
TSUKISHIMA IN
HERE'S WHERE THE REAL CHALLENGE STARTS.
TMP
TMP
...
GOOONG
WAIT, WHY IS THIS BEING MADE OUT TO BE KAGEYAMA VS. TSUKISHIMA?!

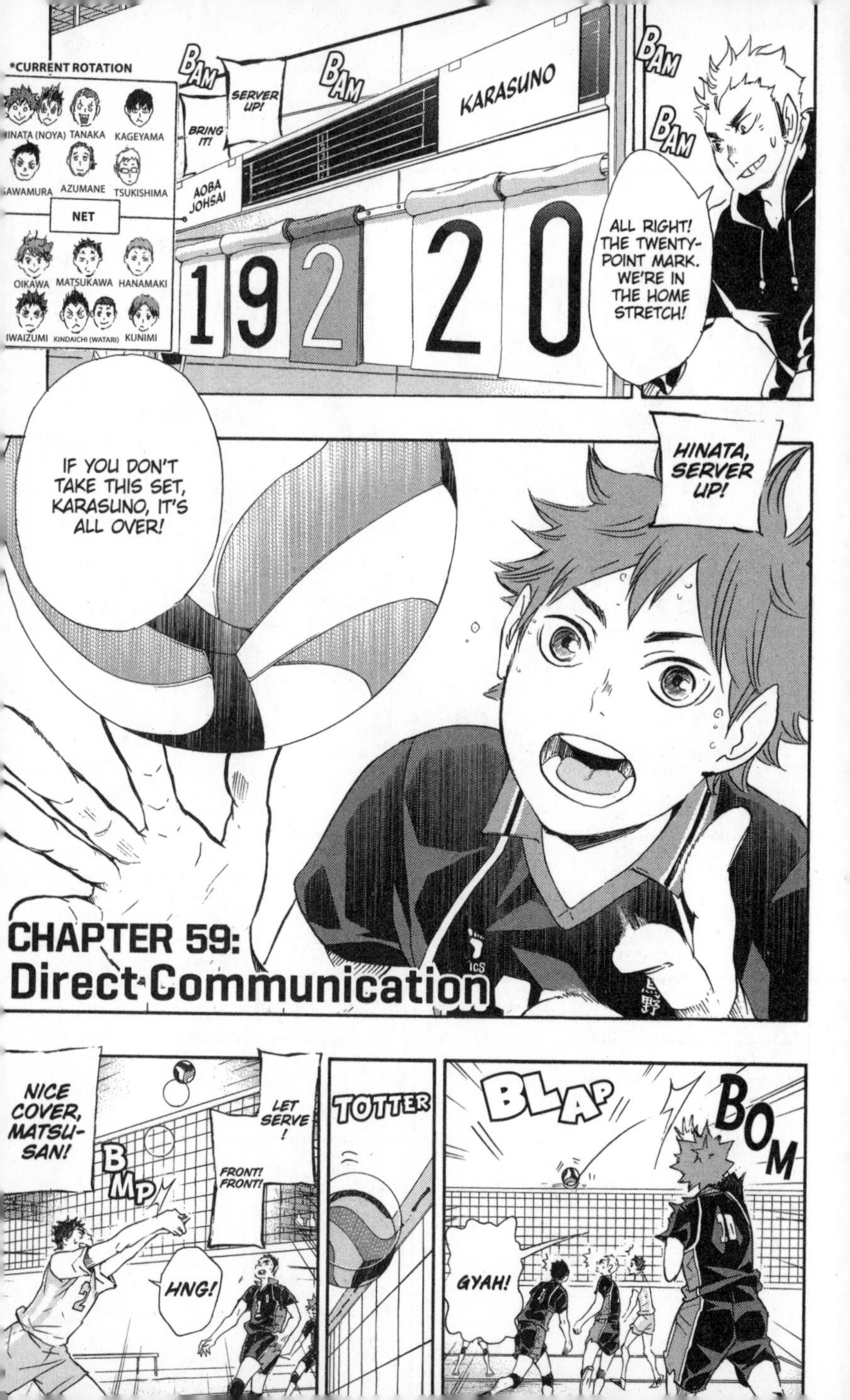
*CURRENT ROTATION
HINATA (NOYA) TANAKA KAGEYAMA
SAWAMURA AZUMANE TSUKISHIMA
NET
OIKAWA MATSUKAWA HANAMAKI
IWAIZUMI KINDAICHI (WATARI) KUNIMI
BAM
BAM
ALL RIGHT! THE TWENTY-POINT MARK. WE'RE IN THE HOME STRETCH!
KARASUNO
BAM
SERVER UP!
BRING IT!
BAM
AOBA JOHSAI
19
20
HINATA, SERVER UP!
IF YOU DON'T TAKE THIS SET, KARASUNO, IT'S ALL OVER!
CHAPTER 59:
Direct Communication
BOM
BLAP
GYAH!
TOTTER
LET SERVE!
FRONT! FRONT!
NICE COVER, MATSU-SAN!
BMP
HNG!

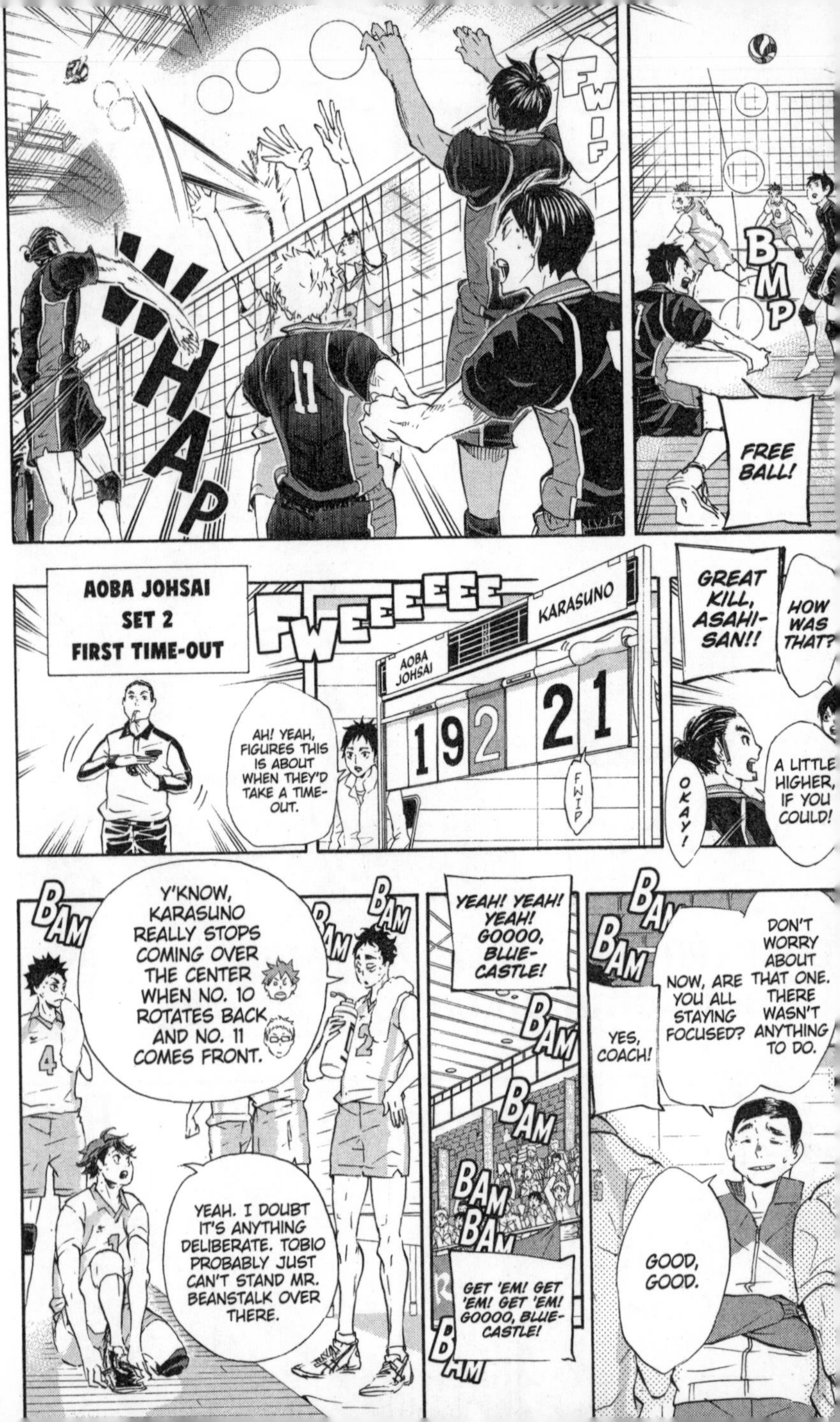
BMP
FREE BALL!
FWIF
WHAP
GREAT KILL, ASAHI-SAN!!
HOW WAS THAT?
A LITTLE HIGHER, IF YOU COULD!
OKAY!
KARASUNO
AOBA JOHSAI
19 2 21
FWIP
FWEEEEEE
AH! YEAH, FIGURES THIS IS ABOUT WHEN THEY'D TAKE A TIME-OUT.
AOBA JOHSAI SET 2 FIRST TIME-OUT
BAM BAM
DON'T WORRY ABOUT THAT ONE. THERE WASN'T ANYTHING TO DO.
NOW, ARE YOU ALL STAYING FOCUSED?
YES, COACH!
GOOD, GOOD.
YEAH! YEAH! YEAH! GOOOO, BLUE-CASTLE!
BAM BAM BAM BAM BAM
GET 'EM! GET 'EM! GET 'EM! GOOOO, BLUE-CASTLE!
BAM
BAM BAM
Y'KNOW, KARASUNO REALLY STOPS COMING OVER THE CENTER WHEN NO. 10 ROTATES BACK AND NO. 11 COMES FRONT.
YEAH. I DOUBT IT'S ANYTHING DELIBERATE. TOBIO PROBABLY JUST CAN'T STAND MR. BEANSTALK OVER THERE.

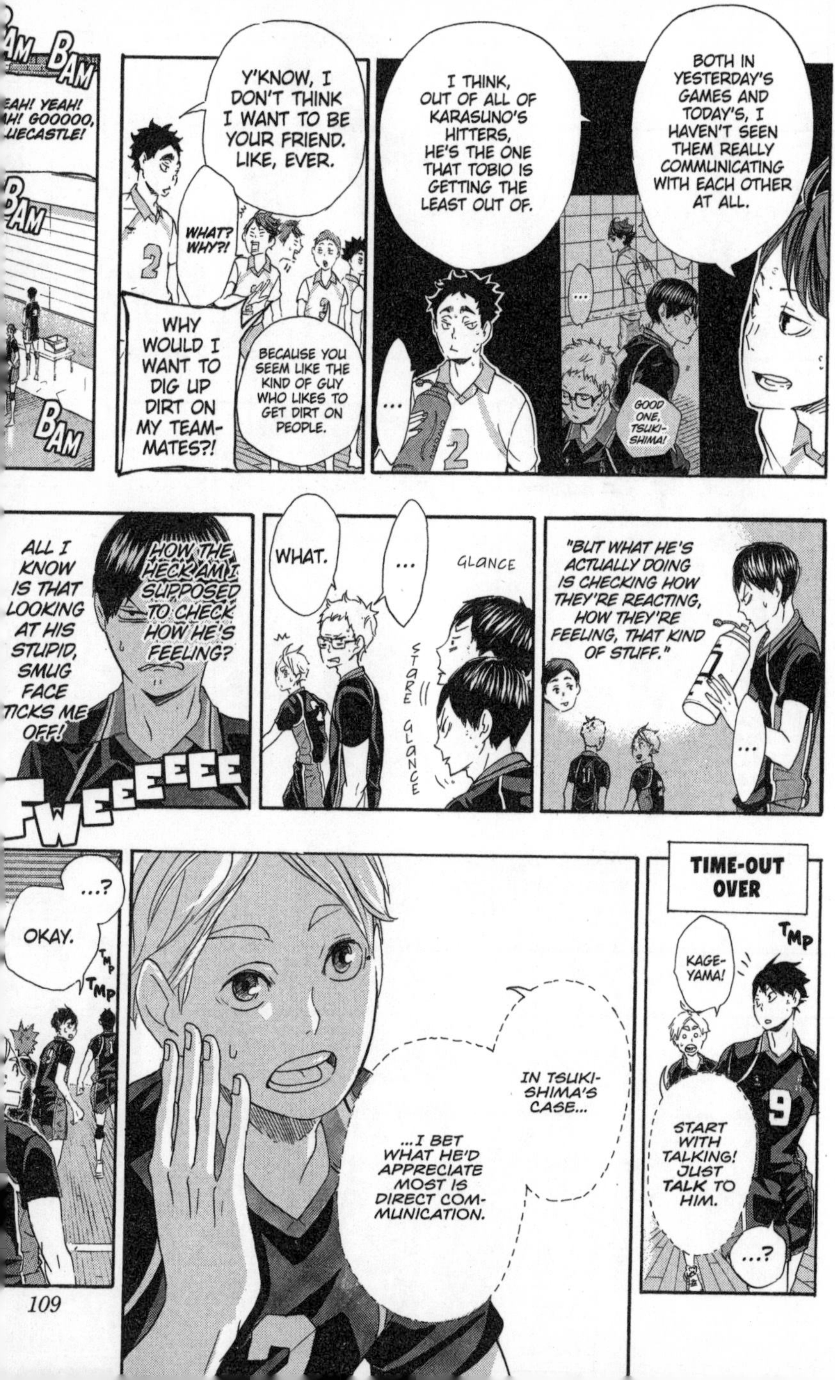
BOTH IN YESTERDAY'S GAMES AND TODAY'S, I HAVEN'T SEEN THEM REALLY COMMUNICATING WITH EACH OTHER AT ALL.
...
GOOD ONE, TSUKI-SHIMA!
I THINK, OUT OF ALL OF KARASUNO'S HITTERS, HE'S THE ONE THAT TOBIO IS GETTING THE LEAST OUT OF.
...
Y'KNOW, I DON'T THINK I WANT TO BE YOUR FRIEND. LIKE, EVER.
WHAT? WHY?!
BECAUSE YOU SEEM LIKE THE KIND OF GUY WHO LIKES TO GET DIRT ON PEOPLE.
WHY WOULD I WANT TO DIG UP DIRT ON MY TEAM-MATES?!
BAM BAM
EAH! YEAH! AH! GOOOOO, UECASTLE!
BAM
BAM
"BUT WHAT HE'S ACTUALLY DOING IS CHECKING HOW THEY'RE REACTING, HOW THEY'RE FEELING, THAT KIND OF STUFF."
...
GLANCE
...
WHAT.
STARE
GLANCE
HOW THE HECK AM I SUPPOSED TO CHECK HOW HE'S FEELING?
ALL I KNOW IS THAT LOOKING AT HIS STUPID, SMUG FACE TICKS ME OFF!
FWEEEEEE
TIME-OUT OVER
TMP
KAGE-YAMA!
START WITH TALKING! JUST TALK TO HIM.
...?
IN TSUKI-SHIMA'S CASE...
...I BET WHAT HE'D APPRECIATE MOST IS DIRECT COM-MUNICATION.
...?
OKAY.
TMP
TMP

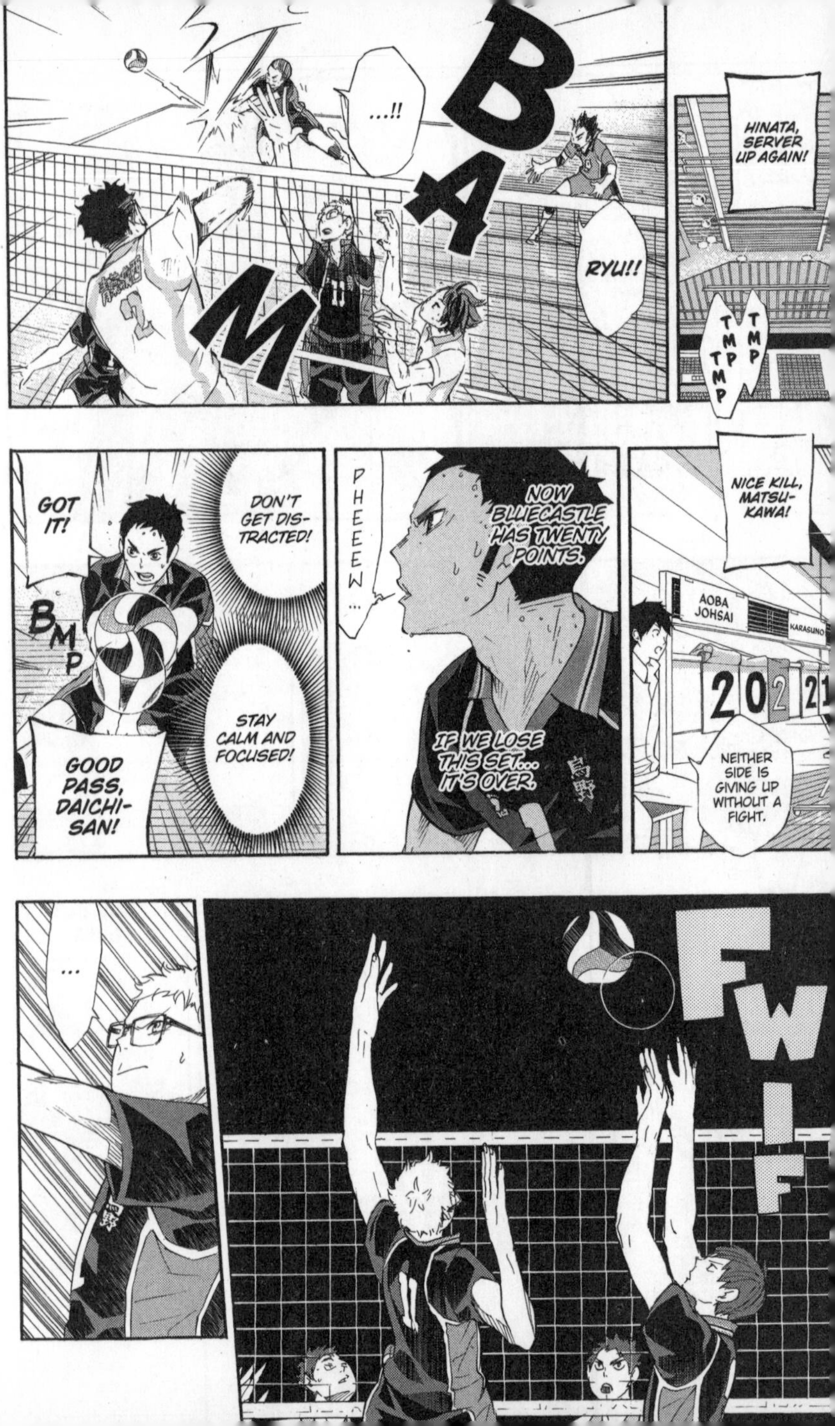
HINATA, SERVER UP AGAIN!
TMP TMP TMP TMP
...!!
BAM
RYU!!
NICE KILL, MATSU-KAWA!
AOBA JOHSAI
KARASUNO
20 21
NEITHER SIDE IS GIVING UP WITHOUT A FIGHT.
PHEEEW...
NOW BLUECASTLE HAS TWENTY POINTS.
IF WE LOSE THIS SET... IT'S OVER.
DON'T GET DIS-TRACTED!
STAY CALM AND FOCUSED!
GOT IT!
BMP
GOOD PASS, DAICHI-SAN!
FWIF
...

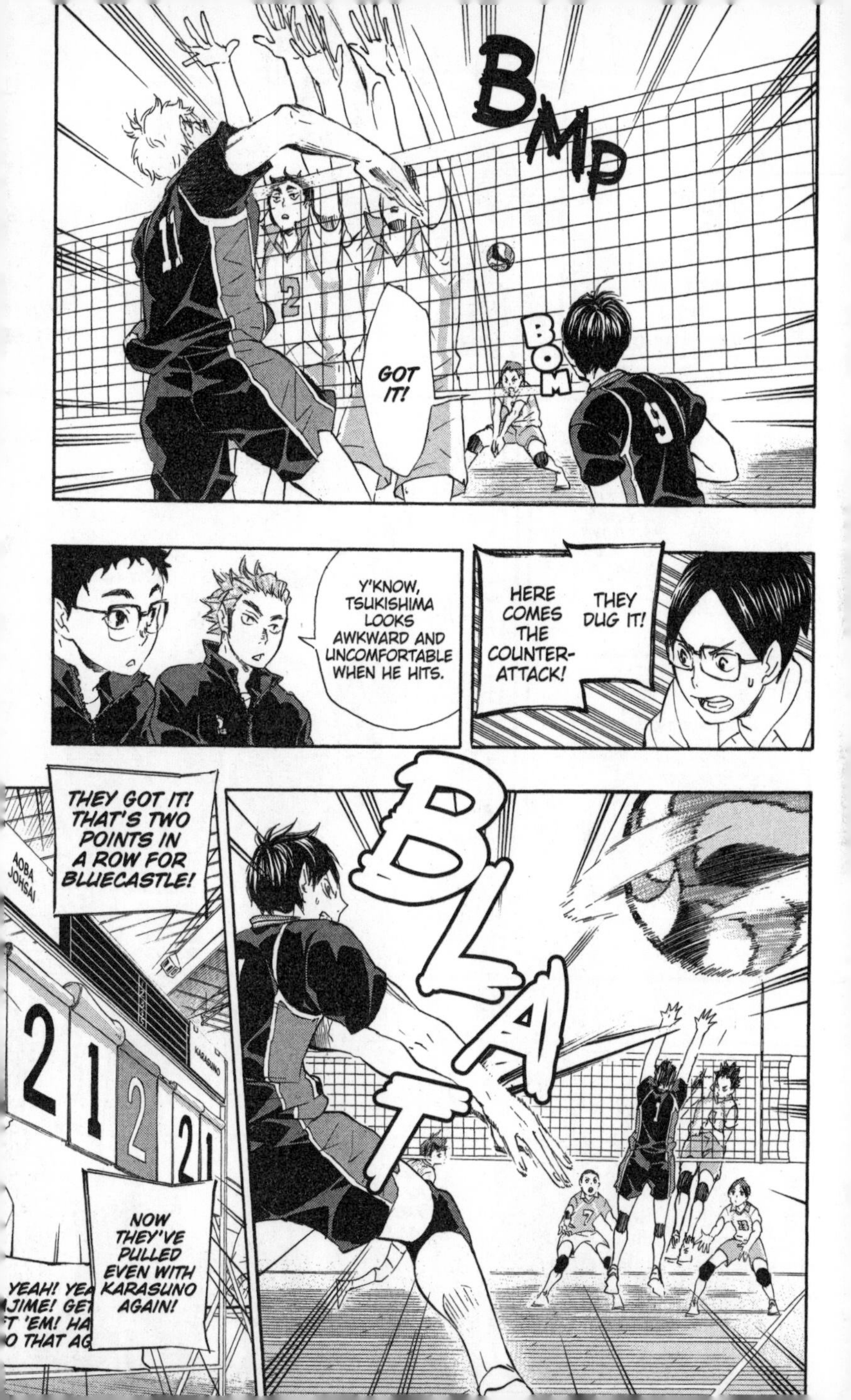
BMP
BOM
GOT IT!
THEY DUG IT!
HERE COMES THE COUNTER-ATTACK!
Y'KNOW, TSUKISHIMA LOOKS AWKWARD AND UNCOMFORTABLE WHEN HE HITS.
BLAT
THEY GOT IT! THAT'S TWO POINTS IN A ROW FOR BLUECASTLE!
AOBA JOHSAI
KARASUNO
NOW THEY'VE PULLED EVEN WITH KARASUNO AGAIN!
YEAH! YEA
JIME! GET
T 'EM! HA
O THAT AG

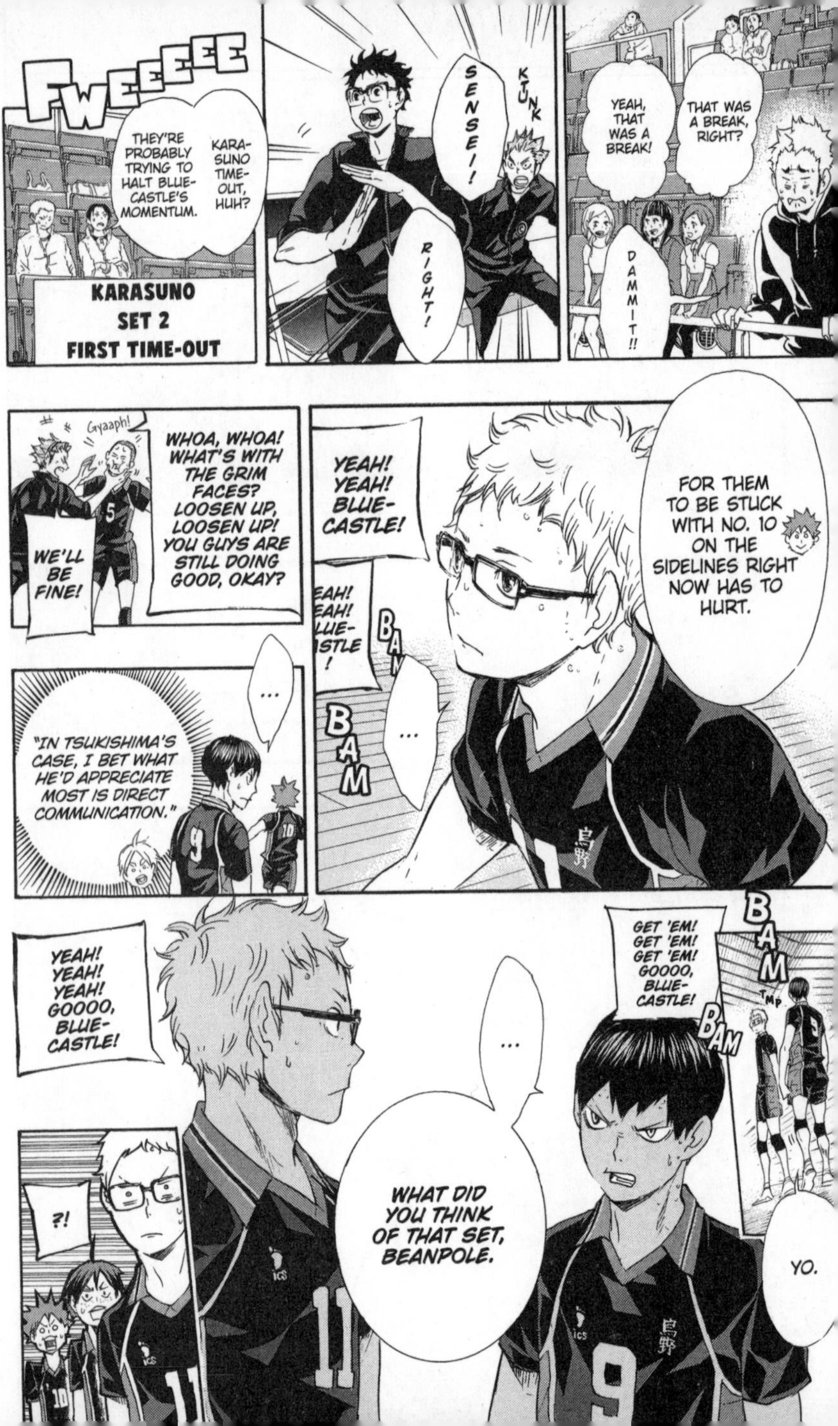
THAT WAS A BREAK, RIGHT?
YEAH, THAT WAS A BREAK!
DAMMIT!!
KTUNK
SENSEI!!
RIGHT!
FWEEEEE
KARA-SUNO TIME-OUT, HUH?
THEY'RE PROBABLY TRYING TO HALT BLUE-CASTLE'S MOMENTUM.
KARASUNO SET 2 FIRST TIME-OUT
FOR THEM TO BE STUCK WITH NO. 10 ON THE SIDELINES RIGHT NOW HAS TO HURT.
YEAH! YEAH! BLUE-CASTLE!
BAM
...
BAM
WHOA, WHOA! WHAT'S WITH THE GRIM FACES? LOOSEN UP, LOOSEN UP! YOU GUYS ARE STILL DOING GOOD, OKAY?
Gyaaph!
WE'LL BE FINE!
...
"IN TSUKISHIMA'S CASE, I BET WHAT HE'D APPRECIATE MOST IS DIRECT COMMUNICATION."
GET 'EM! GET 'EM! GET 'EM! GOOOO, BLUE-CASTLE!
BAM
TMP
BAM
YO.
WHAT DID YOU THINK OF THAT SET, BEANPOLE.
...
YEAH! YEAH! YEAH! GOOOO, BLUE-CASTLE!
?!

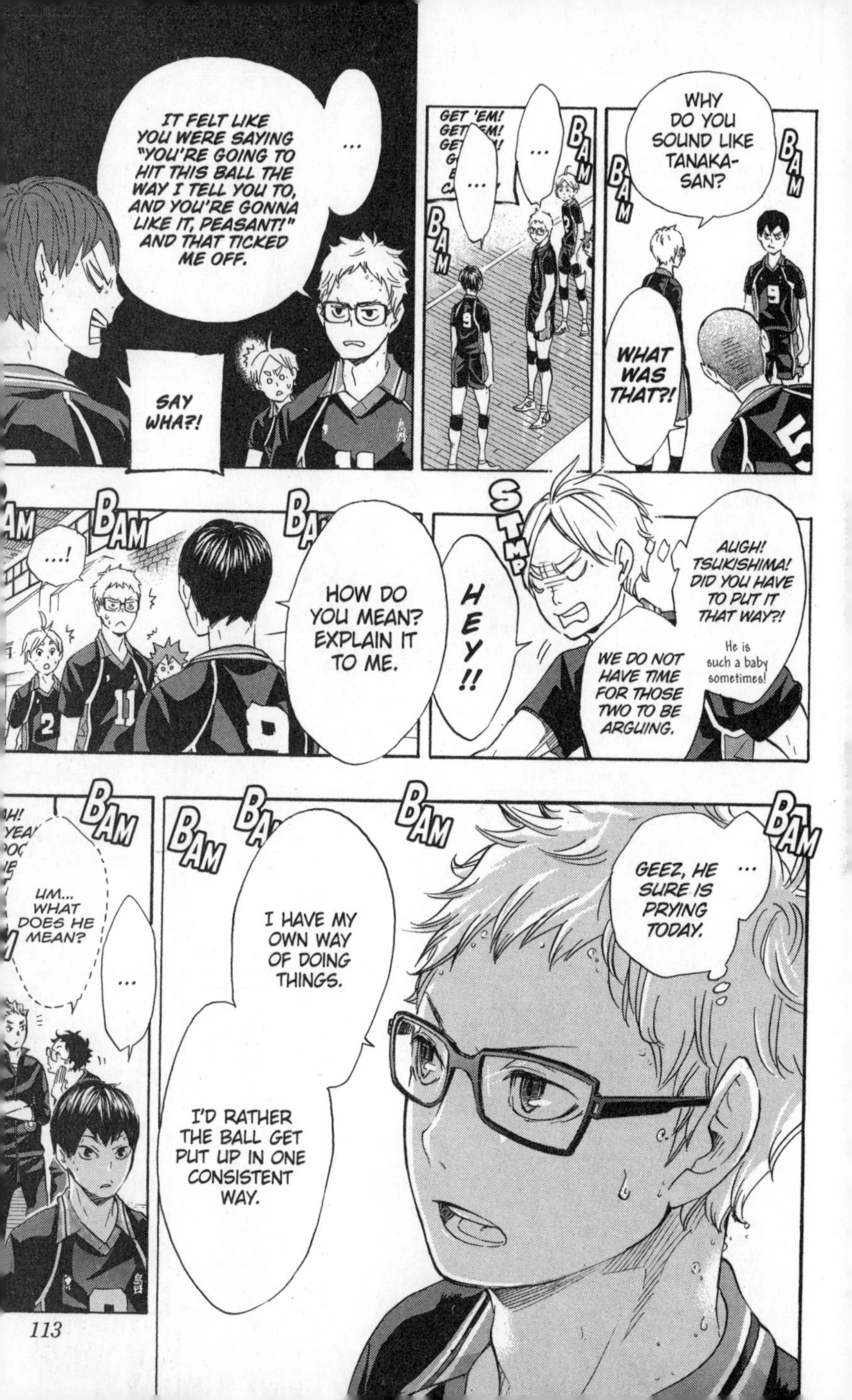

BAM
WHY DO YOU SOUND LIKE TANAKA-SAN?
BAM
WHAT WAS THAT?!
BAM
...
GET 'EM! GET 'EM!
...
IT FELT LIKE YOU WERE SAYING "YOU'RE GOING TO HIT THIS BALL THE WAY I TELL YOU TO, AND YOU'RE GONNA LIKE IT, PEASANT!" AND THAT TICKED ME OFF.
...
SAY WHA?!
STMP
AUGH! TSUKISHIMA! DID YOU HAVE TO PUT IT THAT WAY?!
He is such a baby sometimes!
HEY!!
WE DO NOT HAVE TIME FOR THOSE TWO TO BE ARGUING.
BAM
HOW DO YOU MEAN? EXPLAIN IT TO ME.
BAM
...!
BAM
BAM
...
GEEZ, HE SURE IS PRYING TODAY.
BAM
BAM
I HAVE MY OWN WAY OF DOING THINGS.
I'D RATHER THE BALL GET PUT UP IN ONE CONSISTENT WAY.
BAM
...
UM... WHAT DOES HE MEAN?

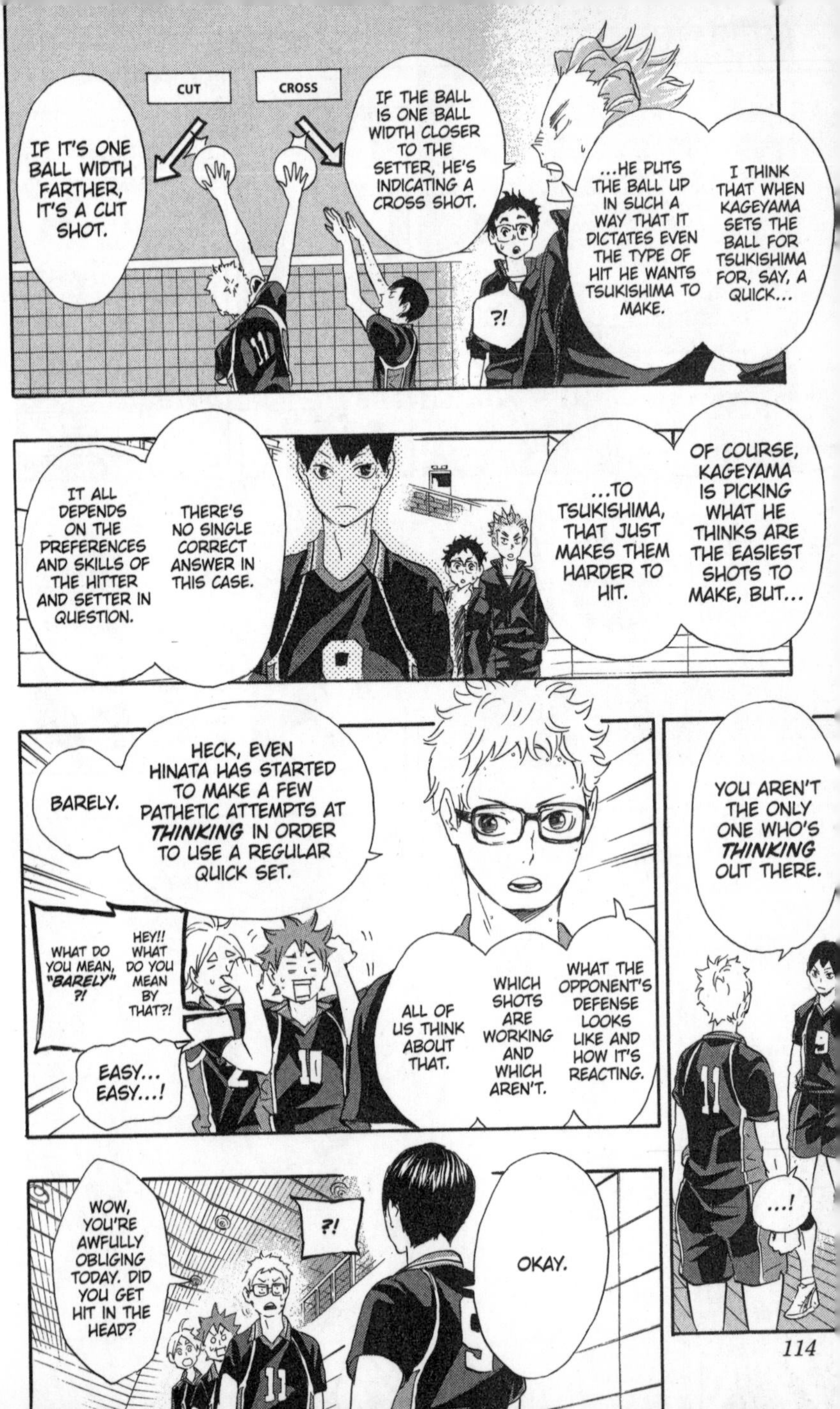
I THINK THAT WHEN KAGEYAMA SETS THE BALL FOR TSUKISHIMA FOR, SAY, A QUICK...
...HE PUTS THE BALL UP IN SUCH A WAY THAT IT DICTATES EVEN THE TYPE OF HIT HE WANTS TSUKISHIMA TO MAKE.
?!
IF THE BALL IS ONE BALL WIDTH CLOSER TO THE SETTER, HE'S INDICATING A CROSS SHOT.
CROSS
CUT
IF IT'S ONE BALL WIDTH FARTHER, IT'S A CUT SHOT.
OF COURSE, KAGEYAMA IS PICKING WHAT HE THINKS ARE THE EASIEST SHOTS TO MAKE, BUT...
...TO TSUKISHIMA, THAT JUST MAKES THEM HARDER TO HIT.
THERE'S NO SINGLE CORRECT ANSWER IN THIS CASE.
IT ALL DEPENDS ON THE PREFERENCES AND SKILLS OF THE HITTER AND SETTER IN QUESTION.
YOU AREN'T THE ONLY ONE WHO'S *THINKING* OUT THERE.
...!
WHAT THE OPPONENT'S DEFENSE LOOKS LIKE AND HOW IT'S REACTING.
WHICH SHOTS ARE WORKING AND WHICH AREN'T.
ALL OF US THINK ABOUT THAT.
HECK, EVEN HINATA HAS STARTED TO MAKE A FEW PATHETIC ATTEMPTS AT *THINKING* IN ORDER TO USE A REGULAR QUICK SET.
BARELY.
HEY!! WHAT DO YOU MEAN BY THAT?!
WHAT DO YOU MEAN, *"BARELY"* ?!
EASY... EASY...!
OKAY.
?!
WOW, YOU'RE AWFULLY OBLIGING TODAY. DID YOU GET HIT IN THE HEAD?

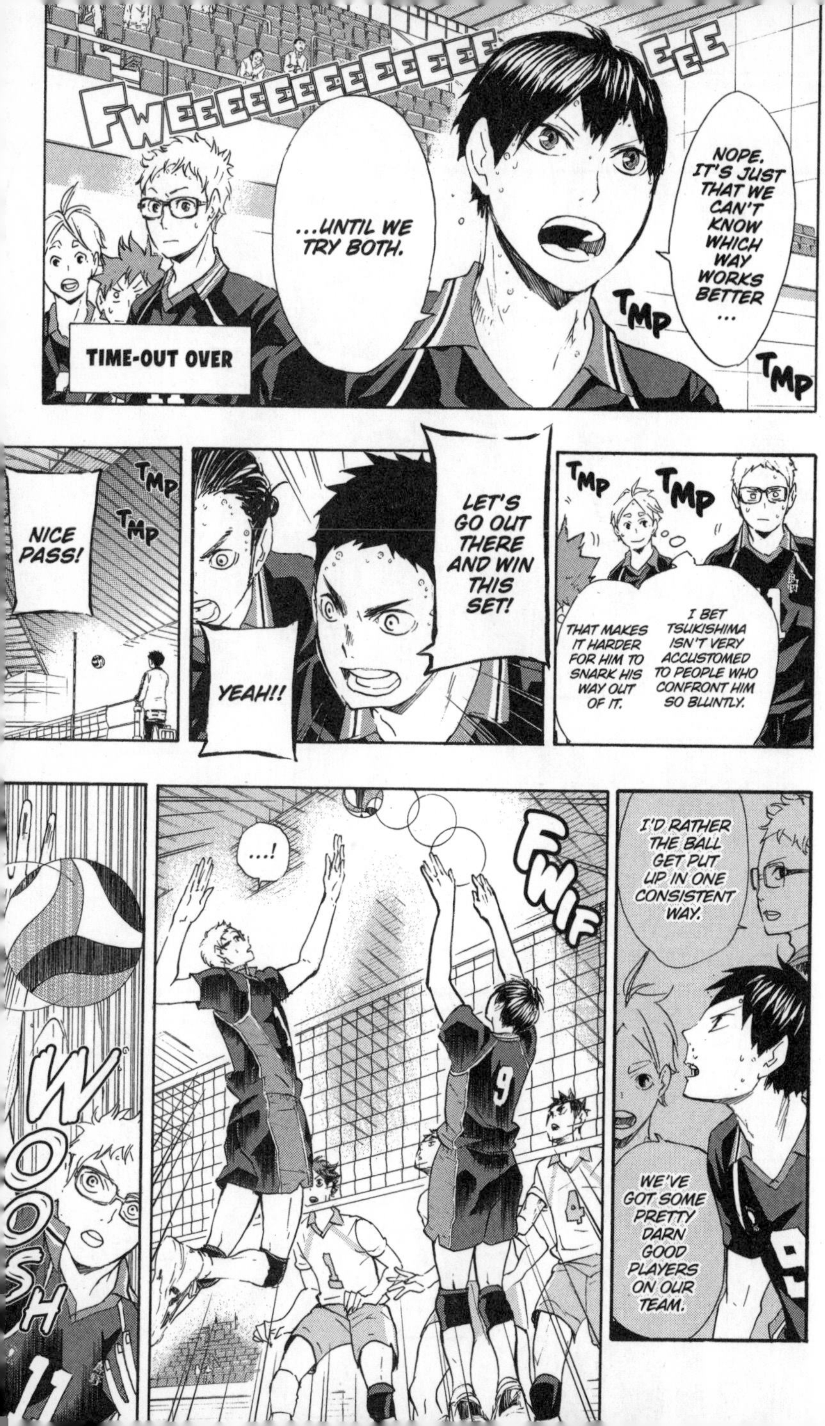
FWEEEEEEEEEEEEEE
EEE
NOPE. IT'S JUST THAT WE CAN'T KNOW WHICH WAY WORKS BETTER...
...UNTIL WE TRY BOTH.
TMP
TMP
TIME-OUT OVER
TMP
TMP
I BET TSUKISHIMA ISN'T VERY ACCUSTOMED TO PEOPLE WHO CONFRONT HIM SO BLUNTLY.
THAT MAKES IT HARDER FOR HIM TO SNARK HIS WAY OUT OF IT.
LET'S GO OUT THERE AND WIN THIS SET!
YEAH!!
TMP
TMP
NICE PASS!
I'D RATHER THE BALL GET PUT UP IN ONE CONSISTENT WAY.
WE'VE GOT SOME PRETTY DARN GOOD PLAYERS ON OUR TEAM.
FWIF
...!
WOOSH

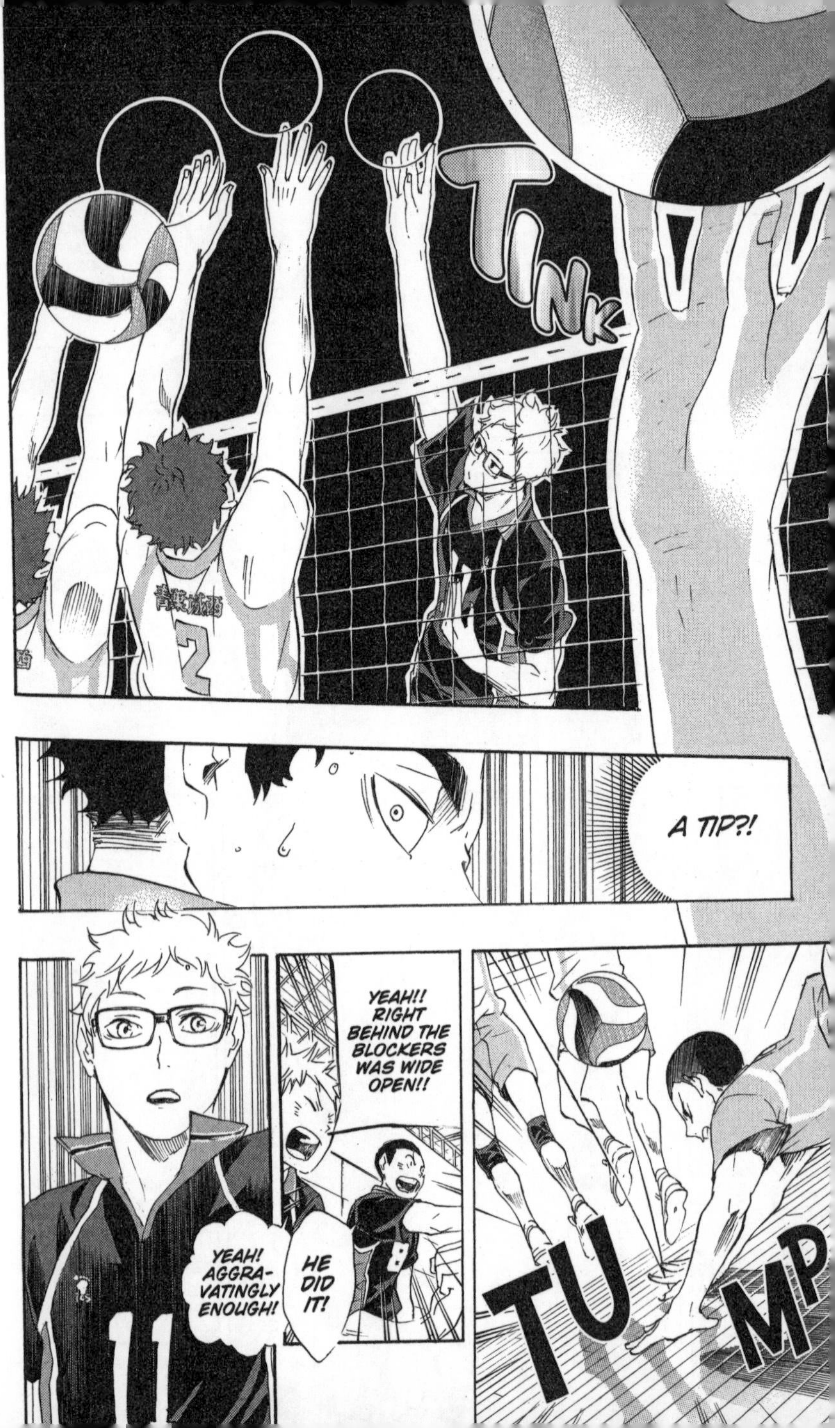
TINK
A TIP?!
TUMP
YEAH!! RIGHT BEHIND THE BLOCKERS WAS WIDE OPEN!!
HE DID IT!
YEAH! AGGRAVATINGLY ENOUGH!

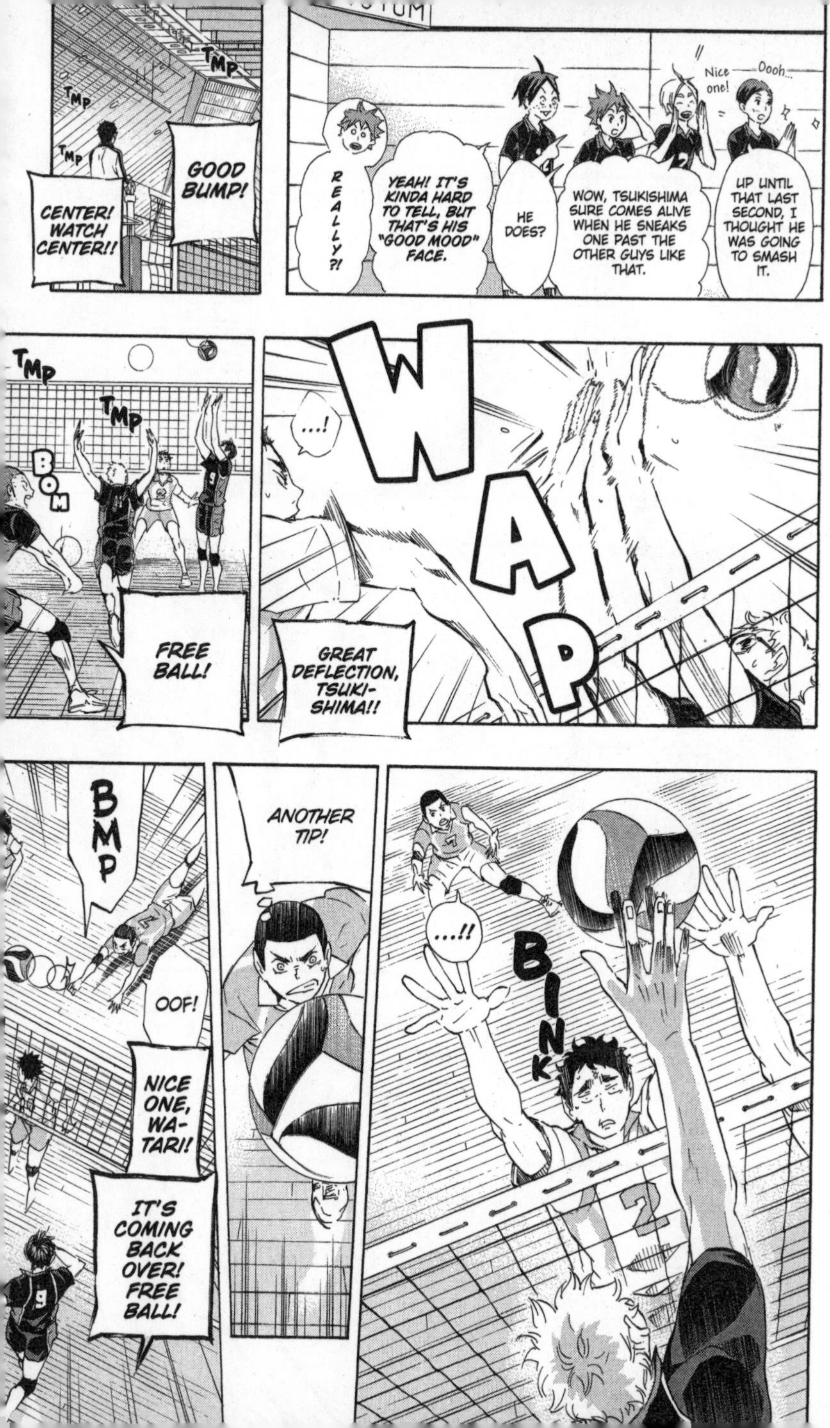
Nice one!
Oooh...
UP UNTIL THAT LAST SECOND, I THOUGHT HE WAS GOING TO SMASH IT.
WOW, TSUKISHIMA SURE COMES ALIVE WHEN HE SNEAKS ONE PAST THE OTHER GUYS LIKE THAT.
HE DOES?
YEAH! IT'S KINDA HARD TO TELL, BUT THAT'S HIS "GOOD MOOD" FACE.
REALLY?!
TMP
TMP
GOOD BUMP!
TMP
CENTER! WATCH CENTER!!
WAP
...!
GREAT DEFLECTION, TSUKI-SHIMA!!
TMP
TMP
BOM
FREE BALL!
...!!
BINK
ANOTHER TIP!
BMP
OOF!
NICE ONE, WA-TARI!
IT'S COMING BACK OVER! FREE BALL!

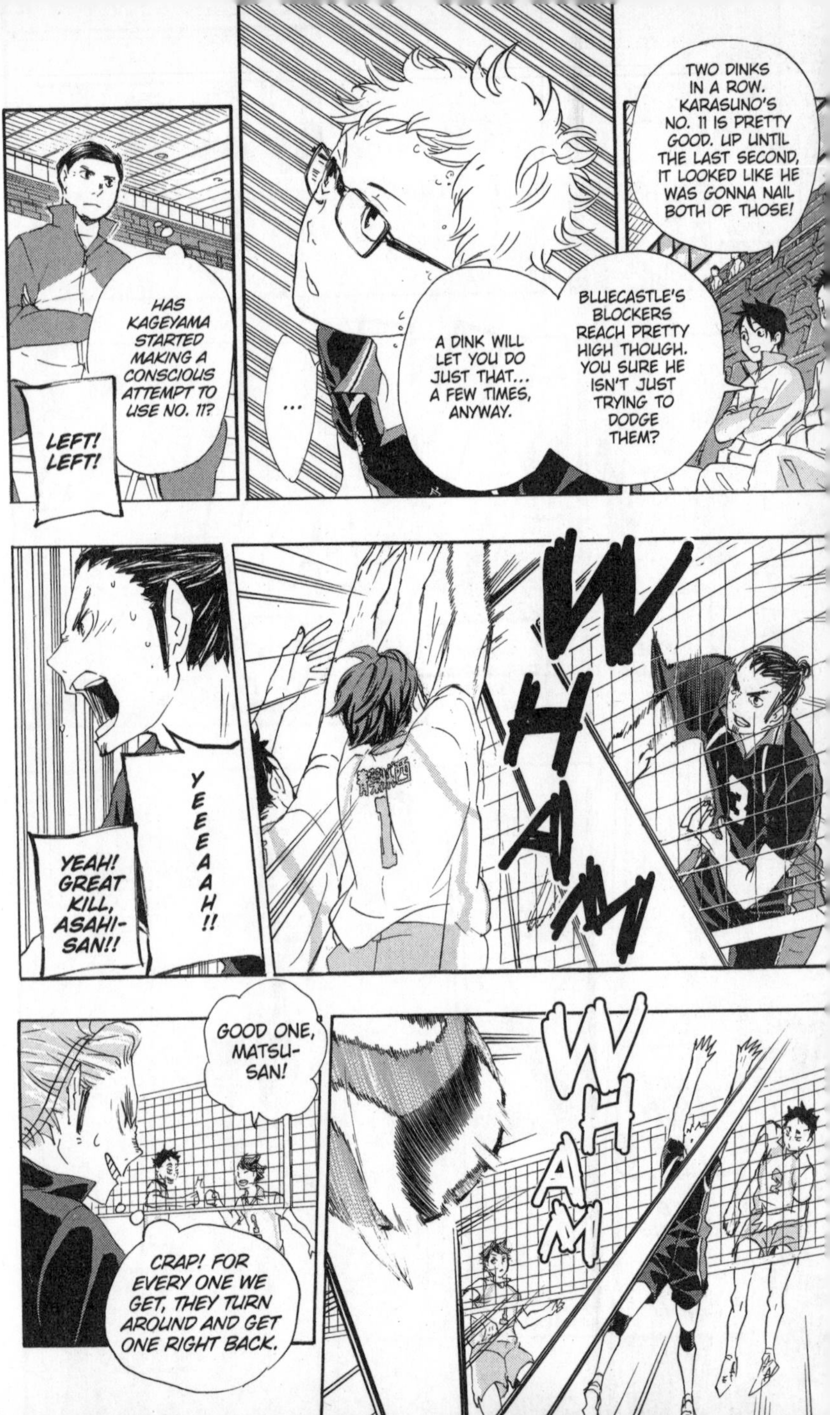
TWO DINKS IN A ROW. KARASUNO'S NO. 11 IS PRETTY GOOD. UP UNTIL THE LAST SECOND, IT LOOKED LIKE HE WAS GONNA NAIL BOTH OF THOSE!
BLUECASTLE'S BLOCKERS REACH PRETTY HIGH THOUGH. YOU SURE HE ISN'T JUST TRYING TO DODGE THEM?
A DINK WILL LET YOU DO JUST THAT... A FEW TIMES, ANYWAY.
...
HAS KAGEYAMA STARTED MAKING A CONSCIOUS ATTEMPT TO USE NO. 11?
LEFT! LEFT!
WHAM
YEEEAAAH!!
YEAH! GREAT KILL, ASAHI-SAN!!
WHAM
GOOD ONE, MATSU-SAN!
CRAP! FOR EVERY ONE WE GET, THEY TURN AROUND AND GET ONE RIGHT BACK.

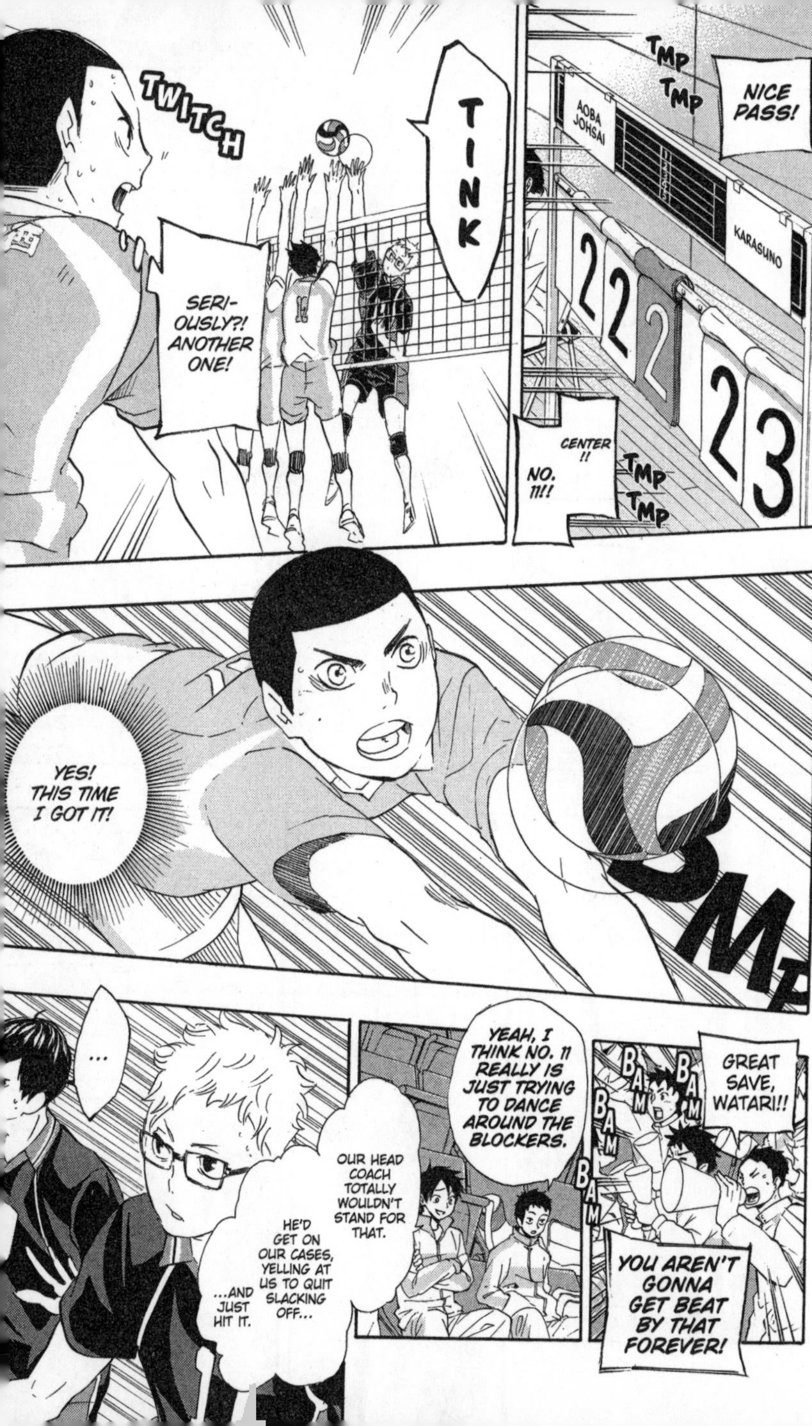
TMP
TMP
NICE PASS!
AOBA JOHSAI
KARASUNO
22
23
CENTER!!
NO. 11!!
TMP
TMP
TINK
TWITCH
SERI-OUSLY?! ANOTHER ONE!
YES! THIS TIME I GOT IT!
SMP
GREAT SAVE, WATARI!!
BAM
BAM
BAM
BAM
BAM
YOU AREN'T GONNA GET BEAT BY THAT FOREVER!
YEAH, I THINK NO. 11 REALLY IS JUST TRYING TO DANCE AROUND THE BLOCKERS.
...
OUR HEAD COACH TOTALLY WOULDN'T STAND FOR THAT.
HE'D GET ON OUR CASES, YELLING AT US TO QUIT SLACKING OFF...
...AND JUST HIT IT.

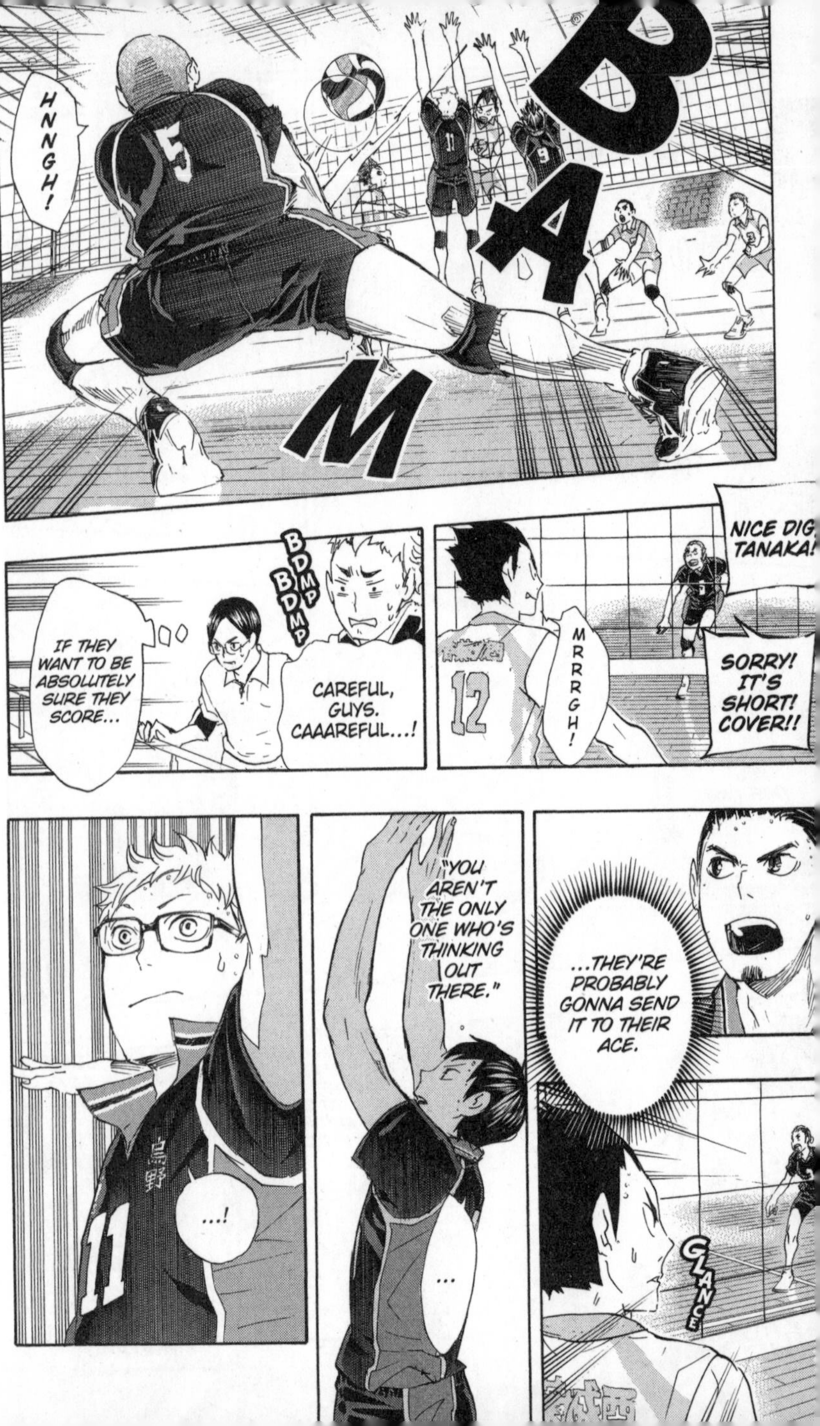
HNNNGH!
BAM
NICE DIG TANAKA!
SORRY! IT'S SHORT! COVER!!
MRRRGH!
BDMP BDMP
CAREFUL, GUYS. CAAAREFUL...!
IF THEY WANT TO BE ABSOLUTELY SURE THEY SCORE...
...THEY'RE PROBABLY GONNA SEND IT TO THEIR ACE.
GLANCE
"YOU AREN'T THE ONLY ONE WHO'S THINKING OUT THERE."
...
...!

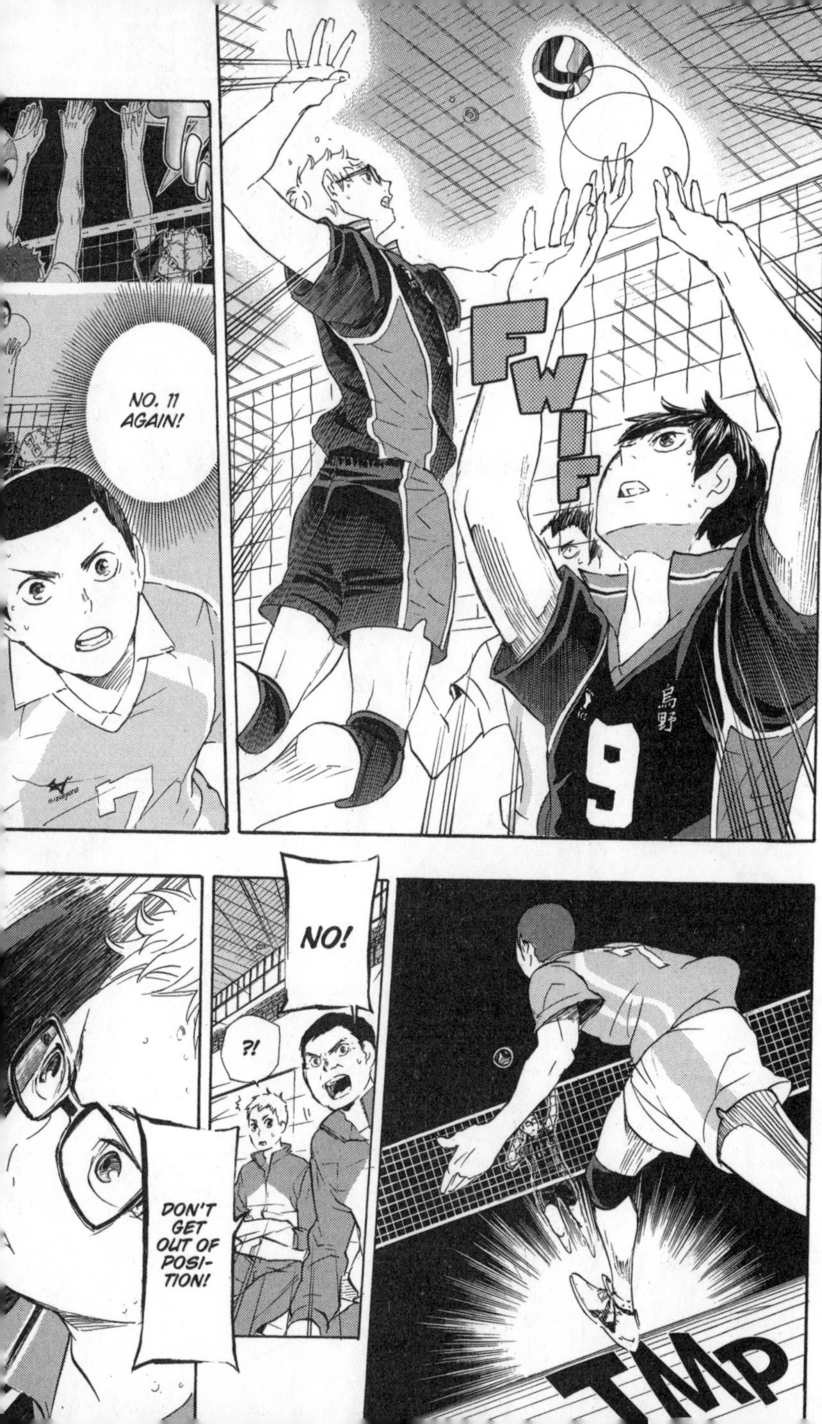
FWIF
NO. 11 AGAIN!
TMP
NO!
?!
DON'T GET OUT OF POSI-TION!

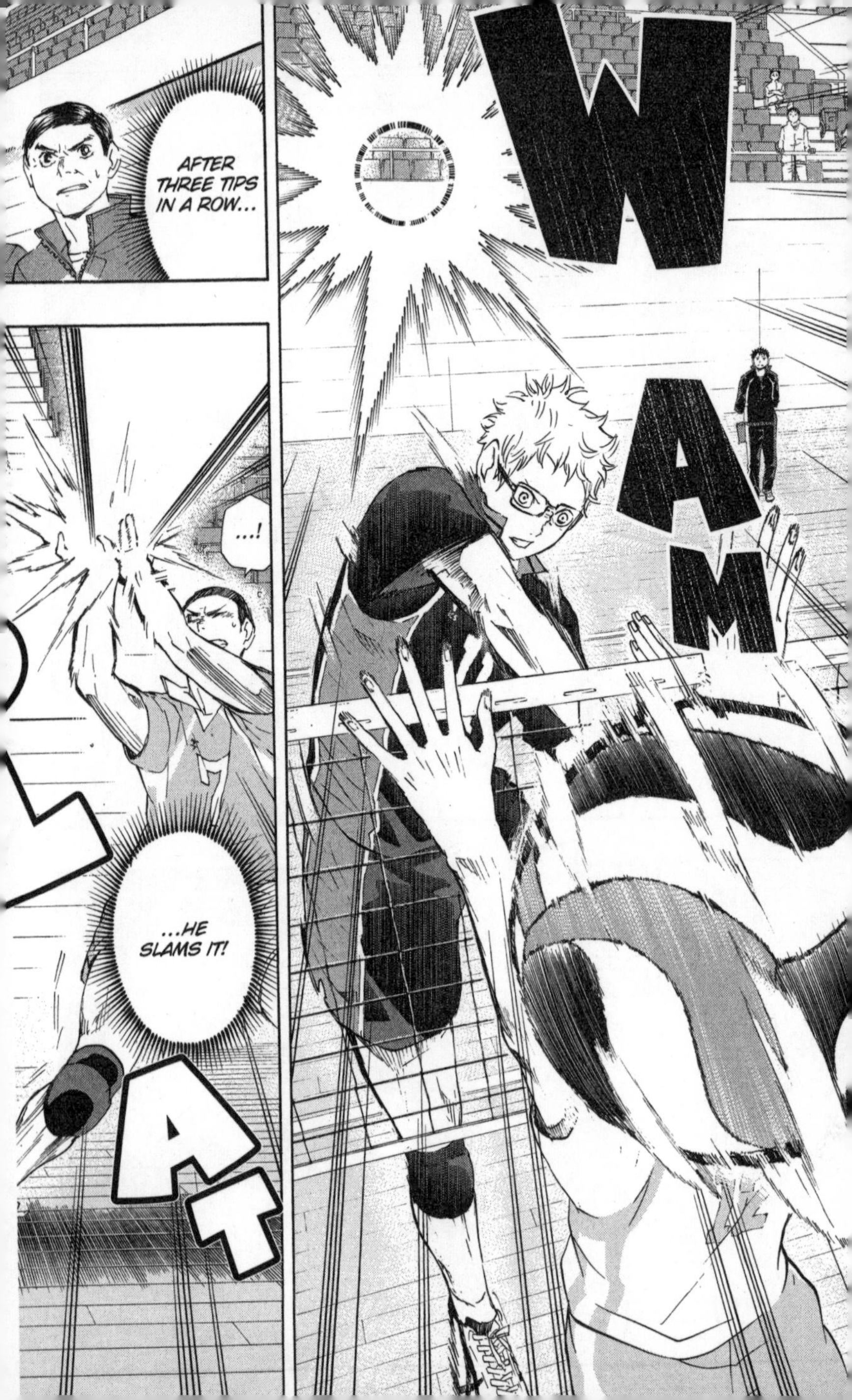
AFTER THREE TIPS IN A ROW...
...!
...HE SLAMS IT!

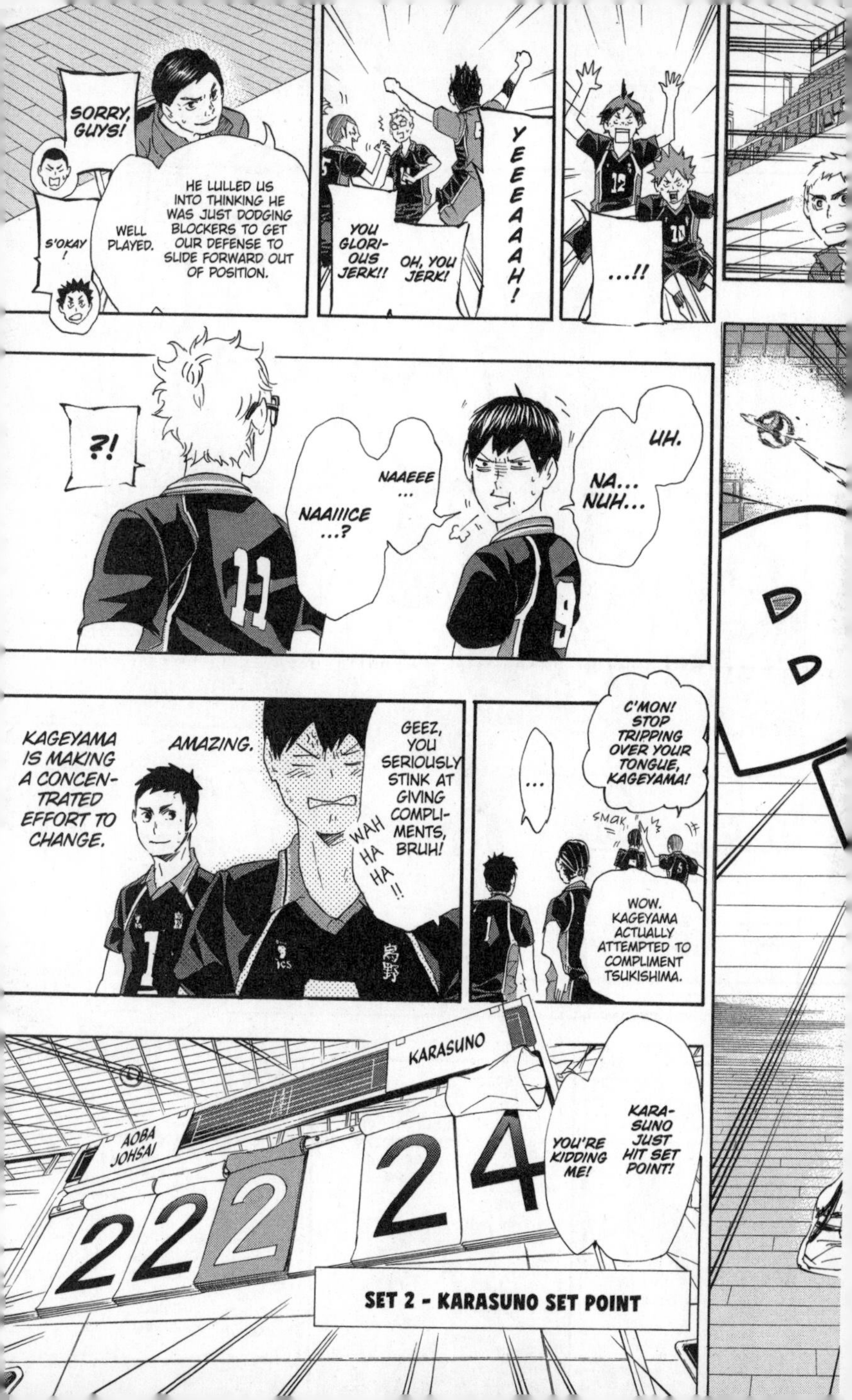
D
D
...!!
YEEEAAAAH!
OH, YOU JERK!
YOU GLORIOUS JERK!!
SORRY, GUYS!
HE LULLED US INTO THINKING HE WAS JUST DODGING BLOCKERS TO GET OUR DEFENSE TO SLIDE FORWARD OUT OF POSITION.
WELL PLAYED.
S'OKAY!
UH.
NA... NUH...
NAAEEE...
NAAIIICE...?
?!
C'MON! STOP TRIPPING OVER YOUR TONGUE, KAGEYAMA!
SMAK
...
WOW. KAGEYAMA ACTUALLY ATTEMPTED TO COMPLIMENT TSUKISHIMA.
GEEZ, YOU SERIOUSLY STINK AT GIVING COMPLIMENTS, BRUH!
WAH HA HA HA!!
AMAZING.
KAGEYAMA IS MAKING A CONCENTRATED EFFORT TO CHANGE.
KARASUNO JUST HIT SET POINT!
YOU'RE KIDDING ME!
KARASUNO
AOBA JOHSAI
22
24
SET 2 - KARASUNO SET POINT

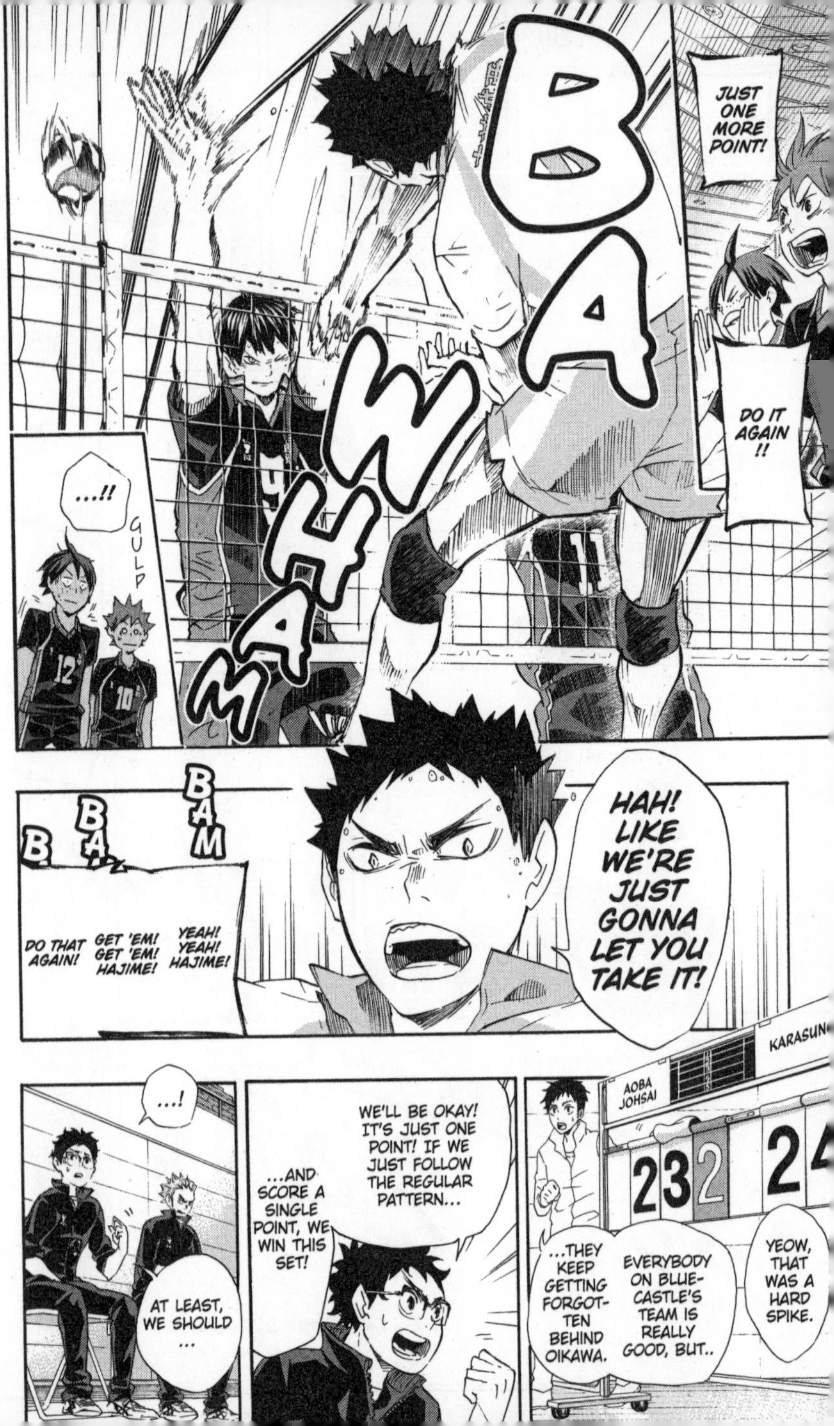
JUST ONE MORE POINT!
BAWHAM
DO IT AGAIN !!
...!!
GULP
HAH! LIKE WE'RE JUST GONNA LET YOU TAKE IT!
B BA BAM
YEAH! YEAH! HAJIME!
GET 'EM! GET 'EM! HAJIME!
DO THAT AGAIN!
KARASUN
AOBA JOHSAI
23
2
24
YEOW, THAT WAS A HARD SPIKE.
EVERYBODY ON BLUE-CASTLE'S TEAM IS REALLY GOOD, BUT..
...THEY KEEP GETTING FORGOT-TEN BEHIND OIKAWA.
WE'LL BE OKAY! IT'S JUST ONE POINT! IF WE JUST FOLLOW THE REGULAR PATTERN...
...AND SCORE A SINGLE POINT, WE WIN THIS SET!
...!
AT LEAST, WE SHOULD ...

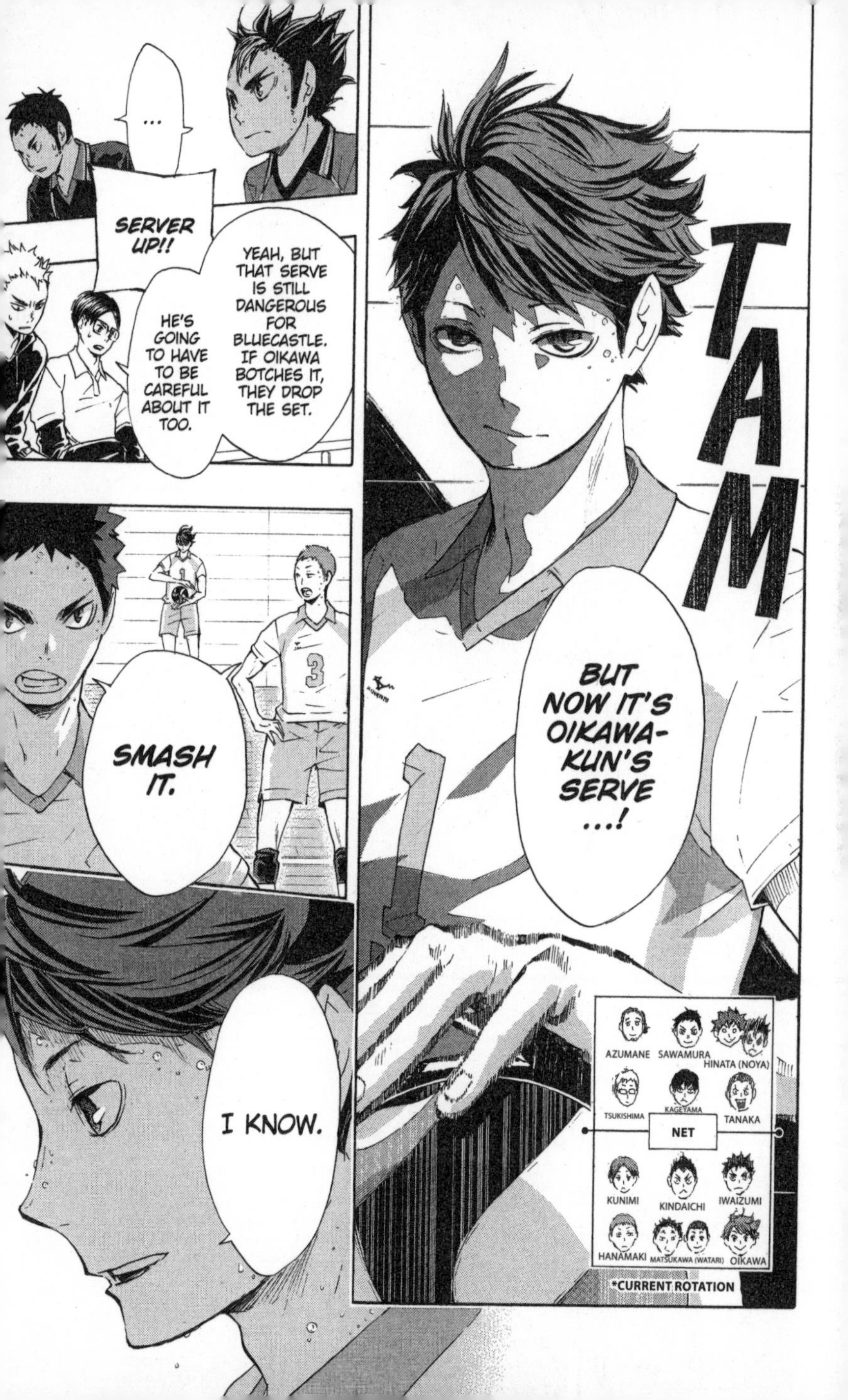
TAM
BUT NOW IT'S OIKAWA-KUN'S SERVE ...!
AZUMANE
SAWAMURA
HINATA (NOYA)
TSUKISHIMA
KAGEYAMA
TANAKA
NET
KUNIMI
KINDAICHI
IWAIZUMI
HANAMAKI
MATSUKAWA (WATARI)
OIKAWA
*CURRENT ROTATION
...
SERVER UP!!
YEAH, BUT THAT SERVE IS STILL DANGEROUS FOR BLUECASTLE. IF OIKAWA BOTCHES IT, THEY DROP THE SET.
HE'S GOING TO HAVE TO BE CAREFUL ABOUT IT TOO.
SMASH IT.
I KNOW.

EARLIER IN THE CHAPTER, COACH UKAI DESCRIBES TSUKISHIMA'S HITTING OF KAGEYAMA'S SETS AS FEELING "IZUI" IN JAPANESE AND "UNCOMFORTABLE" IN ENGLISH. BOTH MYSELF AND MY EDITOR THOUGHT THE WORD *IZUI* WAS ONE THAT MOST JAPANESE PEOPLE WOULD UNDERSTAND. APPARENTLY IT'S A DIALECT WORD NOT WELL-KNOWN OUTSIDE OF THE NORTH.

IN ENGLISH, IT TRANSLATES TO SOMETHING LIKE "AWKWARD," "SLIGHTLY UNCOMFORTABLE" OR "NOT QUITE RIGHT."

EUGH. IZUI...

RUMPLE

*AN EXAMPLE OF THE WORD *IZUI*.

SAY THAT YOU PUT A COAT ON OVER A T-SHIRT, AND ONE OF THE T-SHIRT'S SLEEVES BUNCHES UP INTO A WAD INSIDE THE COAT SLEEVE. YOU WOULD SAY THAT SLIGHTLY UNCOMFORTABLE, AWKWARD FEELING OF THE BUNCHED-UP SLEEVE IS *IZUI*.

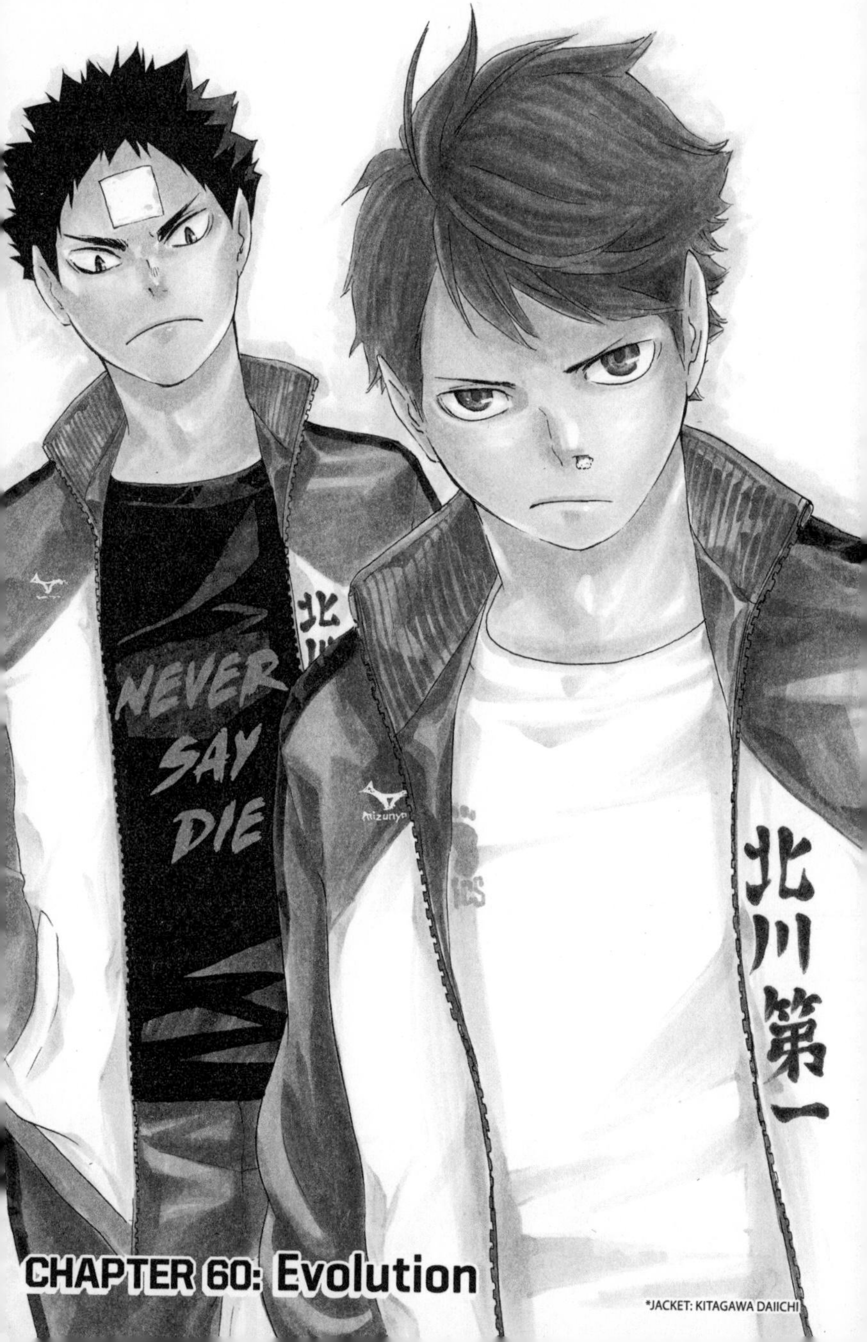
NEVER SAY DIE
北川第一

CHAPTER 60: Evolution

*JACKET: KITAGAWA DAIICHI

HAIKYU!!

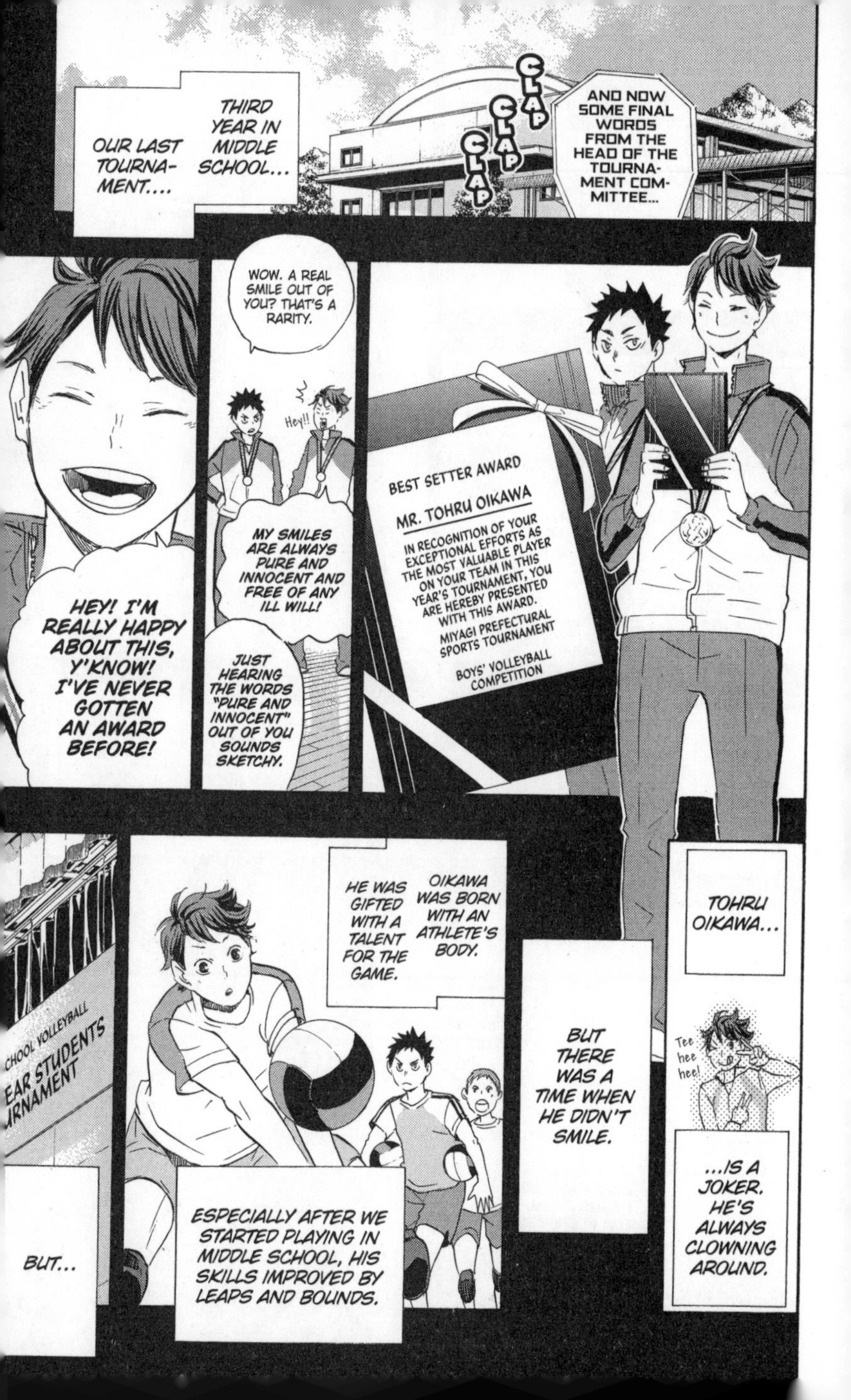
AND NOW SOME FINAL WORDS FROM THE HEAD OF THE TOURNAMENT COMMITTEE...
CLAP
CLAP
CLAP
THIRD YEAR IN MIDDLE SCHOOL...
OUR LAST TOURNAMENT....
BEST SETTER AWARD
MR. TOHRU OIKAWA
IN RECOGNITION OF YOUR EXCEPTIONAL EFFORTS AS THE MOST VALUABLE PLAYER ON YOUR TEAM IN THIS YEAR'S TOURNAMENT, YOU ARE HEREBY PRESENTED WITH THIS AWARD.
MIYAGI PREFECTURAL SPORTS TOURNAMENT
BOYS' VOLLEYBALL COMPETITION
WOW. A REAL SMILE OUT OF YOU? THAT'S A RARITY.
Hey!!
MY SMILES ARE ALWAYS PURE AND INNOCENT AND FREE OF ANY ILL WILL!
JUST HEARING THE WORDS "PURE AND INNOCENT" OUT OF YOU SOUNDS SKETCHY.
HEY! I'M REALLY HAPPY ABOUT THIS, Y'KNOW! I'VE NEVER GOTTEN AN AWARD BEFORE!
TOHRU OIKAWA...
Tee hee hee!
...IS A JOKER. HE'S ALWAYS CLOWNING AROUND.
BUT THERE WAS A TIME WHEN HE DIDN'T SMILE.
OIKAWA WAS BORN WITH AN ATHLETE'S BODY.
HE WAS GIFTED WITH A TALENT FOR THE GAME.
ESPECIALLY AFTER WE STARTED PLAYING IN MIDDLE SCHOOL, HIS SKILLS IMPROVED BY LEAPS AND BOUNDS.
CHOOL VOLLEYBALL
EAR STUDENTS
RNAMENT
BUT...

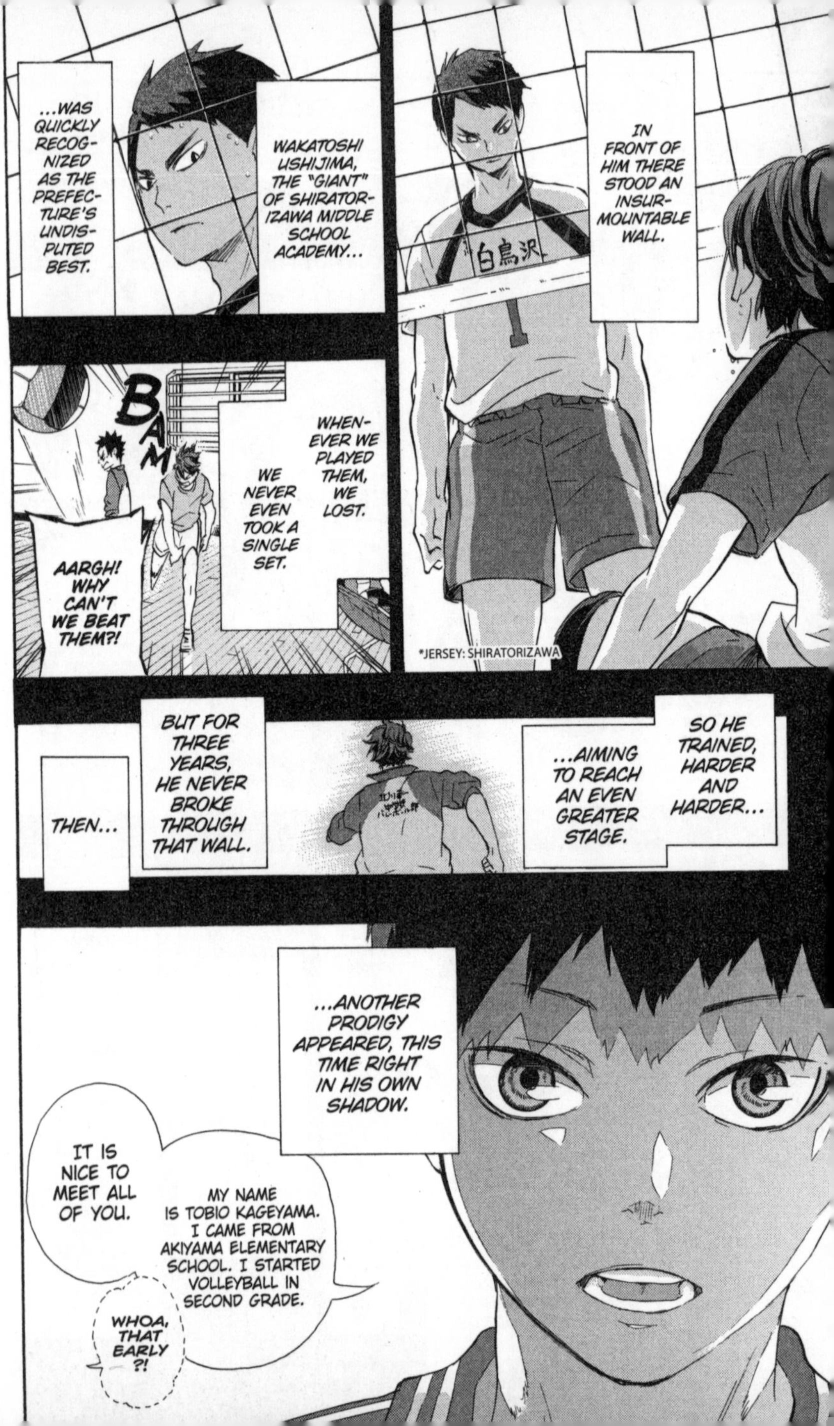
IN FRONT OF HIM THERE STOOD AN INSURMOUNTABLE WALL.
*JERSEY: SHIRATORIZAWA
WAKATOSHI USHIJIMA, THE "GIANT" OF SHIRATORIZAWA MIDDLE SCHOOL ACADEMY...
...WAS QUICKLY RECOGNIZED AS THE PREFECTURE'S UNDISPUTED BEST.
WHENEVER WE PLAYED THEM, WE LOST.
WE NEVER EVEN TOOK A SINGLE SET.
BAM
AARGH! WHY CAN'T WE BEAT THEM?!
SO HE TRAINED, HARDER AND HARDER...
...AIMING TO REACH AN EVEN GREATER STAGE.
BUT FOR THREE YEARS, HE NEVER BROKE THROUGH THAT WALL.
THEN...
...ANOTHER PRODIGY APPEARED, THIS TIME RIGHT IN HIS OWN SHADOW.
IT IS NICE TO MEET ALL OF YOU.
MY NAME IS TOBIO KAGEYAMA. I CAME FROM AKIYAMA ELEMENTARY SCHOOL. I STARTED VOLLEYBALL IN SECOND GRADE.
WHOA, THAT EARLY?!

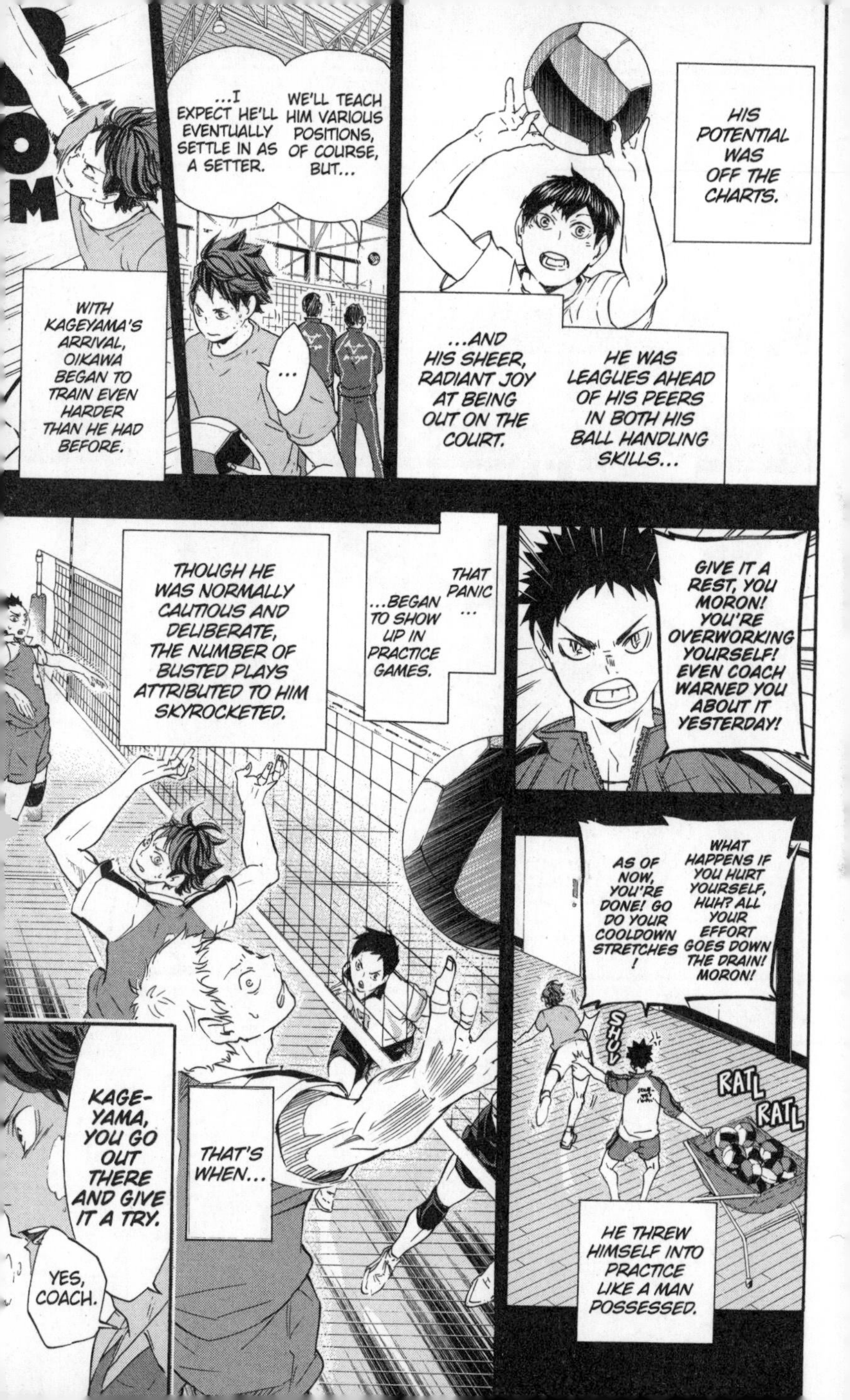
HIS POTENTIAL WAS OFF THE CHARTS.
HE WAS LEAGUES AHEAD OF HIS PEERS IN BOTH HIS BALL HANDLING SKILLS...
...AND HIS SHEER, RADIANT JOY AT BEING OUT ON THE COURT.
WE'LL TEACH HIM VARIOUS POSITIONS, OF COURSE, BUT...
...I EXPECT HE'LL EVENTUALLY SETTLE IN AS A SETTER.
...
WITH KAGEYAMA'S ARRIVAL, OIKAWA BEGAN TO TRAIN EVEN HARDER THAN HE HAD BEFORE.
GIVE IT A REST, YOU MORON! YOU'RE OVERWORKING YOURSELF! EVEN COACH WARNED YOU ABOUT IT YESTERDAY!
WHAT HAPPENS IF YOU HURT YOURSELF, HUH? ALL YOUR EFFORT GOES DOWN THE DRAIN! MORON!
AS OF NOW, YOU'RE DONE! GO DO YOUR COOLDOWN STRETCHES!
SHUV
RATTL
RATTL
HE THREW HIMSELF INTO PRACTICE LIKE A MAN POSSESSED.
THAT PANIC...
...BEGAN TO SHOW UP IN PRACTICE GAMES.
THOUGH HE WAS NORMALLY CAUTIOUS AND DELIBERATE, THE NUMBER OF BUSTED PLAYS ATTRIBUTED TO HIM SKYROCKETED.
THAT'S WHEN...
KAGEYAMA, YOU GO OUT THERE AND GIVE IT A TRY.
YES, COACH.

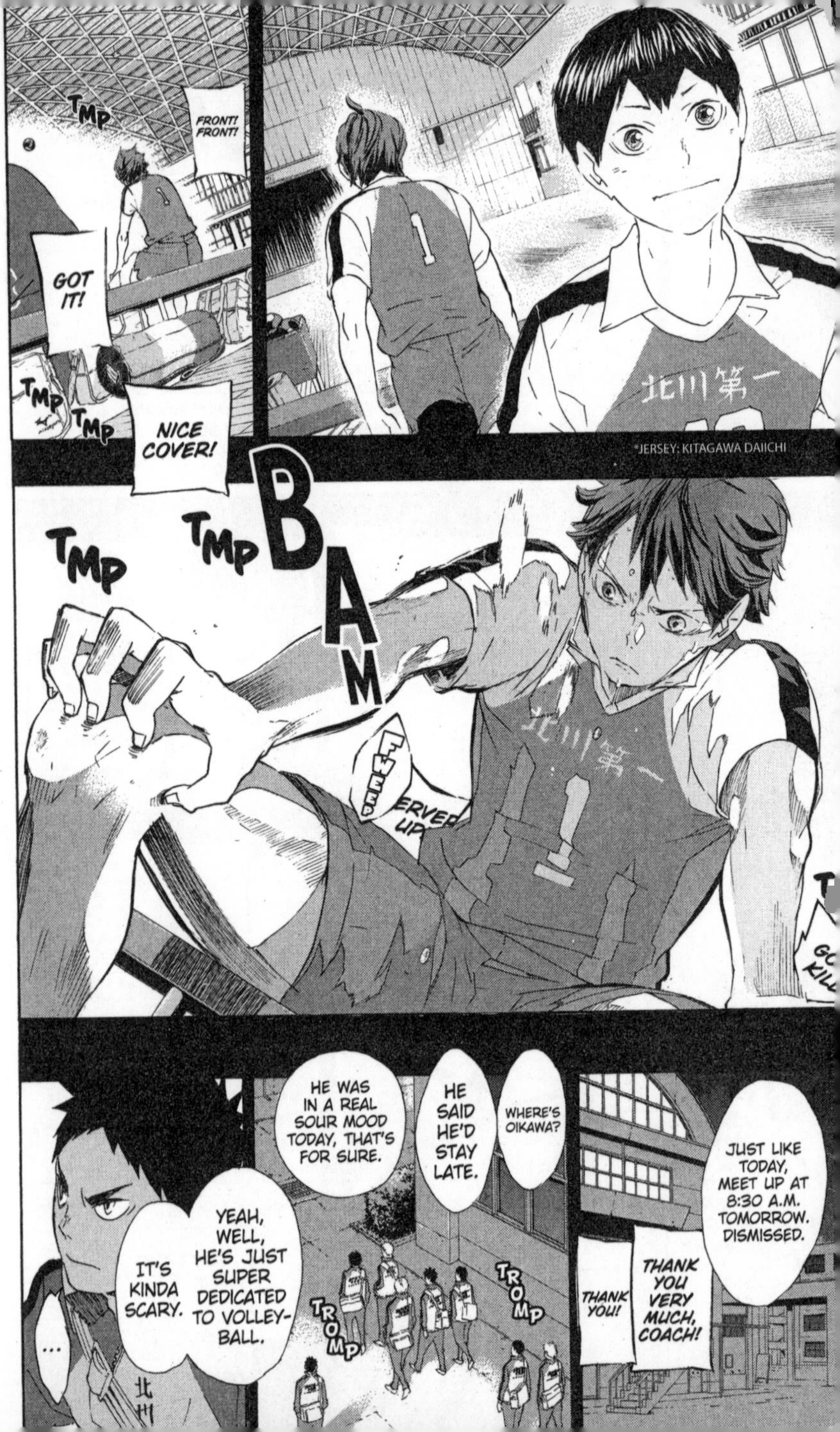

*JERSEY: KITAGAWA DAIICHI
TMP
FRONT! FRONT!
GOT IT!
TMP
TMP
NICE COVER!
TMP
TMP
BAM
FWEEP
WHERE'S OIKAWA?
HE SAID HE'D STAY LATE.
HE WAS IN A REAL SOUR MOOD TODAY, THAT'S FOR SURE.
JUST LIKE TODAY, MEET UP AT 8:30 A.M. TOMORROW. DISMISSED.
THANK YOU VERY MUCH, COACH!
THANK YOU!
TROMP
TROMP
YEAH, WELL, HE'S JUST SUPER DEDICATED TO VOLLEY-BALL.
IT'S KINDA SCARY.
...

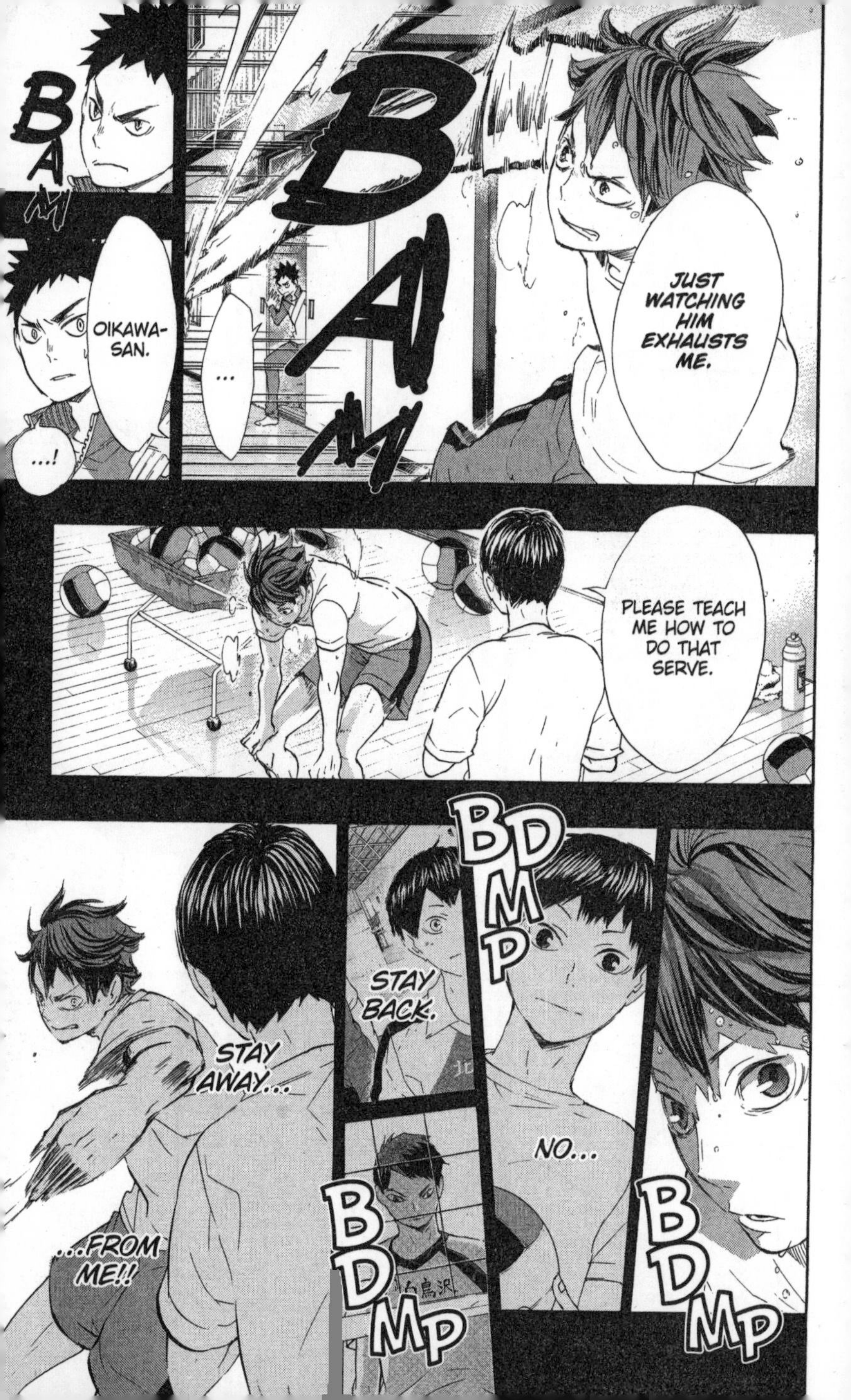
JUST WATCHING HIM EXHAUSTS ME.
BAM
...
BAM
OIKAWA-SAN.
...!
PLEASE TEACH ME HOW TO DO THAT SERVE.
BDMP
BDMP
NO...
STAY BACK.
BDMP
STAY AWAY...
...FROM ME!!

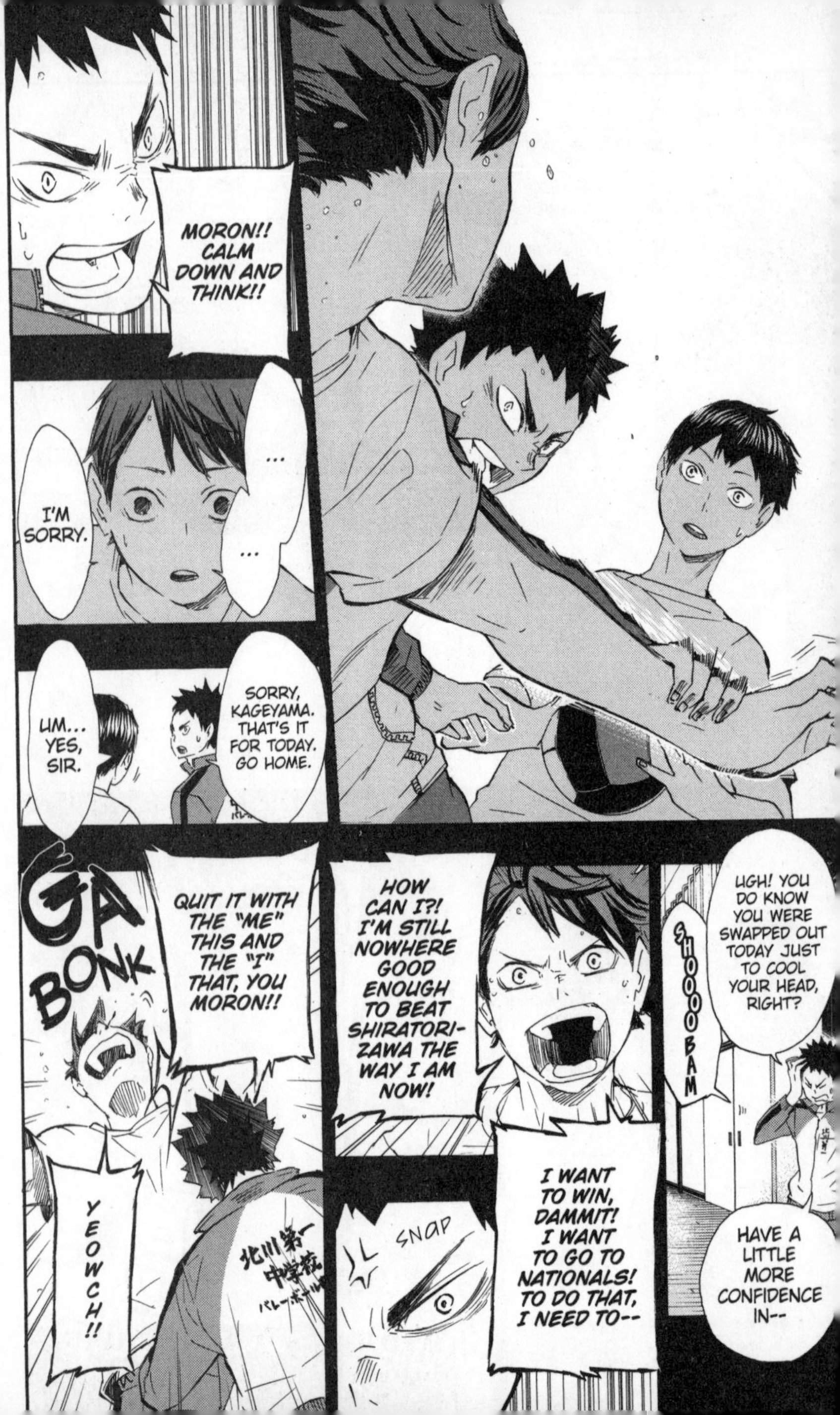
MORON!! CALM DOWN AND THINK!!
...
...
I'M SORRY.
SORRY, KAGEYAMA. THAT'S IT FOR TODAY. GO HOME.
UM... YES, SIR.
UGH! YOU DO KNOW YOU WERE SWAPPED OUT TODAY JUST TO COOL YOUR HEAD, RIGHT?
SHOOOO BAM
HAVE A LITTLE MORE CONFIDENCE IN--
HOW CAN I?! I'M STILL NOWHERE GOOD ENOUGH TO BEAT SHIRATORI-ZAWA THE WAY I AM NOW!
I WANT TO WIN, DAMMIT! I WANT TO GO TO NATIONALS! TO DO THAT, I NEED TO--
SNAP
GA
BONK
QUIT IT WITH THE "ME" THIS AND THE "I" THAT, YOU MORON!!
YEOWCH!!
北川第一中学校

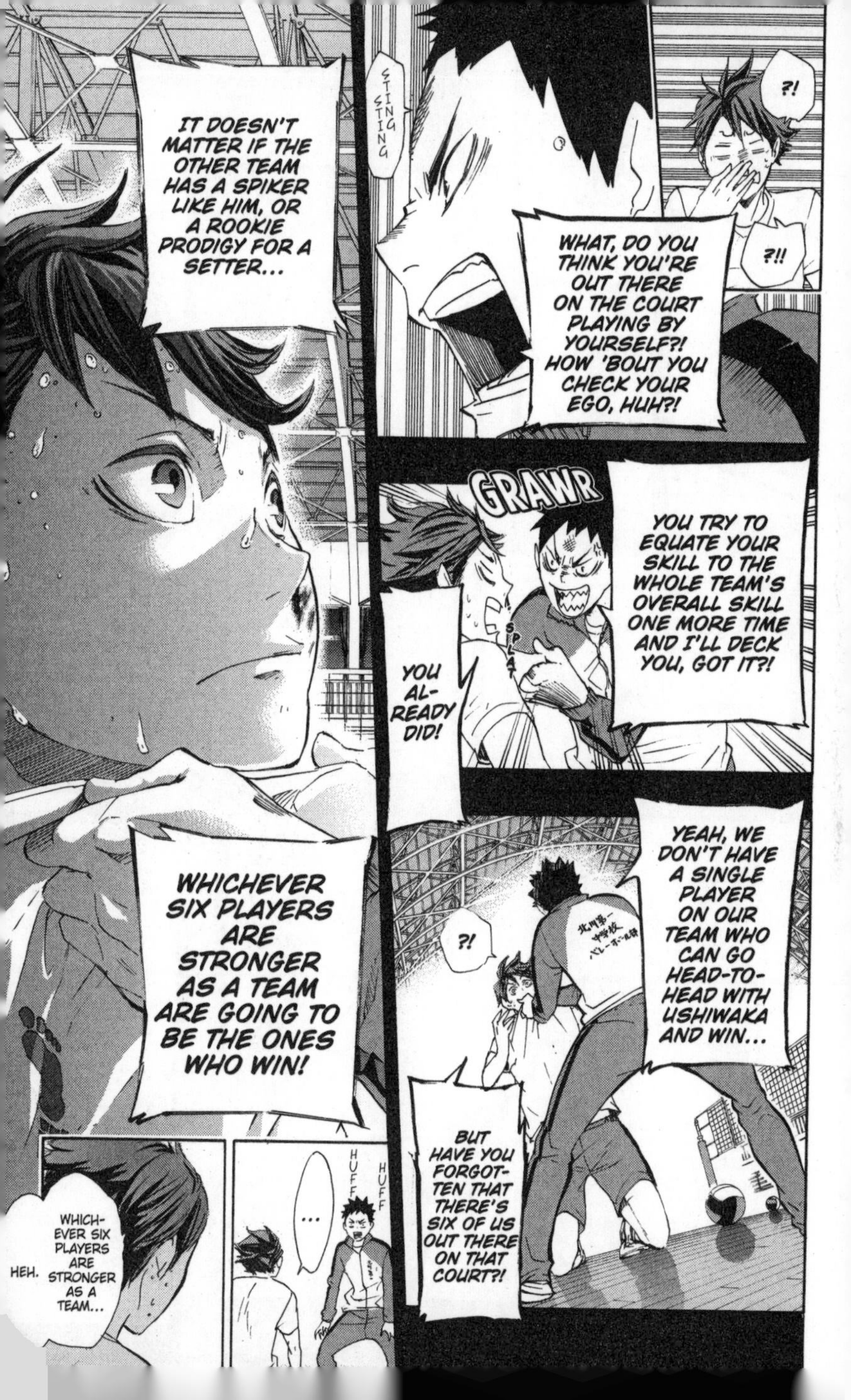
?!
STING STING
?!!
WHAT, DO YOU THINK YOU'RE OUT THERE ON THE COURT PLAYING BY YOURSELF?! HOW 'BOUT YOU CHECK YOUR EGO, HUH?!
GRAWR
YOU TRY TO EQUATE YOUR SKILL TO THE WHOLE TEAM'S OVERALL SKILL ONE MORE TIME AND I'LL DECK YOU, GOT IT?!
SPLAT
YOU AL-READY DID!
YEAH, WE DON'T HAVE A SINGLE PLAYER ON OUR TEAM WHO CAN GO HEAD-TO-HEAD WITH USHIWAKA AND WIN...
?!
BUT HAVE YOU FORGOT-TEN THAT THERE'S SIX OF US OUT THERE ON THAT COURT?!
IT DOESN'T MATTER IF THE OTHER TEAM HAS A SPIKER LIKE HIM, OR A ROOKIE PRODIGY FOR A SETTER...
WHICHEVER SIX PLAYERS ARE STRONGER AS A TEAM ARE GOING TO BE THE ONES WHO WIN!
HUFF HUFF
...
HEH.
WHICH-EVER SIX PLAYERS ARE STRONGER AS A TEAM...

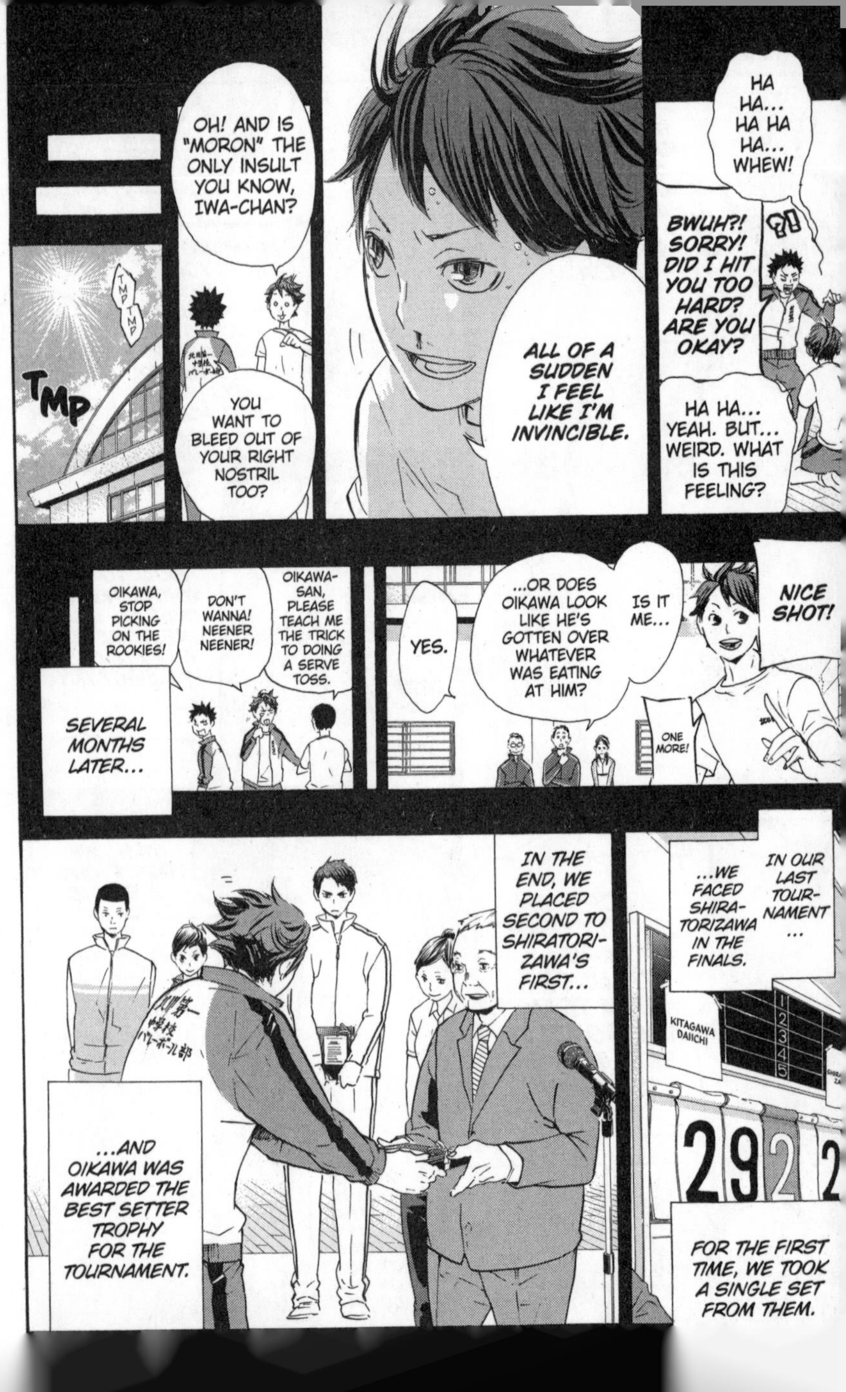
HA HA... HA HA HA... WHEW!
BWUH?! SORRY! DID I HIT YOU TOO HARD? ARE YOU OKAY?
HA HA... YEAH. BUT... WEIRD. WHAT IS THIS FEELING?
ALL OF A SUDDEN I FEEL LIKE I'M INVINCIBLE.
OH! AND IS "MORON" THE ONLY INSULT YOU KNOW, IWA-CHAN?
TMP TMP
TMP
YOU WANT TO BLEED OUT OF YOUR RIGHT NOSTRIL TOO?
NICE SHOT!
ONE MORE!
IS IT ME...
...OR DOES OIKAWA LOOK LIKE HE'S GOTTEN OVER WHATEVER WAS EATING AT HIM?
YES.
OIKAWA-SAN, PLEASE TEACH ME THE TRICK TO DOING A SERVE TOSS.
DON'T WANNA! NEENER NEENER!
OIKAWA, STOP PICKING ON THE ROOKIES!
SEVERAL MONTHS LATER...
IN OUR LAST TOURNAMENT...
...WE FACED SHIRATORIZAWA IN THE FINALS.
KITAGAWA DAIICHI
FOR THE FIRST TIME, WE TOOK A SINGLE SET FROM THEM.
IN THE END, WE PLACED SECOND TO SHIRATORIZAWA'S FIRST...
...AND OIKAWA WAS AWARDED THE BEST SETTER TROPHY FOR THE TOURNAMENT.

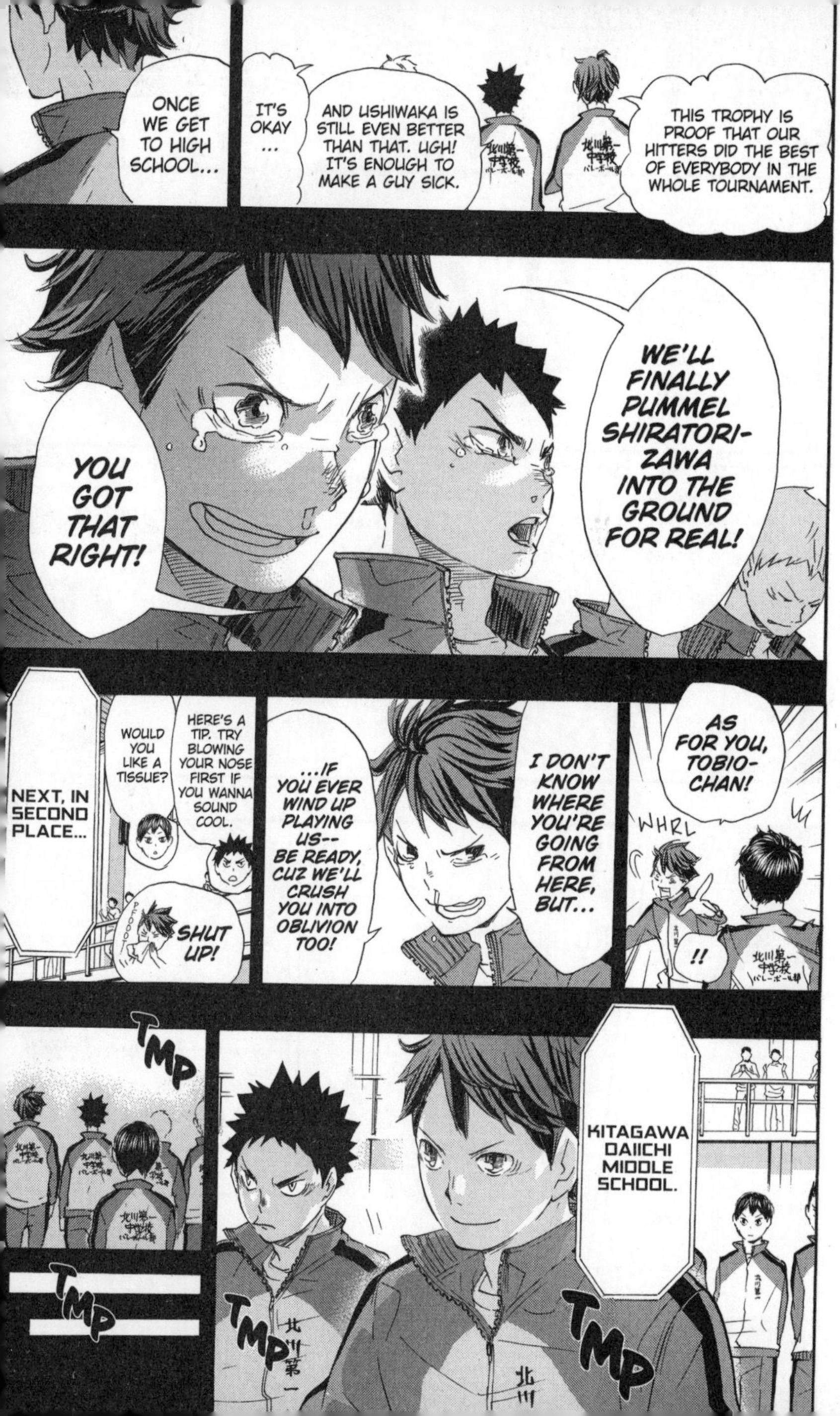
THIS TROPHY IS PROOF THAT OUR HITTERS DID THE BEST OF EVERYBODY IN THE WHOLE TOURNAMENT.
AND USHIWAKA IS STILL EVEN BETTER THAN THAT. UGH! IT'S ENOUGH TO MAKE A GUY SICK.
IT'S OKAY ...
ONCE WE GET TO HIGH SCHOOL...
WE'LL FINALLY PUMMEL SHIRATORI-ZAWA INTO THE GROUND FOR REAL!
YOU GOT THAT RIGHT!
AS FOR YOU, TOBIO-CHAN!
WHRL
!!
I DON'T KNOW WHERE YOU'RE GOING FROM HERE, BUT...
...IF YOU EVER WIND UP PLAYING US-- BE READY, CUZ WE'LL CRUSH YOU INTO OBLIVION TOO!
HERE'S A TIP. TRY BLOWING YOUR NOSE FIRST IF YOU WANNA SOUND COOL.
WOULD YOU LIKE A TISSUE?
PFOOOT
SHUT UP!
NEXT, IN SECOND PLACE...
KITAGAWA DAIICHI MIDDLE SCHOOL.
TMP
TMP
TMP
TMP

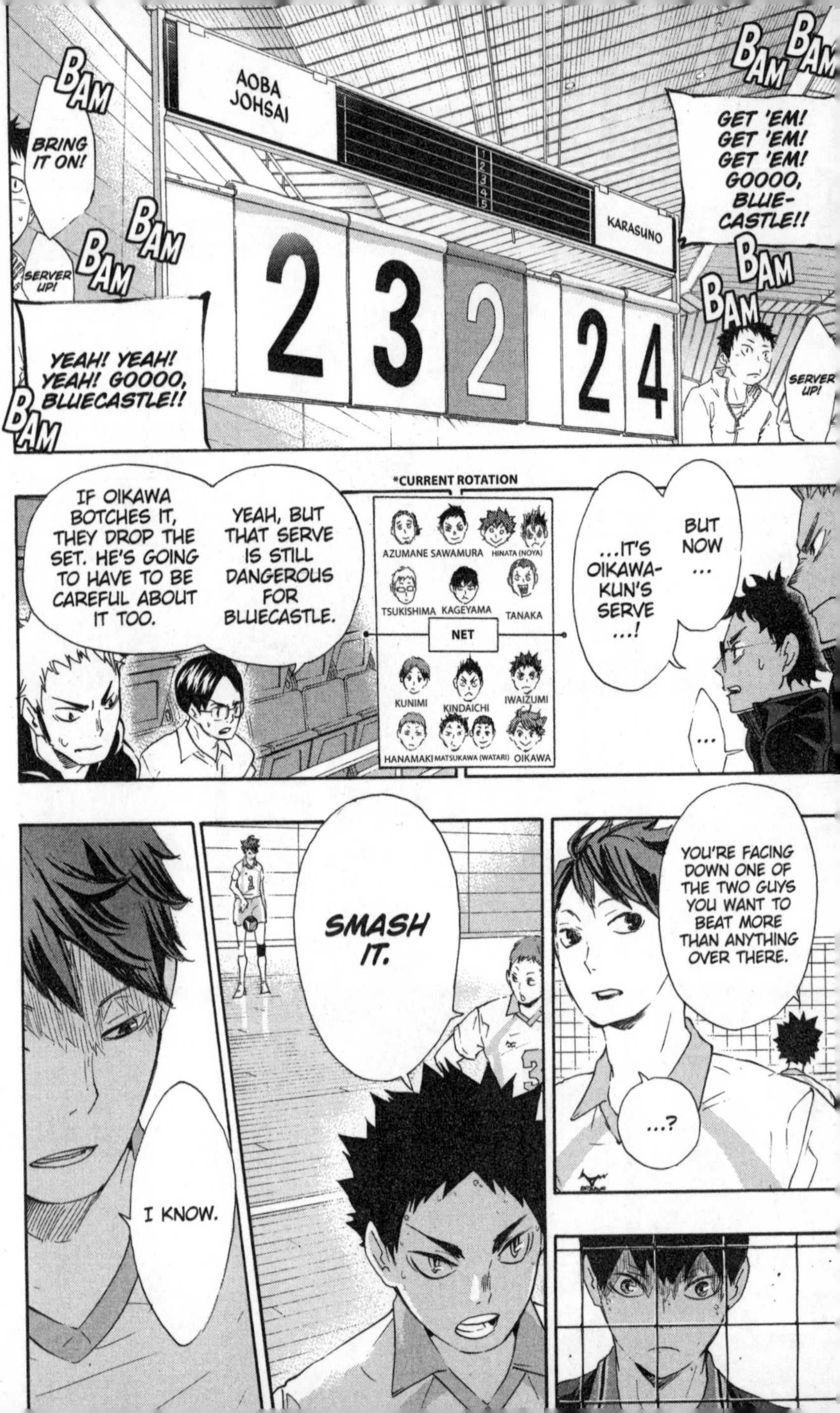
BAM BAM
GET 'EM! GET 'EM! GET 'EM! GOOOO, BLUE-CASTLE!!
BAM BAM
SERVER UP!
AOBA JOHSAI
KARASUNO
23 2 24
BAM
BRING IT ON!
BAM BAM
SERVER UP!
YEAH! YEAH! YEAH! GOOOO, BLUECASTLE!!
BAM
BUT NOW...
...IT'S OIKAWA-KUN'S SERVE...!
...
*CURRENT ROTATION
AZUMANE SAWAMURA HINATA (NOYA)
TSUKISHIMA KAGEYAMA TANAKA
NET
KUNIMI KINDAICHI IWAIZUMI
HANAMAKI MATSUKAWA (WATARI) OIKAWA
IF OIKAWA BOTCHES IT, THEY DROP THE SET. HE'S GOING TO HAVE TO BE CAREFUL ABOUT IT TOO.
YEAH, BUT THAT SERVE IS STILL DANGEROUS FOR BLUECASTLE.
YOU'RE FACING DOWN ONE OF THE TWO GUYS YOU WANT TO BEAT MORE THAN ANYTHING OVER THERE.
...?
SMASH IT.
I KNOW.

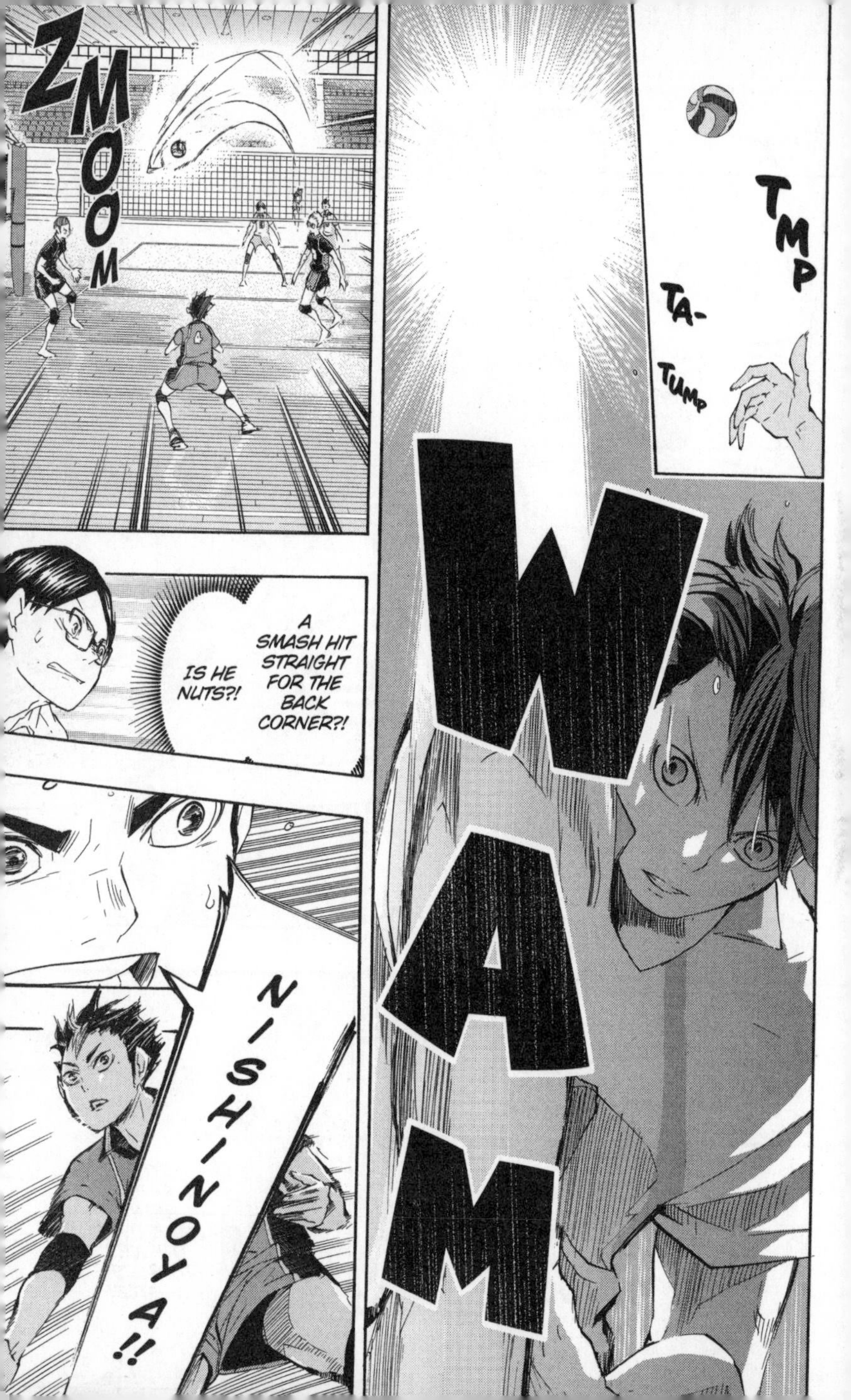
TMP
TA-
TUMP
WAM
ZMOOM
A SMASH HIT STRAIGHT FOR THE BACK CORNER?!
IS HE NUTS?!
NISHINOYA!!

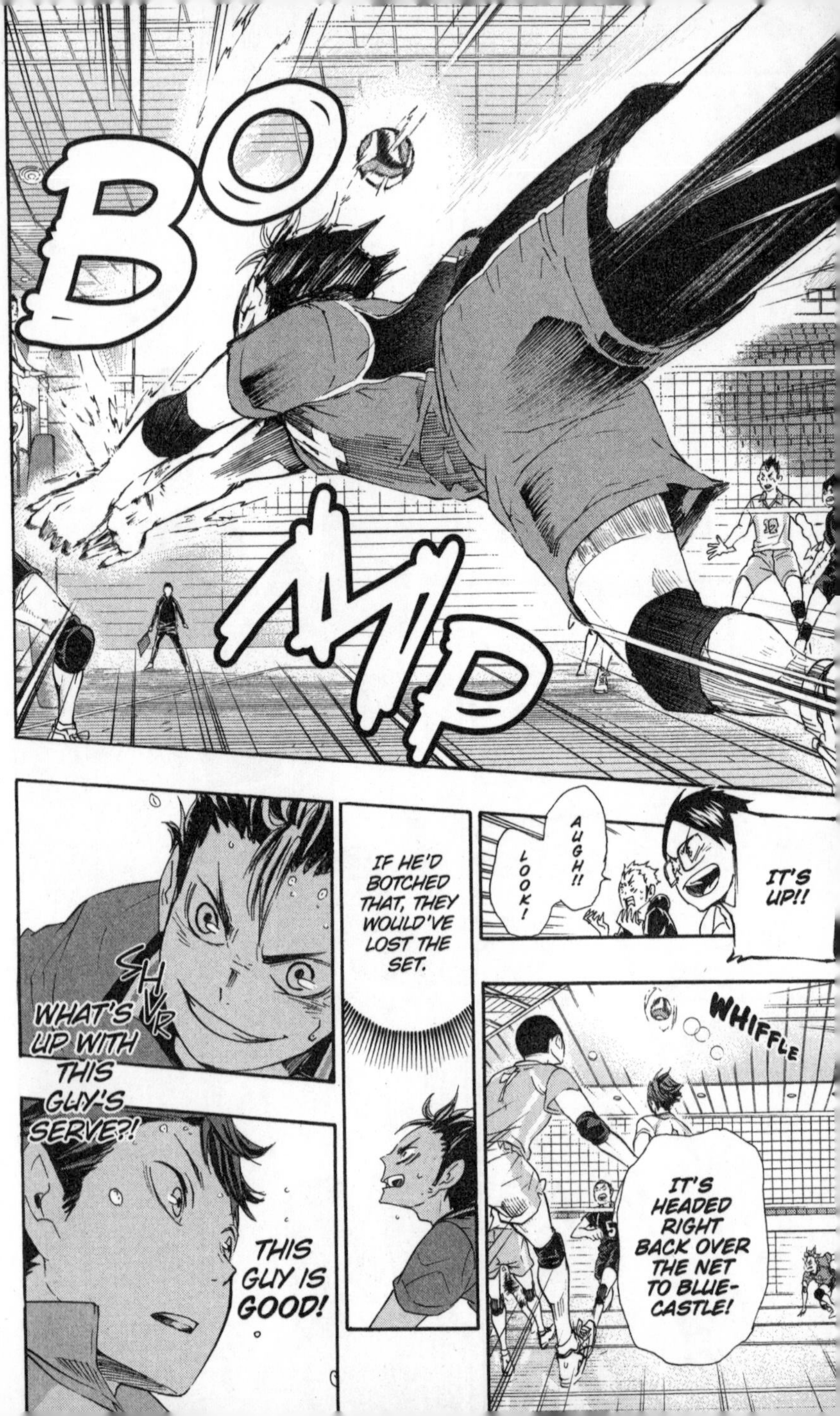
BOOMP
IT'S UP!!
AUGH!! LOOK!
WHIFFLE
IT'S HEADED RIGHT BACK OVER THE NET TO BLUE-CASTLE!
IF HE'D BOTCHED THAT, THEY WOULD'VE LOST THE SET.
SHVR
WHAT'S UP WITH THIS GUY'S SERVE?!
THIS GUY IS GOOD!

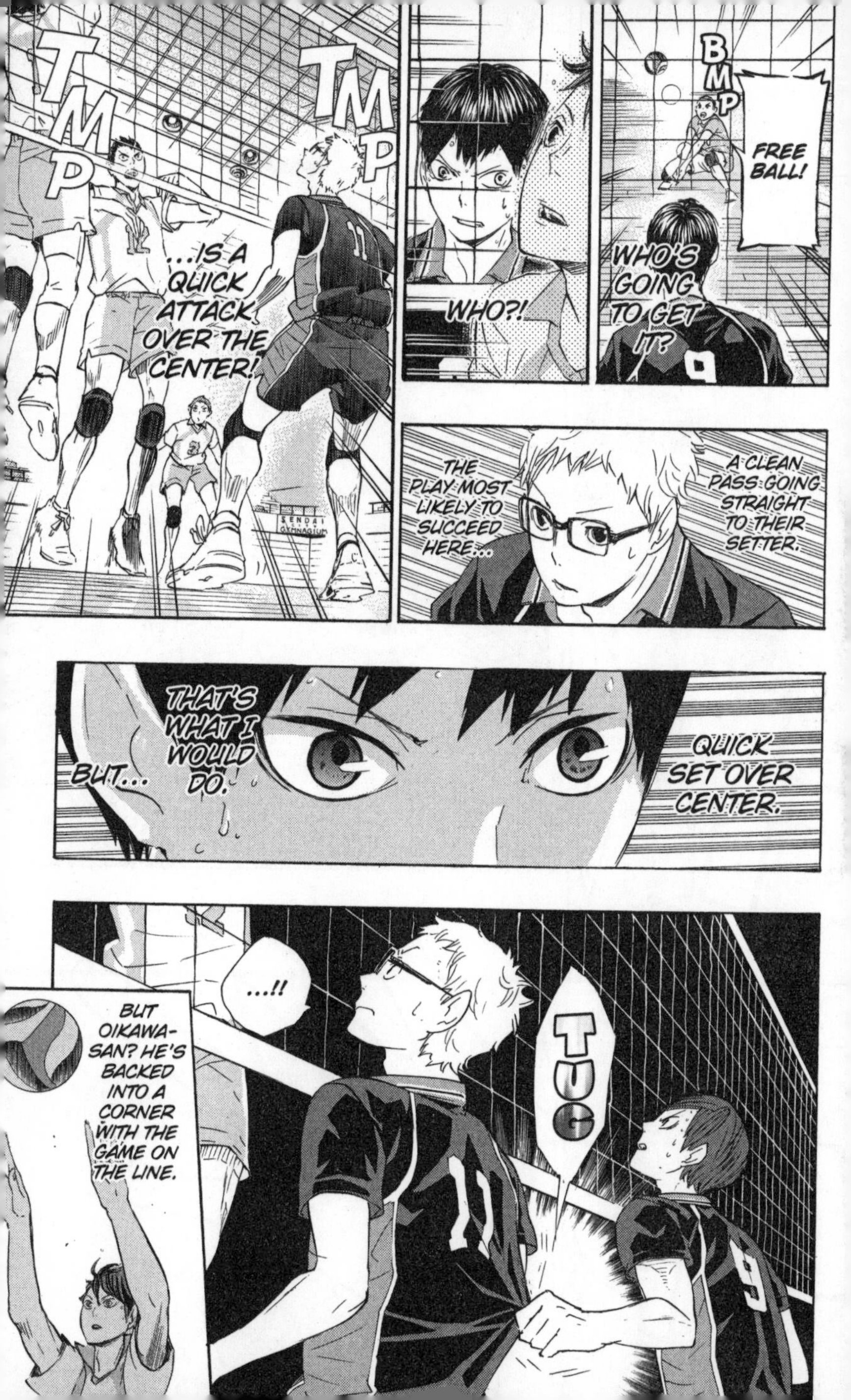
BMP
FREE BALL!
WHO'S GOING TO GET IT?
WHO?!
A CLEAN PASS GOING STRAIGHT TO THEIR SETTER.
THE PLAY MOST LIKELY TO SUCCEED HERE...
TMP
TMP
...IS A QUICK ATTACK OVER THE CENTER!
SENDAI CITY GYMNASIUM
QUICK SET OVER CENTER.
THAT'S WHAT I WOULD DO.
BUT...
...!!
TUG
BUT OIKAWA-SAN? HE'S BACKED INTO A CORNER WITH THE GAME ON THE LINE.

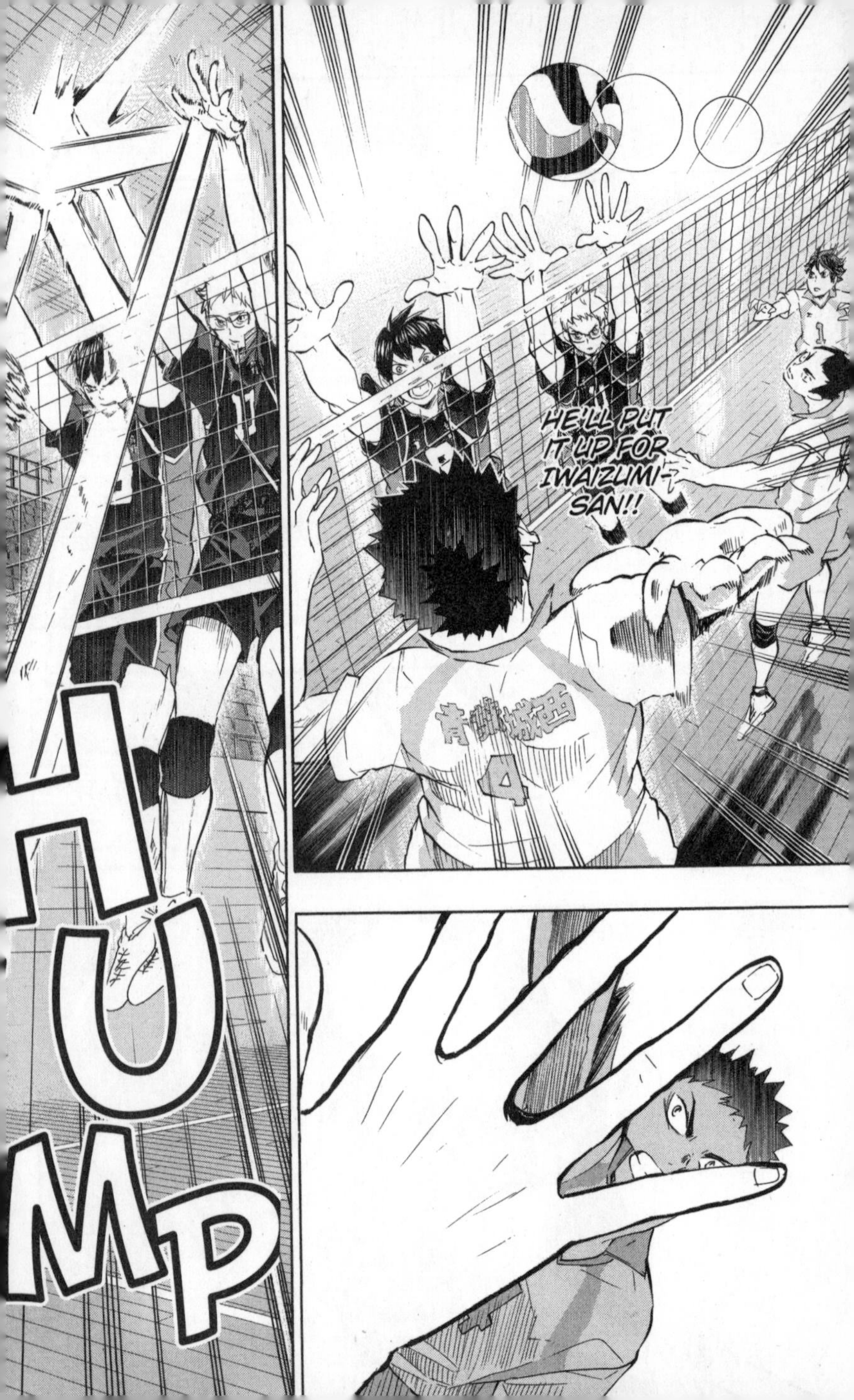
HE'LL PUT IT UP FOR IWAIZUMI-SAN!!
THUMP

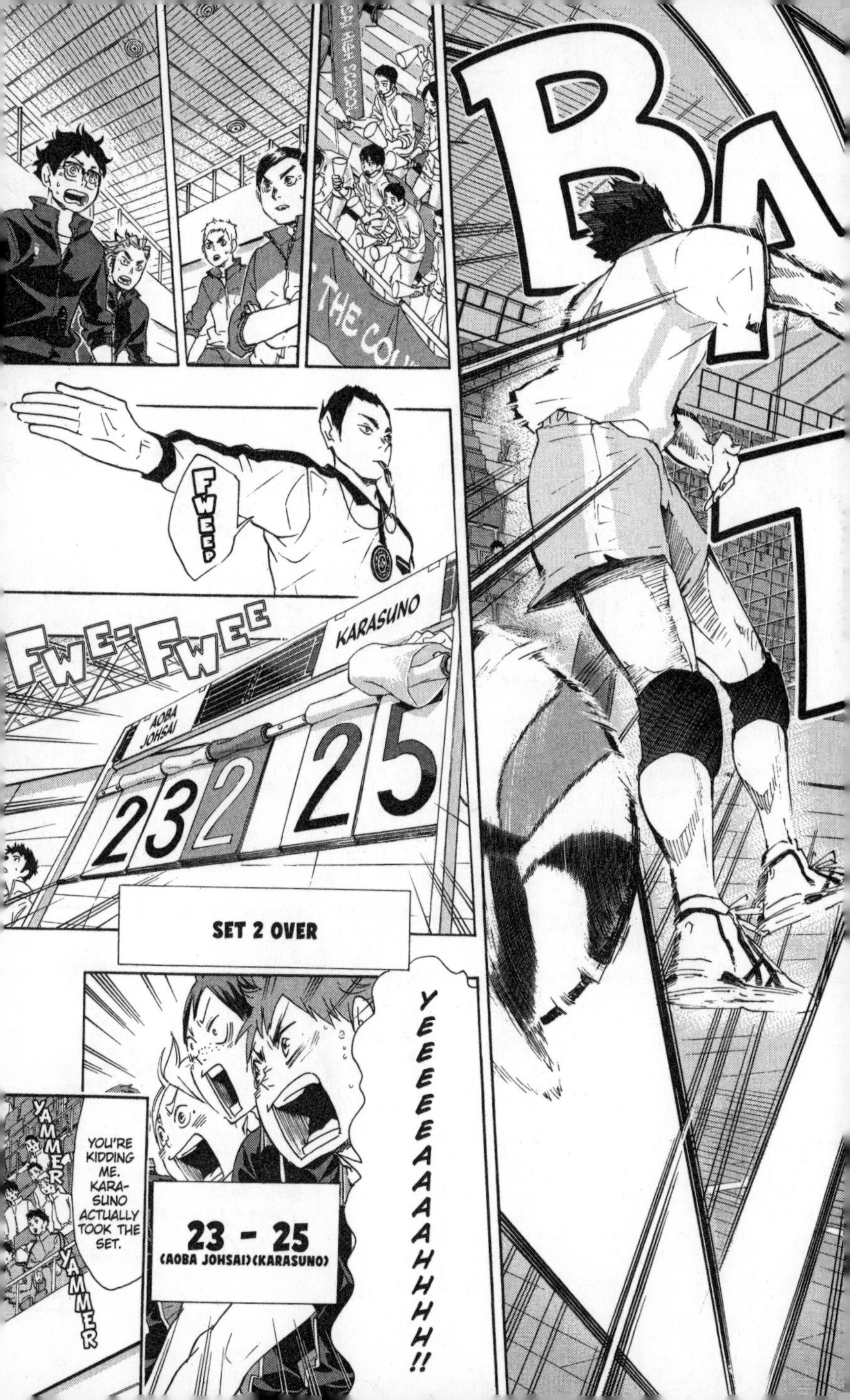
FWEEP
FWE-FWEE
KARASUNO
AOBA JOHSAI
23 2 25
SET 2 OVER
YEEEEEAAAAAHHHHH!!
YAMMER YAMMER
YOU'RE KIDDING ME. KARASUNO ACTUALLY TOOK THE SET.
23 - 25
(AOBA JOHSAI)(KARASUNO)

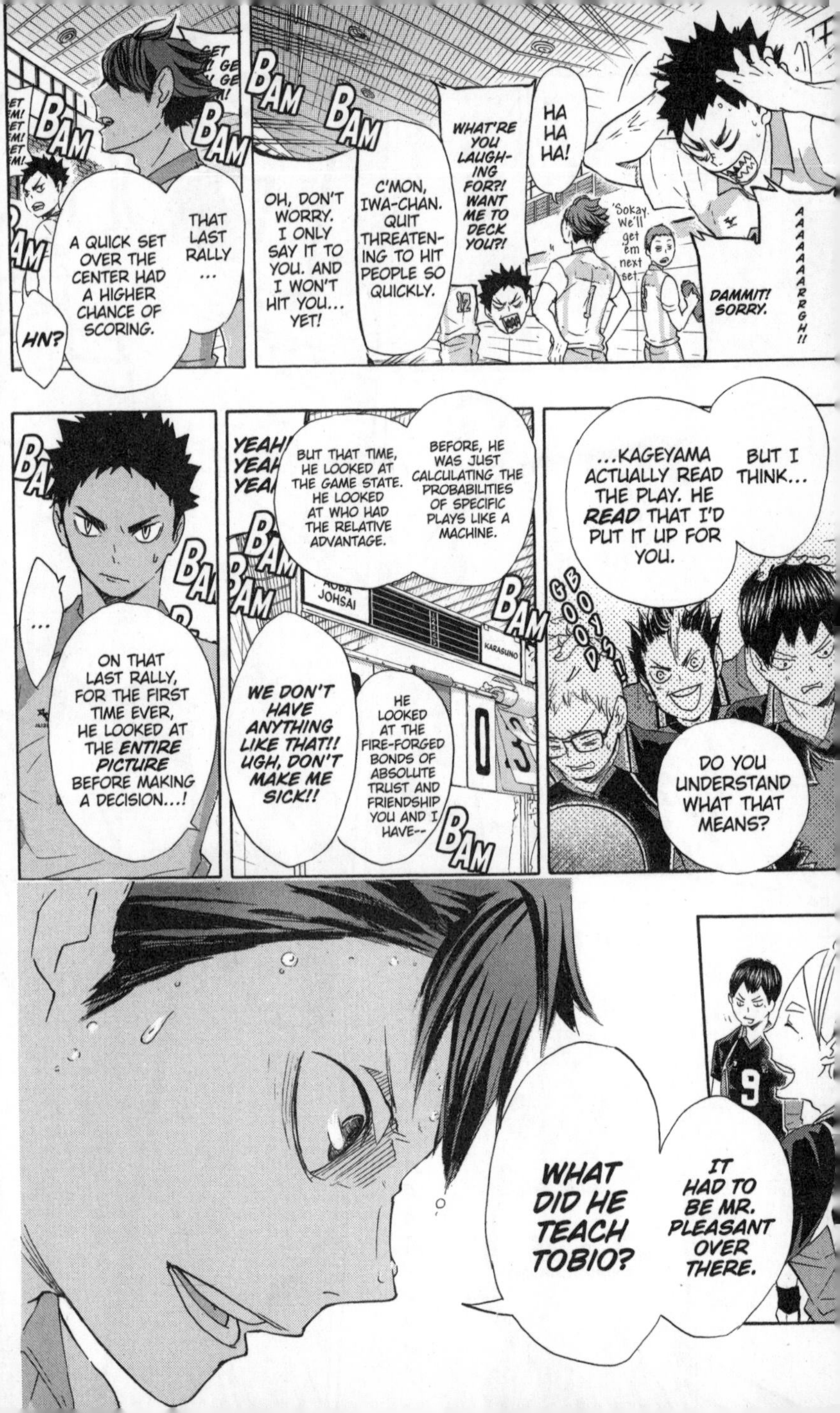
AAAAAAAARRGH!!
DAMMIT! SORRY.
'Sokay. We'll get 'em next set.
HA HA HA!
WHAT'RE YOU LAUGHING FOR?! WANT ME TO DECK YOU?!
C'MON, IWA-CHAN. QUIT THREATENING TO HIT PEOPLE SO QUICKLY.
OH, DON'T WORRY. I ONLY SAY IT TO YOU. AND I WON'T HIT YOU... YET!
BAM
BAM
BAM
BAM
THAT LAST RALLY...
A QUICK SET OVER THE CENTER HAD A HIGHER CHANCE OF SCORING.
HN?
BUT I THINK...
...KAGEYAMA ACTUALLY READ THE PLAY. HE READ THAT I'D PUT IT UP FOR YOU.
DO YOU UNDERSTAND WHAT THAT MEANS?
BEFORE, HE WAS JUST CALCULATING THE PROBABILITIES OF SPECIFIC PLAYS LIKE A MACHINE.
BUT THAT TIME, HE LOOKED AT THE GAME STATE. HE LOOKED AT WHO HAD THE RELATIVE ADVANTAGE.
YEAH! YEAH! YEAH!
BAM
BAM
AOBA JOHSAI
KARASUNO
HE LOOKED AT THE FIRE-FORGED BONDS OF ABSOLUTE TRUST AND FRIENDSHIP YOU AND I HAVE--
WE DON'T HAVE ANYTHING LIKE THAT!! UGH, DON'T MAKE ME SICK!!
BAM
...
ON THAT LAST RALLY, FOR THE FIRST TIME EVER, HE LOOKED AT THE ENTIRE PICTURE BEFORE MAKING A DECISION...!
IT HAD TO BE MR. PLEASANT OVER THERE.
WHAT DID HE TEACH TOBIO?

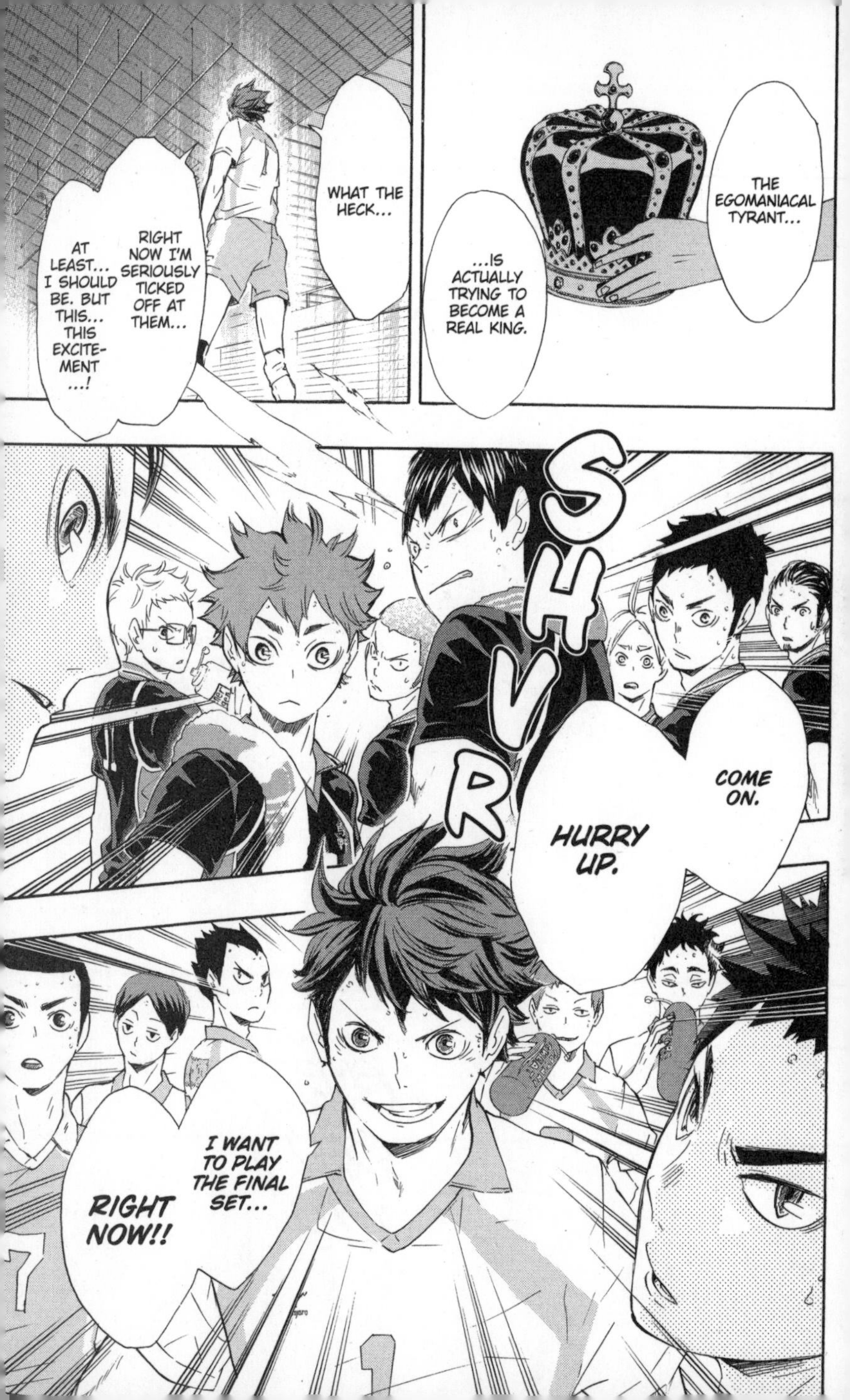
THE EGOMANIACAL TYRANT...
...IS ACTUALLY TRYING TO BECOME A REAL KING.
WHAT THE HECK...
RIGHT NOW I'M SERIOUSLY TICKED OFF AT THEM...
AT LEAST... I SHOULD BE. BUT THIS... THIS EXCITEMENT...!
SHVR
COME ON.
HURRY UP.
I WANT TO PLAY THE FINAL SET...
RIGHT NOW!!

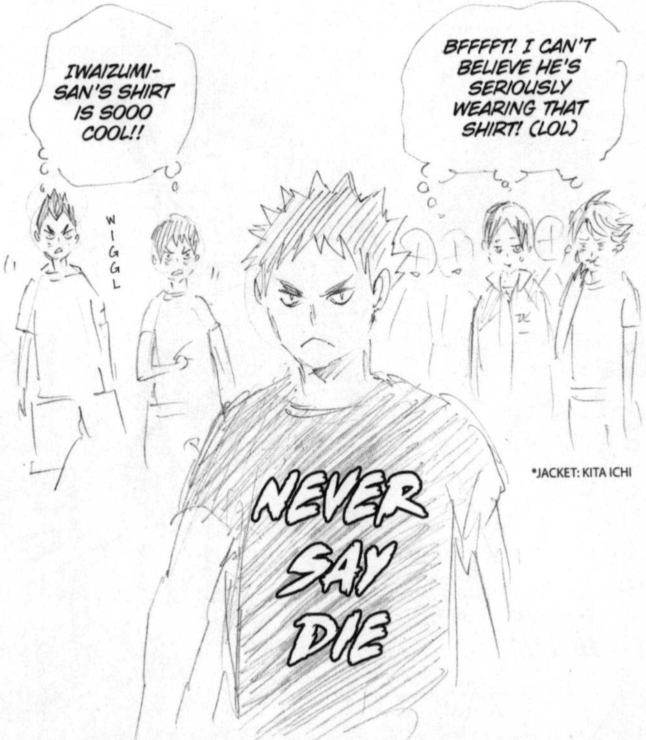
BFFFFT! I CAN'T BELIEVE HE'S SERIOUSLY WEARING THAT SHIRT! (LOL)
IWAIZUMI-SAN'S SHIRT IS SOOO COOL!!
WIGGL
NEVER SAY DIE
*JACKET: KITA ICHI

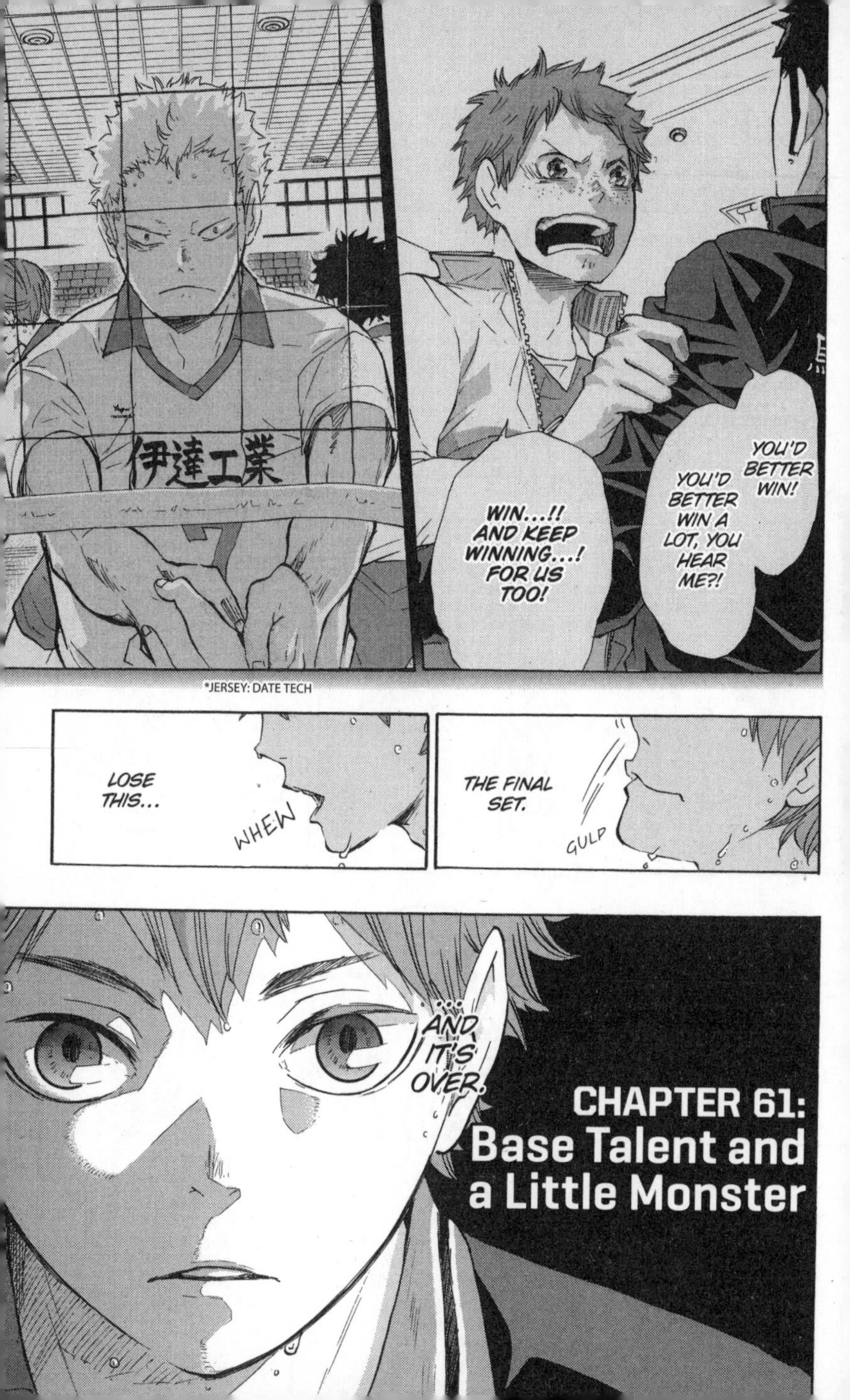
YOU'D BETTER WIN!
YOU'D BETTER WIN A LOT, YOU HEAR ME?!
WIN...!! AND KEEP WINNING...! FOR US TOO!
伊達工業
*JERSEY: DATE TECH
THE FINAL SET.
GULP
LOSE THIS...
WHEW
...AND IT'S OVER.
CHAPTER 61: Base Talent and a Little Monster

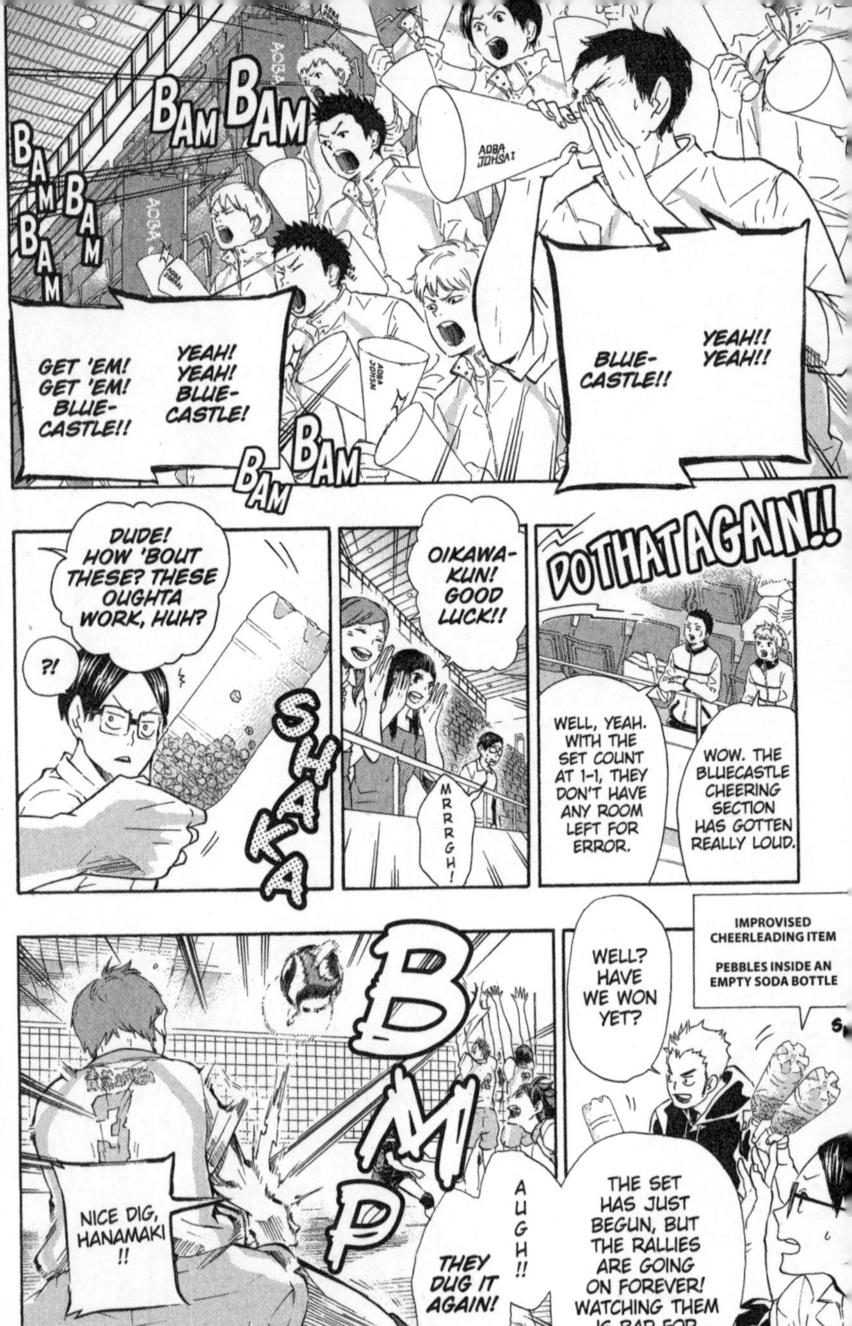
YEAH!! YEAH!!
BLUE-CASTLE!!
BAM BAM
BAM BAM BAM BAM
YEAH! YEAH! BLUE-CASTLE!
GET 'EM! GET 'EM! BLUE-CASTLE!!
BAM BAM
DO THAT AGAIN!!
WOW. THE BLUECASTLE CHEERING SECTION HAS GOTTEN REALLY LOUD.
WELL, YEAH. WITH THE SET COUNT AT 1-1, THEY DON'T HAVE ANY ROOM LEFT FOR ERROR.
OIKAWA-KUN! GOOD LUCK!!
MRRRGH!
DUDE! HOW 'BOUT THESE? THESE OUGHTA WORK, HUH?
?!
SHAKA
IMPROVISED CHEERLEADING ITEM
PEBBLES INSIDE AN EMPTY SODA BOTTLE
WELL? HAVE WE WON YET?
THE SET HAS JUST BEGUN, BUT THE RALLIES ARE GOING ON FOREVER! WATCHING THEM IS BAD FOR MY--
BUMP
AUGH!!
THEY DUG IT AGAIN!
NICE DIG, HANAMAKI!!

*RALLY: WHEN THE BA IS BEING PASSED THROUGH, BETWEEN SERVE AND SCORE.

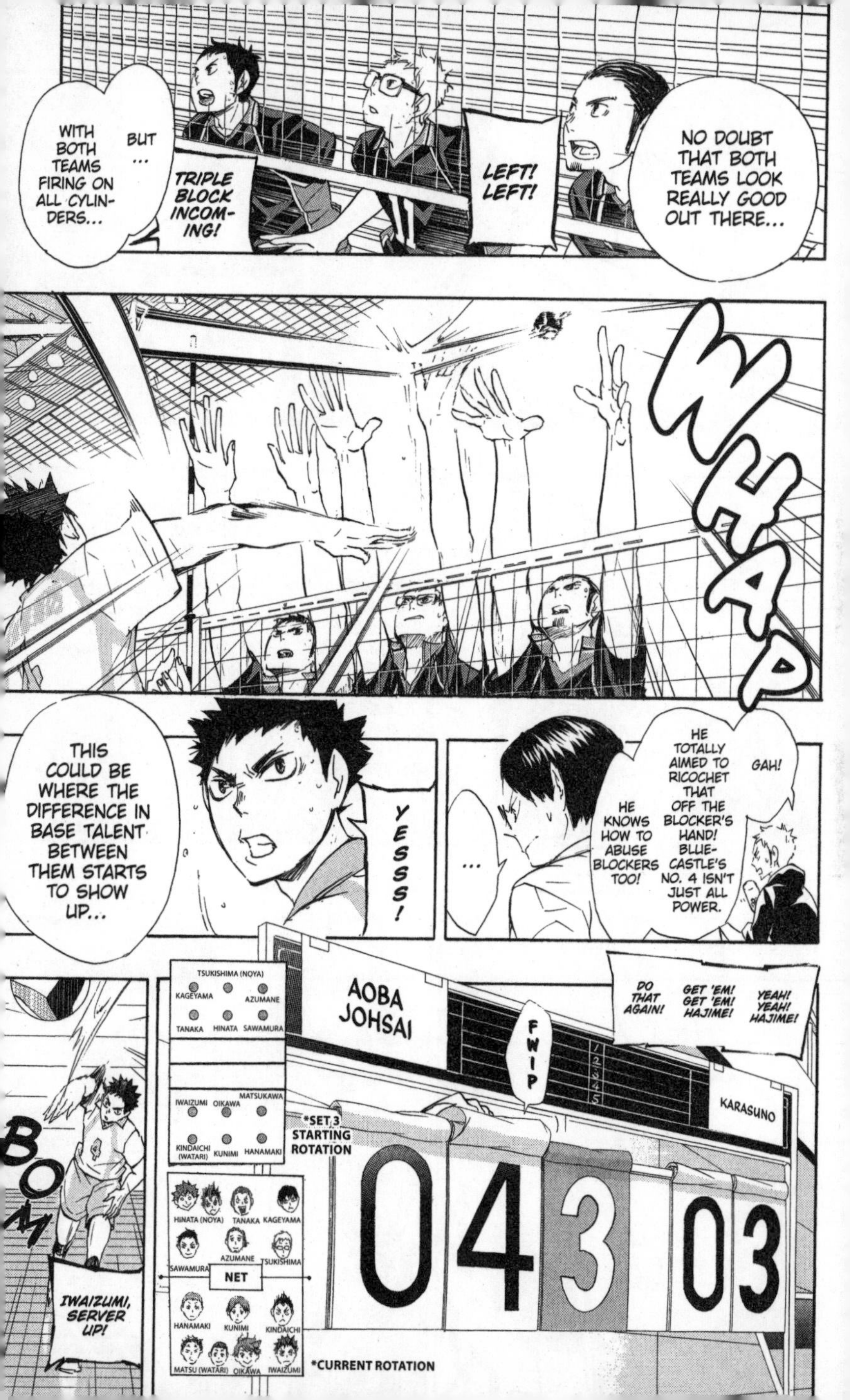
NO DOUBT THAT BOTH TEAMS LOOK REALLY GOOD OUT THERE...
LEFT! LEFT!
TRIPLE BLOCK INCOMING!
BUT ...
WITH BOTH TEAMS FIRING ON ALL CYLINDERS...
WHAP
GAH!
HE TOTALLY AIMED TO RICOCHET THAT OFF THE BLOCKER'S HAND! BLUE-CASTLE'S NO. 4 ISN'T JUST ALL POWER.
HE KNOWS HOW TO ABUSE BLOCKERS TOO!
...
YESSS!
THIS COULD BE WHERE THE DIFFERENCE IN BASE TALENT BETWEEN THEM STARTS TO SHOW UP...
YEAH! YEAH! HAJIME!
GET 'EM! GET 'EM! HAJIME!
DO THAT AGAIN!
AOBA JOHSAI
FWIP
KARASUNO
04 3 03
TSUKISHIMA (NOYA)
KAGEYAMA
AZUMANE
TANAKA
HINATA
SAWAMURA
IWAIZUMI
OIKAWA
MATSUKAWA
KINDAICHI (WATARI)
KUNIMI
HANAMAKI
*SET 3 STARTING ROTATION
HINATA (NOYA)
TANAKA
KAGEYAMA
SAWAMURA
AZUMANE
TSUKISHIMA
NET
HANAMAKI
KUNIMI
KINDAICHI
MATSU (WATARI)
OIKAWA
IWAIZUMI
*CURRENT ROTATION
BOOM
IWAIZUMI, SERVER UP!

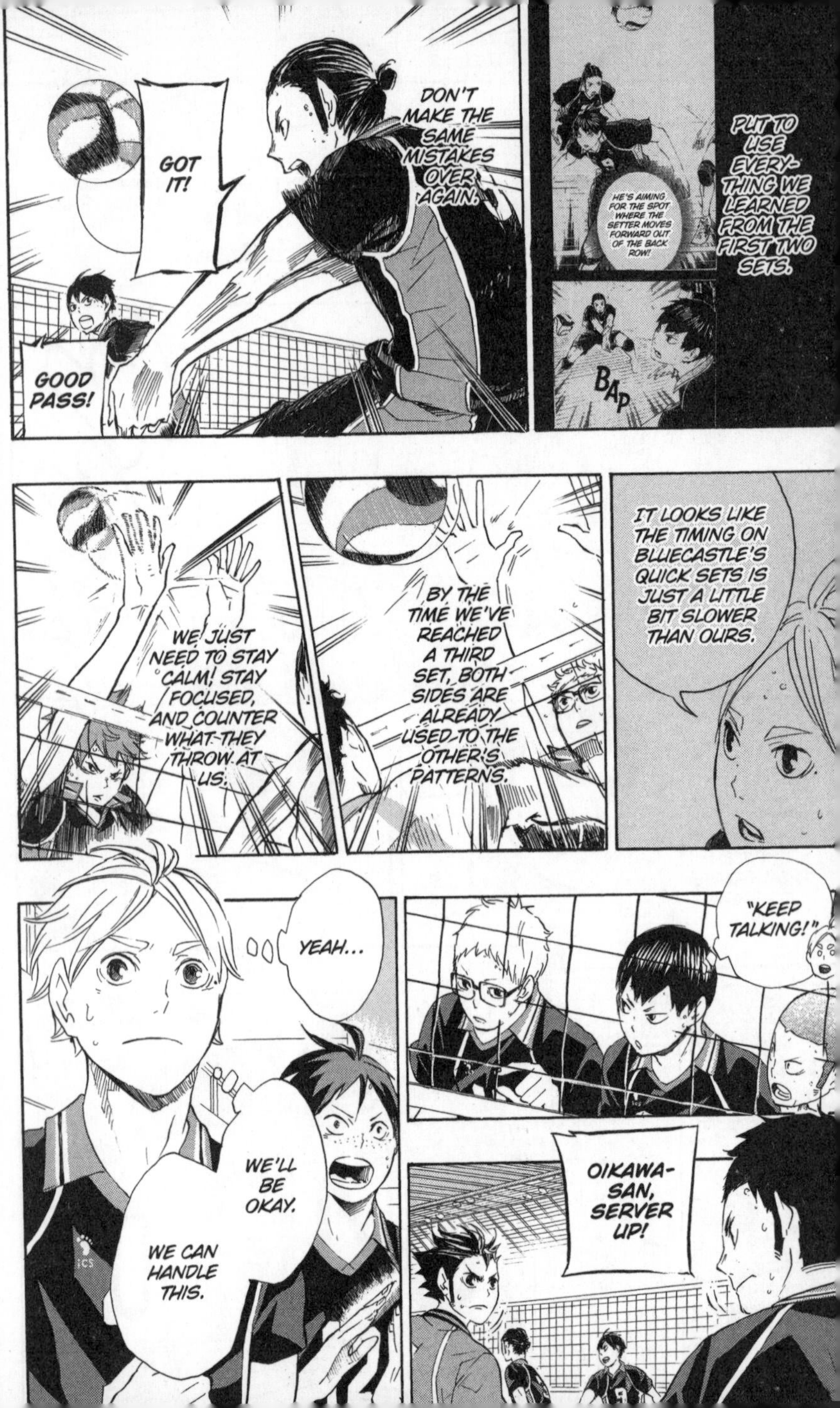
PUT TO USE EVERY-THING WE LEARNED FROM THE FIRST TWO SETS.
HE'S AIMING FOR THE SPOT WHERE THE SETTER MOVES FORWARD OUT OF THE BACK ROW!
BAP
DON'T MAKE THE SAME MISTAKES OVER AGAIN.
GOT IT!
GOOD PASS!
IT LOOKS LIKE THE TIMING ON BLUECASTLE'S QUICK SETS IS JUST A LITTLE BIT SLOWER THAN OURS.
BY THE TIME WE'VE REACHED A THIRD SET, BOTH SIDES ARE ALREADY USED TO THE OTHER'S PATTERNS.
WE JUST NEED TO STAY CALM! STAY FOCUSED, AND COUNTER WHAT THEY THROW AT US.
"KEEP TALKING!"
OIKAWA-SAN, SERVER UP!
YEAH...
WE'LL BE OKAY.
WE CAN HANDLE THIS.

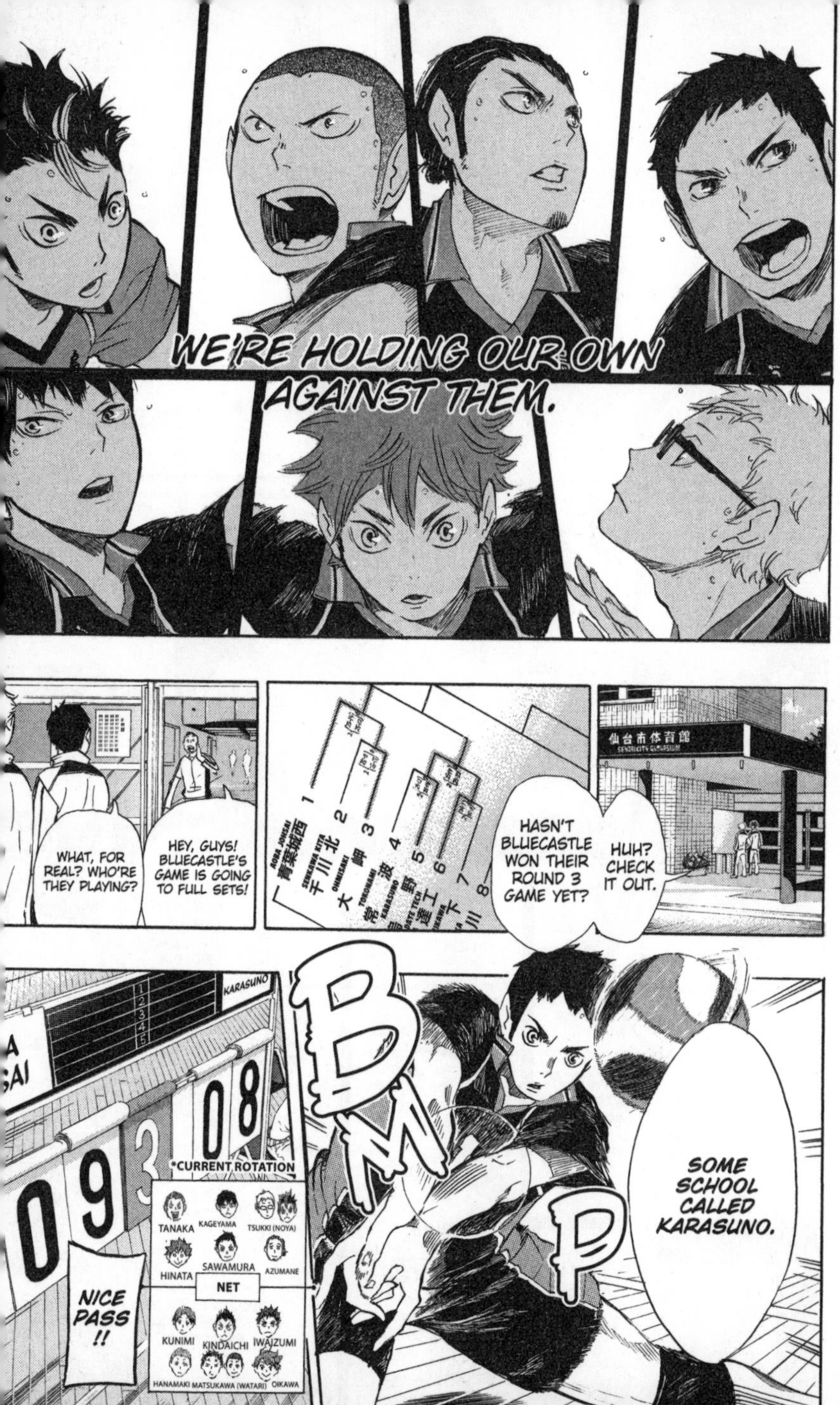
WE'RE HOLDING OUR OWN AGAINST THEM.
仙台市体育館
SENDAI CITY GYMNASIUM
HUH? CHECK IT OUT.
HASN'T BLUECASTLE WON THEIR ROUND 3 GAME YET?
AOBA JOHSAI 青葉城西
SENKAWA KITA 千川北
OHMISAKI 大岬
TOKONAMI 常波
HEY, GUYS! BLUECASTLE'S GAME IS GOING TO FULL SETS!
WHAT, FOR REAL? WHO'RE THEY PLAYING?
SOME SCHOOL CALLED KARASUNO.
BMP
KARASUNO
09 3 08
*CURRENT ROTATION
TANAKA
KAGEYAMA
TSUKKI (NOYA)
HINATA
SAWAMURA
AZUMANE
NET
KUNIMI
KINDAICHI
IWAIZUMI
HANAMAKI
MATSUKAWA (WATARI)
OIKAWA
NICE PASS !!

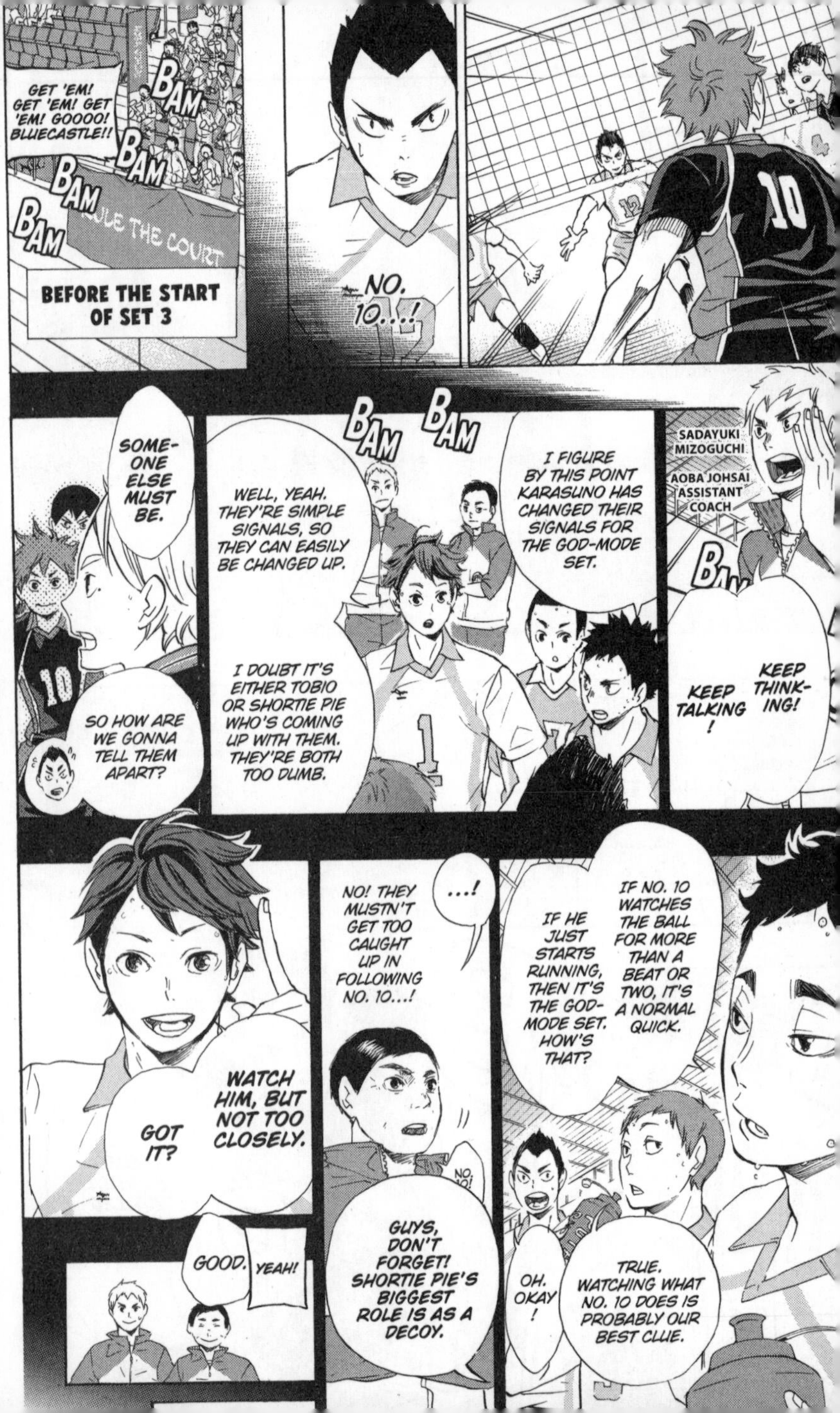
NO. 10...!
BAM
BAM
BAM
BAM
GET 'EM! GET 'EM! GET 'EM! GOOOO! BLUECASTLE!!
BEFORE THE START OF SET 3
SADAYUKI MIZOGUCHI
AOBA JOHSAI ASSISTANT COACH
KEEP THINKING!
KEEP TALKING!
BAM
BAM
I FIGURE BY THIS POINT KARASUNO HAS CHANGED THEIR SIGNALS FOR THE GOD-MODE SET.
WELL, YEAH. THEY'RE SIMPLE SIGNALS, SO THEY CAN EASILY BE CHANGED UP.
I DOUBT IT'S EITHER TOBIO OR SHORTIE PIE WHO'S COMING UP WITH THEM. THEY'RE BOTH TOO DUMB.
SOME-ONE ELSE MUST BE.
SO HOW ARE WE GONNA TELL THEM APART?
IF NO. 10 WATCHES THE BALL FOR MORE THAN A BEAT OR TWO, IT'S A NORMAL QUICK.
IF HE JUST STARTS RUNNING, THEN IT'S THE GOD-MODE SET. HOW'S THAT?
TRUE. WATCHING WHAT NO. 10 DOES IS PROBABLY OUR BEST CLUE.
OH. OKAY!
...!
NO! THEY MUSTN'T GET TOO CAUGHT UP IN FOLLOWING NO. 10...!
NO. NO!
GUYS, DON'T FORGET! SHORTIE PIE'S BIGGEST ROLE IS AS A DECOY.
WATCH HIM, BUT NOT TOO CLOSELY.
GOT IT?
YEAH!
GOOD.

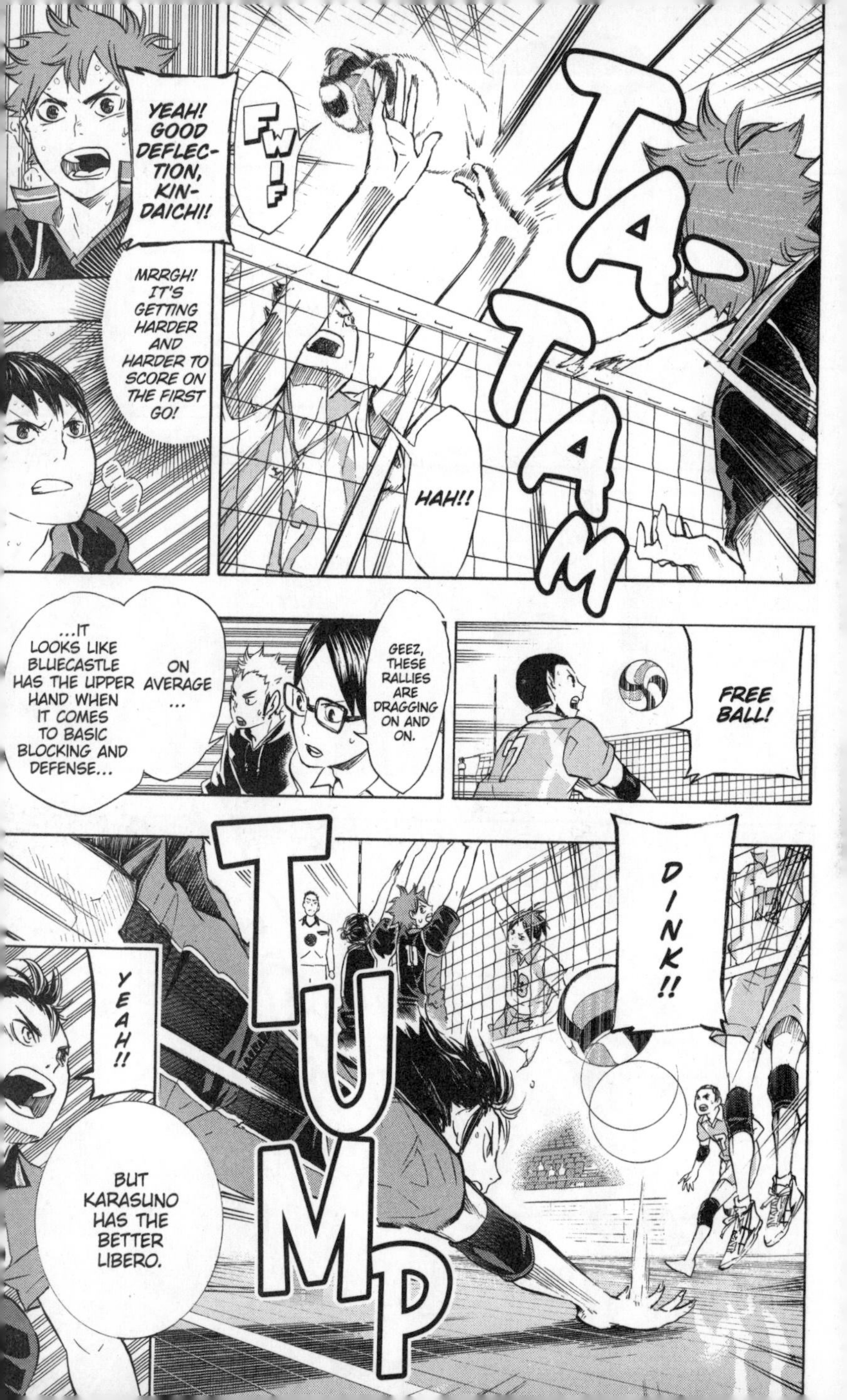
TA-TA-TAM
FWIF
HAH!!
YEAH! GOOD DEFLECTION, KIN-DAICHI!
MRRGH! IT'S GETTING HARDER AND HARDER TO SCORE ON THE FIRST GO!
FREE BALL!
GEEZ, THESE RALLIES ARE DRAGGING ON AND ON.
ON AVERAGE...
...IT LOOKS LIKE BLUECASTLE HAS THE UPPER HAND WHEN IT COMES TO BASIC BLOCKING AND DEFENSE...
DINK!!
TUMP
YEAH!!
BUT KARASUNO HAS THE BETTER LIBERO.

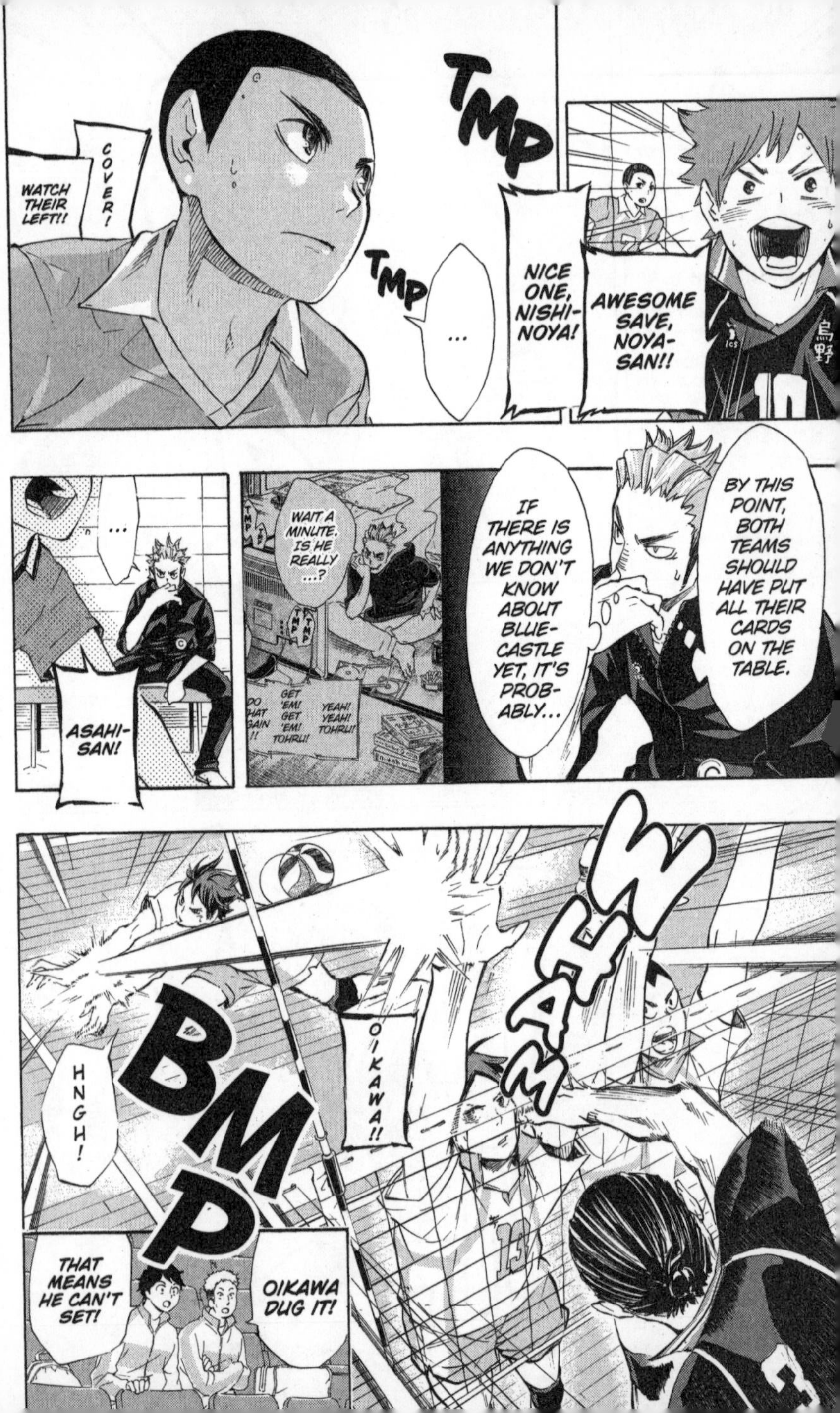
AWESOME SAVE, NOYA-SAN!!
NICE ONE, NISHI-NOYA!
TMP
TMP
...
COVER!
WATCH THEIR LEFT!!
BY THIS POINT, BOTH TEAMS SHOULD HAVE PUT ALL THEIR CARDS ON THE TABLE.
IF THERE IS ANYTHING WE DON'T KNOW ABOUT BLUE-CASTLE YET, IT'S PROBABLY...
WAIT A MINUTE. IS HE REALLY ...?
TMP
TMP
TMP
TMP
YEAH! YEAH! TOHRU!
GET 'EM! GET 'EM! TOHRU!
...
ASAHI-SAN!
WHAM
OIKAWA!!
BMP
HNGH!
OIKAWA DUG IT!
THAT MEANS HE CAN'T SET!

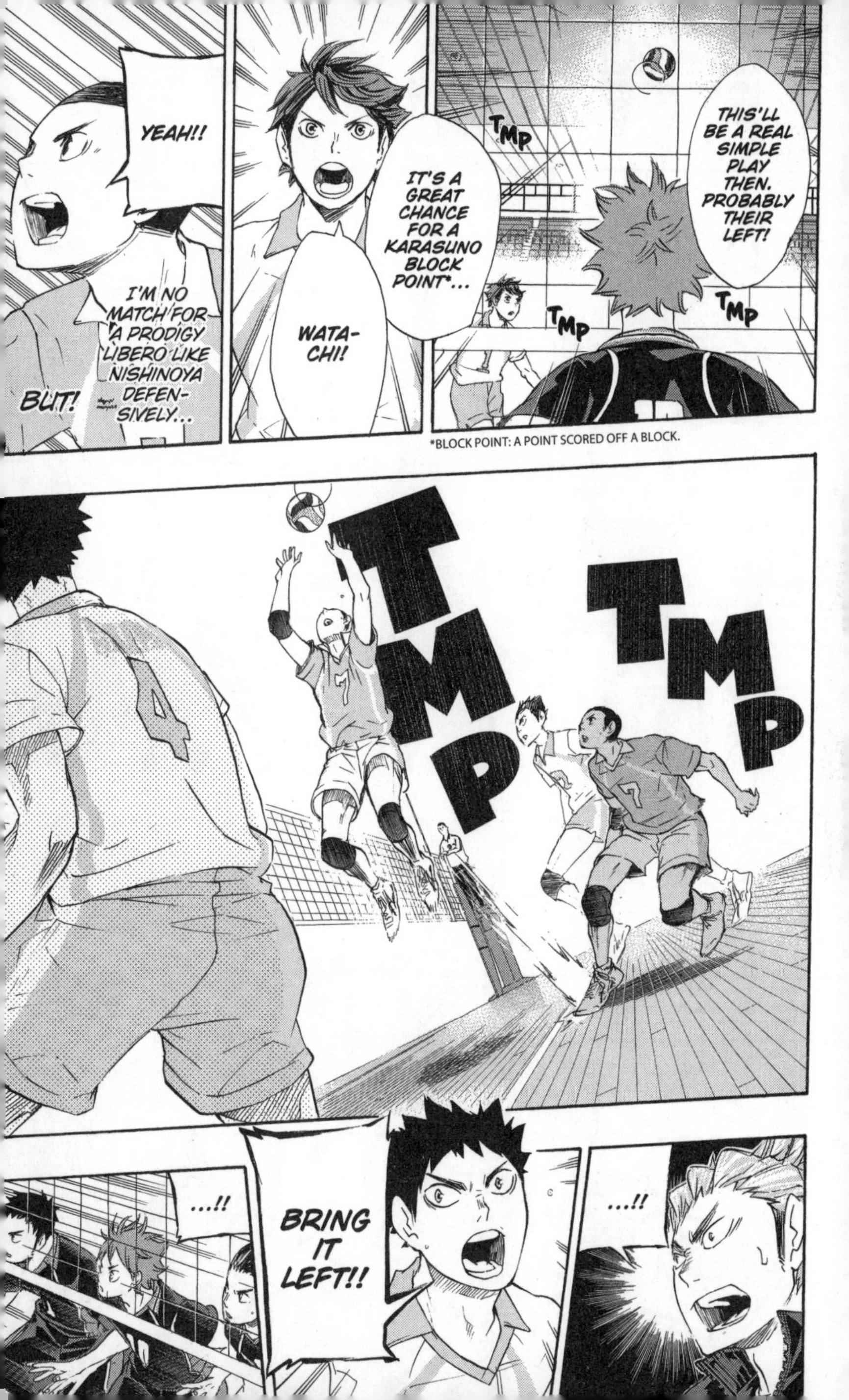
THIS'LL BE A REAL SIMPLE PLAY THEN. PROBABLY THEIR LEFT!
TMP
TMP
TMP
IT'S A GREAT CHANCE FOR A KARASUNO BLOCK POINT*...
WATA-CHI!
YEAH!!
I'M NO MATCH FOR A PRODIGY LIBERO LIKE NISHINOYA DEFENSIVELY...
BUT!
TMP
TMP
...!!
BRING IT LEFT!!
...!!

*BLOCK POINT: A POINT SCORED OFF A BLOCK.

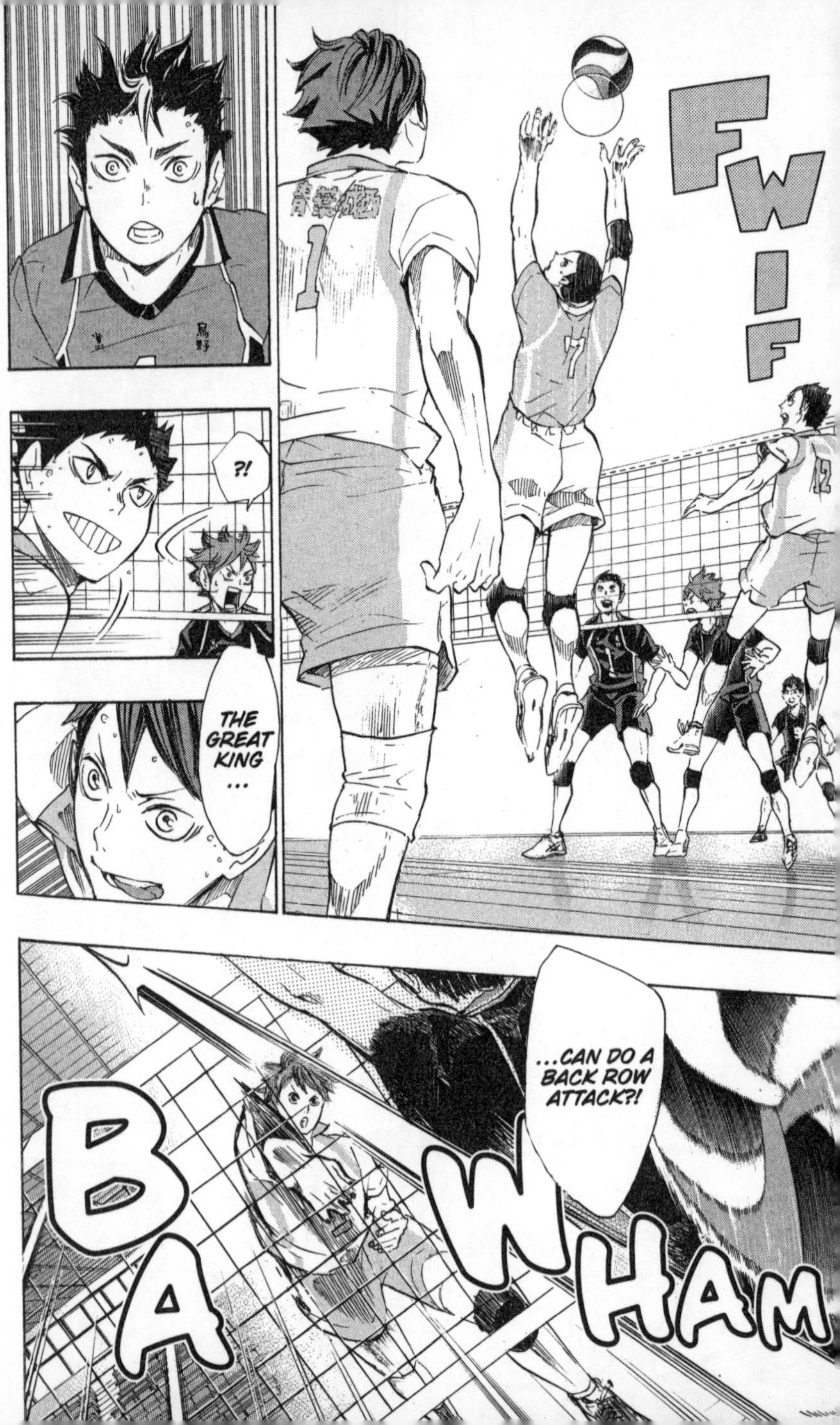
FWIF
?!
THE GREAT KING ...
...CAN DO A BACK ROW ATTACK?!
BAWHAM

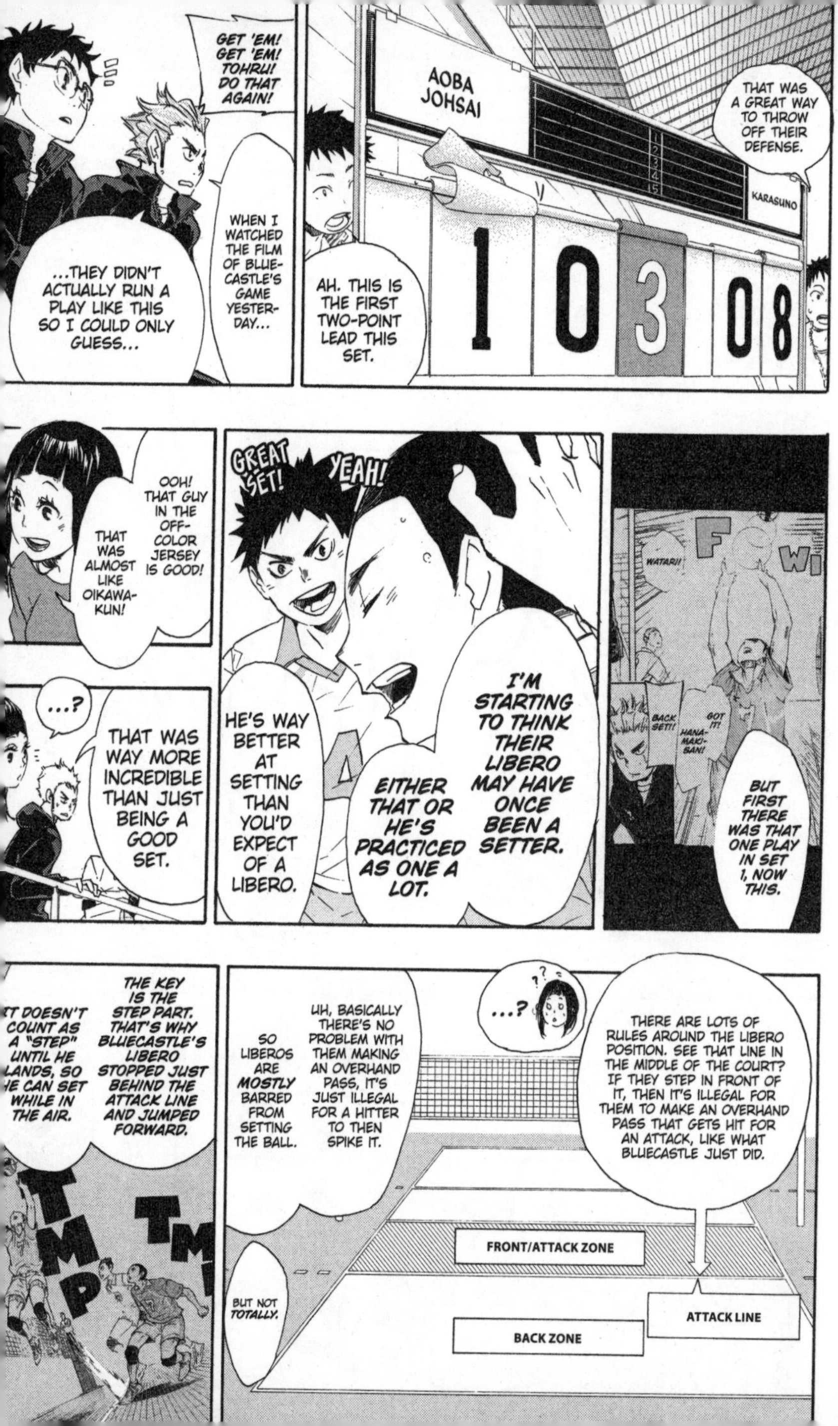
THAT WAS A GREAT WAY TO THROW OFF THEIR DEFENSE.
AOBA JOHSAI
KARASUNO
10 3 08
AH. THIS IS THE FIRST TWO-POINT LEAD THIS SET.
GET 'EM! GET 'EM! TOHRU! DO THAT AGAIN!
WHEN I WATCHED THE FILM OF BLUE-CASTLE'S GAME YESTER-DAY...
...THEY DIDN'T ACTUALLY RUN A PLAY LIKE THIS SO I COULD ONLY GUESS...
F
WI
WATARI!!
BACK SET!!
GOT IT!
HANA-MAKI-SAN!
BUT FIRST THERE WAS THAT ONE PLAY IN SET 1, NOW THIS.
GREAT SET!
YEAH!
I'M STARTING TO THINK THEIR LIBERO MAY HAVE ONCE BEEN A SETTER.
EITHER THAT OR HE'S PRACTICED AS ONE A LOT.
HE'S WAY BETTER AT SETTING THAN YOU'D EXPECT OF A LIBERO.
OOH! THAT GUY IN THE OFF-COLOR JERSEY IS GOOD!
THAT WAS ALMOST LIKE OIKAWA-KUN!
...?
THAT WAS WAY MORE INCREDIBLE THAN JUST BEING A GOOD SET.
...?
THERE ARE LOTS OF RULES AROUND THE LIBERO POSITION. SEE THAT LINE IN THE MIDDLE OF THE COURT? IF THEY STEP IN FRONT OF IT, THEN IT'S ILLEGAL FOR THEM TO MAKE AN OVERHAND PASS THAT GETS HIT FOR AN ATTACK, LIKE WHAT BLUECASTLE JUST DID.
UH, BASICALLY THERE'S NO PROBLEM WITH THEM MAKING AN OVERHAND PASS, IT'S JUST ILLEGAL FOR A HITTER TO THEN SPIKE IT.
SO LIBEROS ARE MOSTLY BARRED FROM SETTING THE BALL.
BUT NOT TOTALLY.
FRONT/ATTACK ZONE
ATTACK LINE
BACK ZONE
THE KEY IS THE STEP PART. THAT'S WHY BLUECASTLE'S LIBERO STOPPED JUST BEHIND THE ATTACK LINE AND JUMPED FORWARD.
T DOESN'T COUNT AS A "STEP" UNTIL HE LANDS, SO E CAN SET WHILE IN THE AIR.
TMP
TM

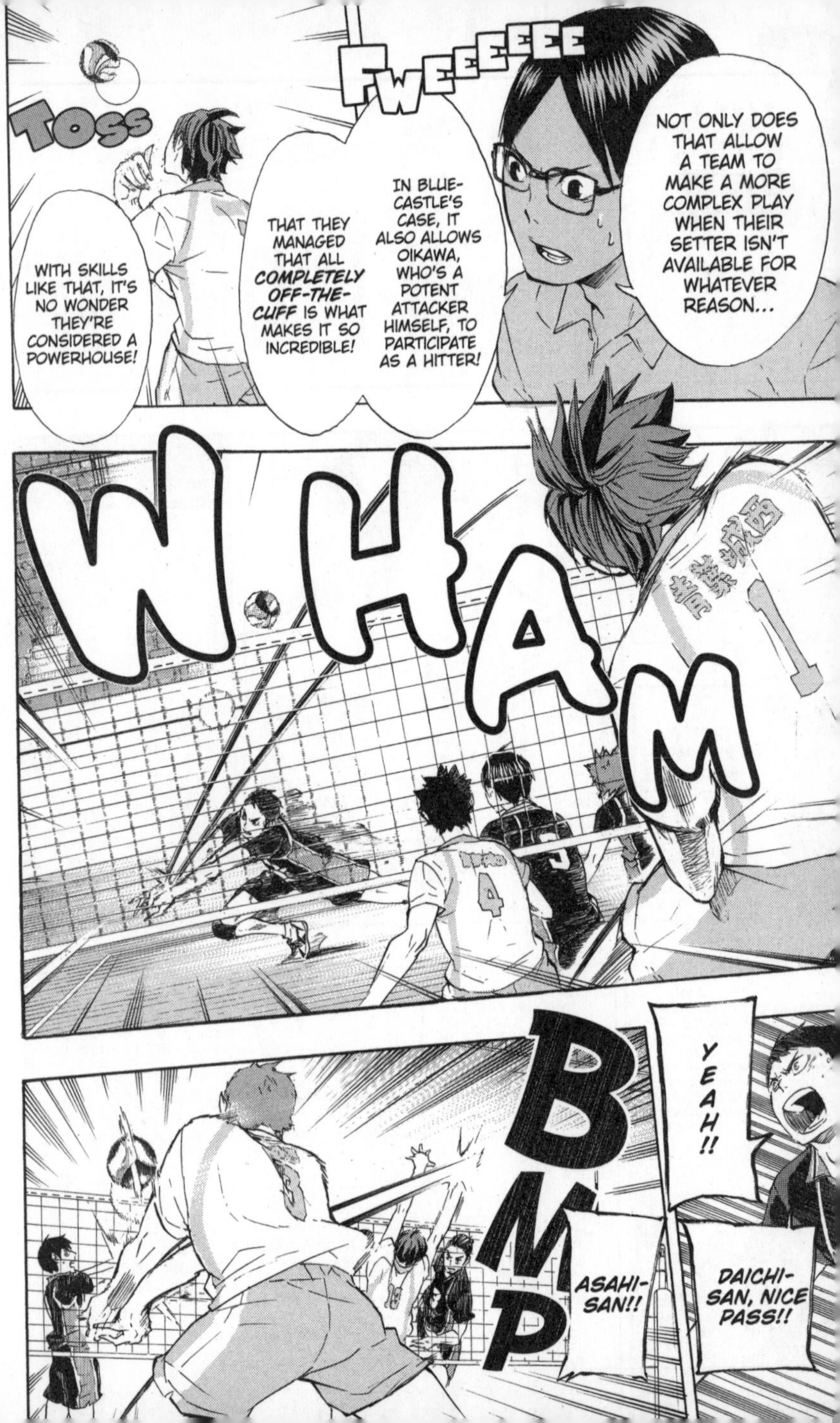

FWEEEEEE
NOT ONLY DOES THAT ALLOW A TEAM TO MAKE A MORE COMPLEX PLAY WHEN THEIR SETTER ISN'T AVAILABLE FOR WHATEVER REASON...
IN BLUE-CASTLE'S CASE, IT ALSO ALLOWS OIKAWA, WHO'S A POTENT ATTACKER HIMSELF, TO PARTICIPATE AS A HITTER!
THAT THEY MANAGED THAT ALL *COMPLETELY OFF-THE-CUFF* IS WHAT MAKES IT SO INCREDIBLE!
TOSS
WITH SKILLS LIKE THAT, IT'S NO WONDER THEY'RE CONSIDERED A POWERHOUSE!
WHAM
YEAH!!
BMP
DAICHI-SAN, NICE PASS!!
ASAHI-SAN!!

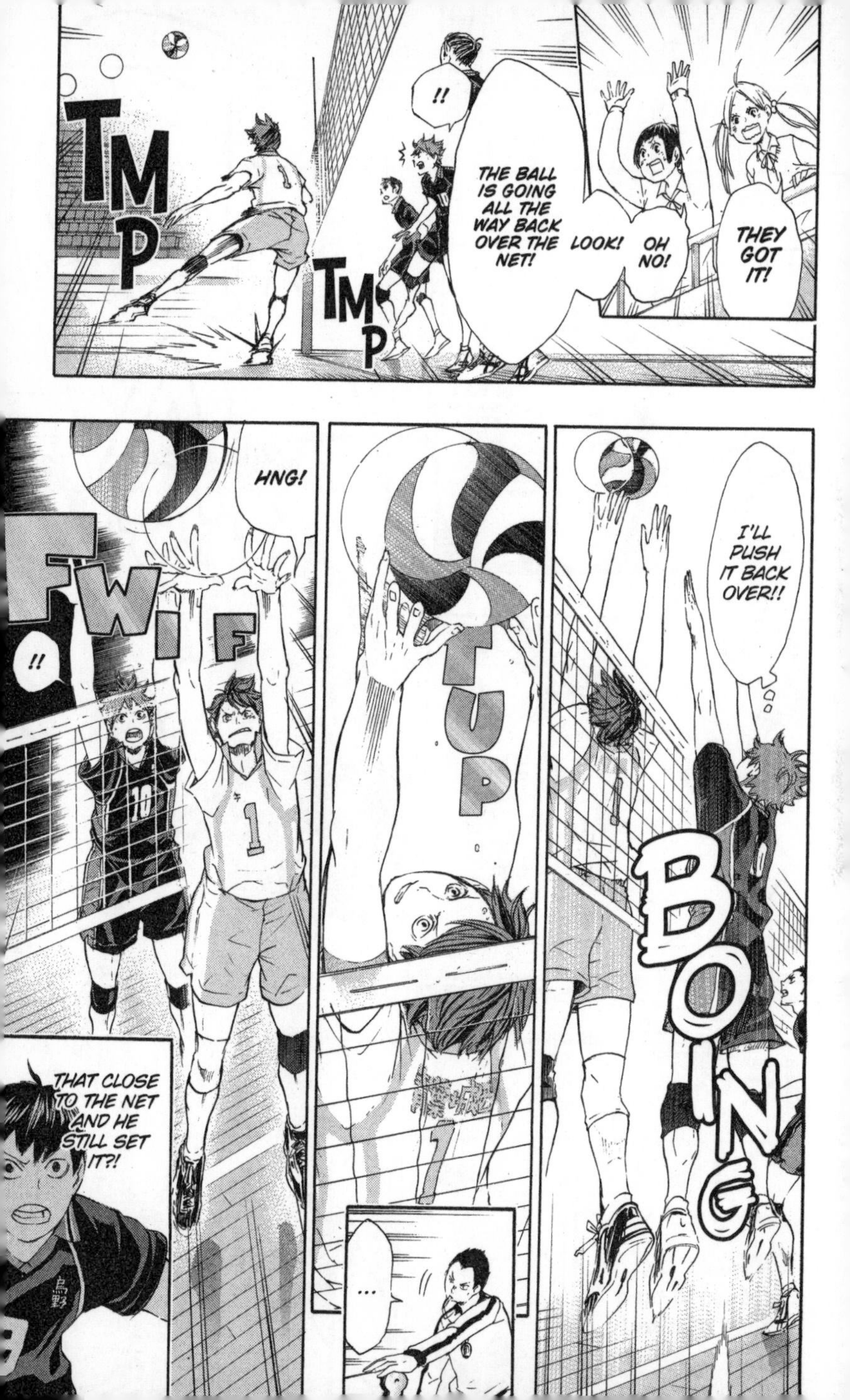
THEY GOT IT!
OH NO!
LOOK!
THE BALL IS GOING ALL THE WAY BACK OVER THE NET!
!!
TMP
TMP
I'LL PUSH IT BACK OVER!!
BOING
TUP
...
HNG!
FWIF
!!
THAT CLOSE TO THE NET AND HE STILL SET IT?!

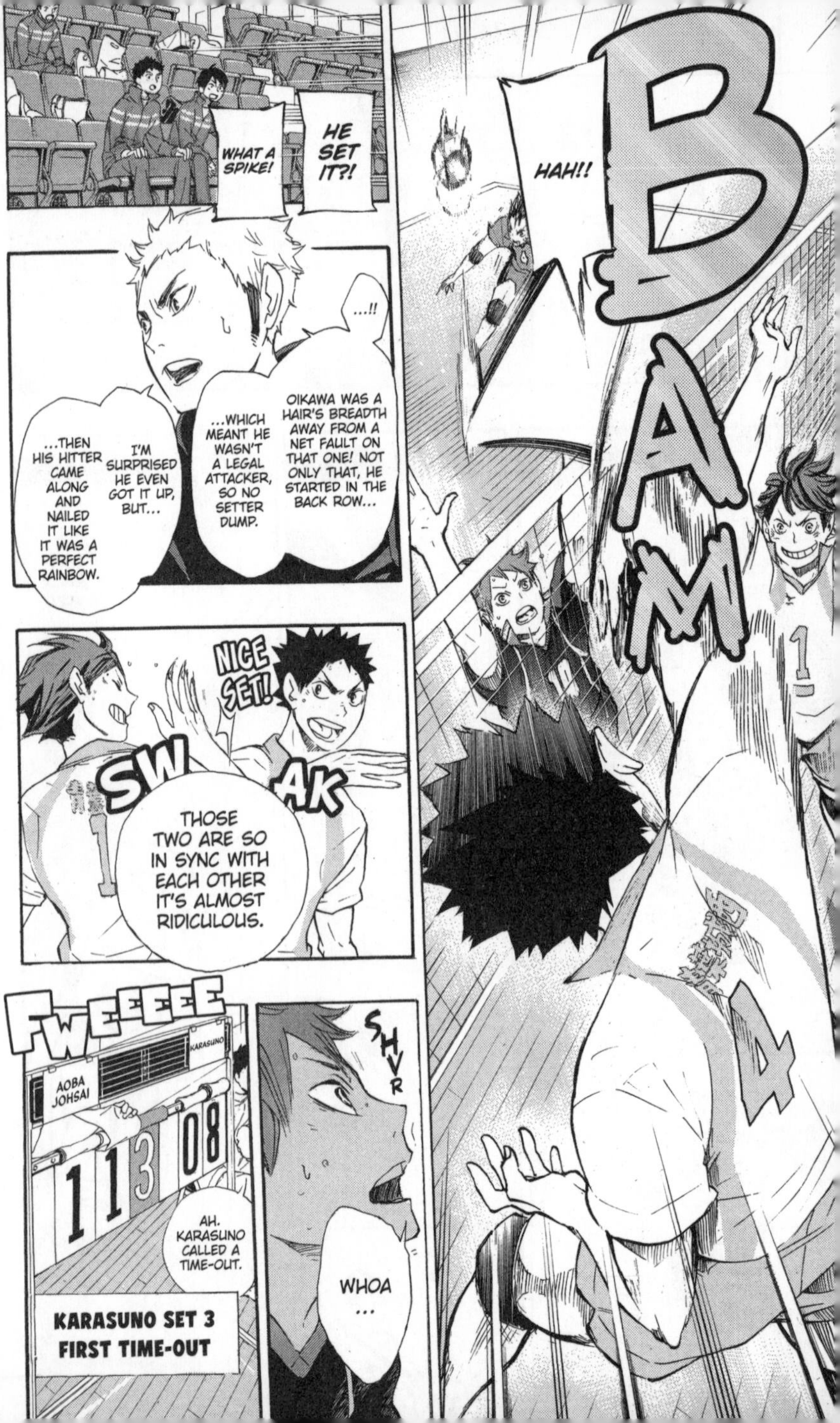
HAH!!
BAM
HE SET IT?!
WHAT A SPIKE!
...!!
OIKAWA WAS A HAIR'S BREADTH AWAY FROM A NET FAULT ON THAT ONE! NOT ONLY THAT, HE STARTED IN THE BACK ROW...
...WHICH MEANT HE WASN'T A LEGAL ATTACKER, SO NO SETTER DUMP.
I'M SURPRISED HE EVEN GOT IT UP, BUT...
...THEN HIS HITTER CAME ALONG AND NAILED IT LIKE IT WAS A PERFECT RAINBOW.
NICE SET!
SWAK
THOSE TWO ARE SO IN SYNC WITH EACH OTHER IT'S ALMOST RIDICULOUS.
SHVR
AH. KARASUNO CALLED A TIME-OUT.
WHOA ...
FWEEEEE
KARASUNO
AOBA JOHSAI
11 13 08
KARASUNO SET 3 FIRST TIME-OUT

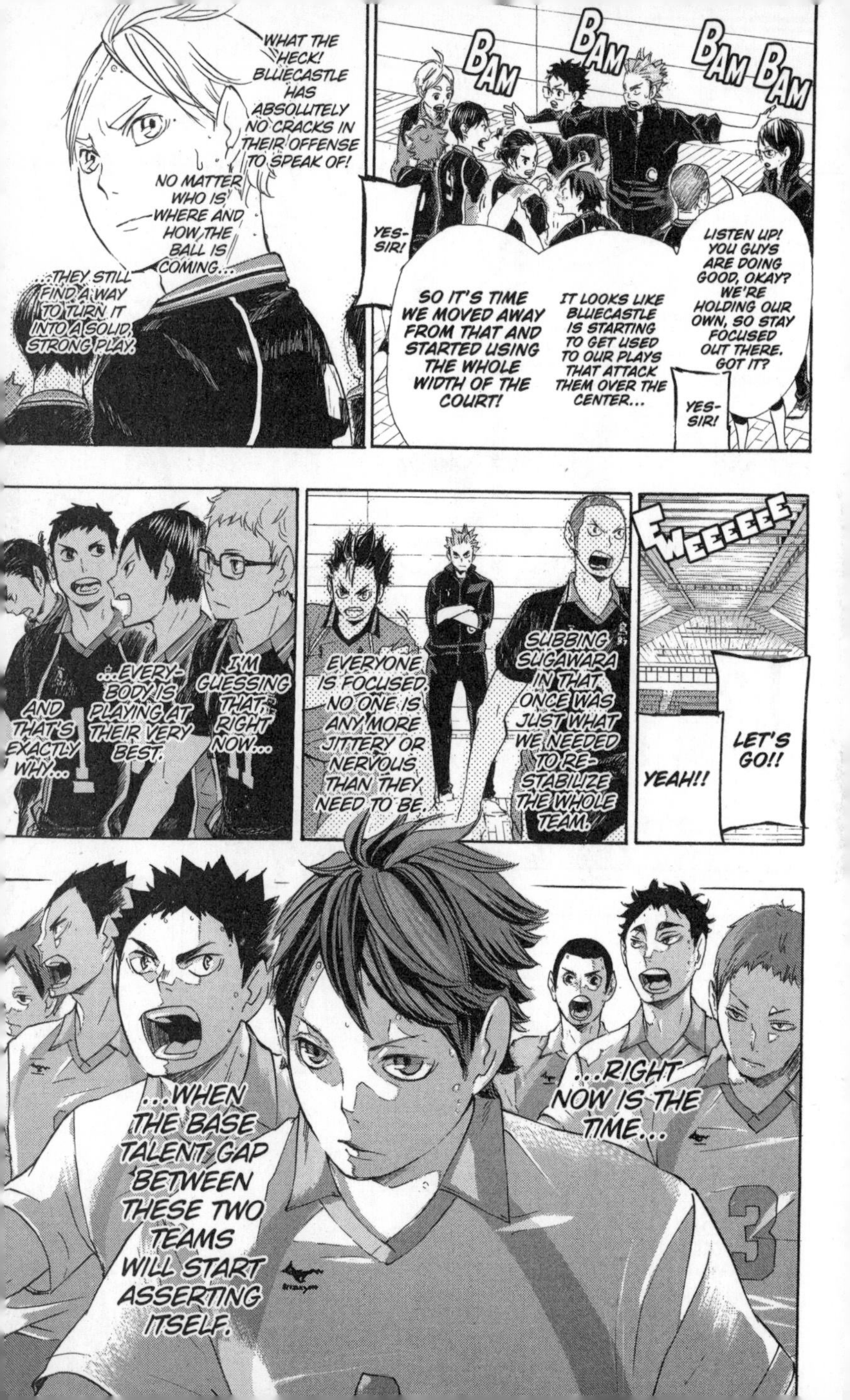
BAM BAM BAM BAM
LISTEN UP! YOU GUYS ARE DOING GOOD, OKAY? WE'RE HOLDING OUR OWN, SO STAY FOCUSED OUT THERE. GOT IT?
YES-SIR!
IT LOOKS LIKE BLUECASTLE IS STARTING TO GET USED TO OUR PLAYS THAT ATTACK THEM OVER THE CENTER...
SO IT'S TIME WE MOVED AWAY FROM THAT AND STARTED USING THE WHOLE WIDTH OF THE COURT!
YES-SIR!
WHAT THE HECK! BLUECASTLE HAS ABSOLUTELY NO CRACKS IN THEIR OFFENSE TO SPEAK OF!
NO MATTER WHO IS, WHERE AND HOW THE BALL IS COMING...
...THEY STILL FIND A WAY TO TURN IT INTO A SOLID, STRONG PLAY.
FWEEEEEE
LET'S GO!!
YEAH!!
SUBBING SUGAWARA IN THAT ONCE WAS JUST WHAT WE NEEDED TO RE-STABILIZE THE WHOLE TEAM.
EVERYONE IS FOCUSED. NO ONE IS ANY MORE JITTERY OR NERVOUS THAN THEY NEED TO BE.
I'M GUESSING THAT, RIGHT NOW...
...EVERYBODY IS PLAYING AT THEIR VERY BEST.
AND THAT'S EXACTLY WHY...
...RIGHT NOW IS THE TIME...
...WHEN THE BASE TALENT GAP BETWEEN THESE TWO TEAMS WILL START ASSERTING ITSELF.

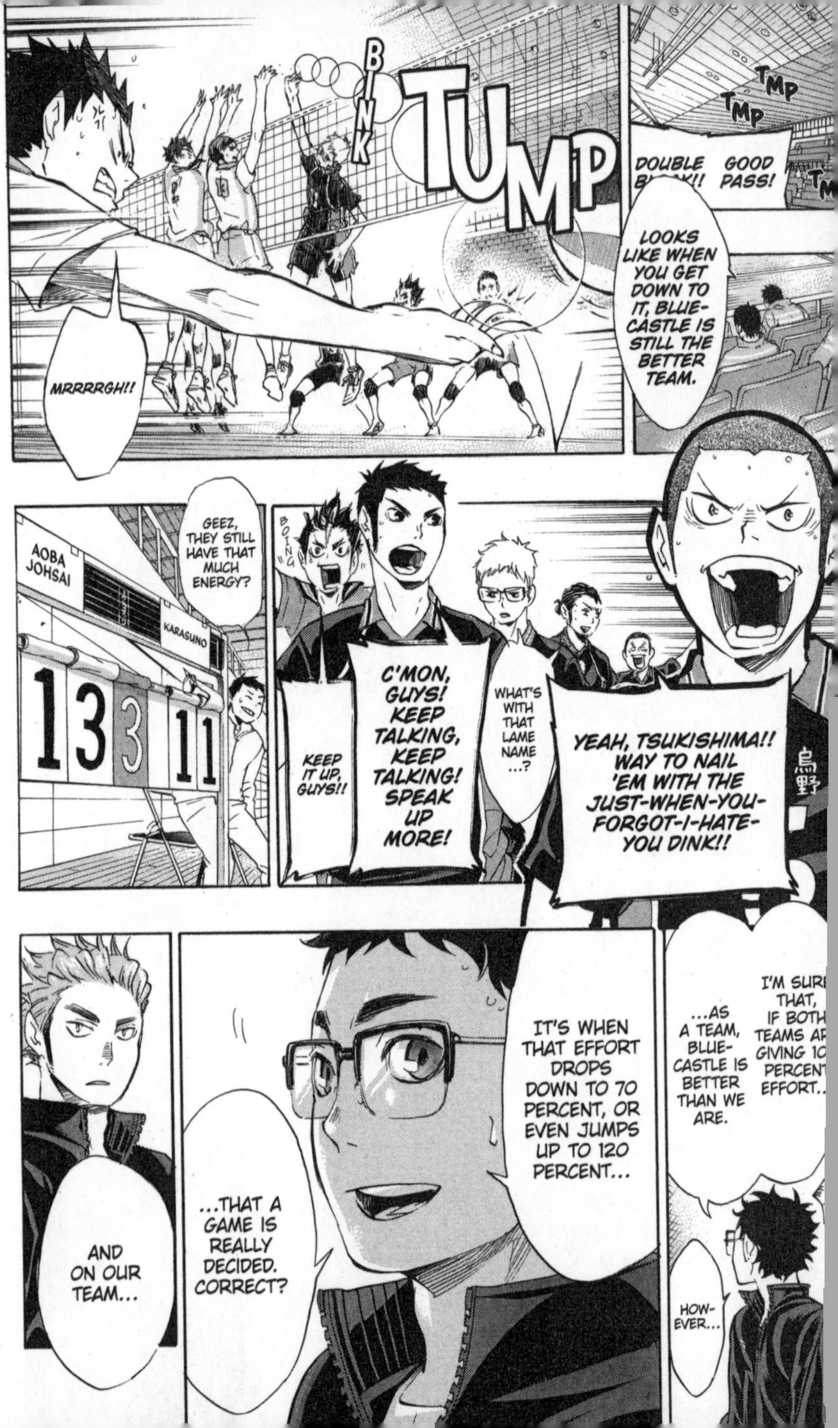
TMP
TMP
TM
GOOD PASS!
DOUBLE BLOCK!!
LOOKS LIKE WHEN YOU GET DOWN TO IT, BLUE-CASTLE IS STILL THE BETTER TEAM.
TUMP
BINK
MRRRRGH!!
YEAH, TSUKISHIMA!! WAY TO NAIL 'EM WITH THE JUST-WHEN-YOU-FORGOT-I-HATE-YOU DINK!!
WHAT'S WITH THAT LAME NAME ...?
C'MON, GUYS! KEEP TALKING, KEEP TALKING! SPEAK UP MORE!
KEEP IT UP, GUYS!!
BOING
GEEZ, THEY STILL HAVE THAT MUCH ENERGY?
AOBA JOHSAI
KARASUNO
13
3
11
I'M SUR THAT, IF BOTH TEAMS AR GIVING 10 PERCENT EFFORT..
...AS A TEAM, BLUE-CASTLE IS BETTER THAN WE ARE.
HOW-EVER...
IT'S WHEN THAT EFFORT DROPS DOWN TO 70 PERCENT, OR EVEN JUMPS UP TO 120 PERCENT...
...THAT A GAME IS REALLY DECIDED. CORRECT?
AND ON OUR TEAM...

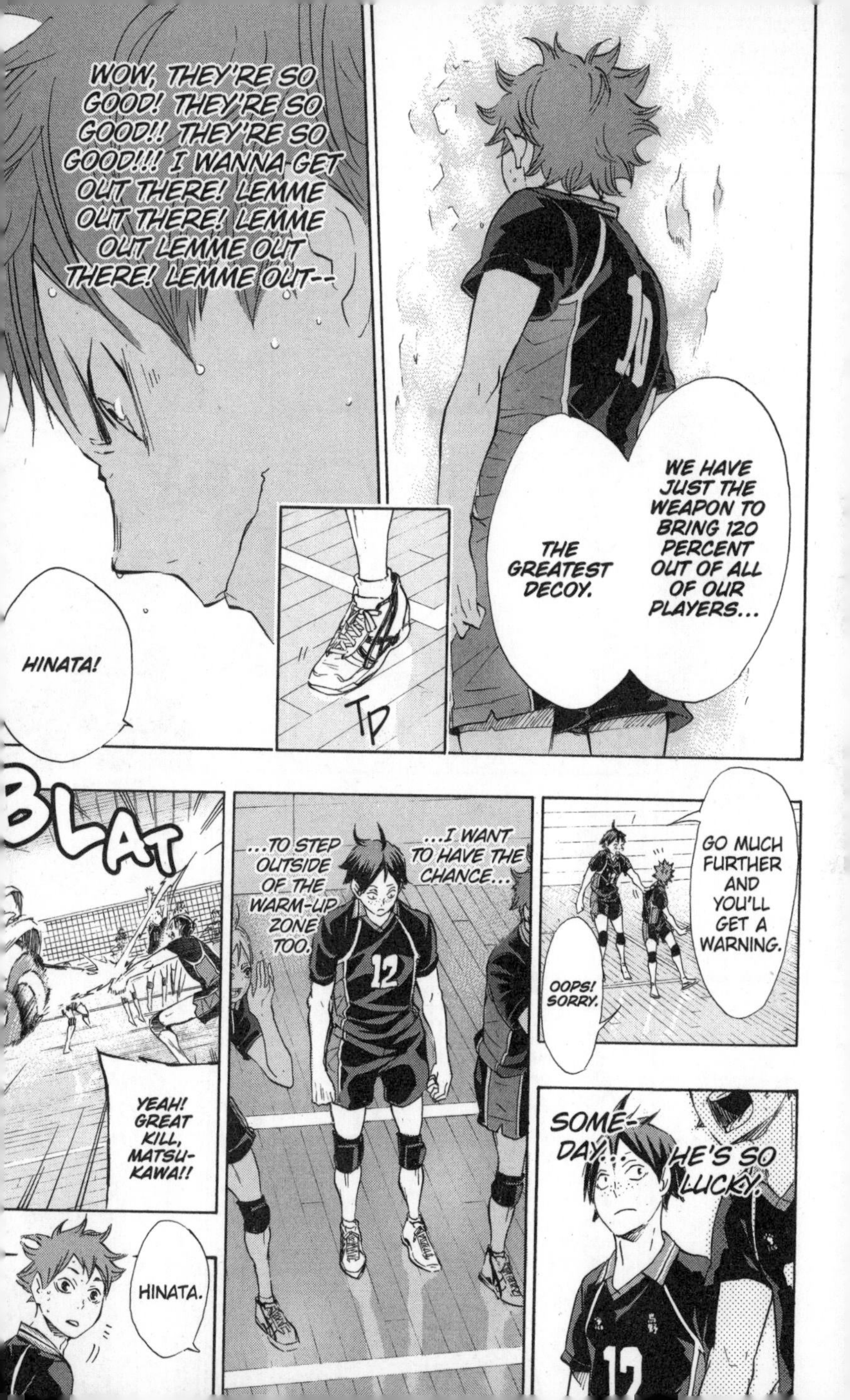
WE HAVE JUST THE WEAPON TO BRING 120 PERCENT OUT OF ALL OF OUR PLAYERS...
THE GREATEST DECOY.
TP
WOW, THEY'RE SO GOOD! THEY'RE SO GOOD!! THEY'RE SO GOOD!!! I WANNA GET OUT THERE! LEMME OUT THERE! LEMME OUT LEMME OUT THERE! LEMME OUT--
HINATA!
GO MUCH FURTHER AND YOU'LL GET A WARNING.
OOPS! SORRY.
SOME-DAY...
HE'S SO LUCKY.
...I WANT TO HAVE THE CHANCE...
...TO STEP OUTSIDE OF THE WARM-UP ZONE TOO.
BLAT
YEAH! GREAT KILL, MATSU-KAWA!!
HINATA.

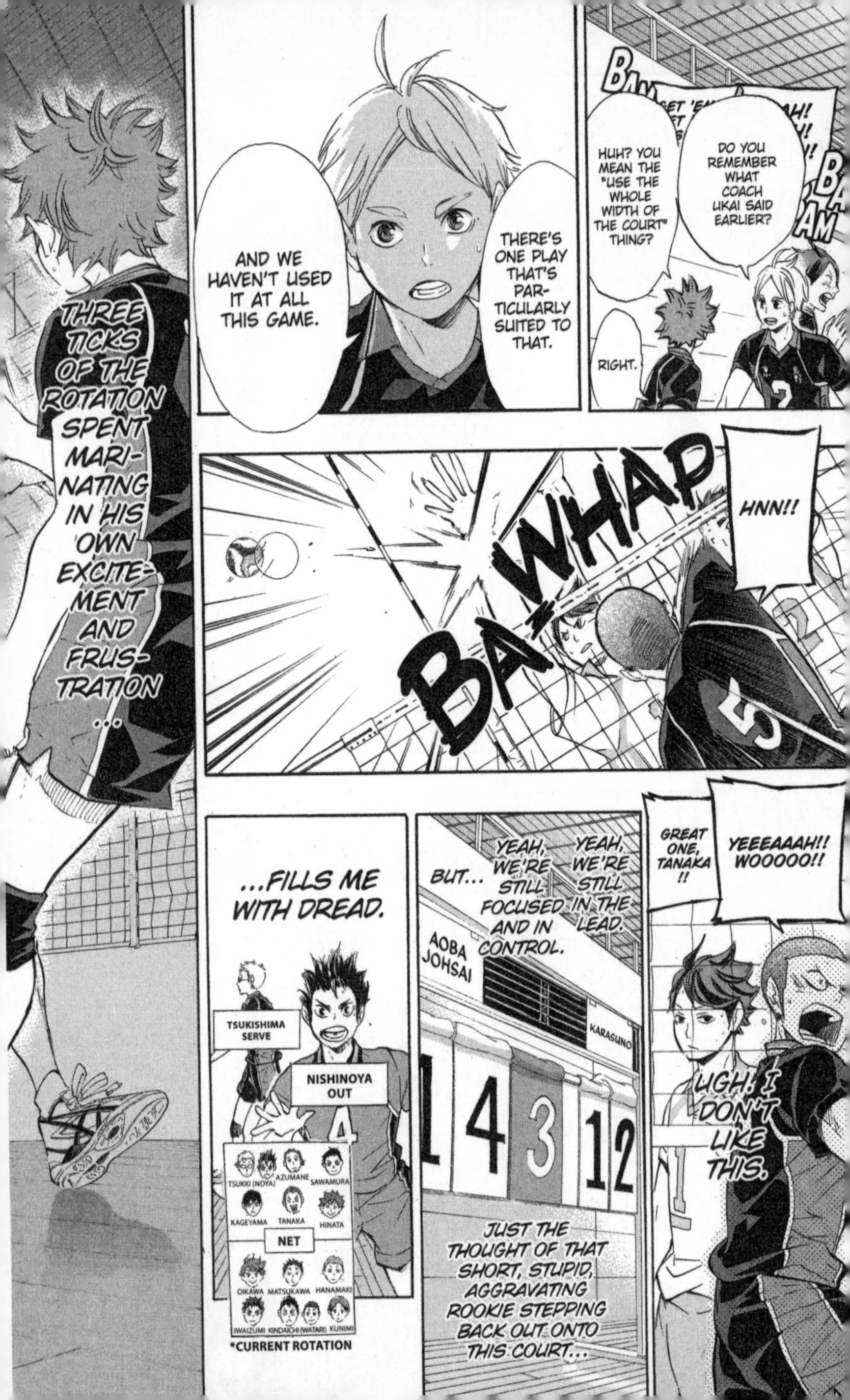
DO YOU REMEMBER WHAT COACH UKAI SAID EARLIER?
HUH? YOU MEAN THE "USE THE WHOLE WIDTH OF THE COURT" THING?
RIGHT.
THERE'S ONE PLAY THAT'S PAR-TICULARLY SUITED TO THAT.
AND WE HAVEN'T USED IT AT ALL THIS GAME.
HNN!!
BA WHAP
YEEEAAAH!! WOOOOO!!
GREAT ONE, TANAKA!!
UGH. I DON'T LIKE THIS.
YEAH, WE'RE STILL IN THE LEAD.
YEAH, WE'RE STILL FOCUSED AND IN CONTROL.
BUT...
AOBA JOHSAI
KARASUNO
1 4 3 12
JUST THE THOUGHT OF THAT SHORT, STUPID, AGGRAVATING ROOKIE STEPPING BACK OUT ONTO THIS COURT...
...FILLS ME WITH DREAD.
TSUKISHIMA SERVE
NISHINOYA OUT
TSUKKI (NOYA) AZUMANE SAWAMURA
KAGEYAMA TANAKA HINATA
NET
OIKAWA MATSUKAWA HANAMAKI
IWAIZUMI KINDAICHI (WATARI) KUNIMI
*CURRENT ROTATION
THREE TICKS OF THE ROTATION SPENT MARI-NATING IN HIS OWN EXCITE-MENT AND FRUS-TRATION...

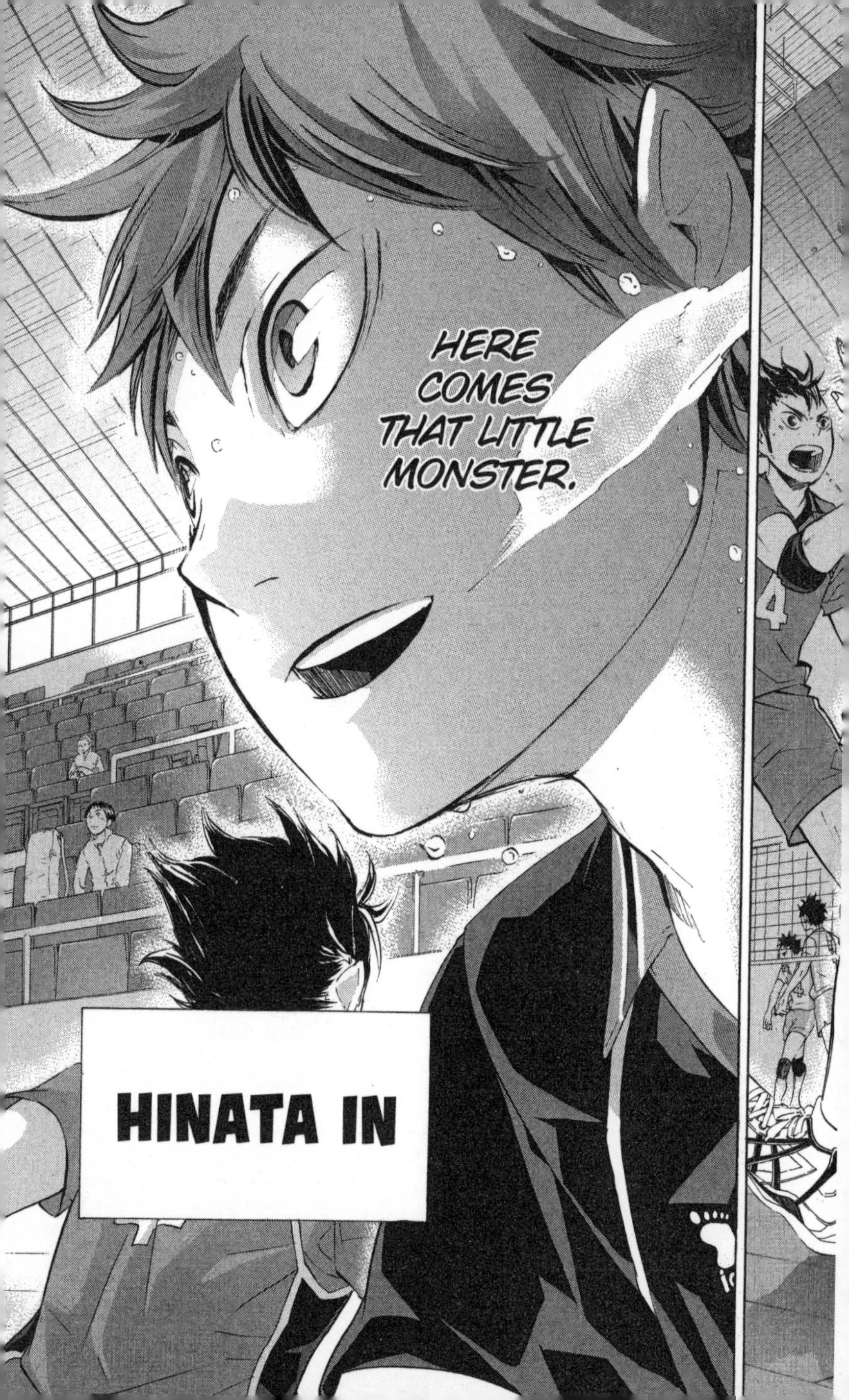
HERE COMES THAT LITTLE MONSTER.
HINATA IN

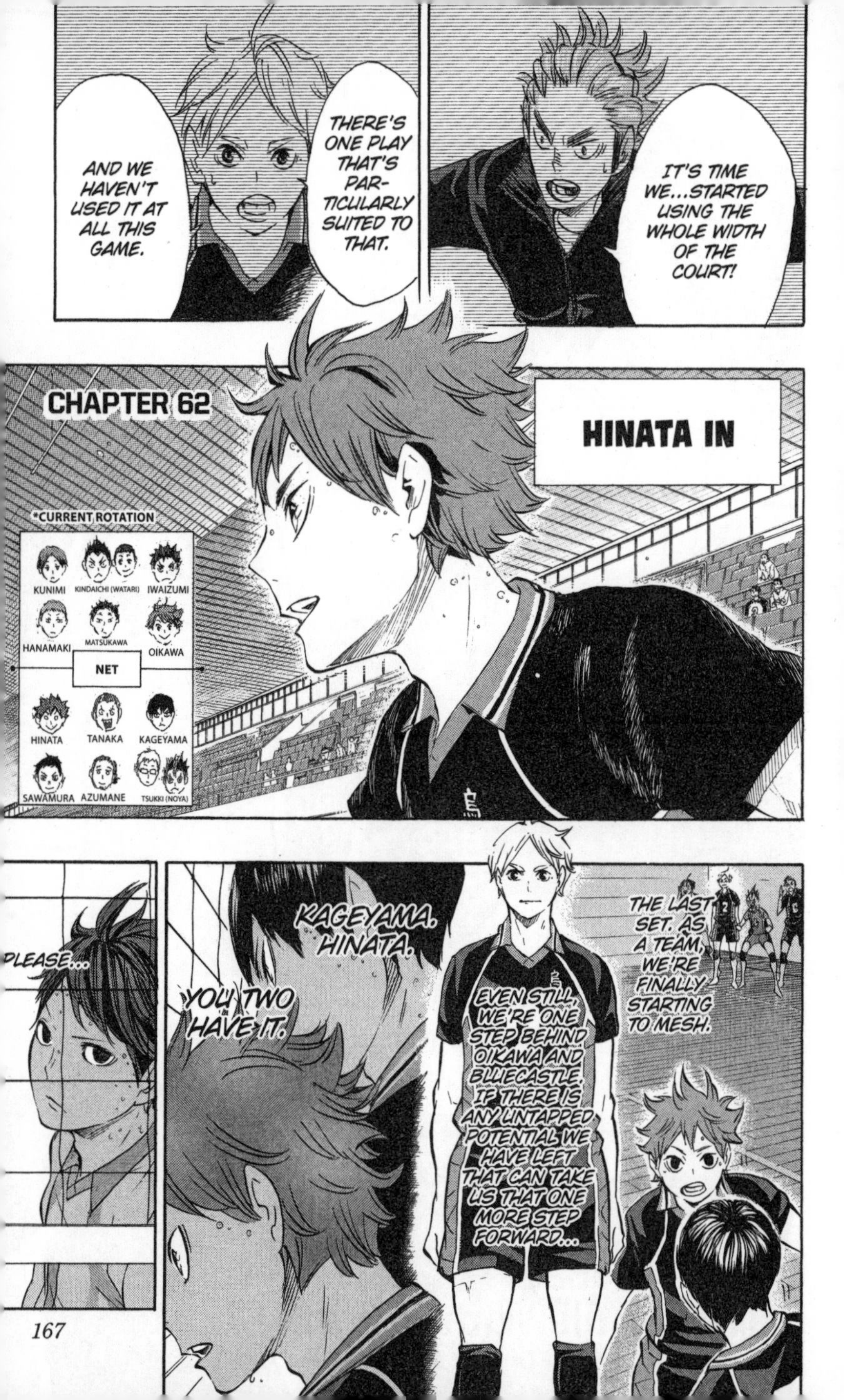
IT'S TIME WE...STARTED USING THE WHOLE WIDTH OF THE COURT!
THERE'S ONE PLAY THAT'S PAR-TICULARLY SUITED TO THAT.
AND WE HAVEN'T USED IT AT ALL THIS GAME.
CHAPTER 62
HINATA IN
*CURRENT ROTATION
KUNIMI
KINDAICHI (WATARI)
IWAIZUMI
HANAMAKI
MATSUKAWA
OIKAWA
NET
HINATA
TANAKA
KAGEYAMA
SAWAMURA
AZUMANE
TSUKKI (NOYA)
THE LAST SET. AS A TEAM, WE'RE FINALLY STARTING TO MESH.
EVEN STILL, WE'RE ONE STEP BEHIND OIKAWA AND BLUECASTLE. IF THERE IS ANY UNTAPPED POTENTIAL WE HAVE LEFT THAT CAN TAKE US THAT ONE MORE STEP FORWARD...
KAGEYAMA. HINATA.
YOU TWO HAVE IT.
PLEASE...

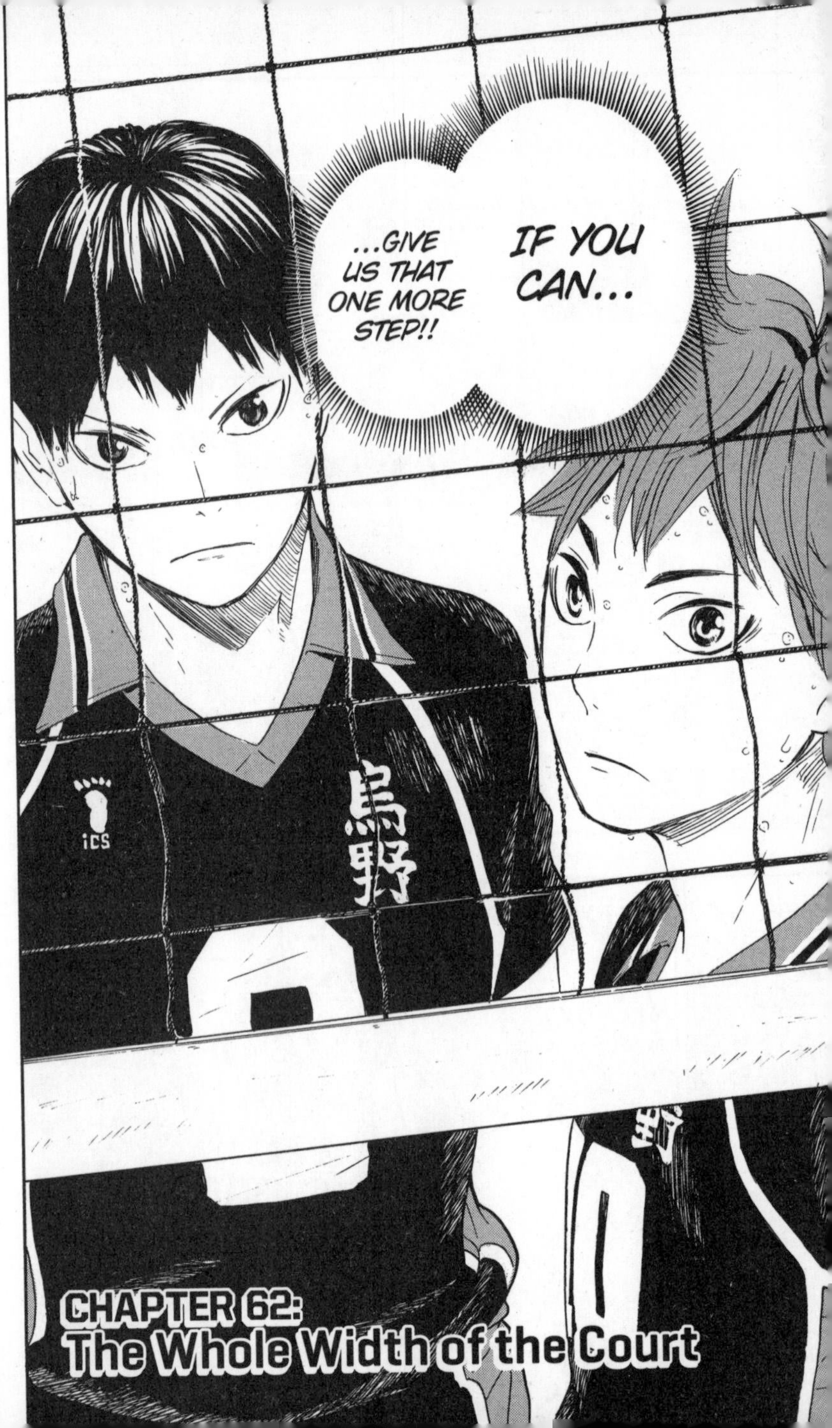
IF YOU CAN...
...GIVE US THAT ONE MORE STEP!!
烏野

CHAPTER 62: The Whole Width of the Court

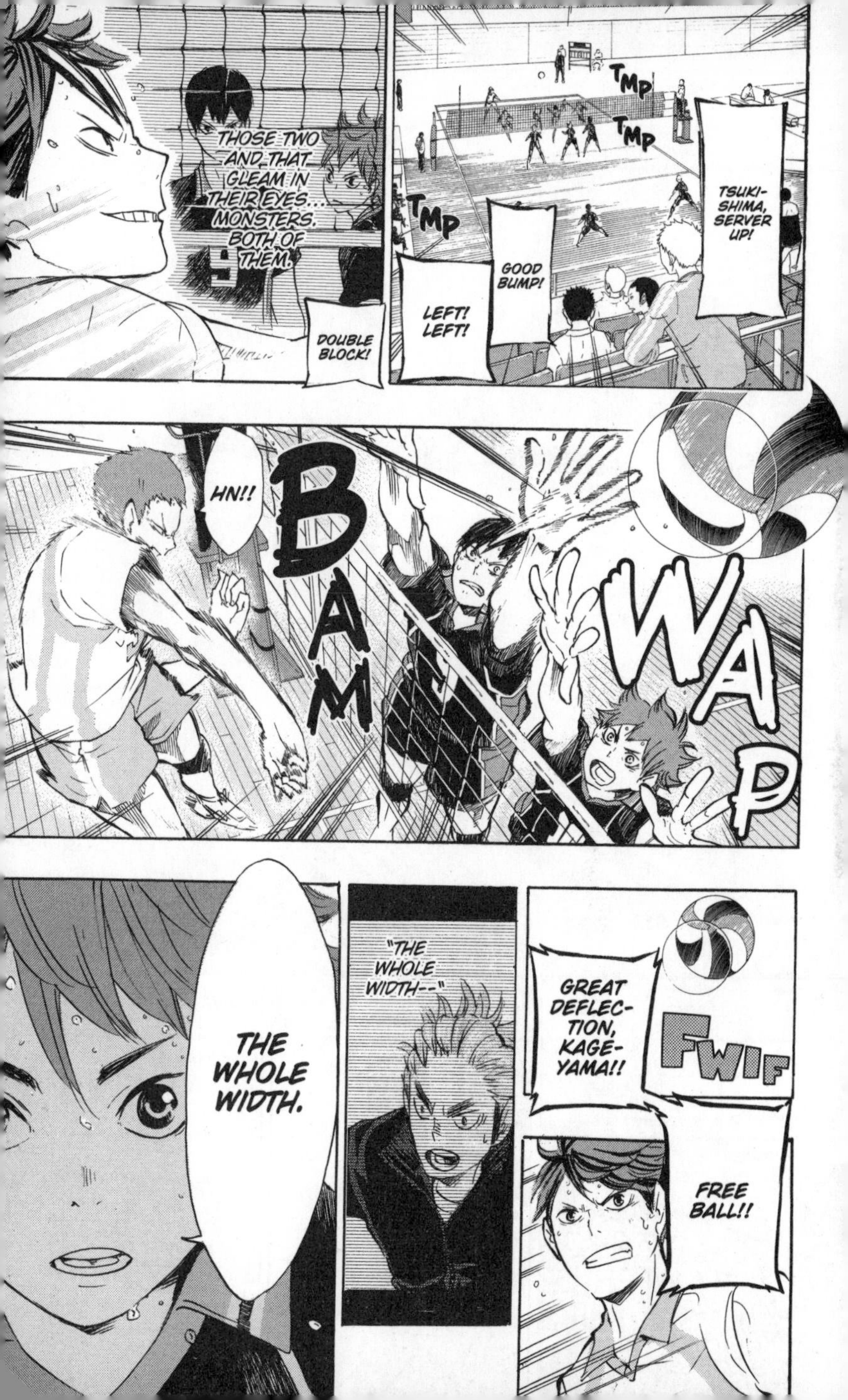
TSUKI-SHIMA, SERVER UP!
TMP
TMP
GOOD BUMP!
LEFT! LEFT!
TMP
THOSE TWO AND THAT GLEAM IN THEIR EYES... MONSTERS. BOTH OF THEM.
DOUBLE BLOCK!
WAP
BAM
HN!!
GREAT DEFLECTION, KAGEYAMA!!
FWIF
FREE BALL!!
"THE WHOLE WIDTH--"
THE WHOLE WIDTH.

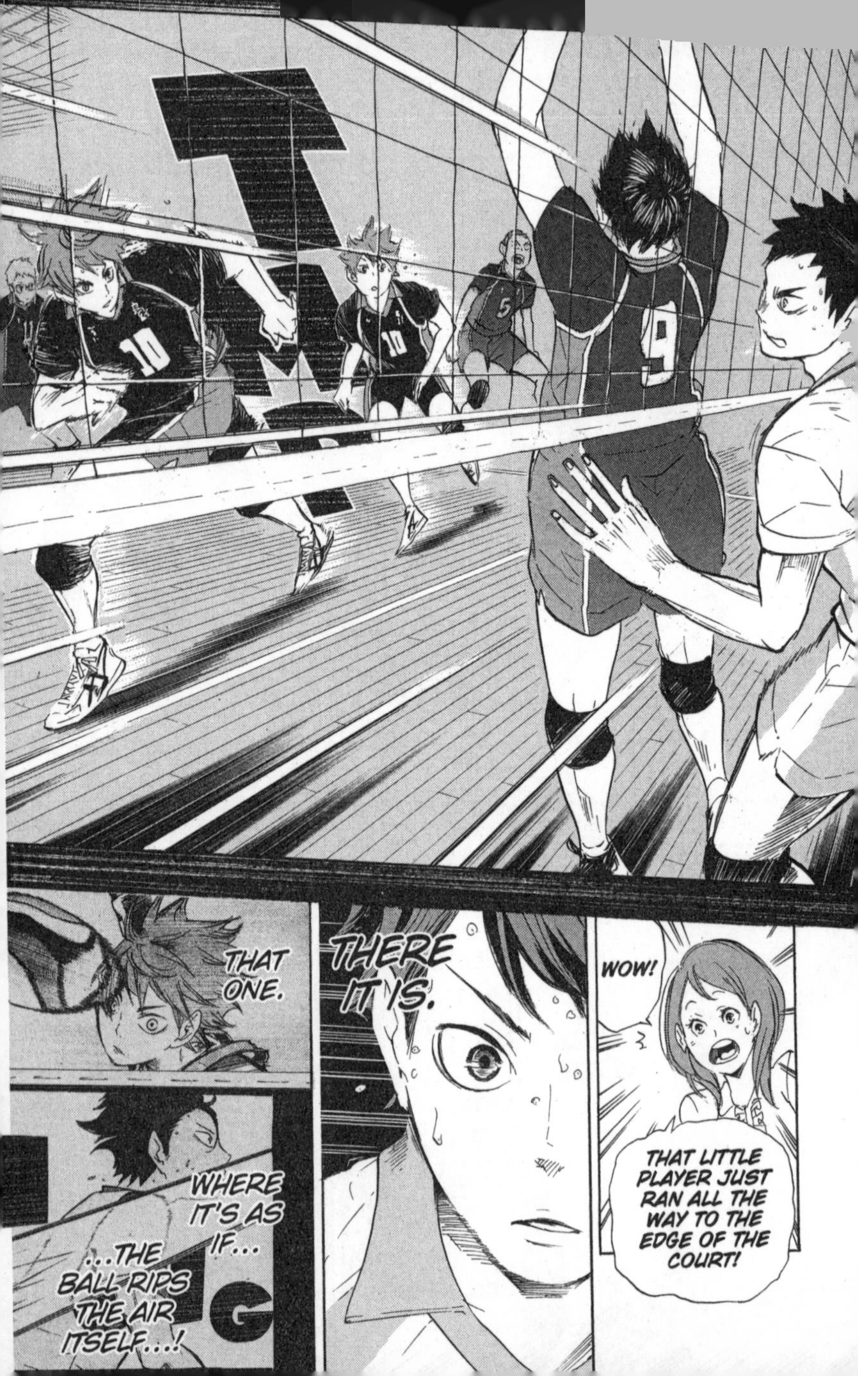
WOW!
THAT LITTLE PLAYER JUST RAN ALL THE WAY TO THE EDGE OF THE COURT!
THERE IT IS.
THAT ONE.
WHERE IT'S AS IF...
...THE BALL RIPS THE AIR ITSELF...!
G

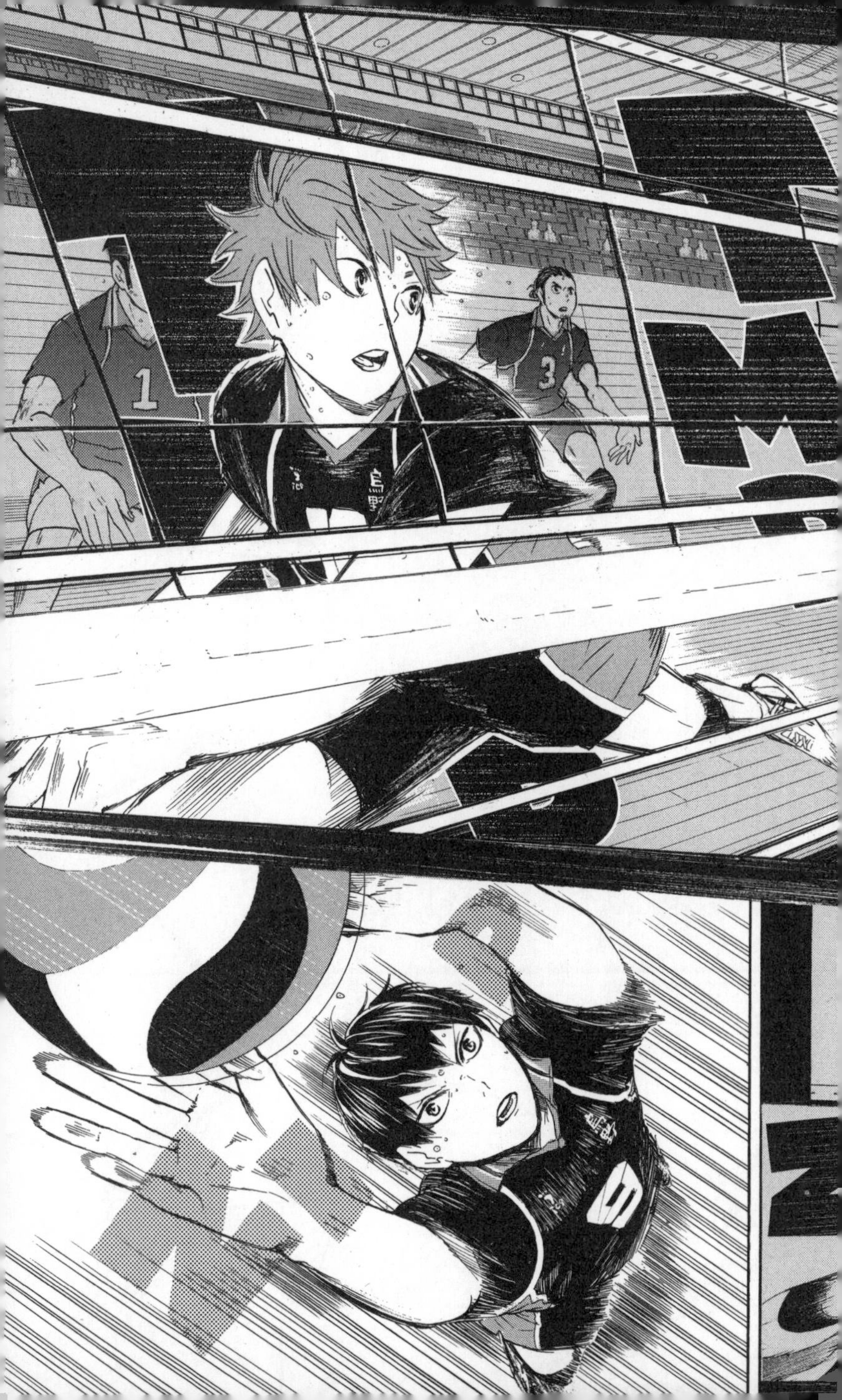

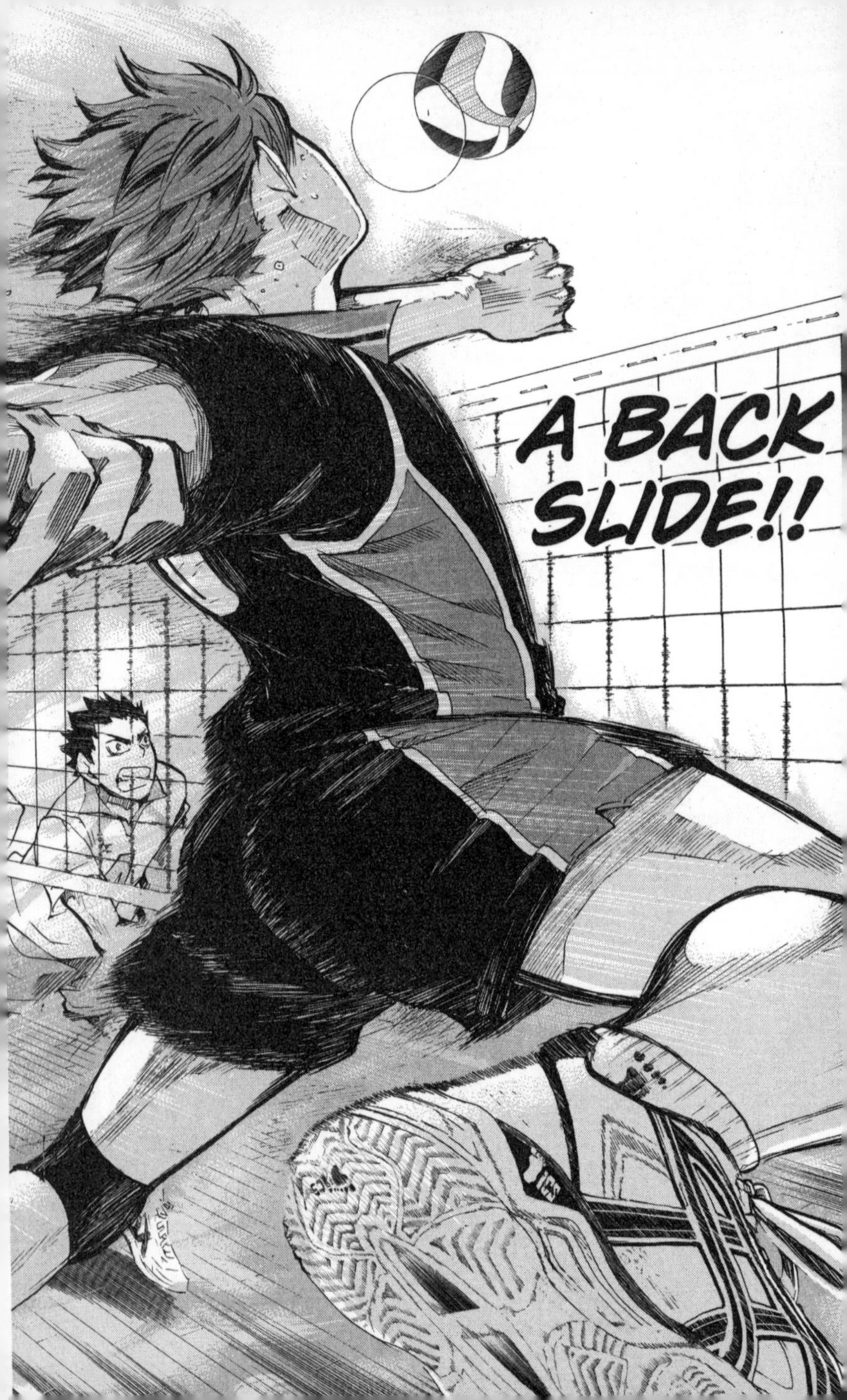
A BACK SLIDE!!

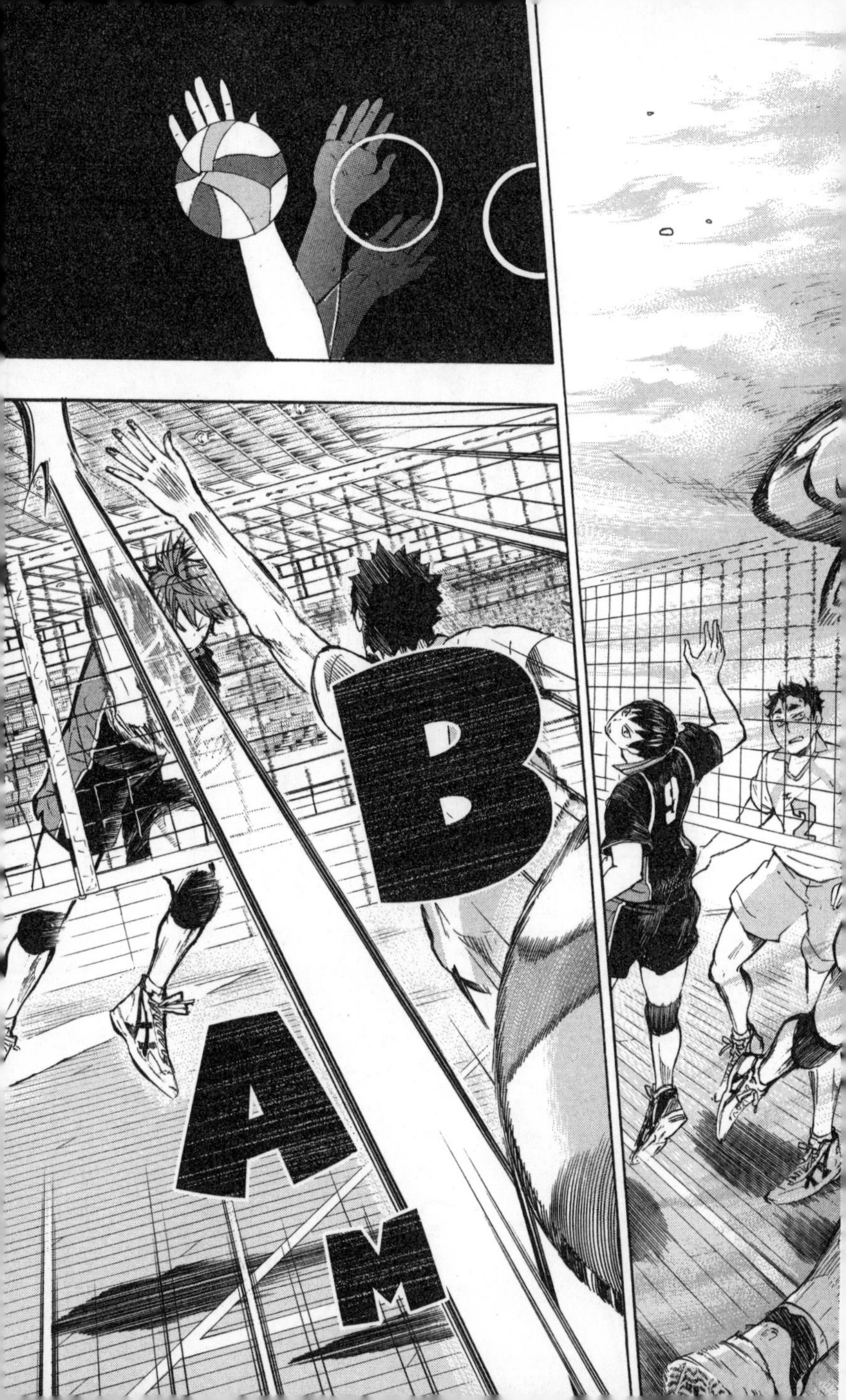
BAM

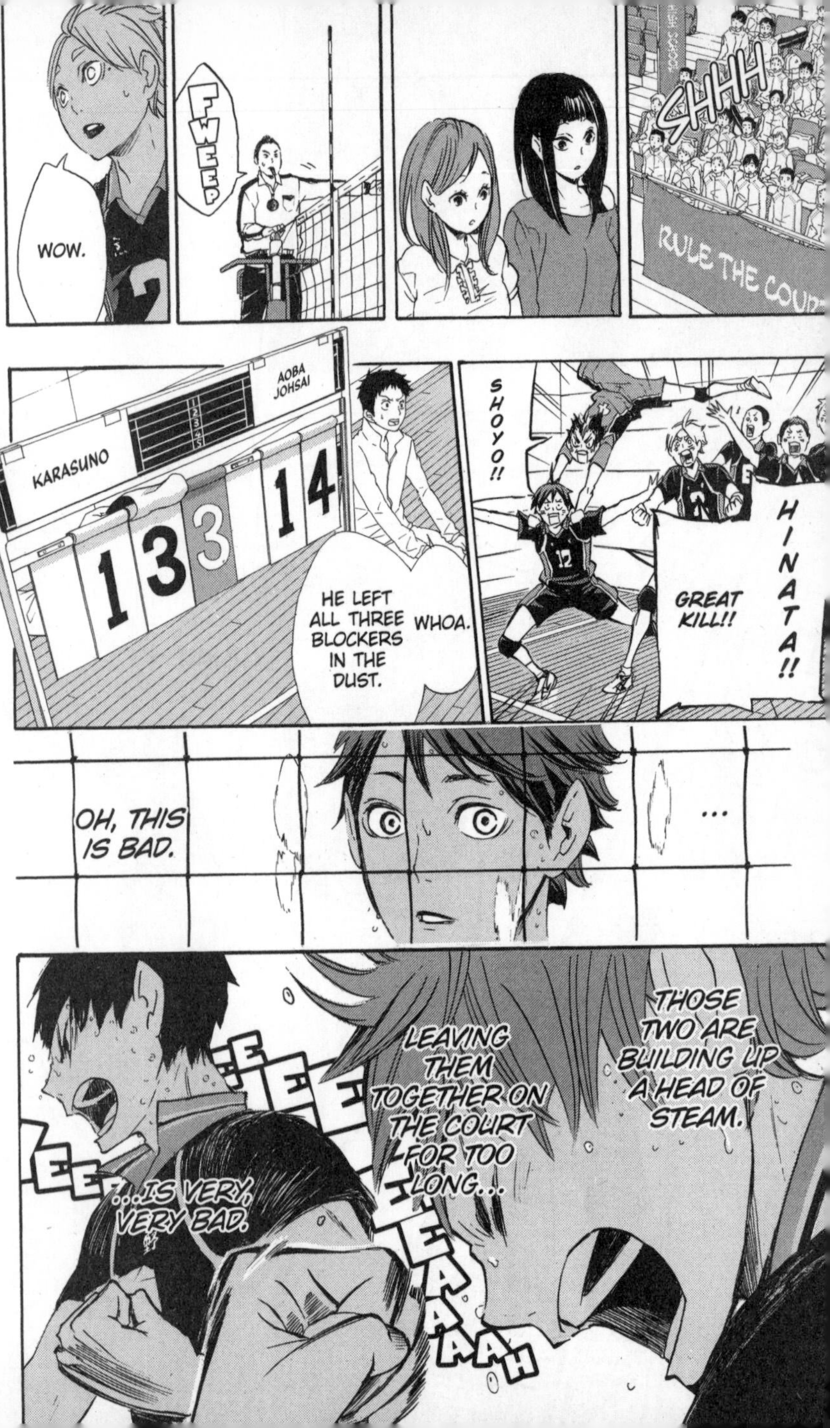
SHHH
RULE THE COU
FWEEP
WOW.
SHOYO!!
HINATA!!
GREAT KILL!!
WHOA.
HE LEFT ALL THREE BLOCKERS IN THE DUST.
AOBA JOHSAI
KARASUNO
13
3
14
...
OH, THIS IS BAD.
THOSE TWO ARE BUILDING UP A HEAD OF STEAM.
LEAVING THEM TOGETHER ON THE COURT FOR TOO LONG...
...IS VERY, VERY BAD.

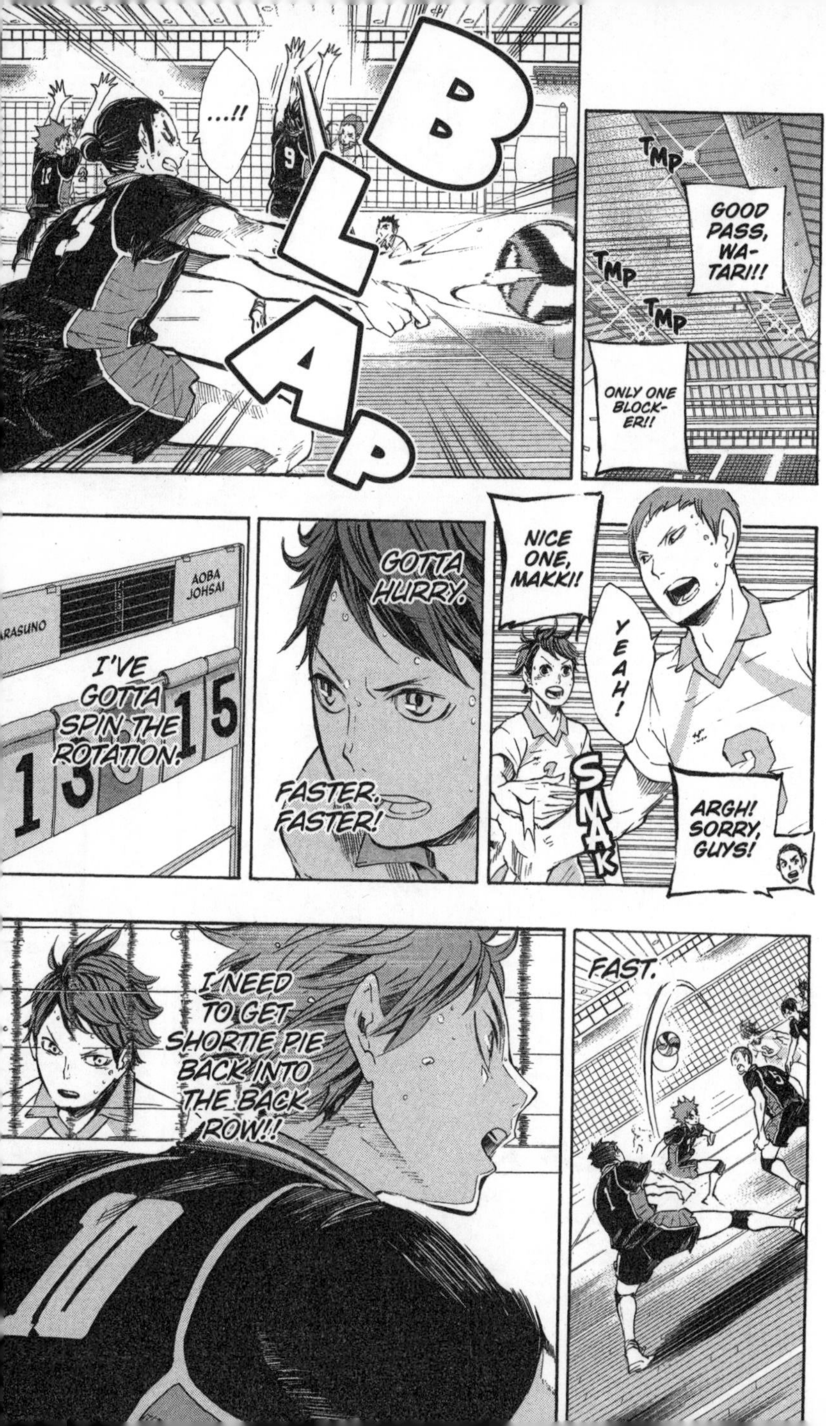
TMP
TMP
TMP
GOOD PASS, WATARI!!
ONLY ONE BLOCKER!!
...!!
BLAP
NICE ONE, MAKKI!
YEAH!
SMAK
ARGH! SORRY, GUYS!
GOTTA HURRY.
FASTER. FASTER!
AOBA JOHSAI
ARASUNO
I'VE GOTTA SPIN THE ROTATION.
15
13
FAST.
I NEED TO GET SHORTIE PIE BACK INTO THE BACK ROW!!

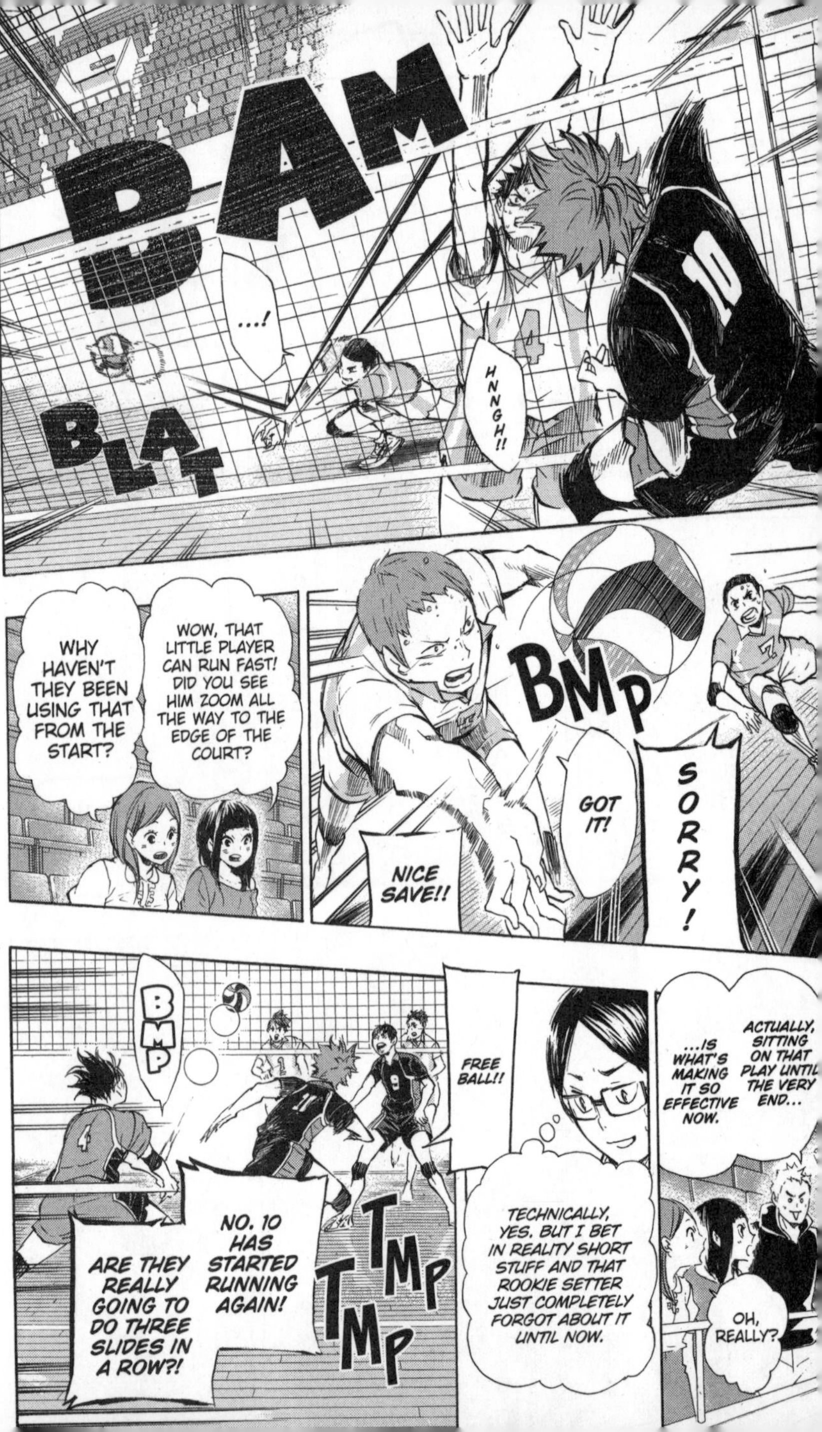
BAM
HNNGH!!
...!
BLAT
BMP
SORRY!
GOT IT!
NICE SAVE!!
WOW, THAT LITTLE PLAYER CAN RUN FAST! DID YOU SEE HIM ZOOM ALL THE WAY TO THE EDGE OF THE COURT?
WHY HAVEN'T THEY BEEN USING THAT FROM THE START?
ACTUALLY, SITTING ON THAT PLAY UNTIL THE VERY END...
...IS WHAT'S MAKING IT SO EFFECTIVE NOW.
OH, REALLY?
FREE BALL!!
TECHNICALLY, YES. BUT I BET IN REALITY SHORT STUFF AND THAT ROOKIE SETTER JUST COMPLETELY FORGOT ABOUT IT UNTIL NOW.
BMP
NO. 10 HAS STARTED RUNNING AGAIN!
TMP TMP
ARE THEY REALLY GOING TO DO THREE SLIDES IN A ROW?!

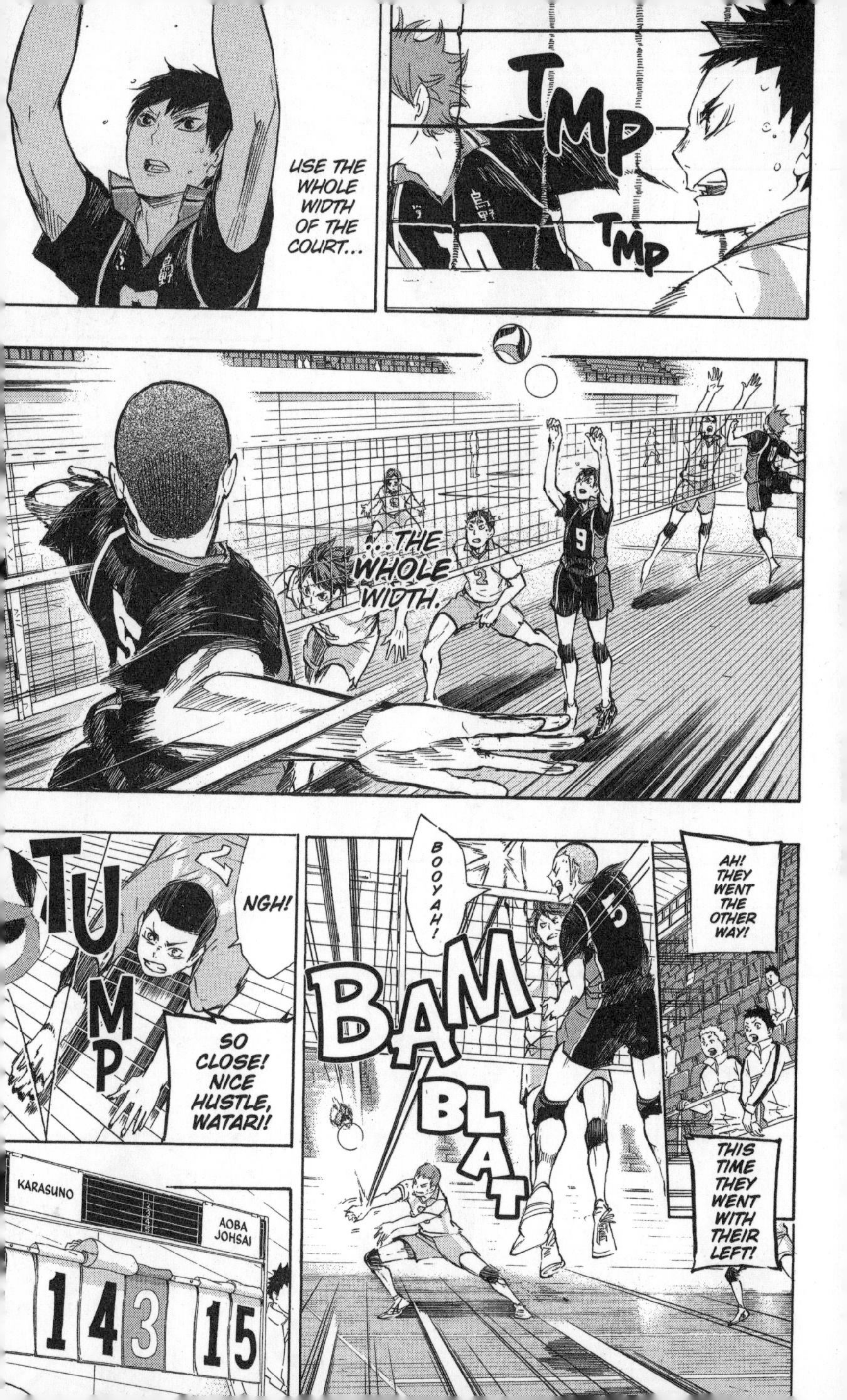
TMP
TMP
USE THE WHOLE WIDTH OF THE COURT...
...THE WHOLE WIDTH.
AH! THEY WENT THE OTHER WAY!
BOOYAH!
BAM
THIS TIME THEY WENT WITH THEIR LEFT!
BLAT
NGH!
TUMP
SO CLOSE! NICE HUSTLE, WATARI!
KARASUNO
AOBA JOHSAI
14
3
15

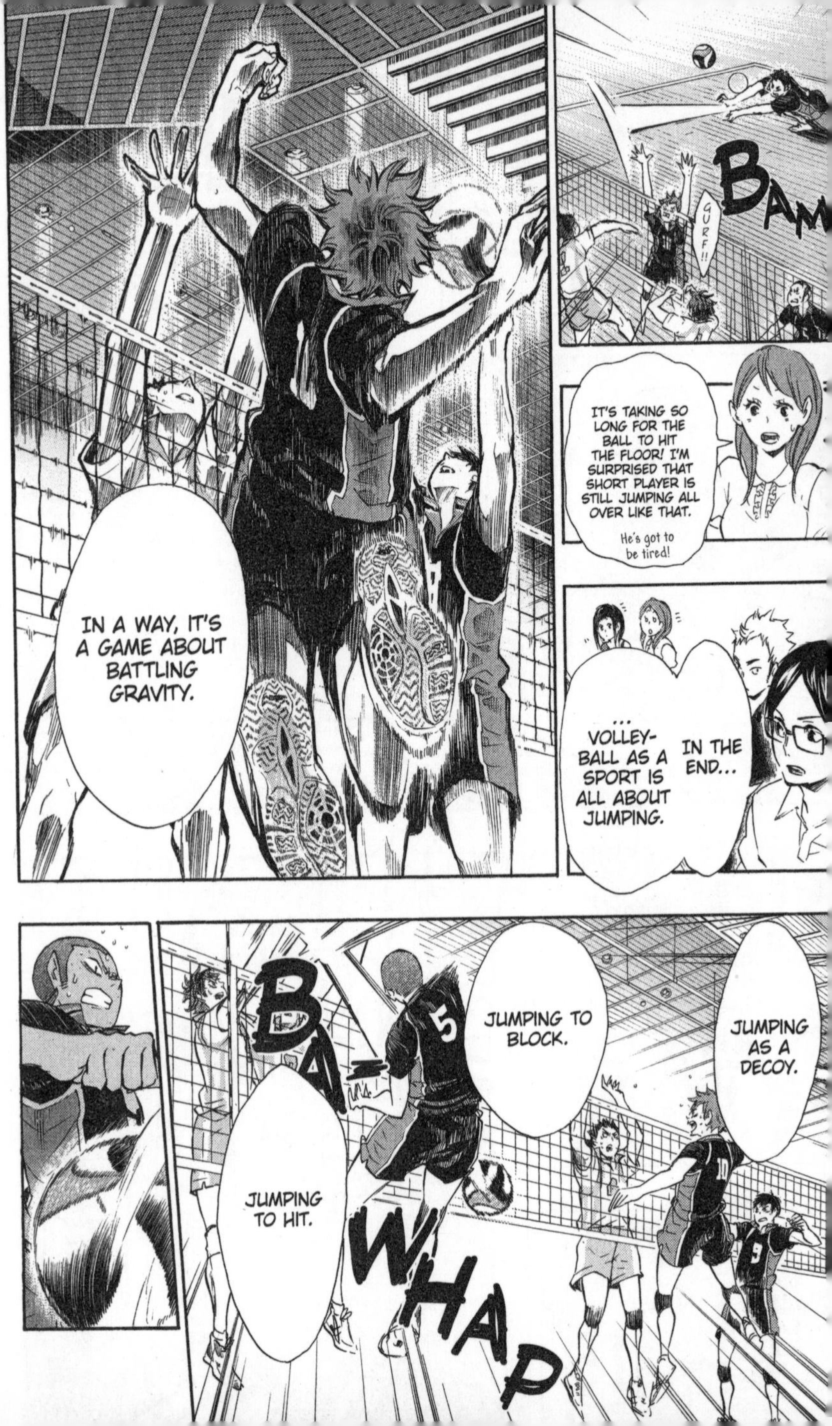
BAM
GURF!!
IT'S TAKING SO LONG FOR THE BALL TO HIT THE FLOOR! I'M SURPRISED THAT SHORT PLAYER IS STILL JUMPING ALL OVER LIKE THAT.
He's got to be tired!
IN THE END...
... VOLLEYBALL AS A SPORT IS ALL ABOUT JUMPING.
IN A WAY, IT'S A GAME ABOUT BATTLING GRAVITY.
JUMPING AS A DECOY.
JUMPING TO BLOCK.
BA
JUMPING TO HIT.
WHAP

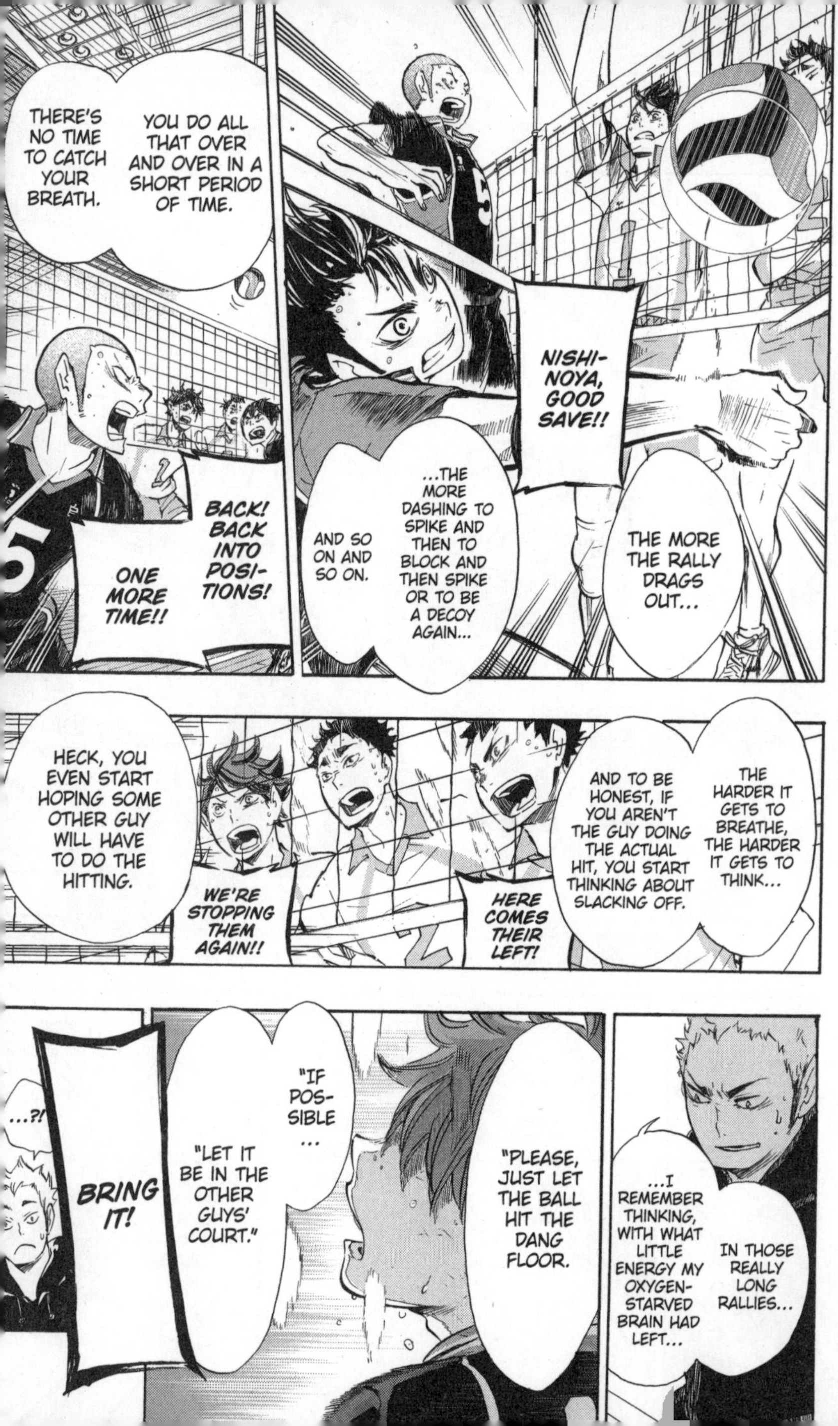
THE MORE THE RALLY DRAGS OUT...
NISHINOYA, GOOD SAVE!!
...THE MORE DASHING TO SPIKE AND THEN TO BLOCK AND THEN SPIKE OR TO BE A DECOY AGAIN...
AND SO ON AND SO ON.
YOU DO ALL THAT OVER AND OVER IN A SHORT PERIOD OF TIME.
THERE'S NO TIME TO CATCH YOUR BREATH.
BACK! BACK INTO POSI-TIONS!
ONE MORE TIME!!
THE HARDER IT GETS TO BREATHE, THE HARDER IT GETS TO THINK...
AND TO BE HONEST, IF YOU AREN'T THE GUY DOING THE ACTUAL HIT, YOU START THINKING ABOUT SLACKING OFF.
HERE COMES THEIR LEFT!
WE'RE STOPPING THEM AGAIN!!
HECK, YOU EVEN START HOPING SOME OTHER GUY WILL HAVE TO DO THE HITTING.
IN THOSE REALLY LONG RALLIES...
...I REMEMBER THINKING, WITH WHAT LITTLE ENERGY MY OXYGEN-STARVED BRAIN HAD LEFT...
"PLEASE, JUST LET THE BALL HIT THE DANG FLOOR.
"IF POS-SIBLE...
"LET IT BE IN THE OTHER GUYS' COURT."
BRING IT!
...?!

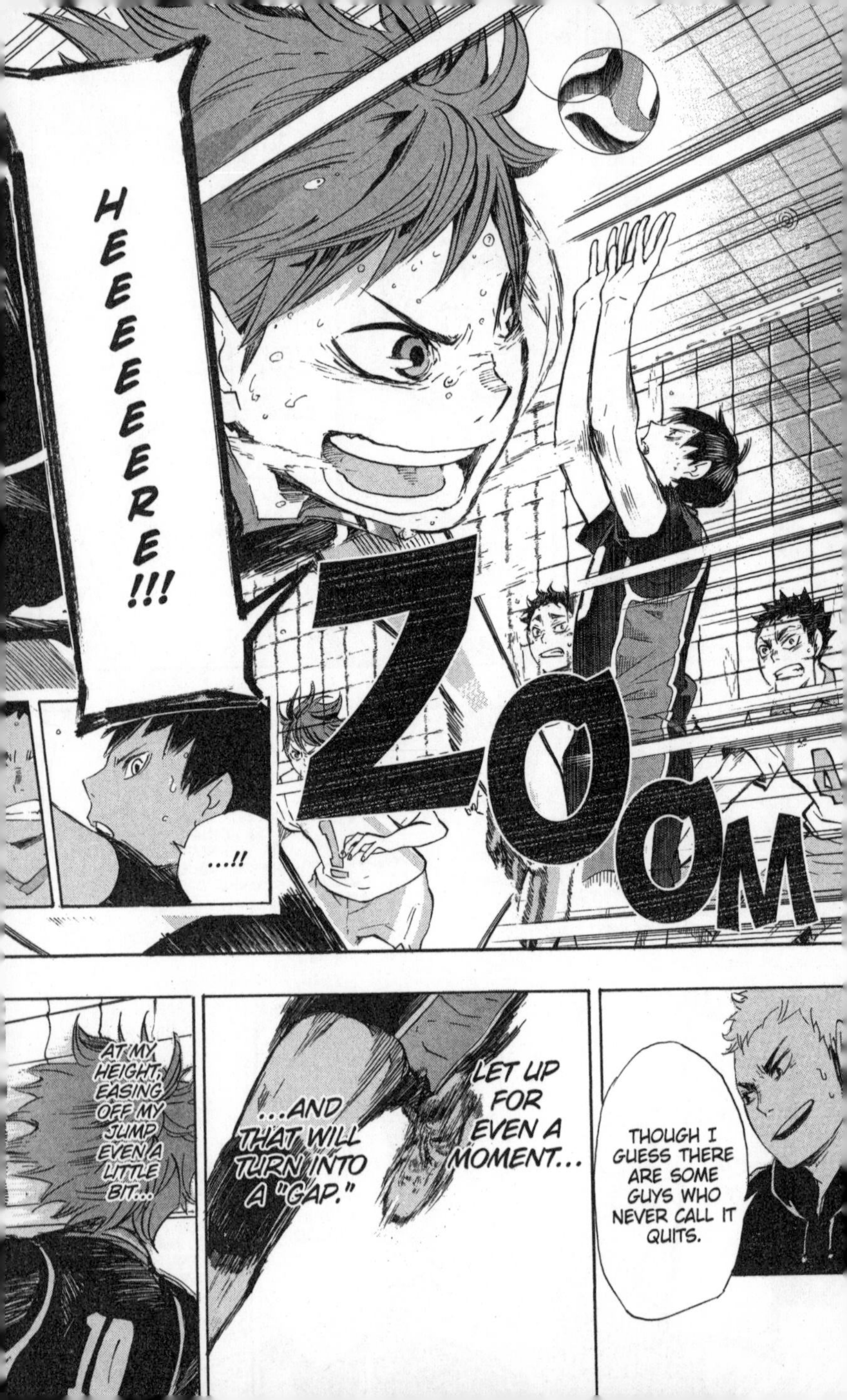
HEEEEEEERE!!!
ZOOM
...!!
THOUGH I GUESS THERE ARE SOME GUYS WHO NEVER CALL IT QUITS.
LET UP FOR EVEN A MOMENT...
...AND THAT WILL TURN INTO A "GAP."
AT MY HEIGHT, EASING OFF MY JUMP EVEN A LITTLE BIT...

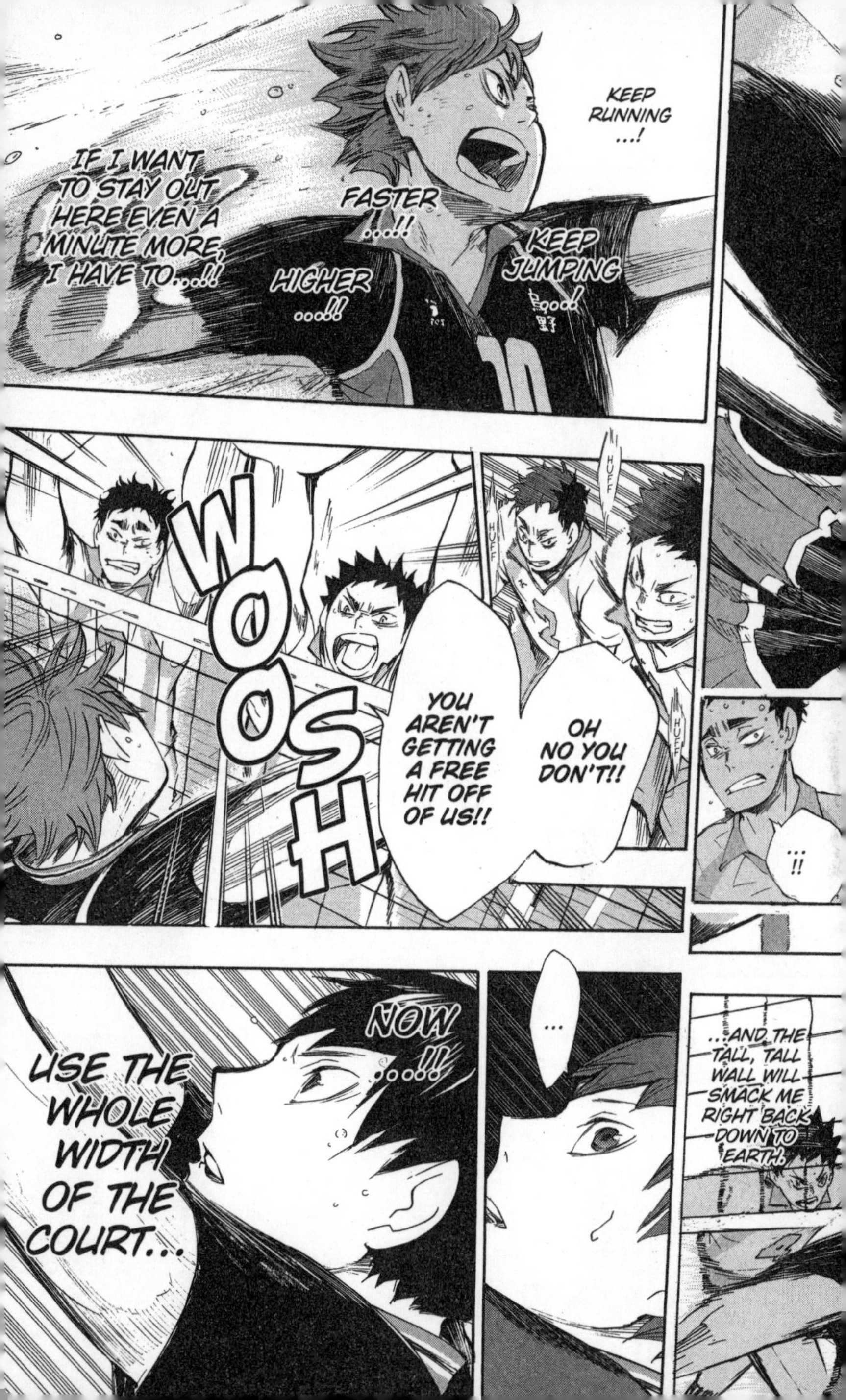
KEEP RUNNING ...!
KEEP JUMPING ...!
FASTER ...!!
HIGHER ...!!
IF I WANT TO STAY OUT HERE EVEN A MINUTE MORE, I HAVE TO...!!
...!!
HUFF
HUFF
OH NO YOU DON'T!!
HUFF
YOU AREN'T GETTING A FREE HIT OFF OF US!!
WOOSH
...AND THE TALL, TALL WALL WILL SMACK ME RIGHT BACK DOWN TO EARTH.
...
NOW ...!!
USE THE WHOLE WIDTH OF THE COURT...

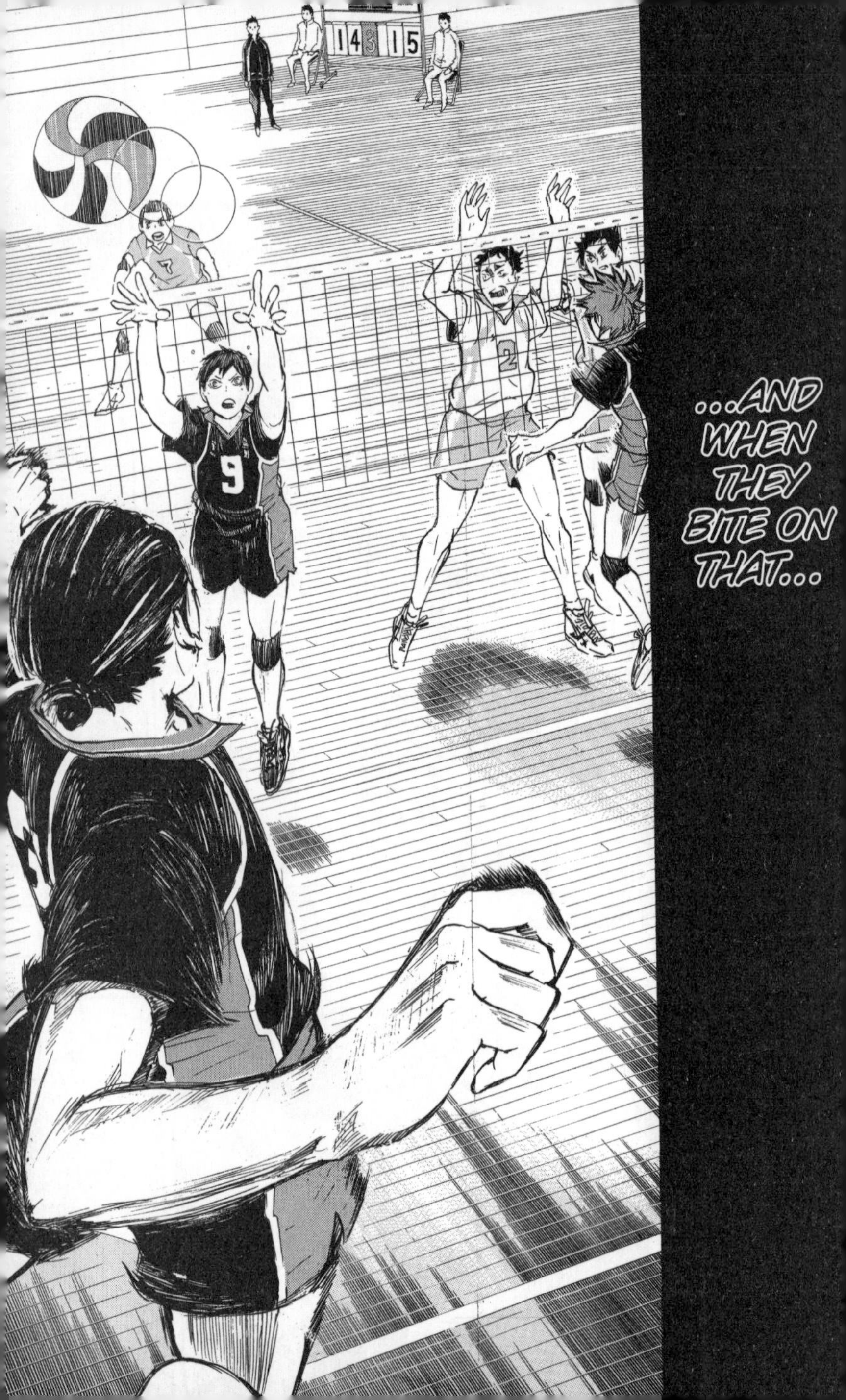
14 3 15
...AND WHEN THEY BITE ON THAT...

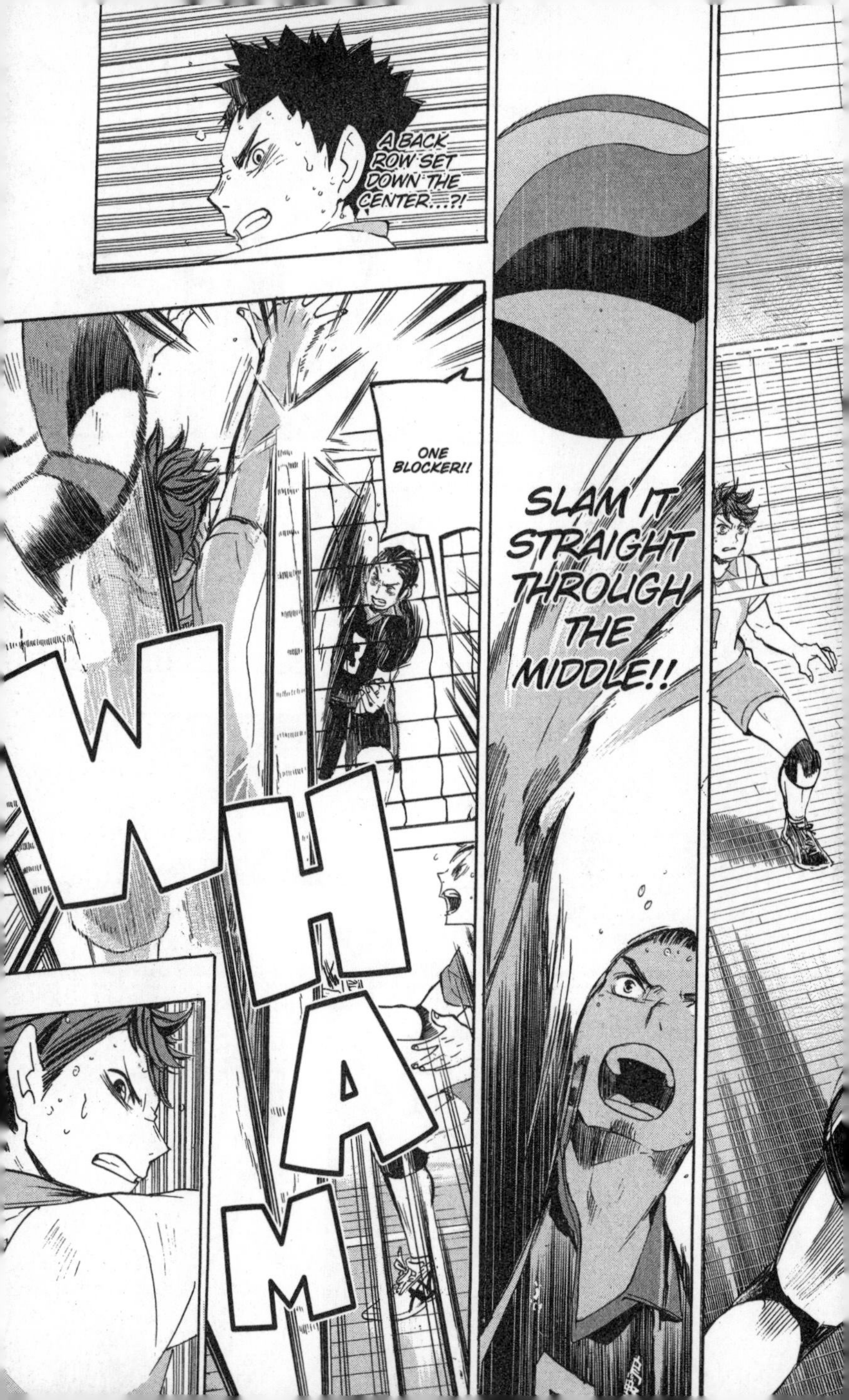
SLAM IT STRAIGHT THROUGH THE MIDDLE!!
A BACK ROW SET DOWN THE CENTER...?!
ONE BLOCKER!!
WHAM

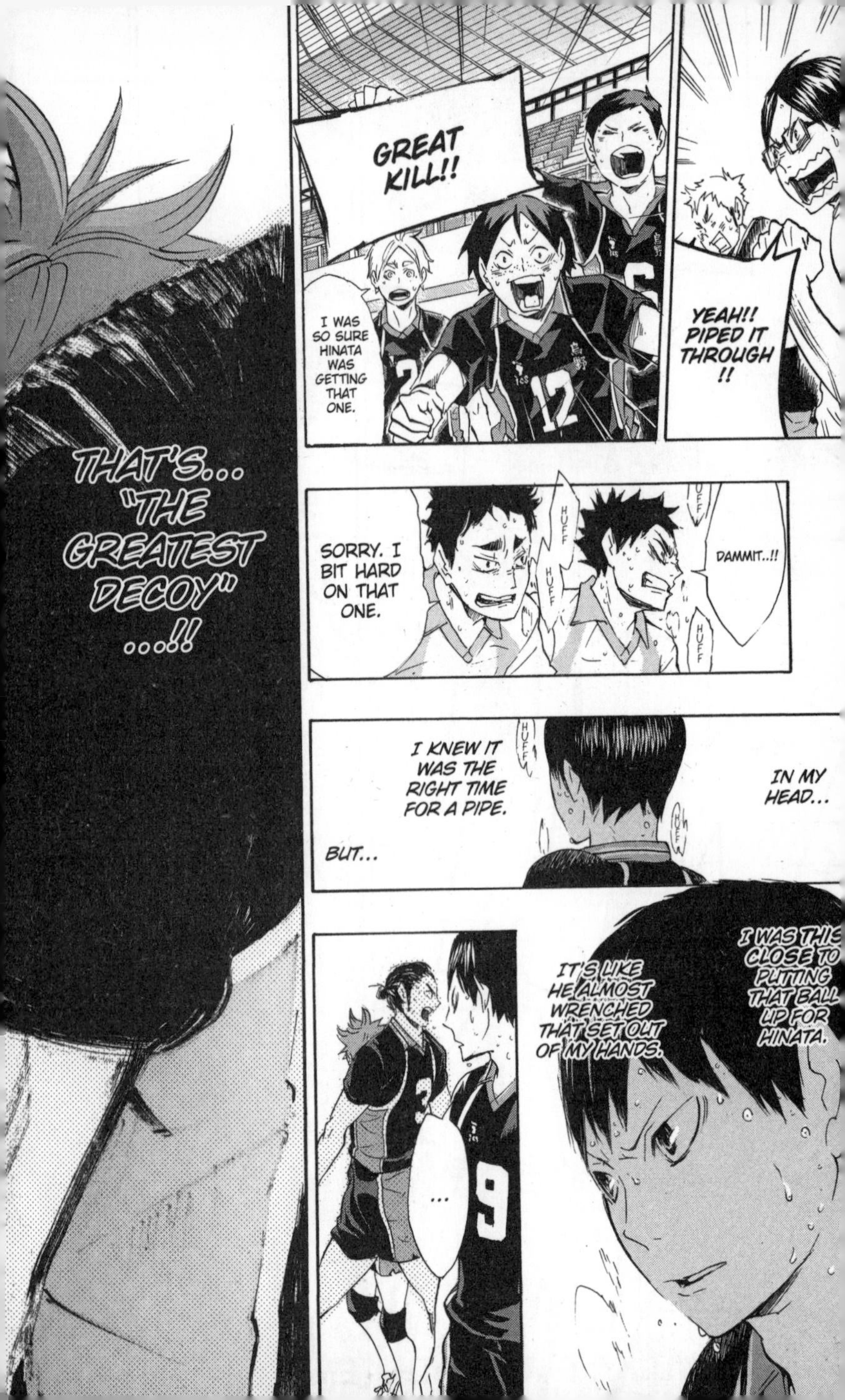
YEAH!! PIPED IT THROUGH !!
GREAT KILL!!
I WAS SO SURE HINATA WAS GETTING THAT ONE.
HUFF
DAMMIT..!!
HUFF
HUFF
SORRY. I BIT HARD ON THAT ONE.
HUFF
IN MY HEAD...
HUFF
HUFF
I KNEW IT WAS THE RIGHT TIME FOR A PIPE.
BUT...
I WAS THIS CLOSE TO PUTTING THAT BALL UP FOR HINATA.
IT'S LIKE HE ALMOST WRENCHED THAT SET OUT OF MY HANDS.
...
THAT'S... "THE GREATEST DECOY" ...!!

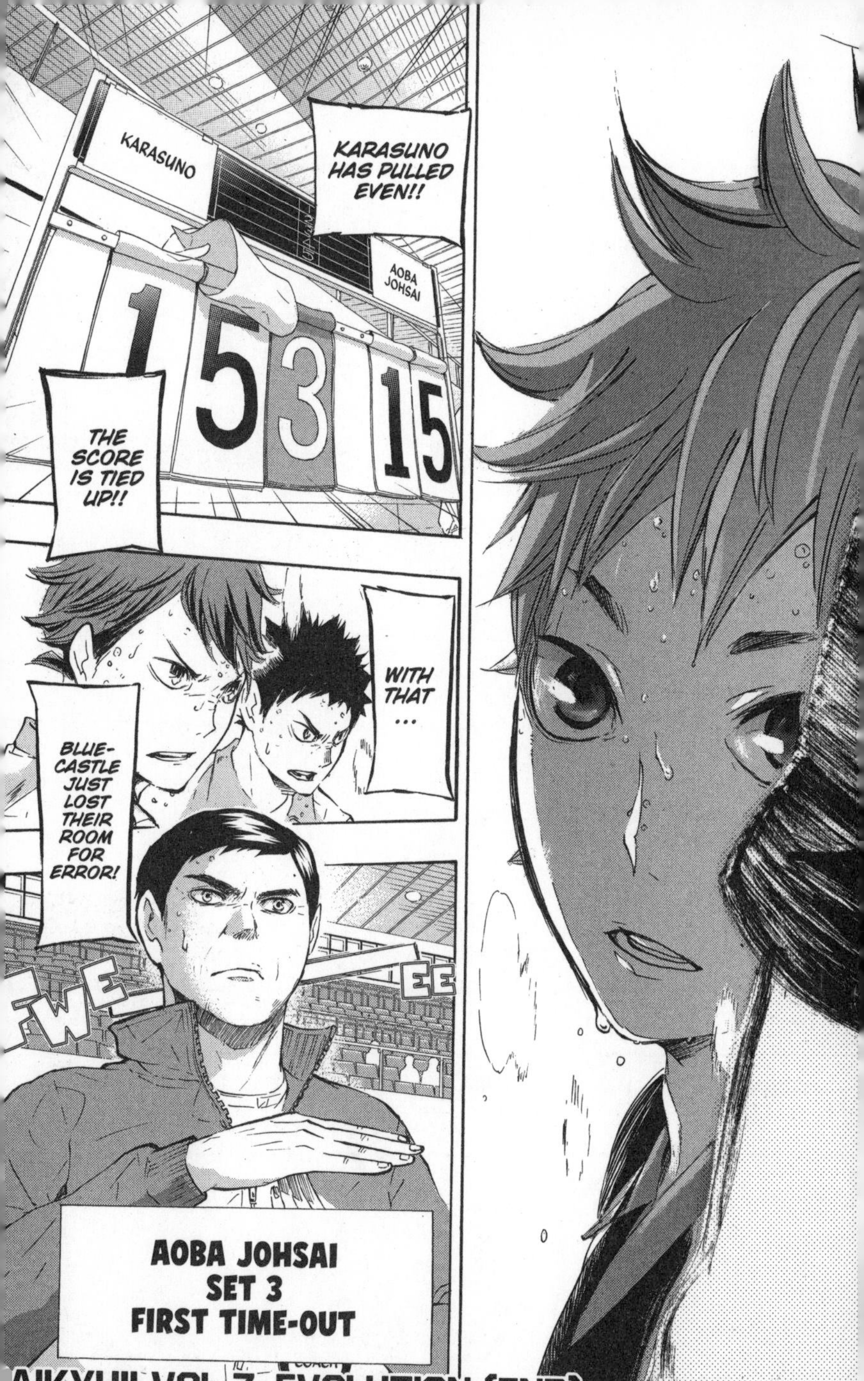
KARASUNO HAS PULLED EVEN!!
KARASUNO
AOBA JOHSAI
THE SCORE IS TIED UP!!
WITH THAT...
BLUE-CASTLE JUST LOST THEIR ROOM FOR ERROR!
FWE-EE
AOBA JOHSAI SET 3 FIRST TIME-OUT

AIKYU!! VOL 7: EVOLUTION (END)

ISSEI MATSUKAWA

AOBA JOHSAI HIGH SCHOOL
CLASS 3-1

POSITION:
MIDDLE BLOCKER

HEIGHT: 6'2"

WEIGHT: 163 LBS.
(AS OF APRIL, 3RD YEAR OF HIGH SCHOOL)

BIRTHDAY: MARCH 1

FAVORITE FOOD:
CHEESEBURGERS

CURRENT WORRY:
PEOPLE SAY HIS SCHOOL UNIFORM DOESN'T LOOK GOOD ON HIM.

ABILITY PARAMETERS
(5-POINT SCALE)

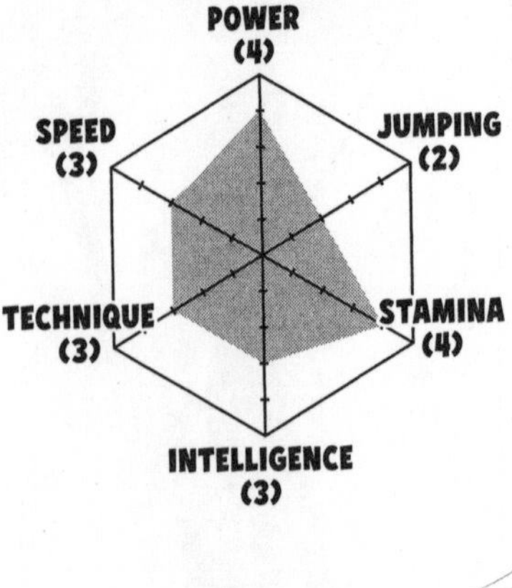
POWER
(4)
JUMPING
(2)
STAMINA
(4)
INTELLIGENCE
(3)
TECHNIQUE
(3)
SPEED
(3)

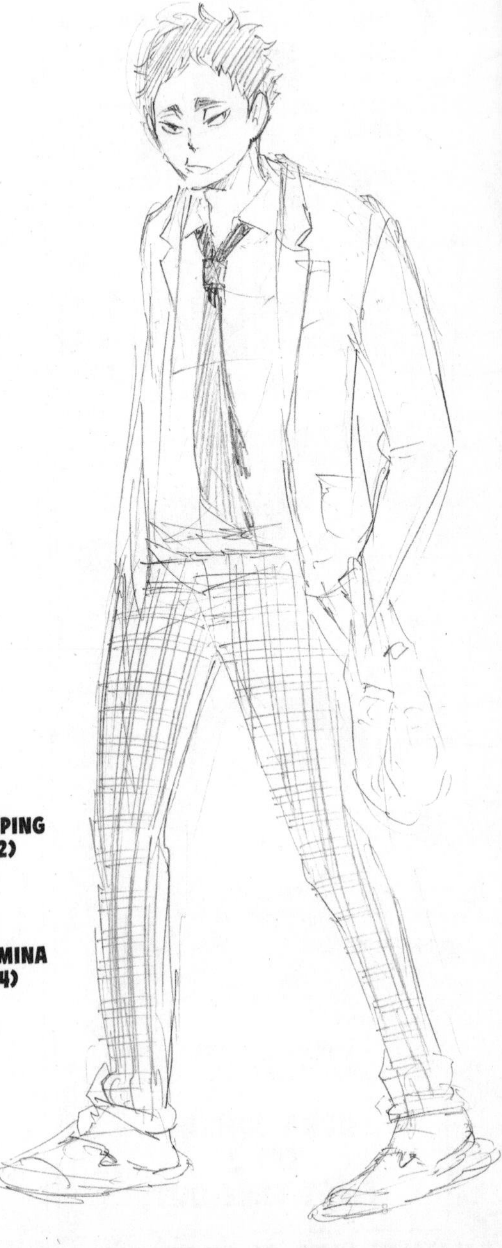

TAKAHIRO HANAMAKI

AOBA JOHSAI HIGH SCHOOL
CLASS 3-3

POSITION:
WING SPIKER

HEIGHT: 6'1"

WEIGHT: 159 LBS.
(AS OF APRIL, 3RD YEAR OF HIGH SCHOOL)

BIRTHDAY: JANUARY 27

FAVORITE FOOD:
CREAM PUFFS

CURRENT WORRY:
NO MATTER HOW HARD HE TRIES, HE CAN'T SEEM TO BEAT IWAIZUMI AT ARM WRESTLING.

ABILITY PARAMETERS
(5-POINT SCALE)

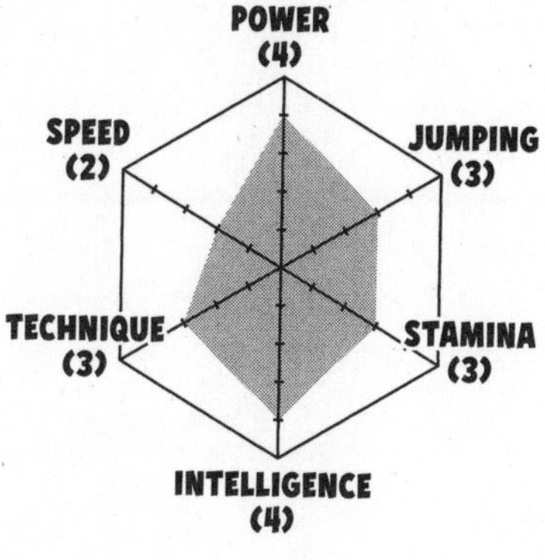
POWER
(4)
JUMPING
(3)
STAMINA
(3)
INTELLIGENCE
(4)
TECHNIQUE
(3)
SPEED
(2)

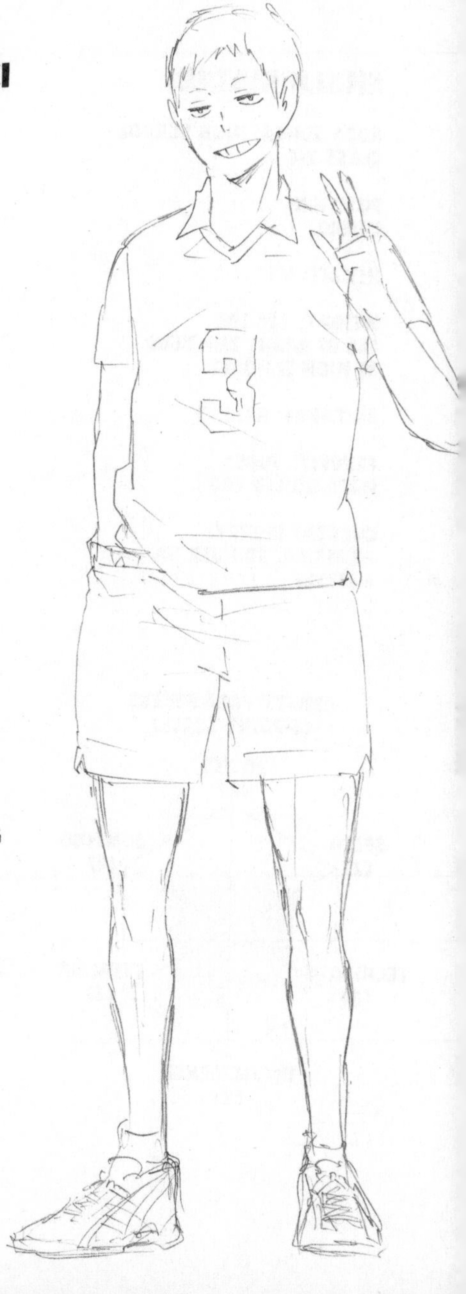
3

SHINJI WATARI

**AOBA JOHSAI HIGH SCHOOL
CLASS 2-6**

**POSITION:
LIBERO**

HEIGHT: 5'7"

**WEIGHT: 138 LBS.
(AS OF APRIL, 2ND YEAR
OF HIGH SCHOOL)**

BIRTHDAY: APRIL 3

**FAVORITE FOOD:
HARD-BOILED EGGS**

**CURRENT WORRY:
HE WANTS TO BULK UP
A LITTLE.**

**ABILITY PARAMETERS
(5-POINT SCALE)**

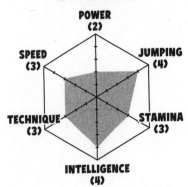

POWER
(2)

JUMPING
(4)

SPEED
(3)

STAMINA
(3)

TECHNIQUE
(3)

INTELLIGENCE
(4)

AKIRA KUNIMI

AOBA JOHSAI HIGH SCHOOL
CLASS 1-6

POSITION:
WING SPIKER

HEIGHT: 6'0"

WEIGHT: 146 LBS.
(AS OF APRIL, 1ST YEAR
OF HIGH SCHOOL)

BIRTHDAY: MARCH 25

FAVORITE FOOD:
SALTED CARAMEL

CURRENT WORRY:
IT'S HARD TO STAY AWAKE
IN CLASS.

ABILITY PARAMETERS
(5-POINT SCALE)

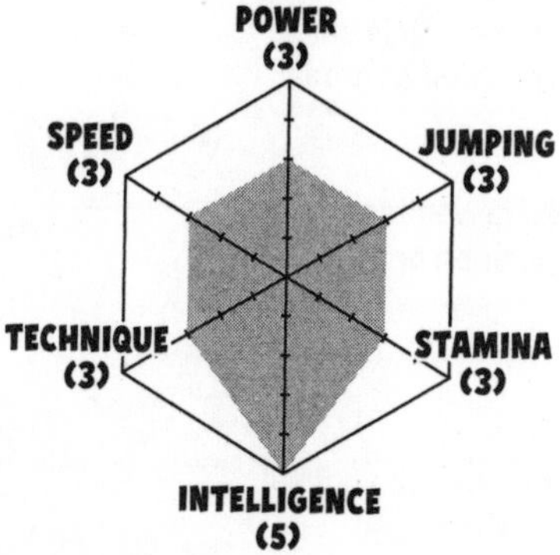
POWER (3)
JUMPING (3)
STAMINA (3)
INTELLIGENCE (5)
TECHNIQUE (3)
SPEED (3)

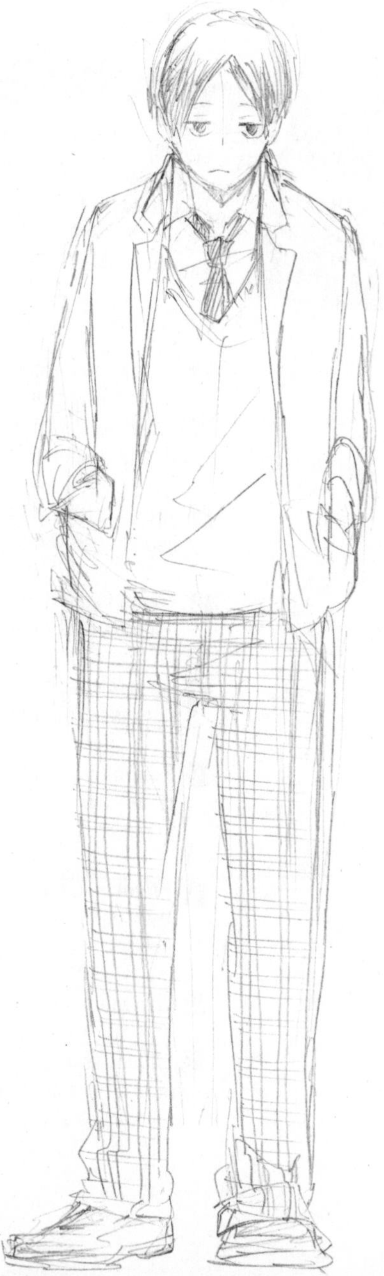

EDITOR'S NOTES

The English edition of Haikyu!! maintains the honorifics used in the original Japanese version. For those of you who are new to these terms, here's a brief explanation to help with your reading experience!

When saying someone's name in Japanese, a suffix is often attached to indicate how familiar the speaker is with the person. Some are more polite and respectful, while others are endearing.

1 **-kun** is often used for young men or boys, usually someone you are familiar with.

2 **-chan** is used for young children and can be used as a term of endearment.

3 **-san** is used for someone you respect or are not close to, or to be polite.

4 **Senpai** is used for someone who is older than you or in a higher position or grade in school.

5 **Kohai** is used for someone who is younger than you or in a lower position or grade in school.

6 **Sensei** means teacher.

7 **Bluecastle** is a nickname for Aoba Johsai. It is a combination of *Ao* (blue) and *Joh* (castle).

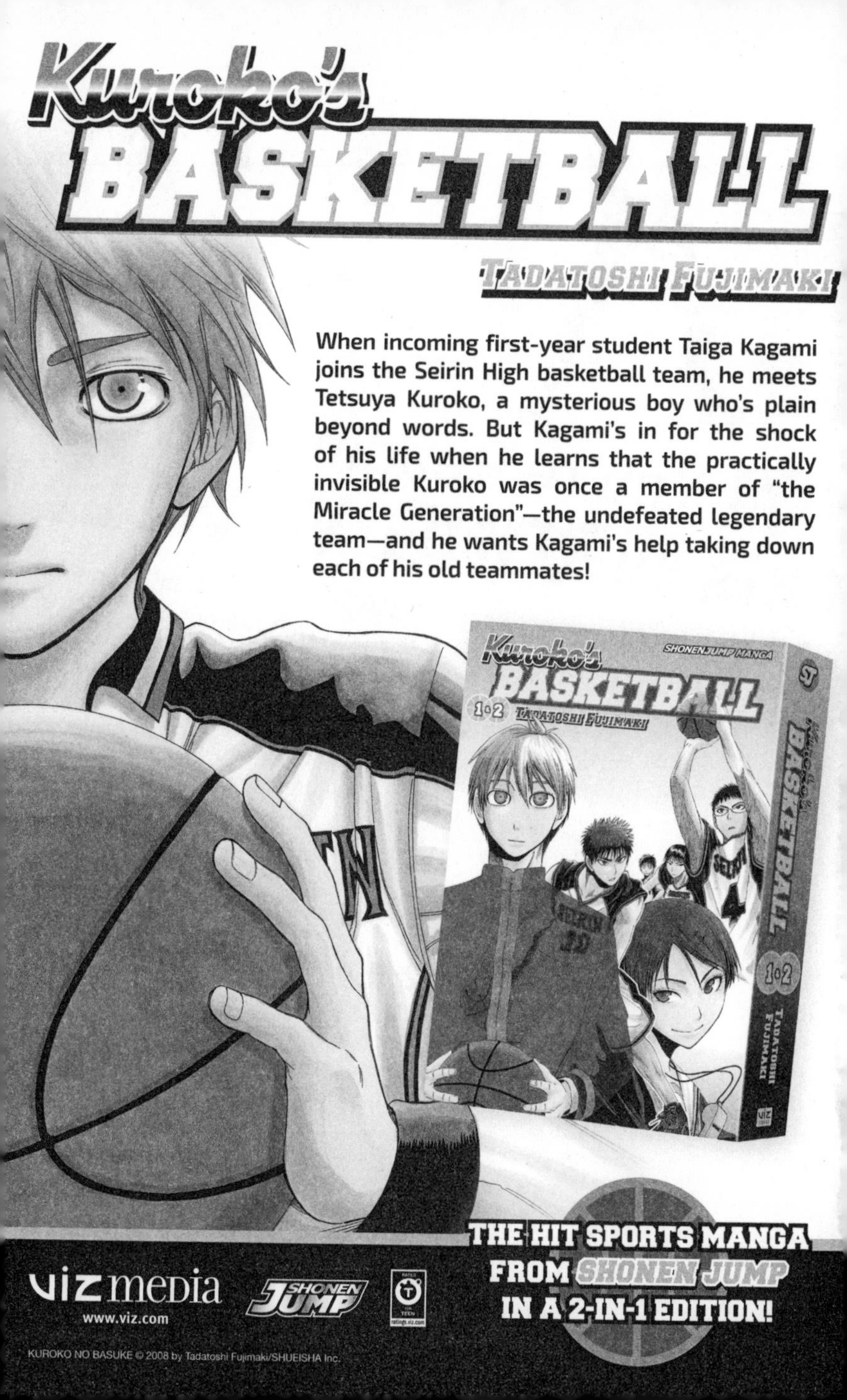

You're Reading the WRONG WAY!

HAIKYU!! reads from right to left, starting in the upper-right corner. Japanese is read from right to left, meaning that action, sound effects and word-balloon order are completely reversed from English order.

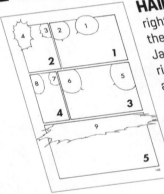